SO-AWU-581

Blood on the Tracks

volume

3

Shuzo
Oshimi

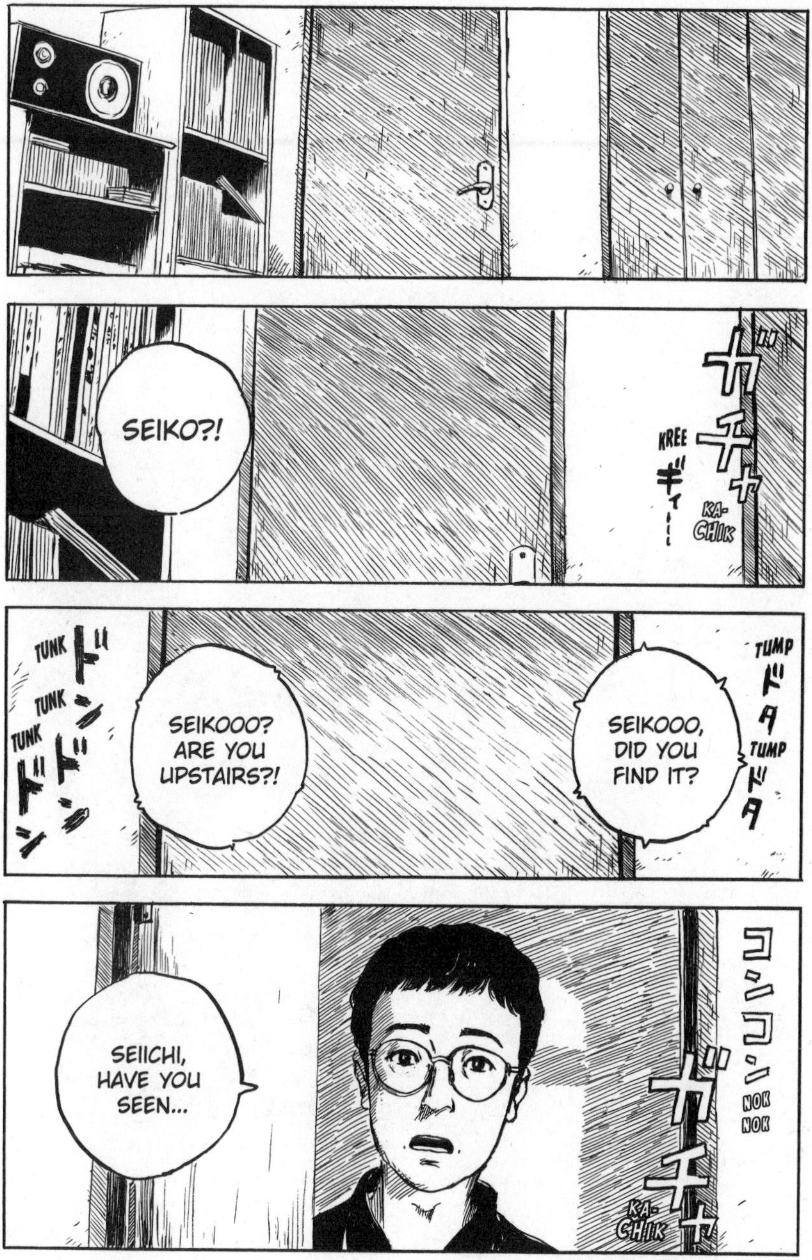
ガチャ
KA-CHIK
KREE
ギィ…
SEIKO?!
TUMP
ドタ
TUMP
ドタ
SEIKOOO, DID YOU FIND IT?
SEIKOOO? ARE YOU UPSTAIRS?!
TUNK
TUNK
TUNK
コンコン
NOK NOK
ガチャ
KA-CHIK
SEIICHI, HAVE YOU SEEN...

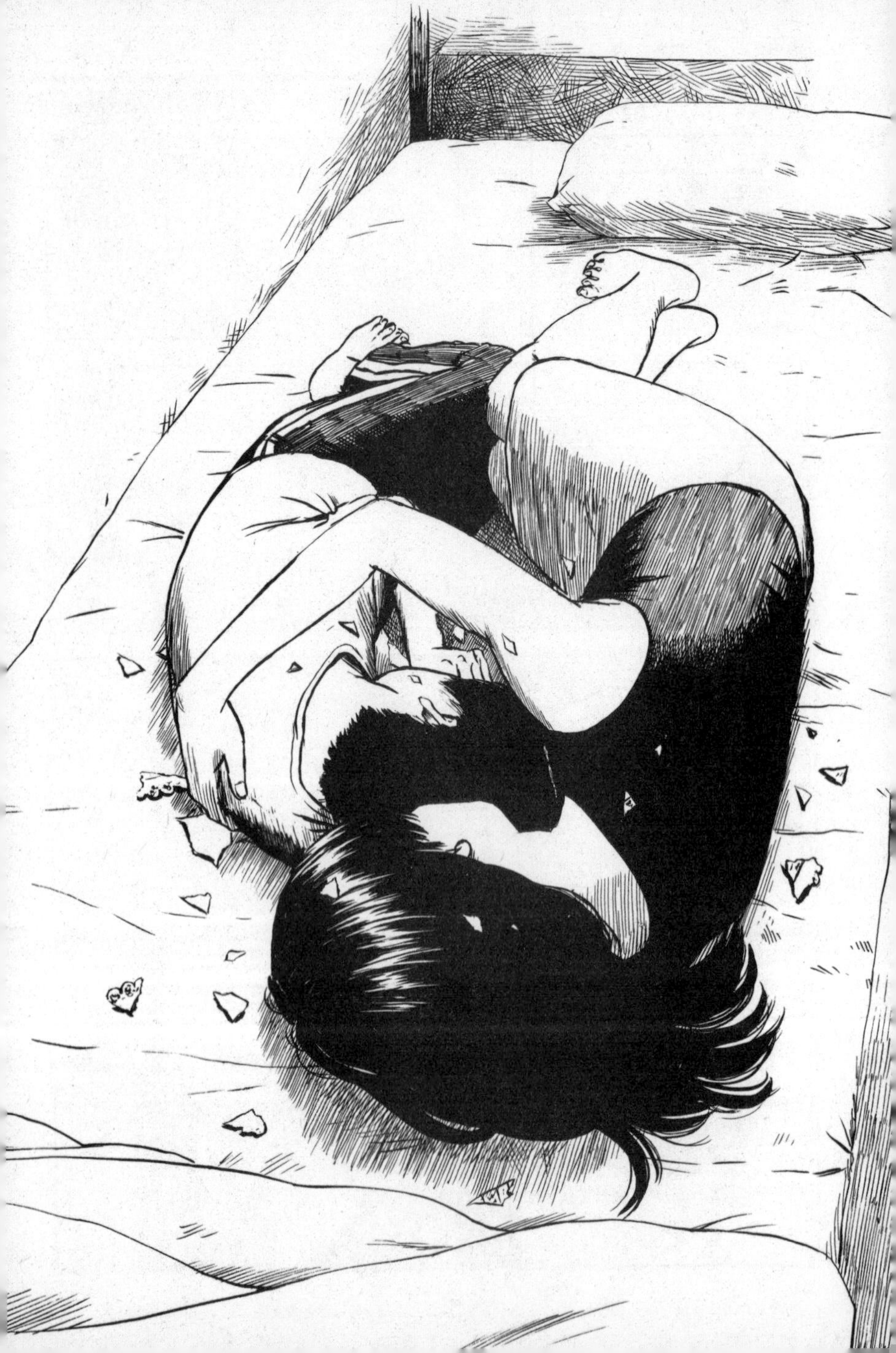

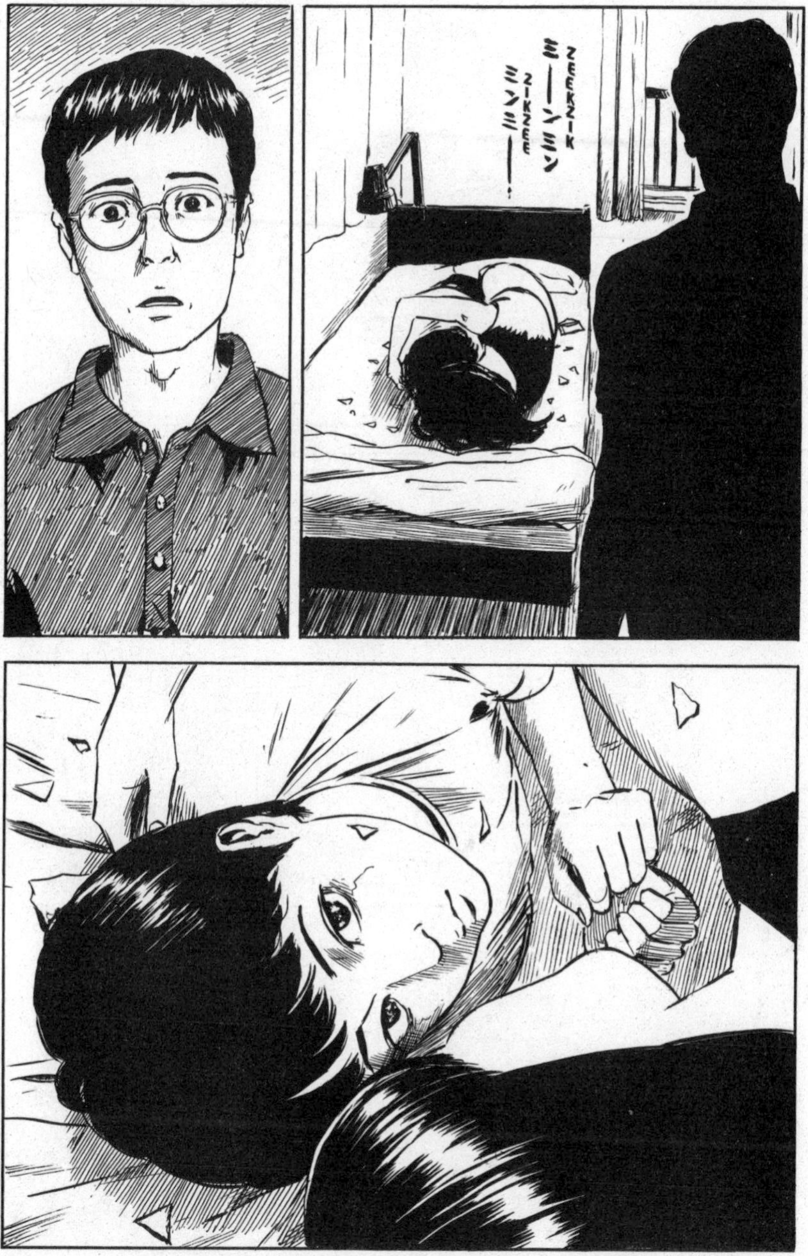
ZEEKZIK
ミーンミン
ZIKZEE
ミンミー！

WH- WHAT'S GOING ON?
DID SOMETHING HAPPEN?
Love
you
WHAT'S THIS PAPER?
WHY'S IT ALL RIPPED UP?

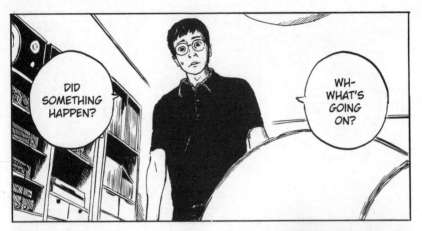

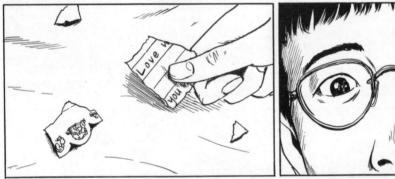

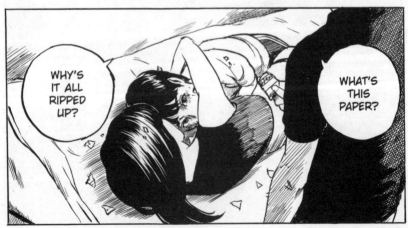

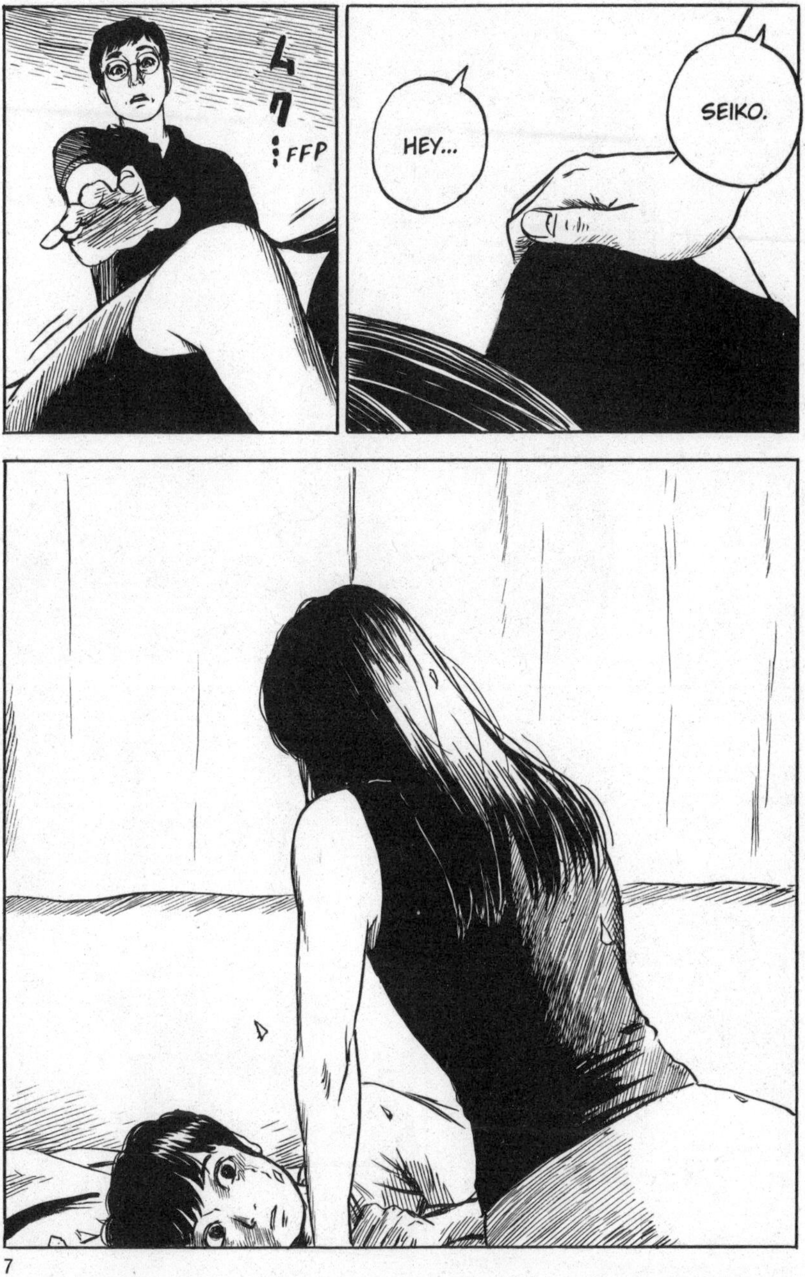
SEIKO.
HEY...
ムク...
FFP

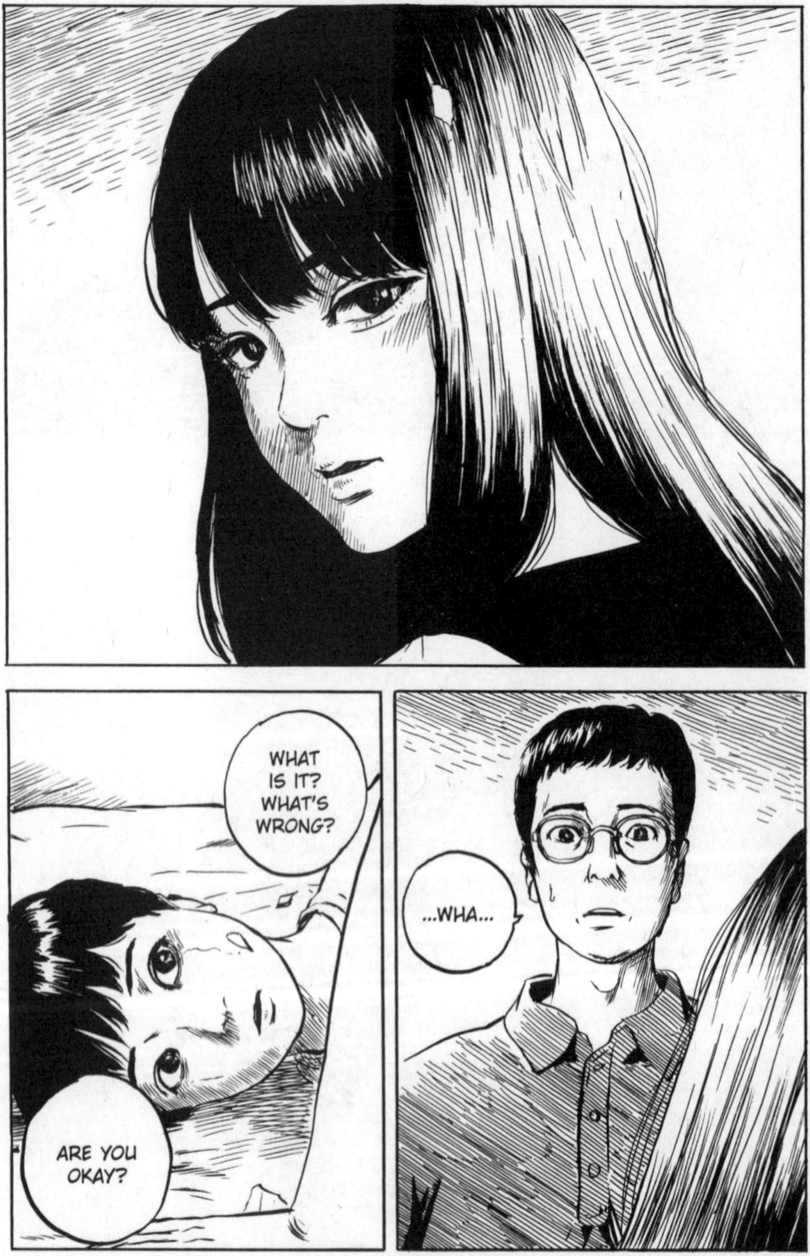
...WHA...
WHAT IS IT? WHAT'S WRONG?
ARE YOU OKAY?

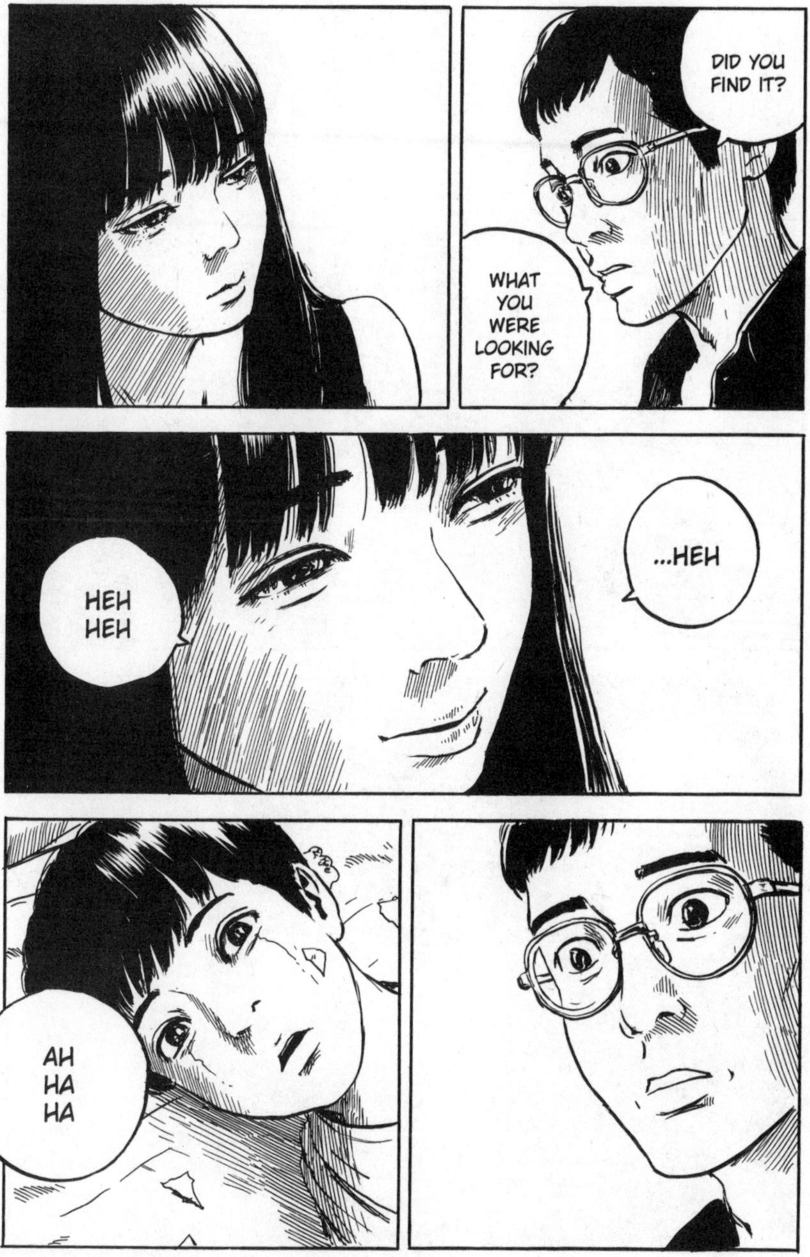
DID YOU FIND IT?
WHAT YOU WERE LOOKING FOR?
...HEH
HEH HEH
AH HA HA

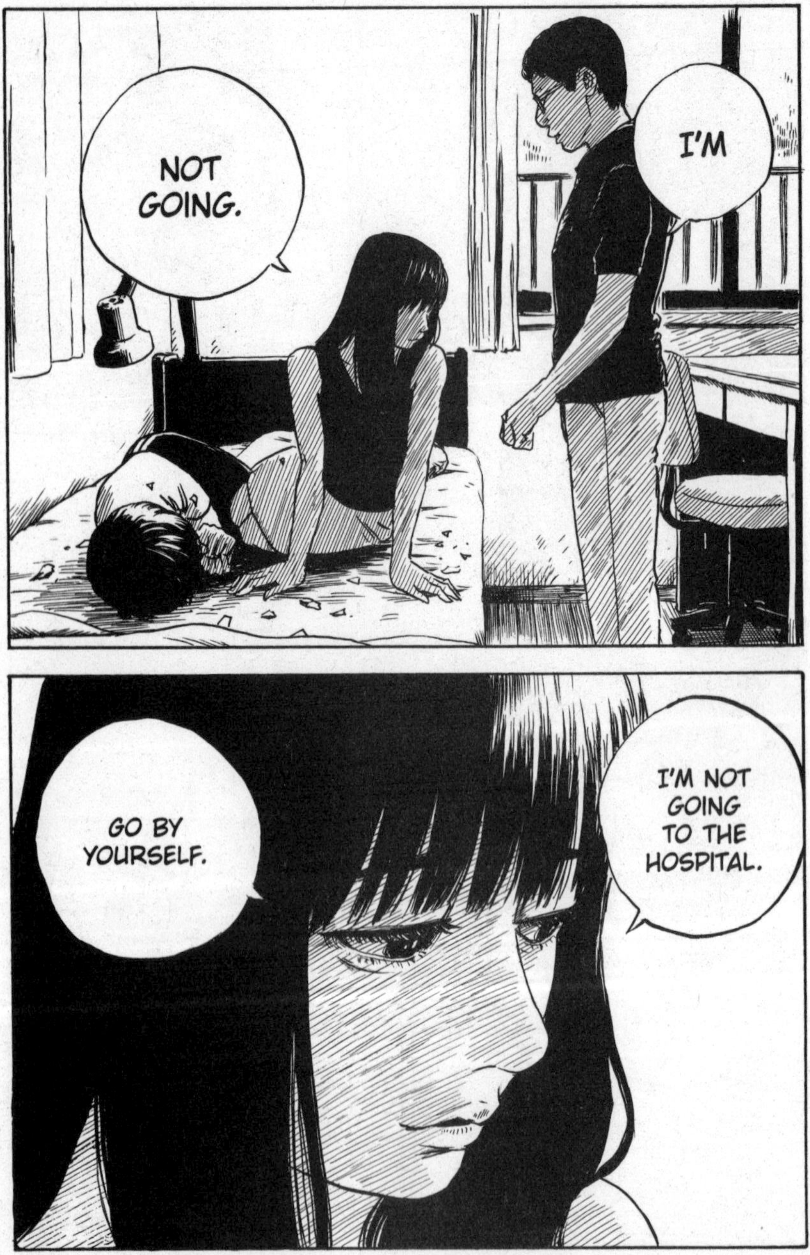
I'M
NOT GOING.
I'M NOT GOING TO THE HOSPITAL.
GO BY YOURSELF.

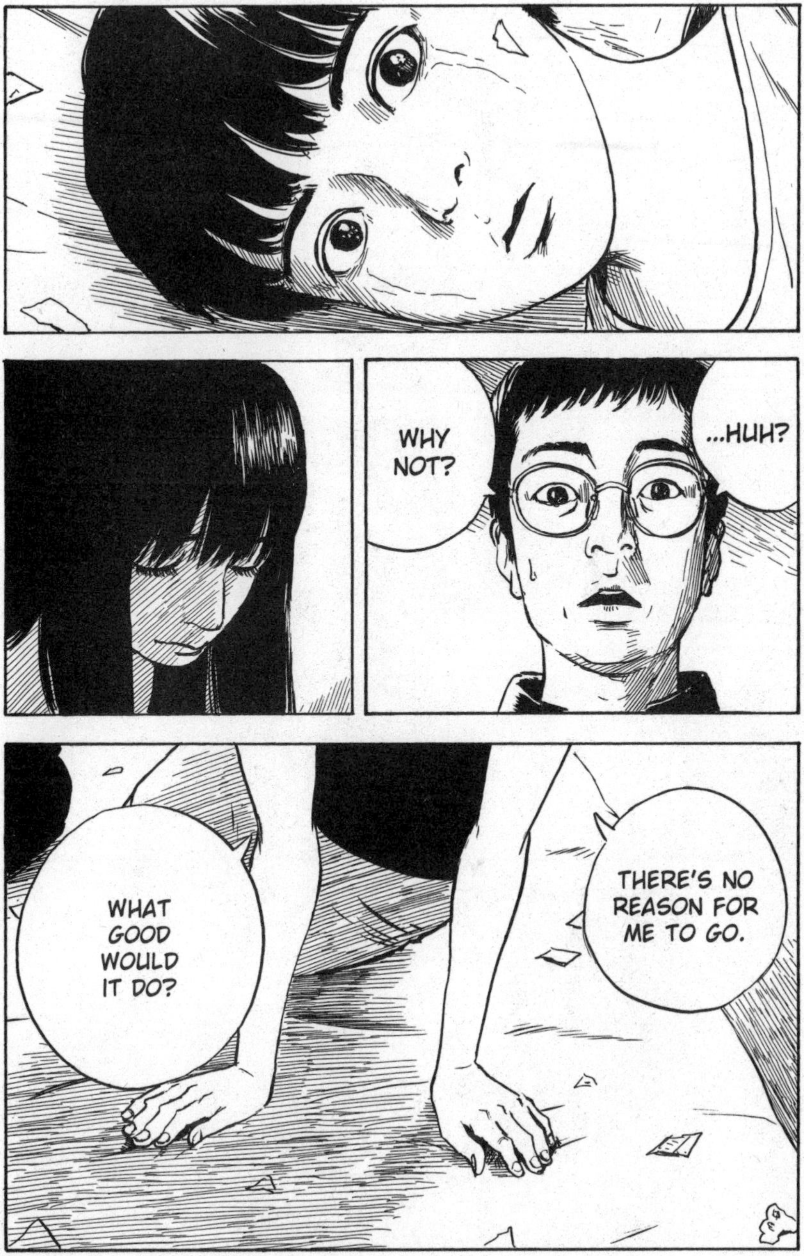
...HUH?
WHY NOT?
THERE'S NO REASON FOR ME TO GO.
WHAT GOOD WOULD IT DO?

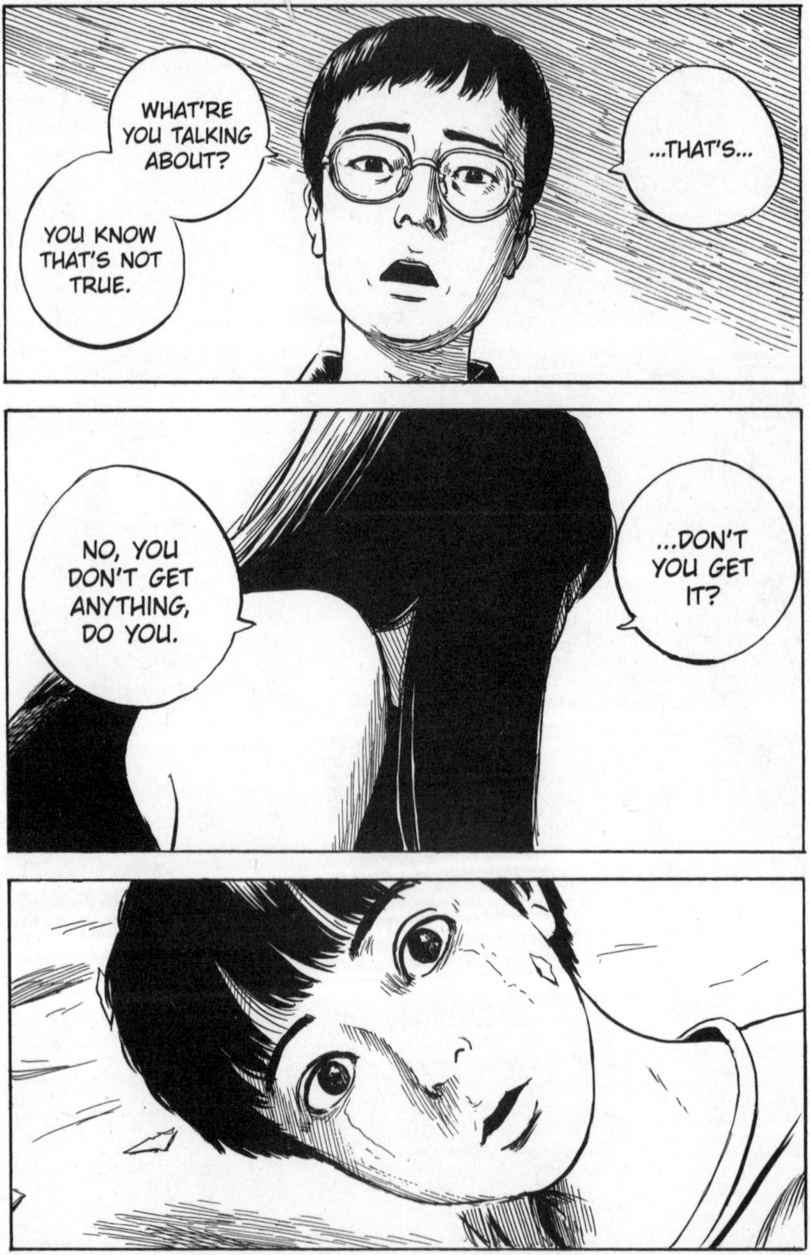
...THAT'S...
WHAT'RE YOU TALKING ABOUT?
YOU KNOW THAT'S NOT TRUE.
...DON'T YOU GET IT?
NO, YOU DON'T GET ANYTHING, DO YOU.

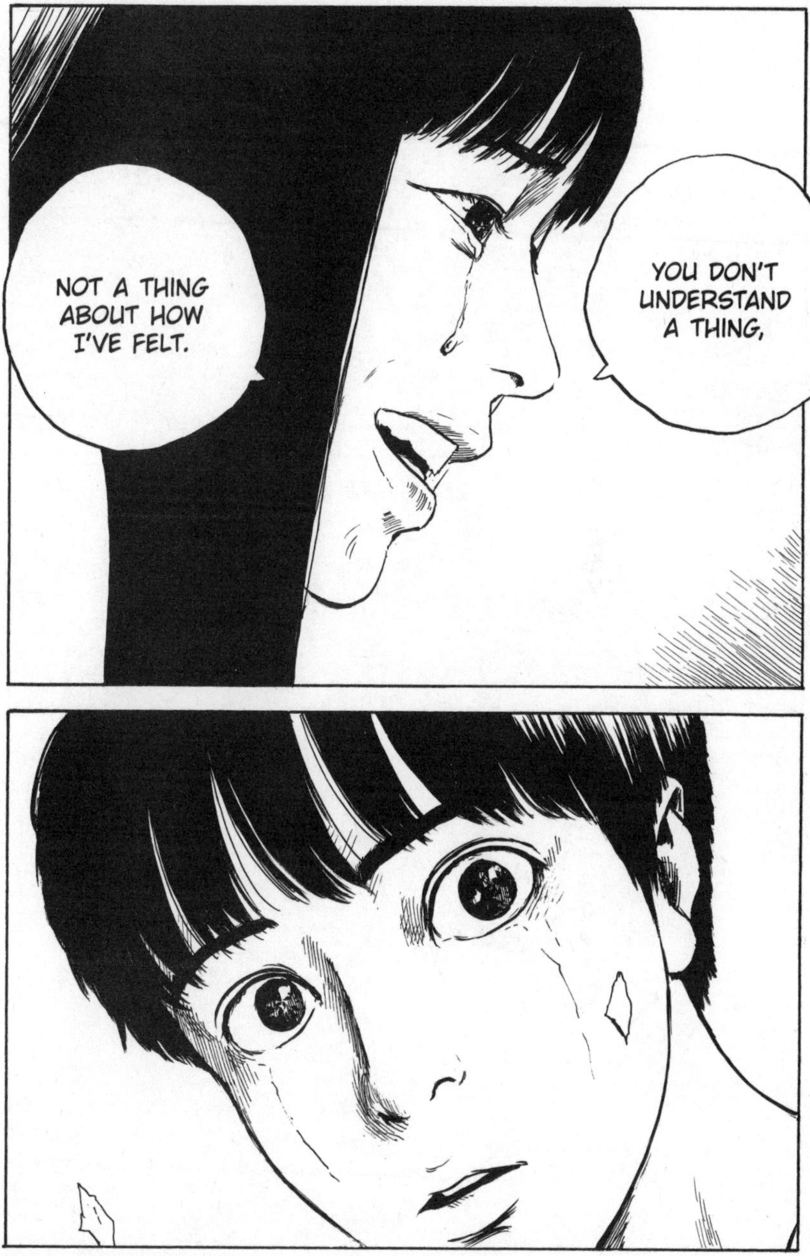
YOU DON'T UNDERSTAND A THING,
NOT A THING ABOUT HOW I'VE FELT.

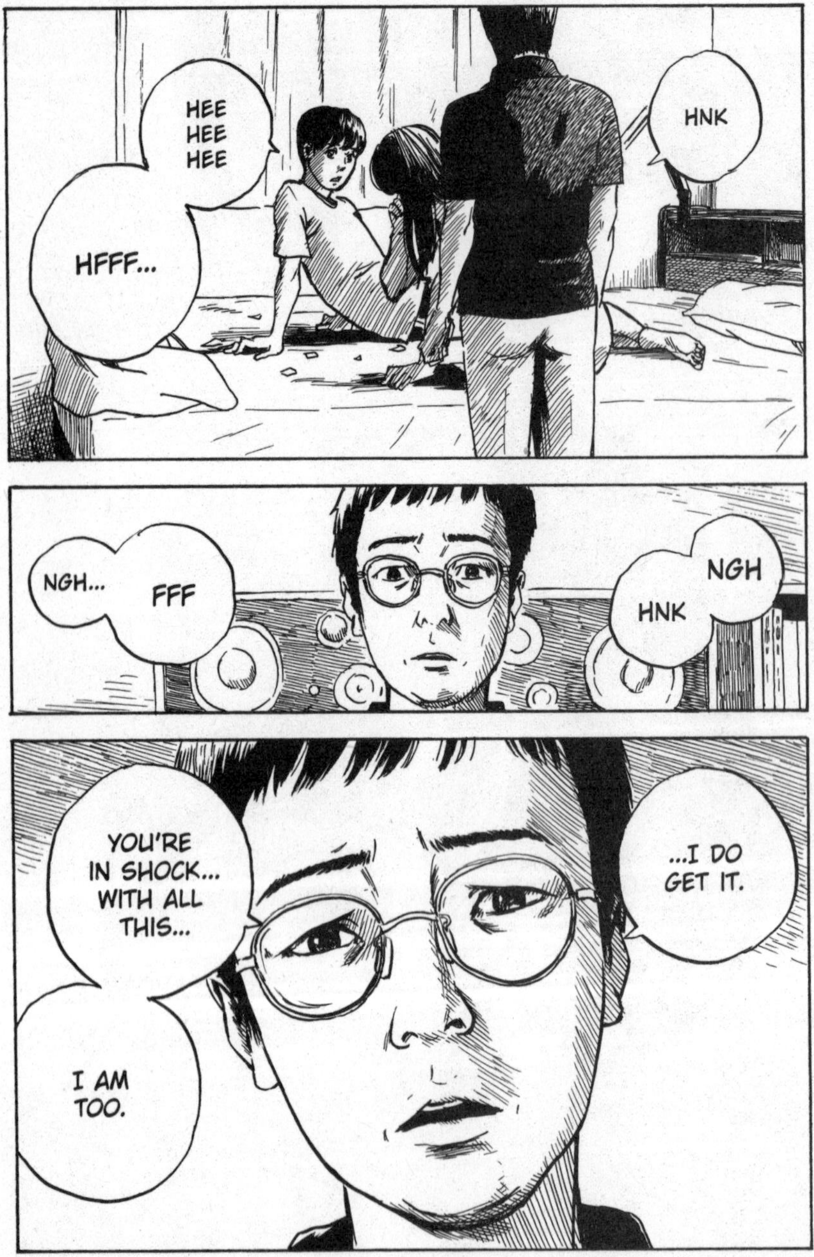
HNK
HEE HEE HEE
HFFF...
NGH HNK
NGH... FFF
...I DO GET IT.
YOU'RE IN SHOCK... WITH ALL THIS...
I AM TOO.

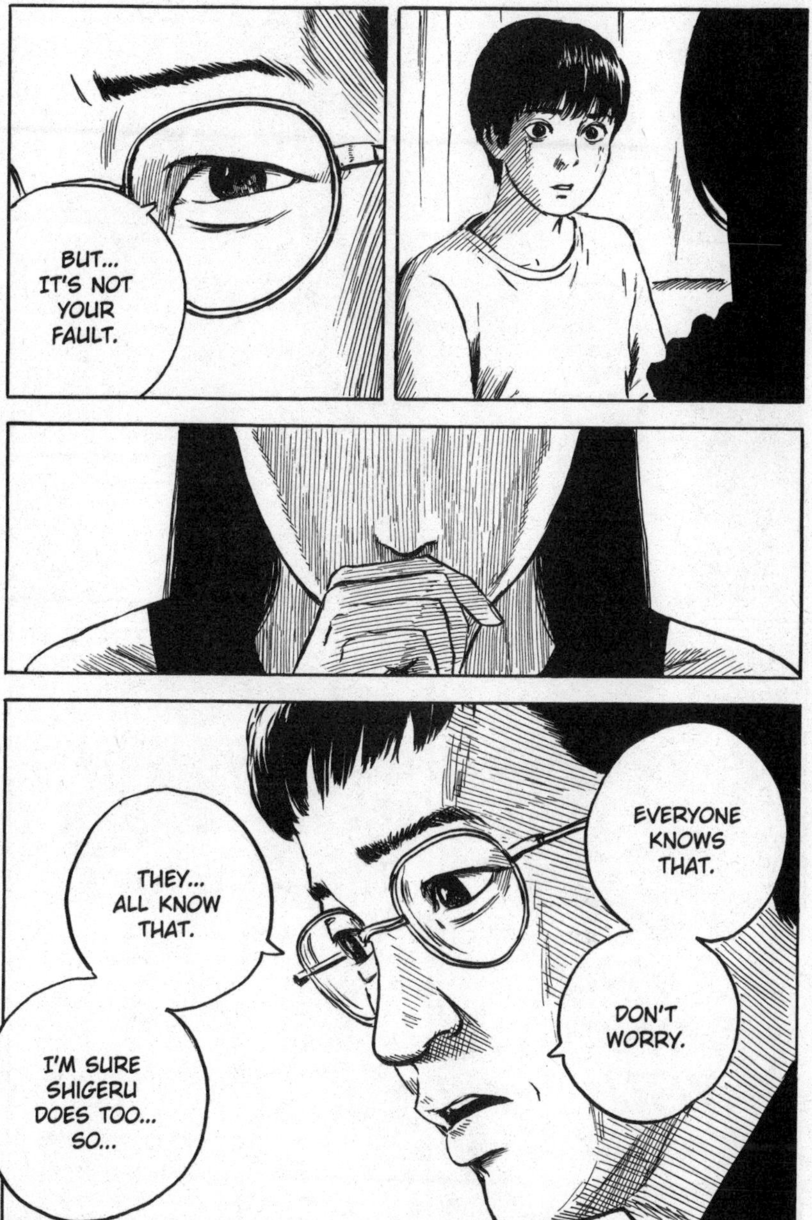
BUT... IT'S NOT YOUR FAULT.
EVERYONE KNOWS THAT.
DON'T WORRY.
THEY... ALL KNOW THAT.
I'M SURE SHIGERU DOES TOO... SO...

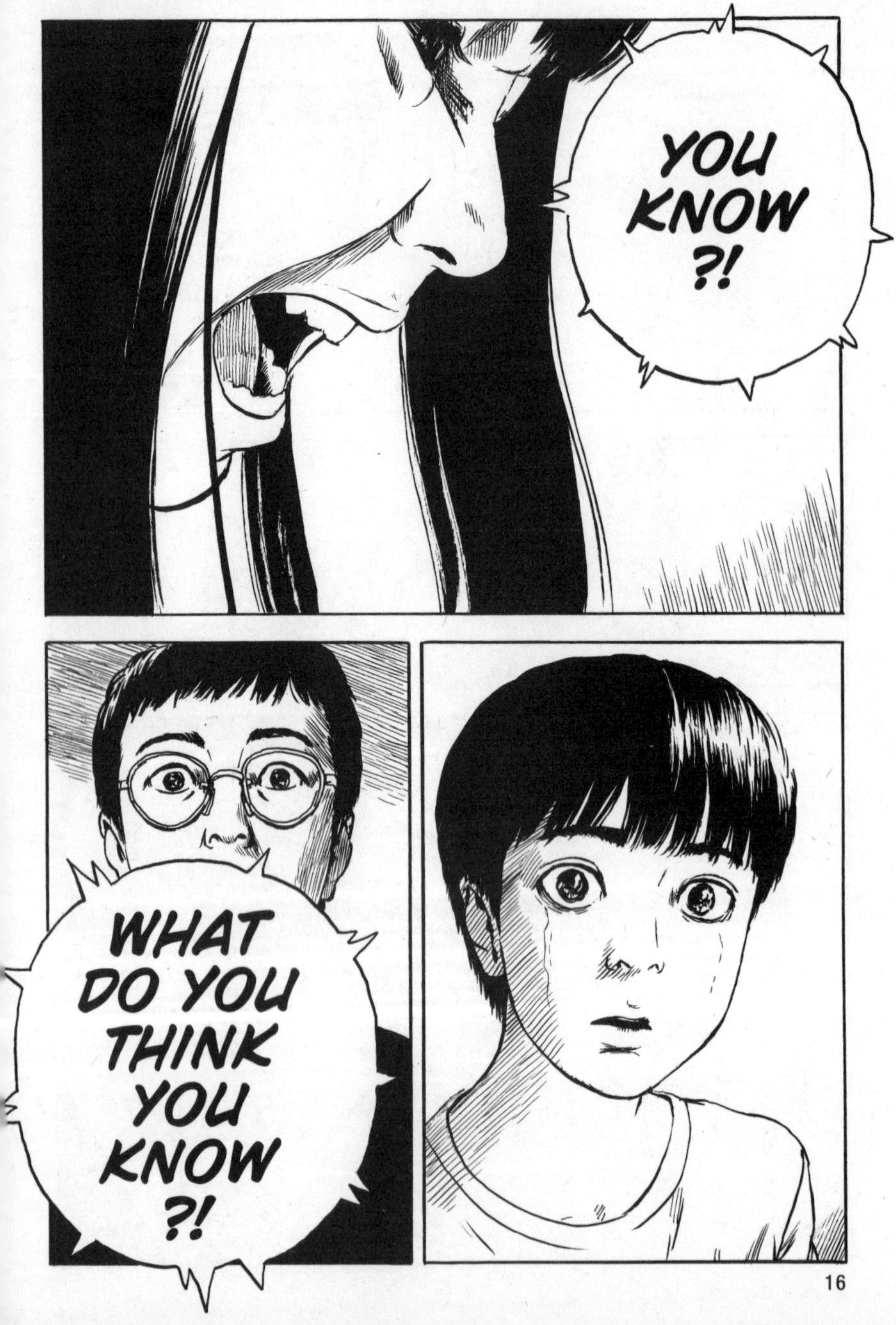
YOU KNOW ?!
WHAT DO YOU THINK YOU KNOW ?!

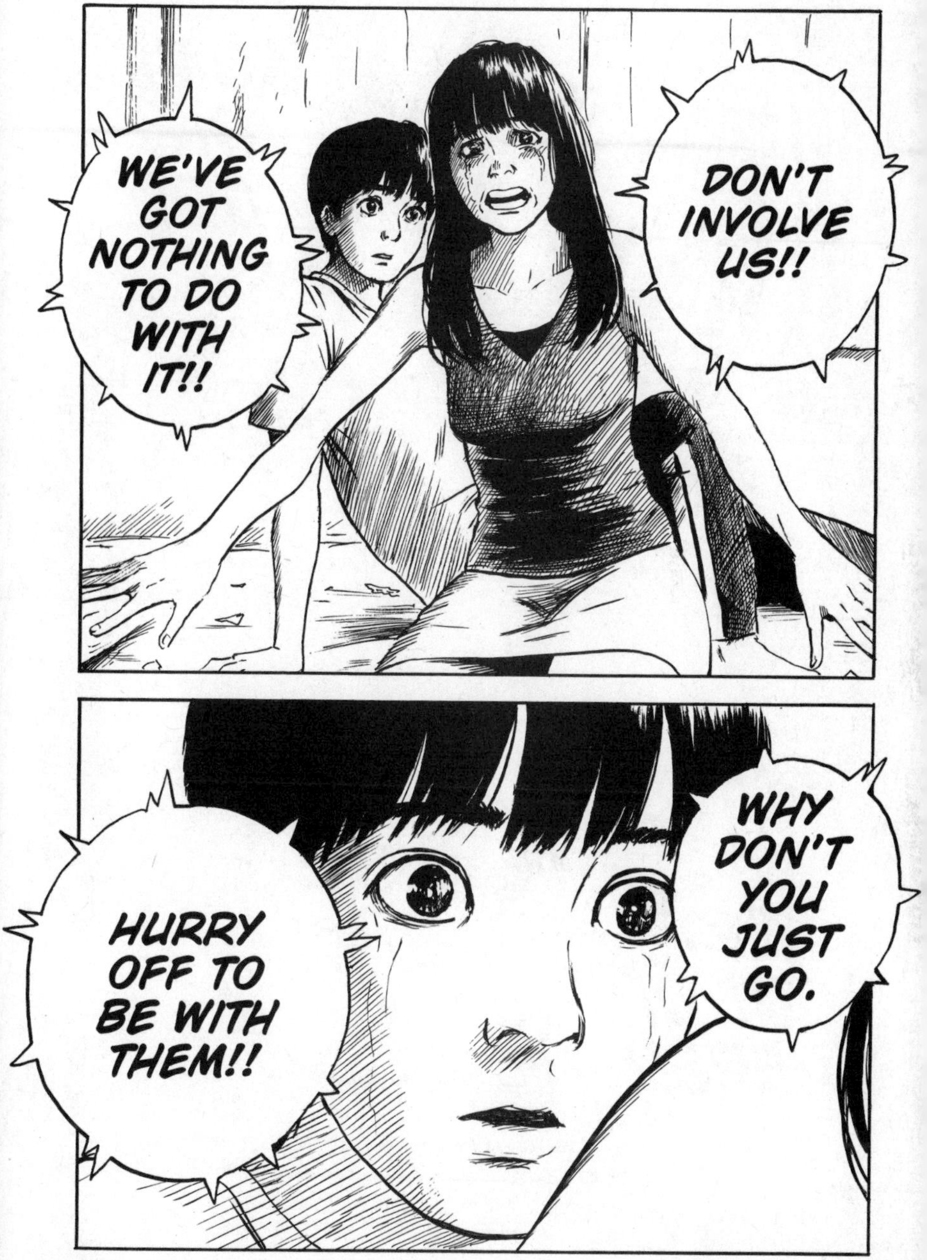
DON'T INVOLVE US!!
WE'VE GOT NOTHING TO DO WITH IT!!
WHY DON'T YOU JUST GO.
HURRY OFF TO BE WITH THEM!!

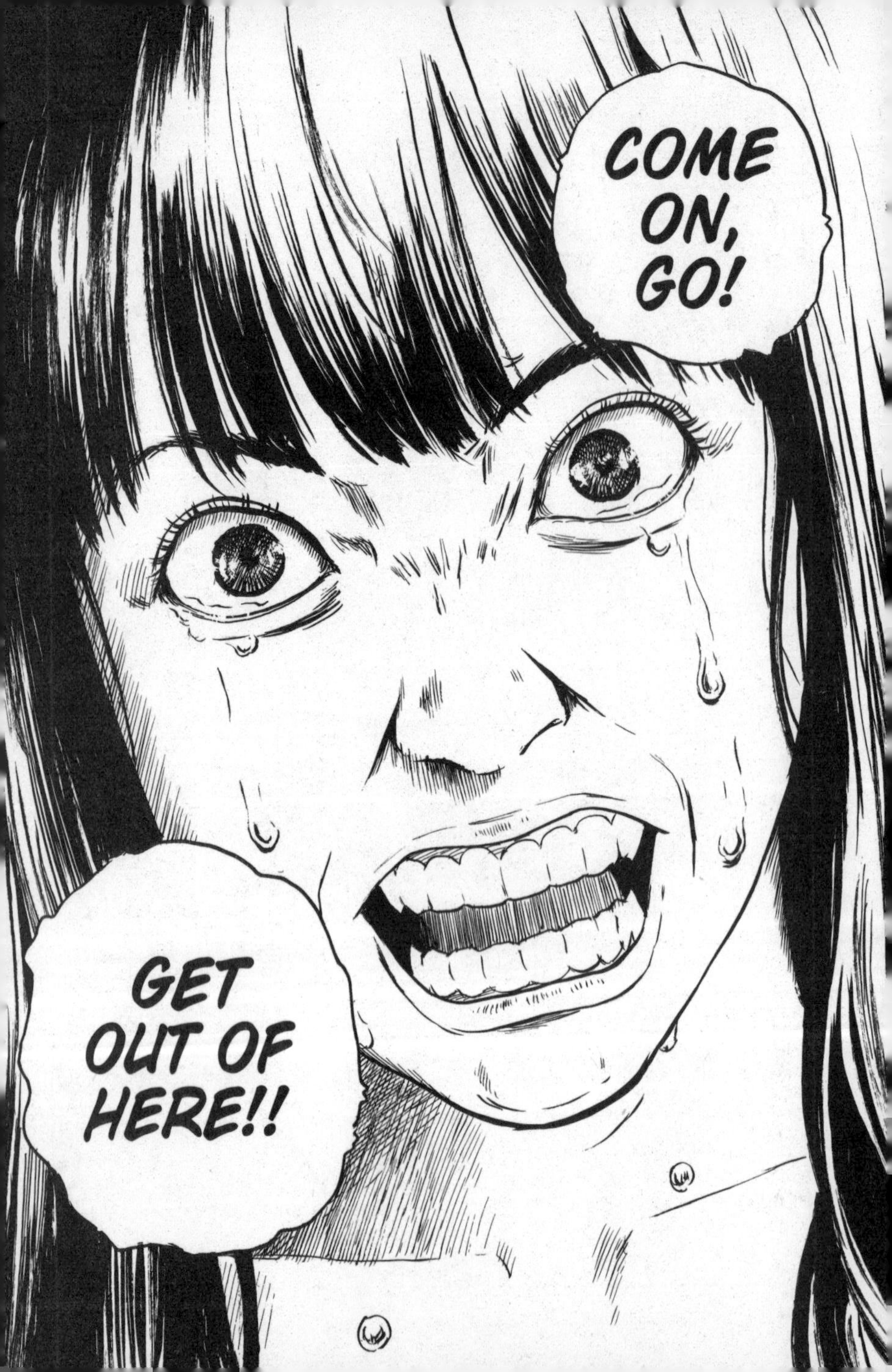
COME ON, GO!
GET OUT OF HERE!!

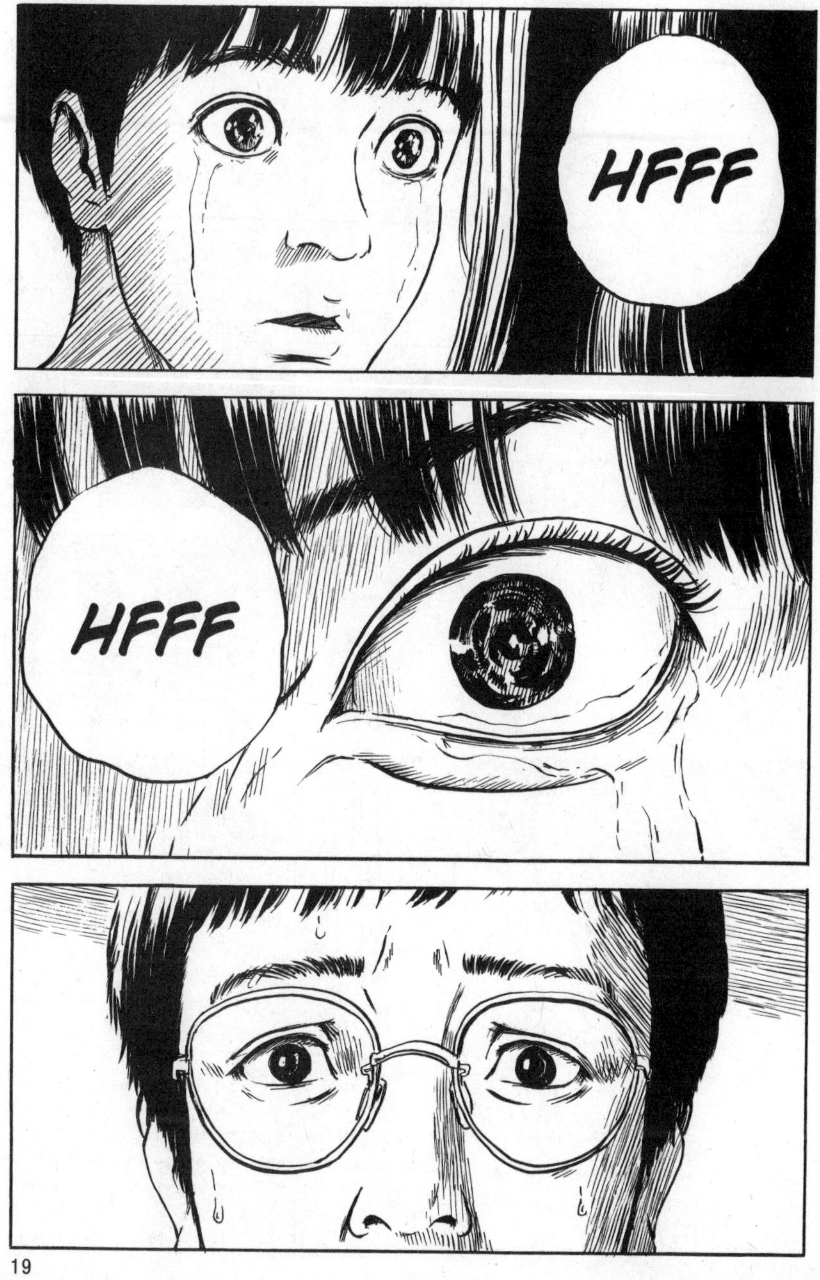
HFFF
HFFF

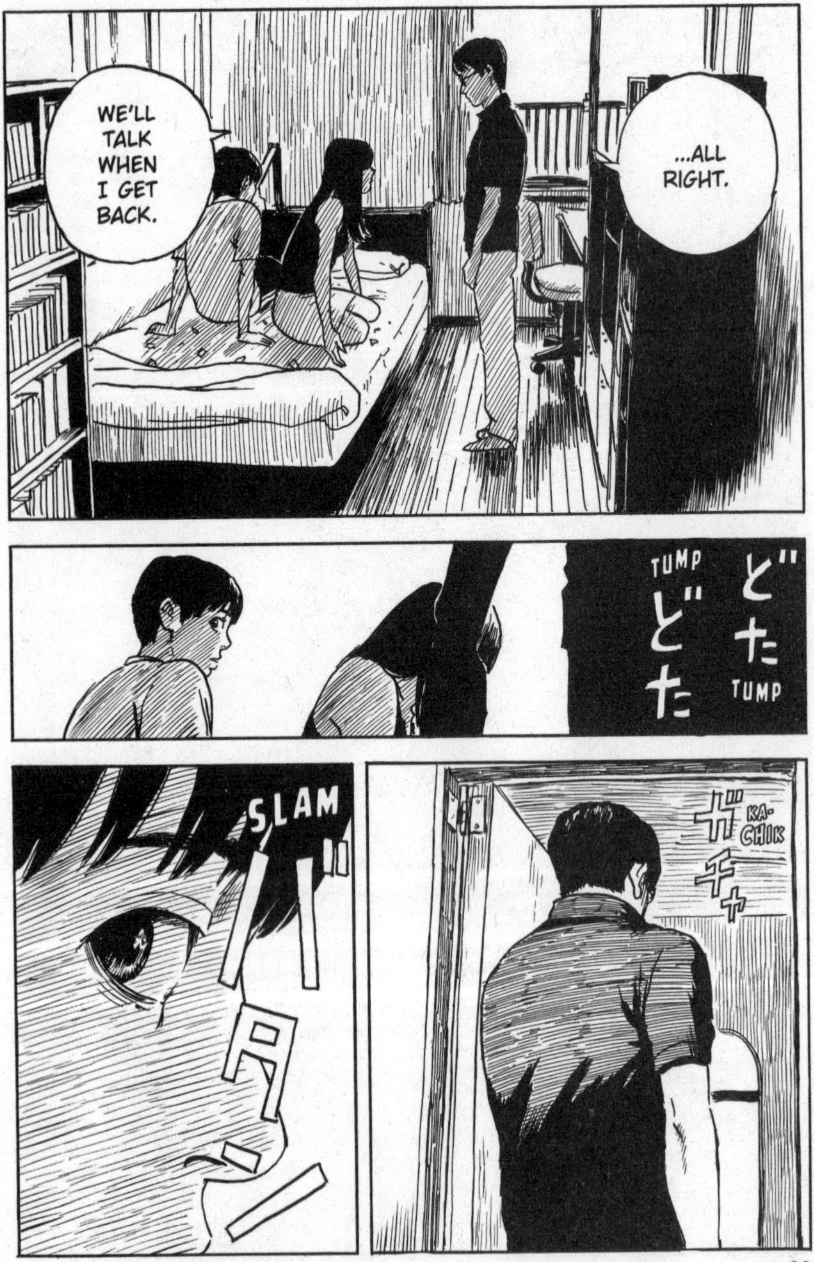
...ALL RIGHT.
WE'LL TALK WHEN I GET BACK.
TUMP
どたどた
TUMP
KA-CHIK
ガチャ
SLAM

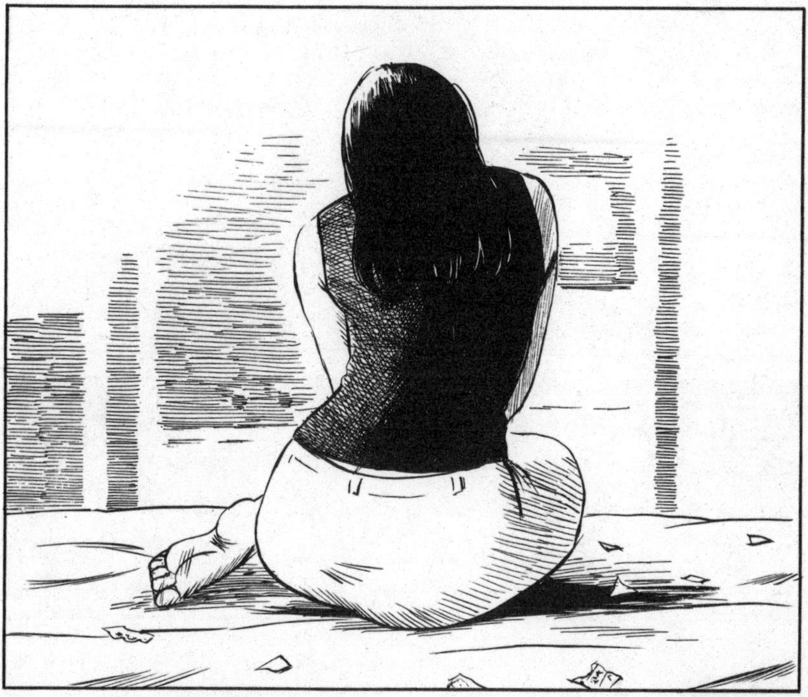
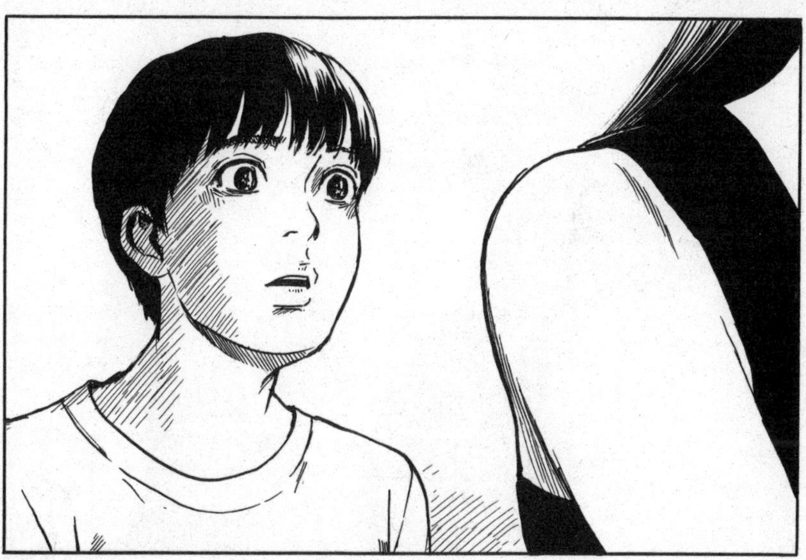

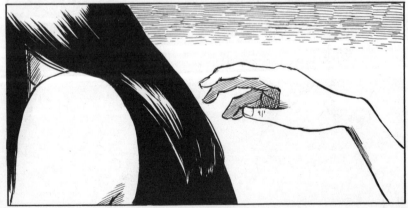

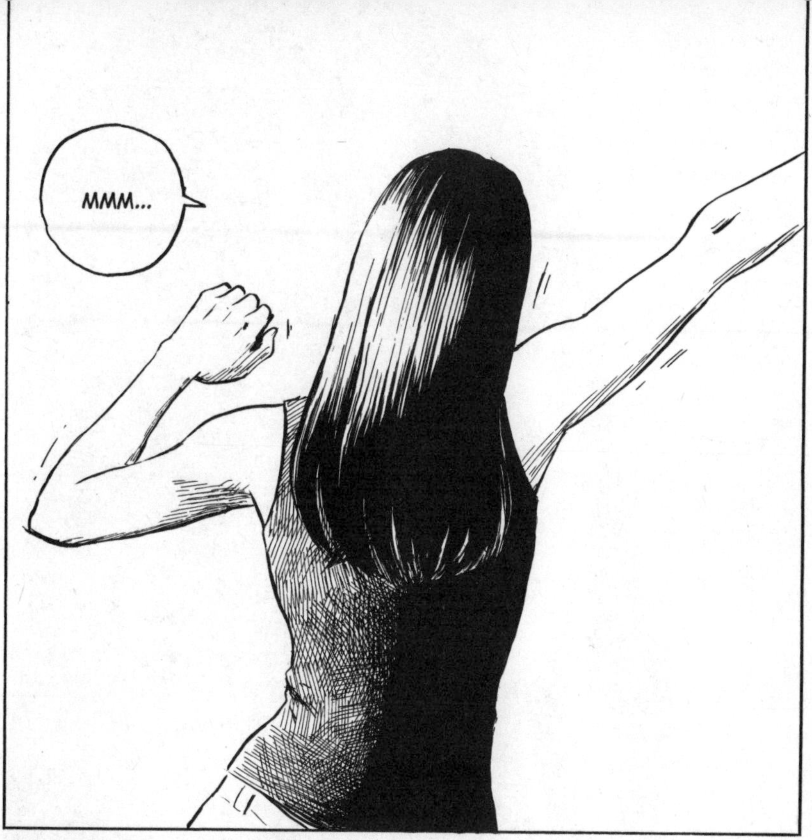
MMM...
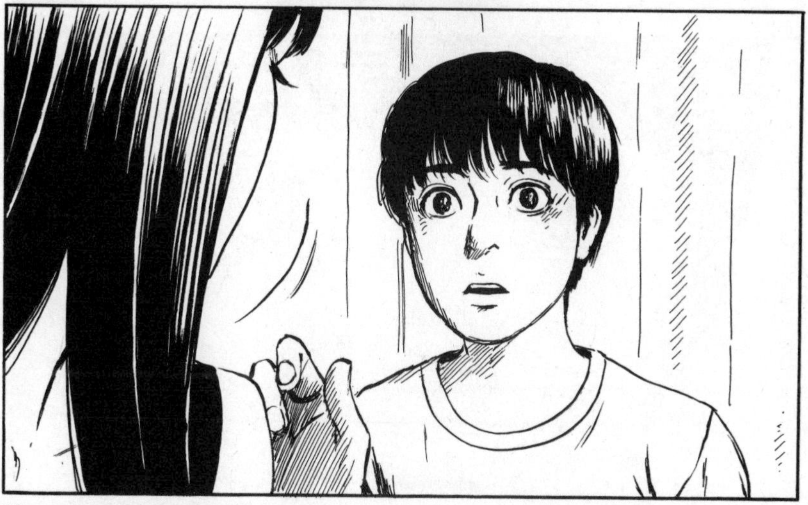

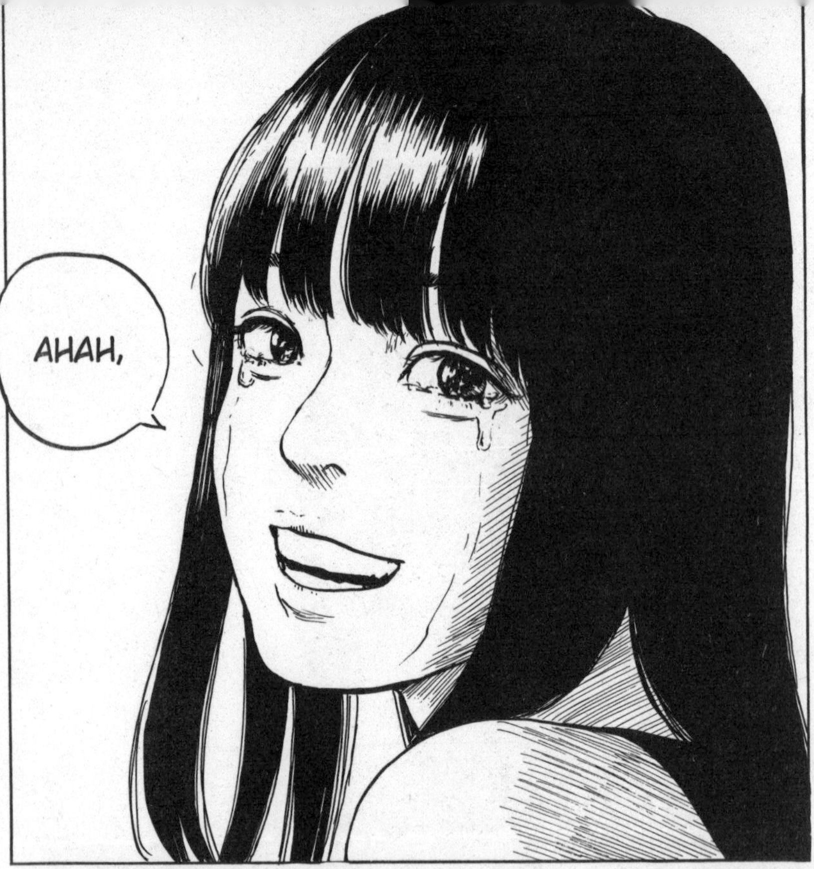
AHAH,

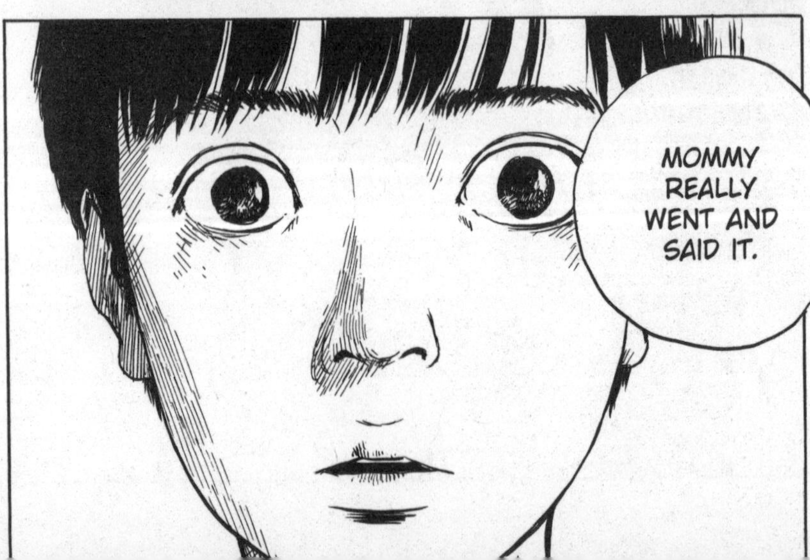
MOMMY REALLY WENT AND SAID IT.

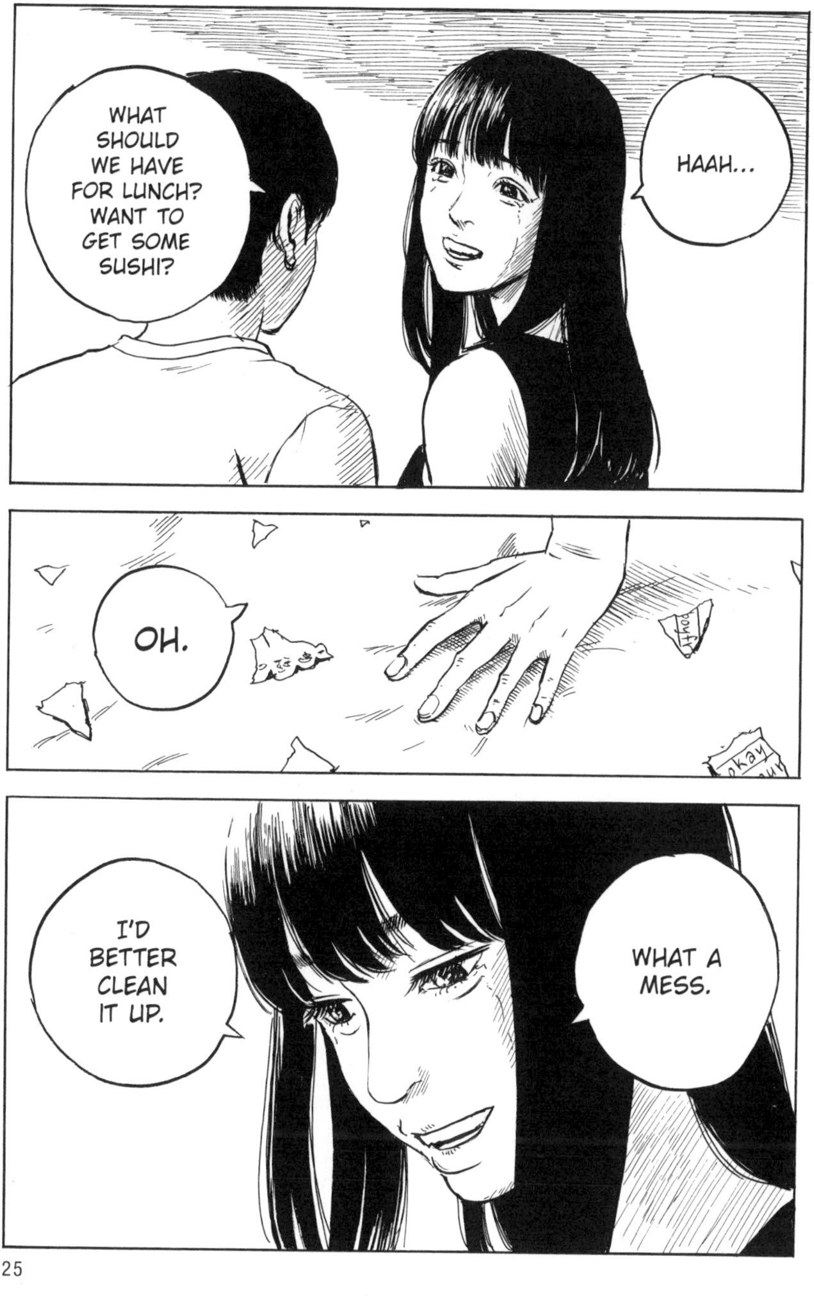
HAAH...
WHAT SHOULD WE HAVE FOR LUNCH? WANT TO GET SOME SUSHI?
OH.
WHAT A MESS.
I'D BETTER CLEAN IT UP.

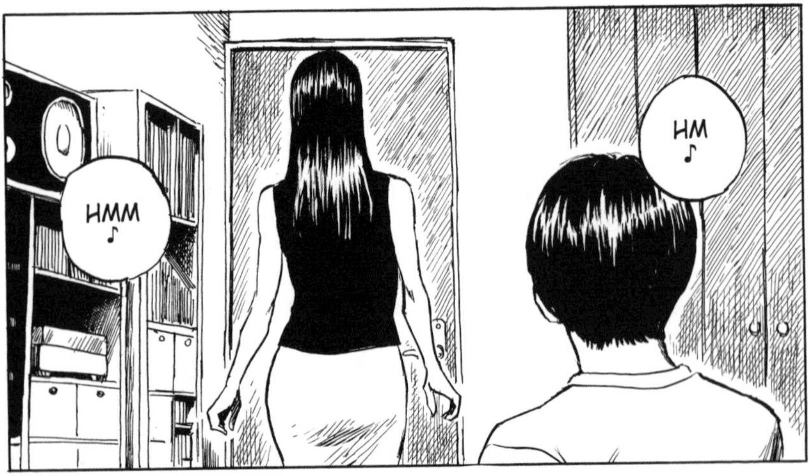
HM ♪
HMM ♪

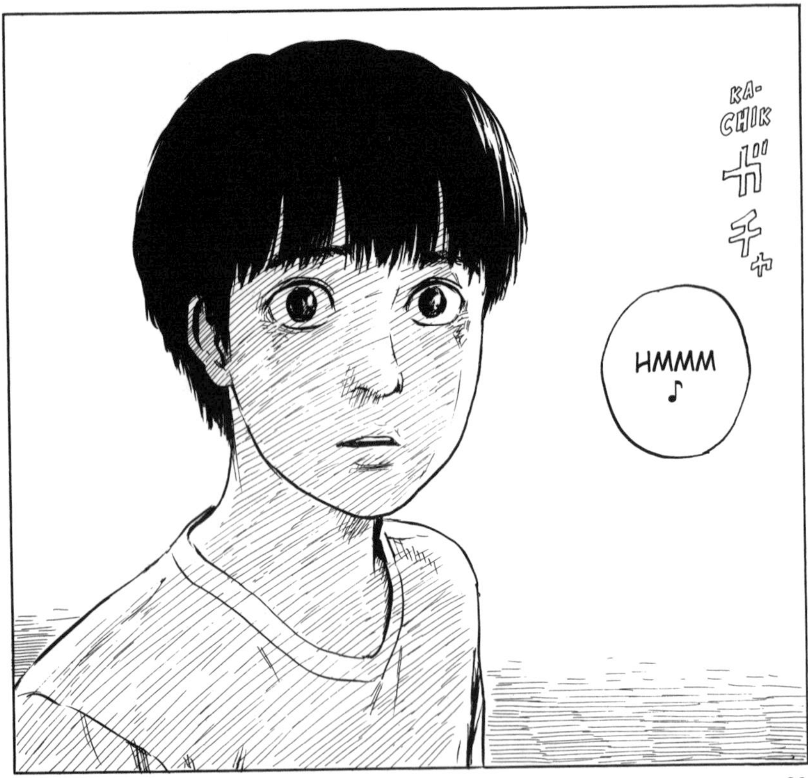
KA-CHIK ガチャ
HMMM ♪

CHAPTER 17 Tryst

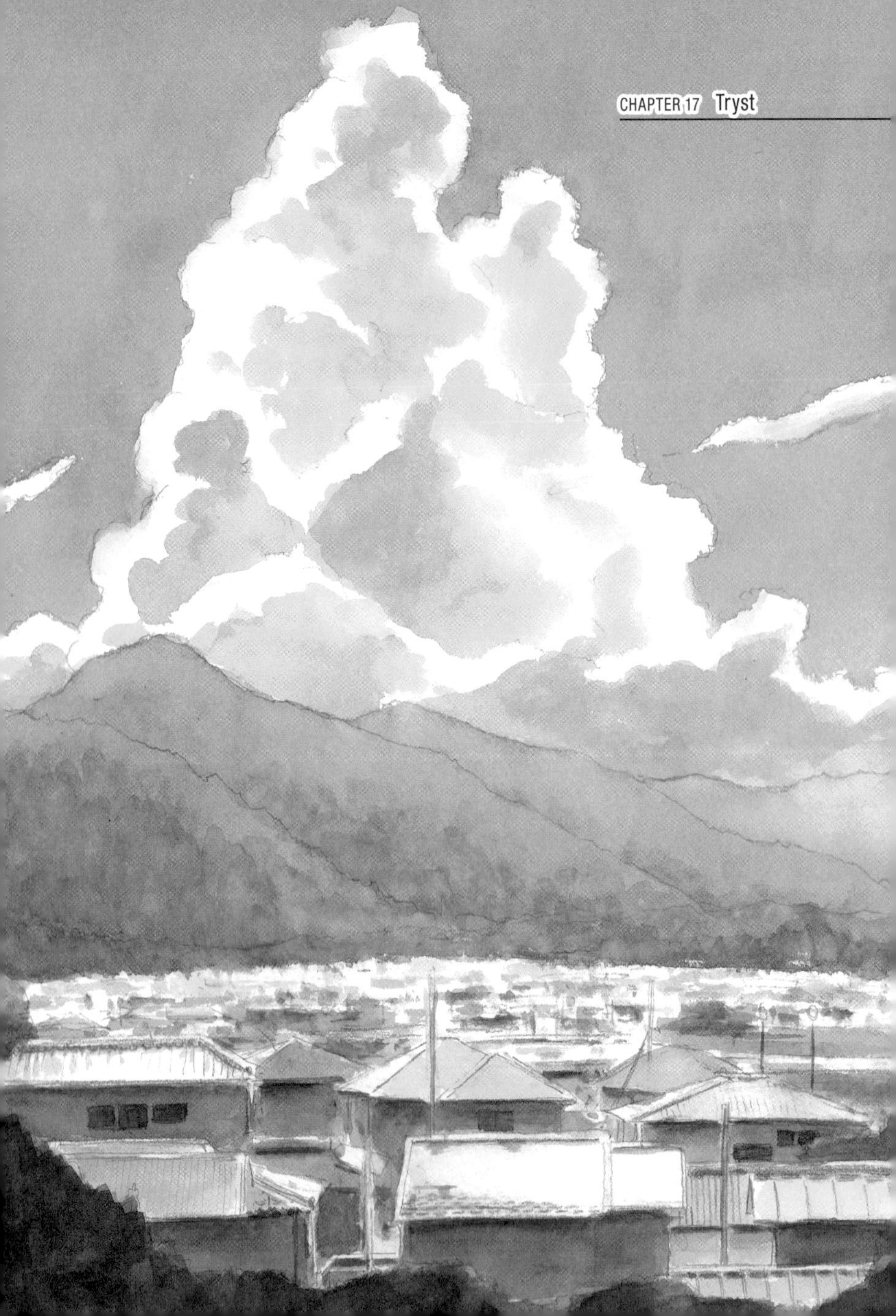

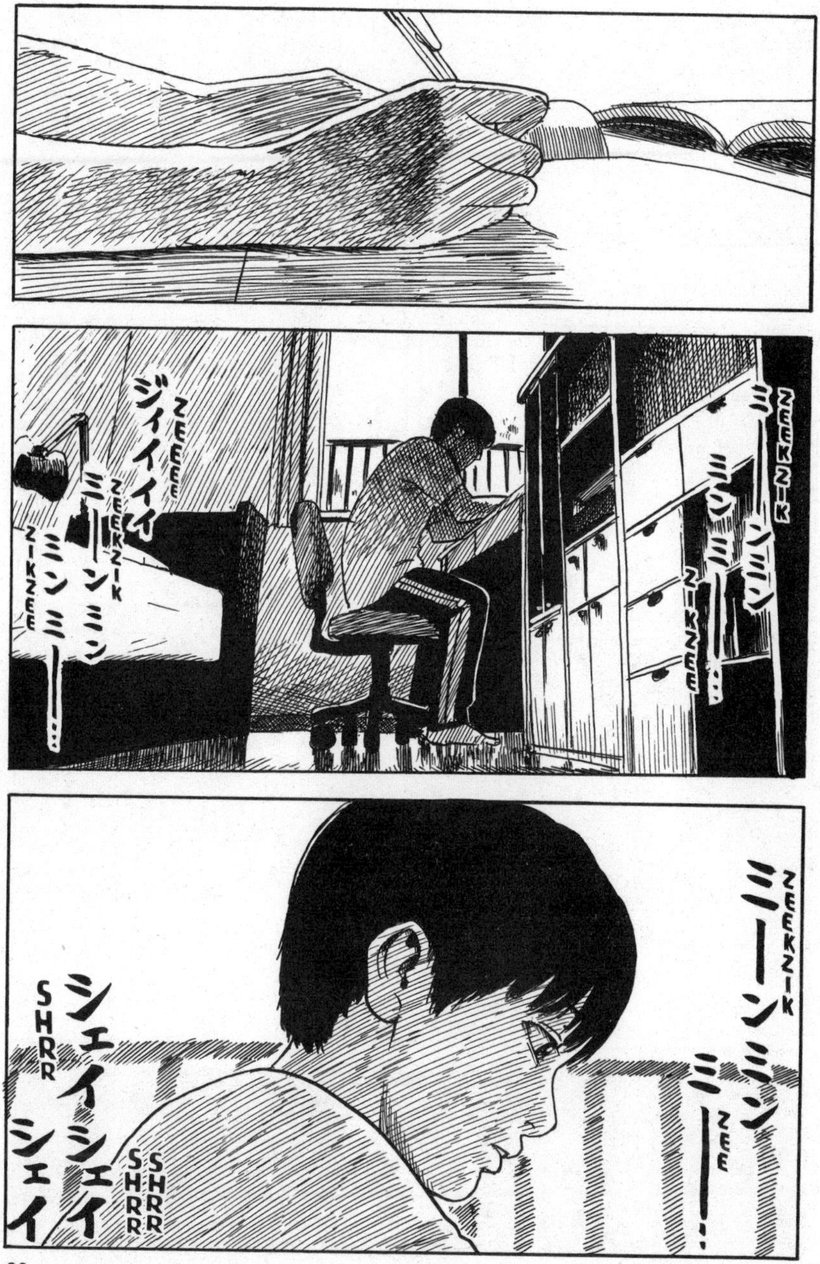
ZEEKZIK
ミーンミン
ミンミー…
ZIKZEE
ZEEEE
ジイイイ
ZEEKZIK
ミーンミン
ミンミー…
ZIKZEE
ZEEKZIK
ミーンミンミー!!
ZEE
SHRR
シェイシェイ
SHRR
シェイ
SHRR

Mommy didn't say anything else after that.

About Shige or about Fukiishi.

And we didn't go to the hospital to see Shige even once,

for three whole weeks.

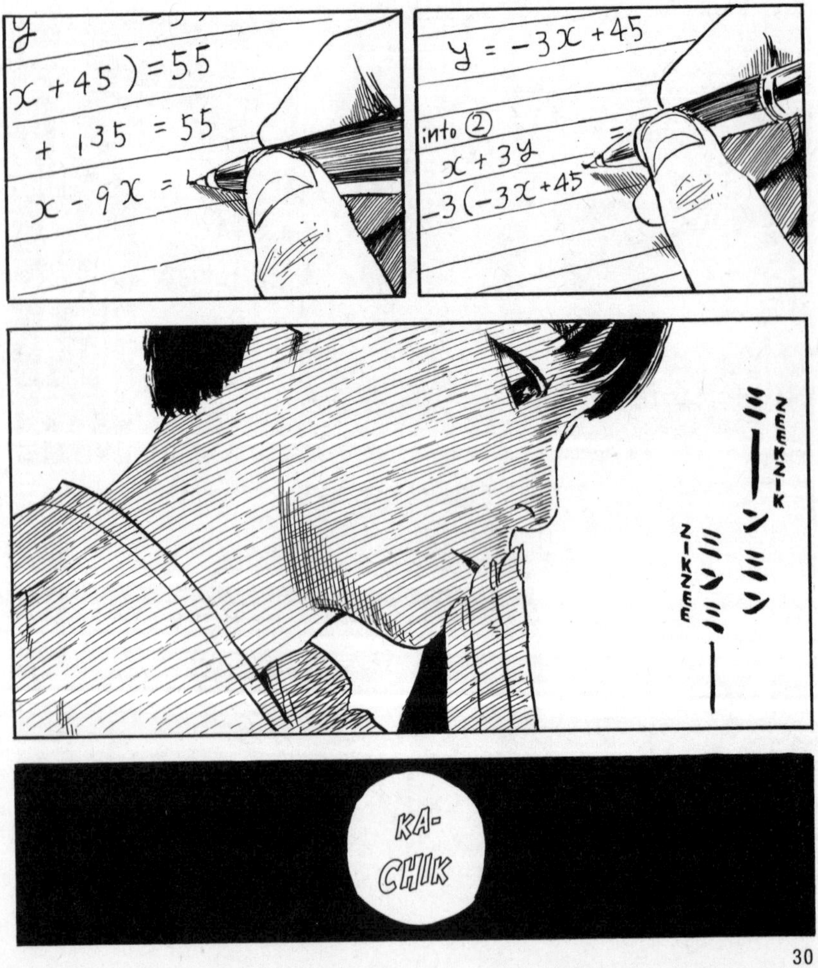
y = -3x + 45
into ②
x + 3y
-3(-3x+45
x + 45) = 55
+ 135 = 55
x - 9x =
ミーンミンミンミー
ZEEKZIK
ZIKZEE
KA-CHIK

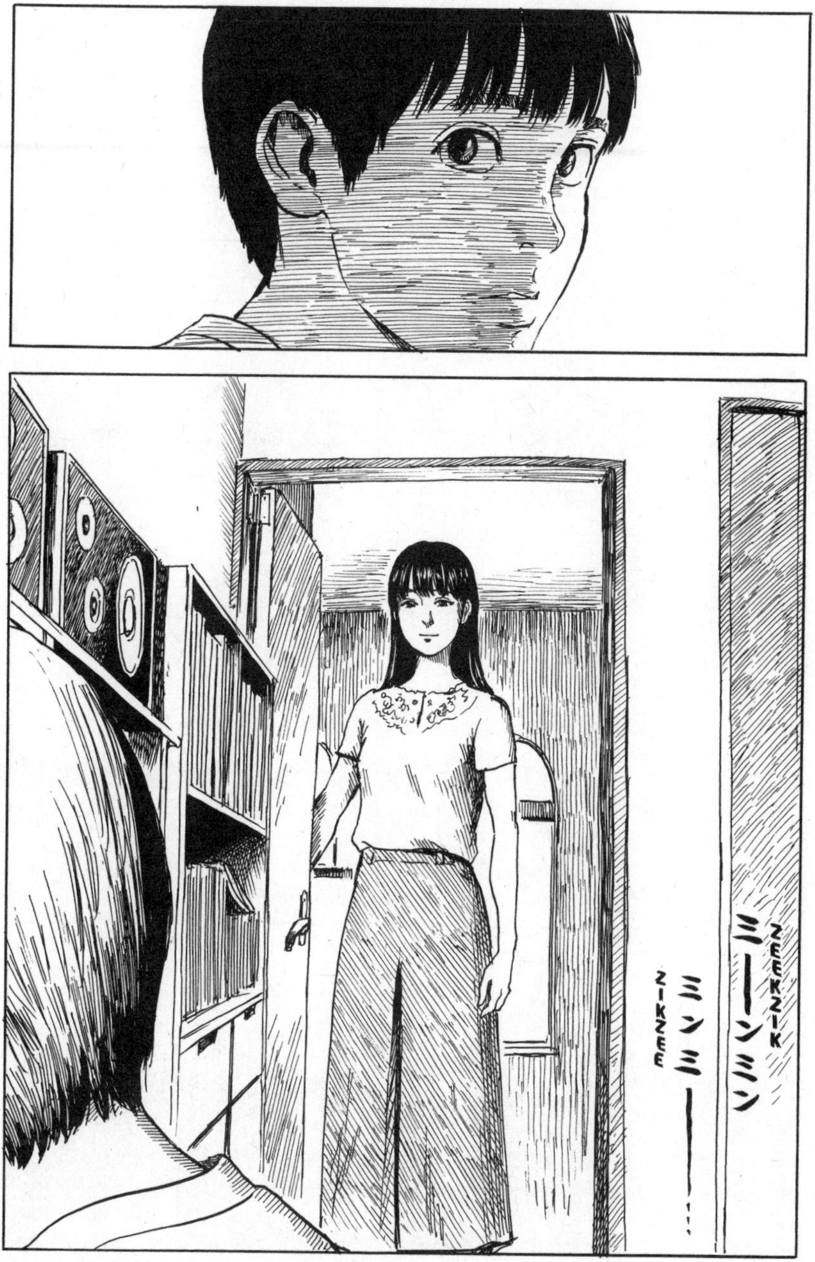
ミーンミン
ZEEKZIK
ミンミーー…
ZIKZEE

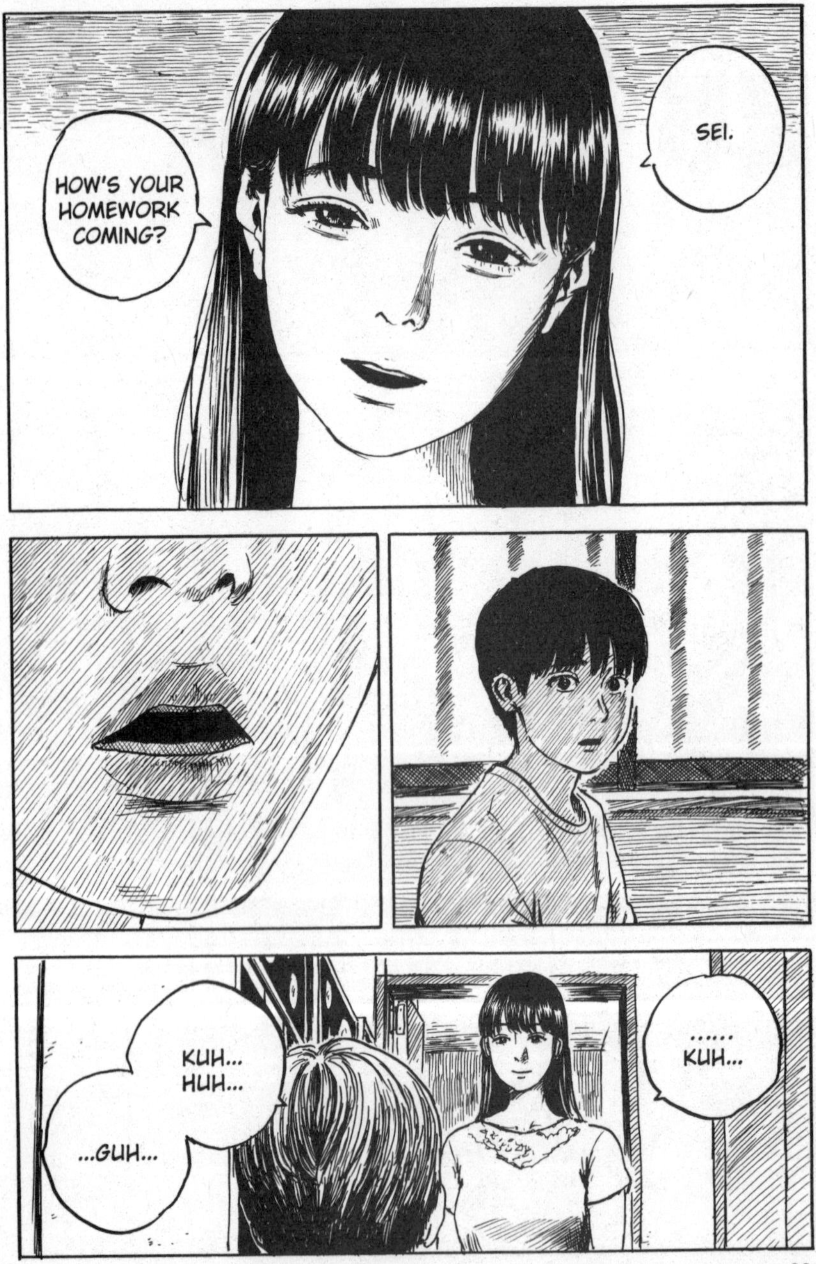
SEI.
HOW'S YOUR HOMEWORK COMING?
...... KUH...
KUH... HUH...
...GUH...

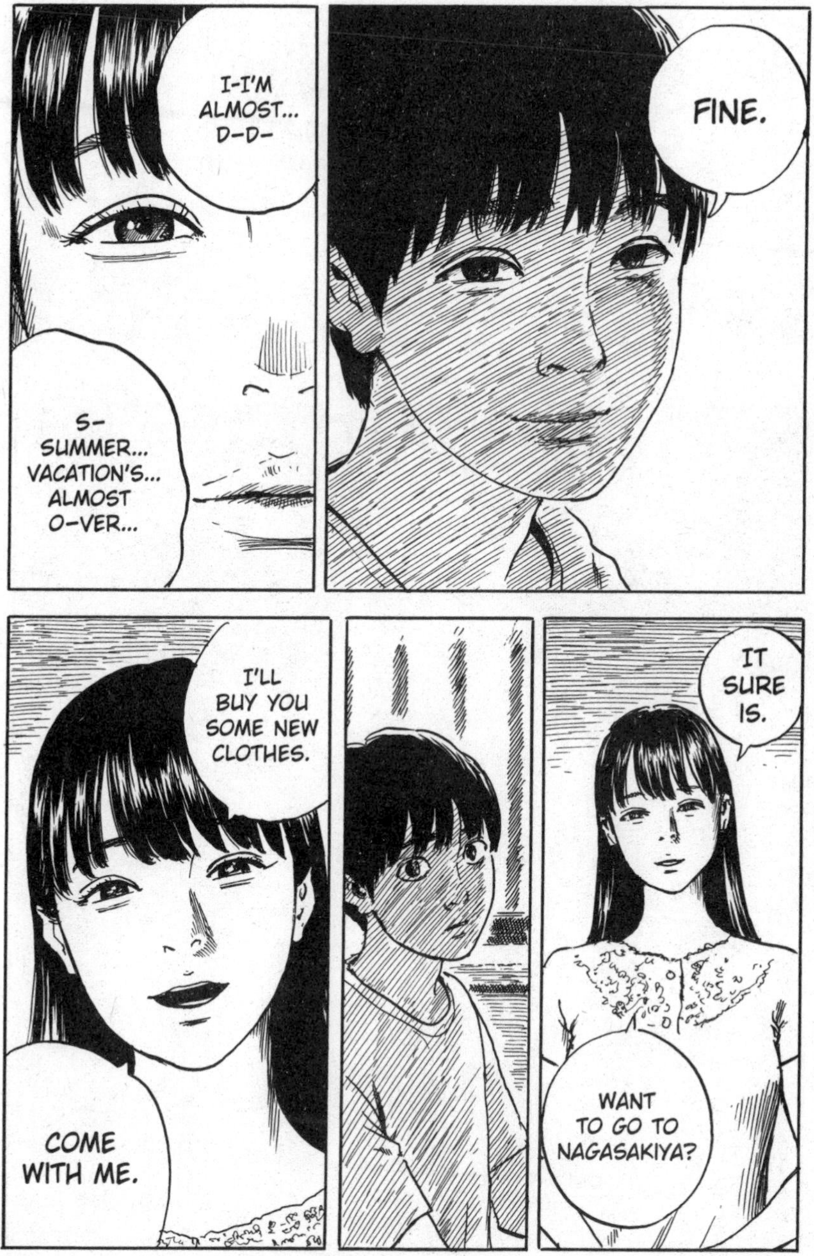
FINE.
I-I'M ALMOST... D-D-
S- SUMMER... VACATION'S... ALMOST O-VER...
IT SURE IS.
WANT TO GO TO NAGASAKIYA?
I'LL BUY YOU SOME NEW CLOTHES.
COME WITH ME.

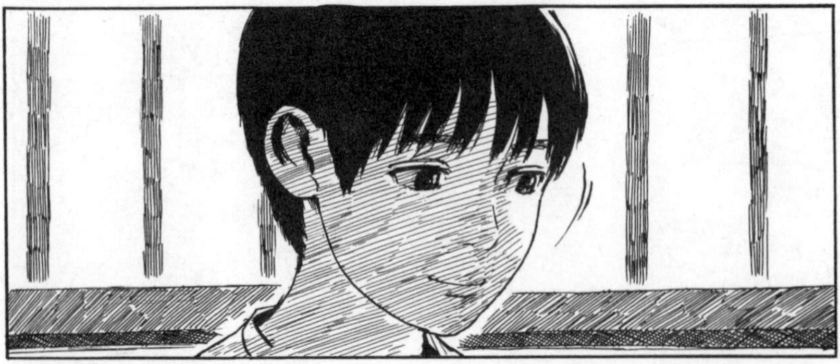

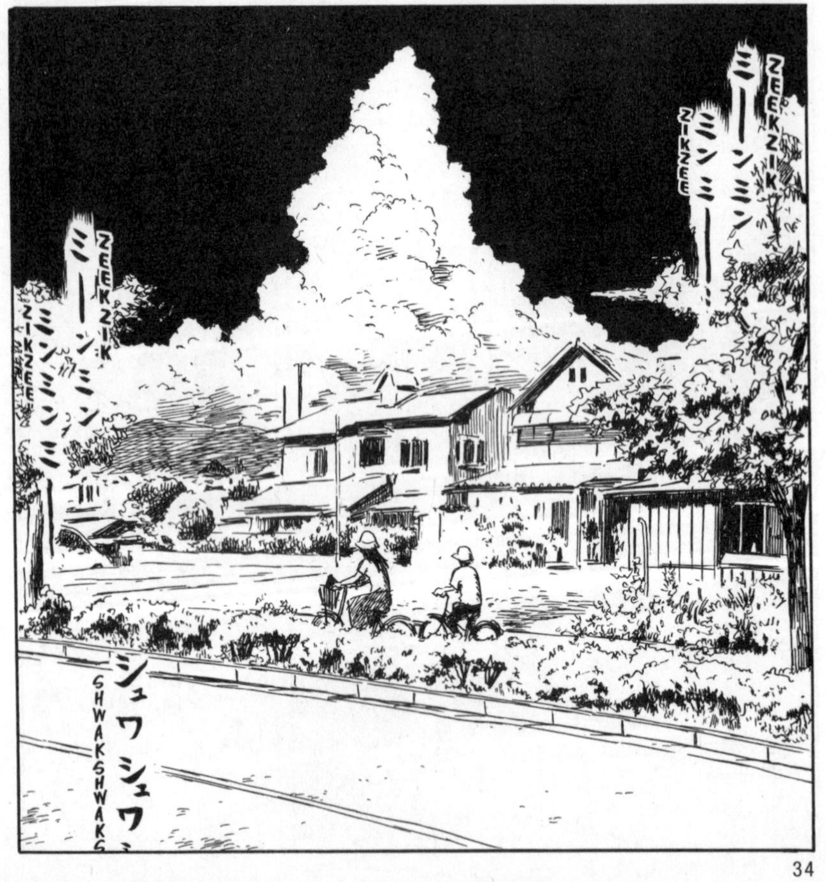
ミーンミンミンミー…
ZEEKZIK
ZIKZEE
ミーンミンミンミ
ZEEKZIK
ZIKZEE
シュワシュワ
SHWAKSHWAK

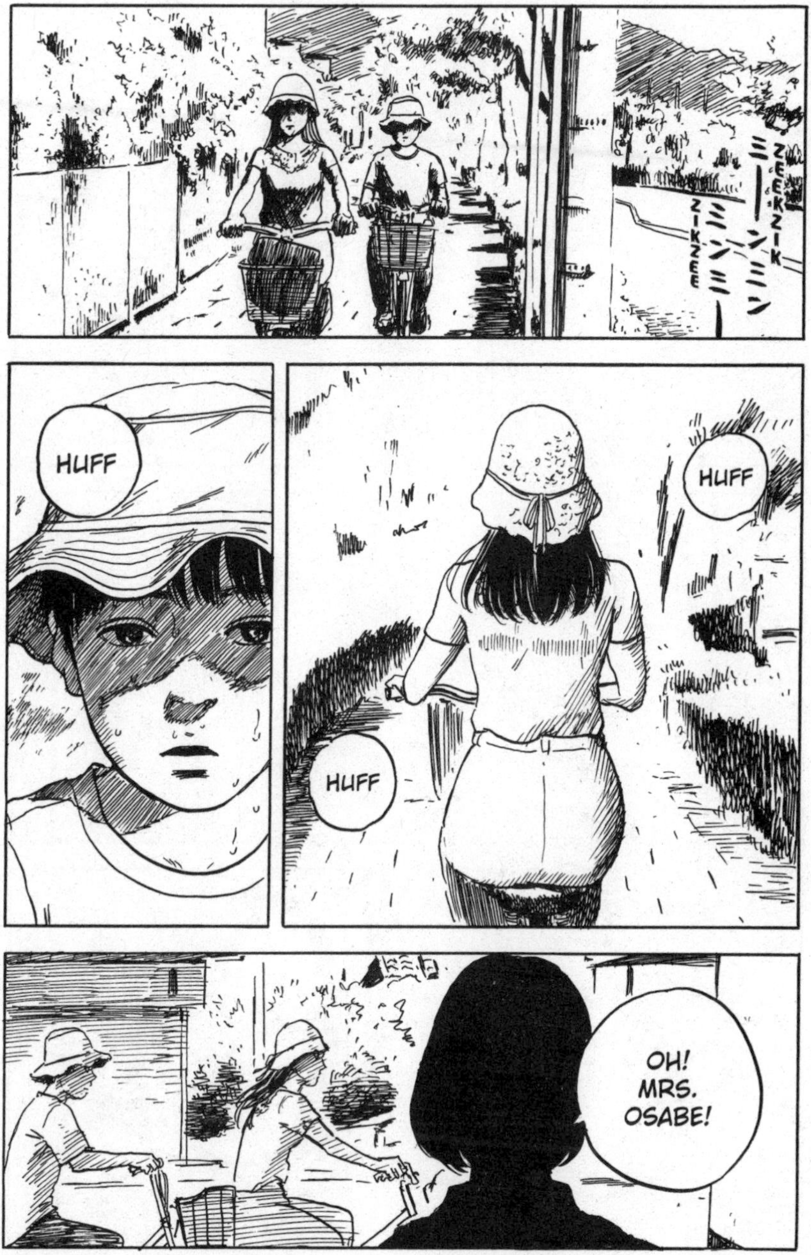
ZEEKZIK
ミーンミンミン
ZIKZEE
ミンミンミー
HUFF
HUFF
HUFF
OH! MRS. OSABE!

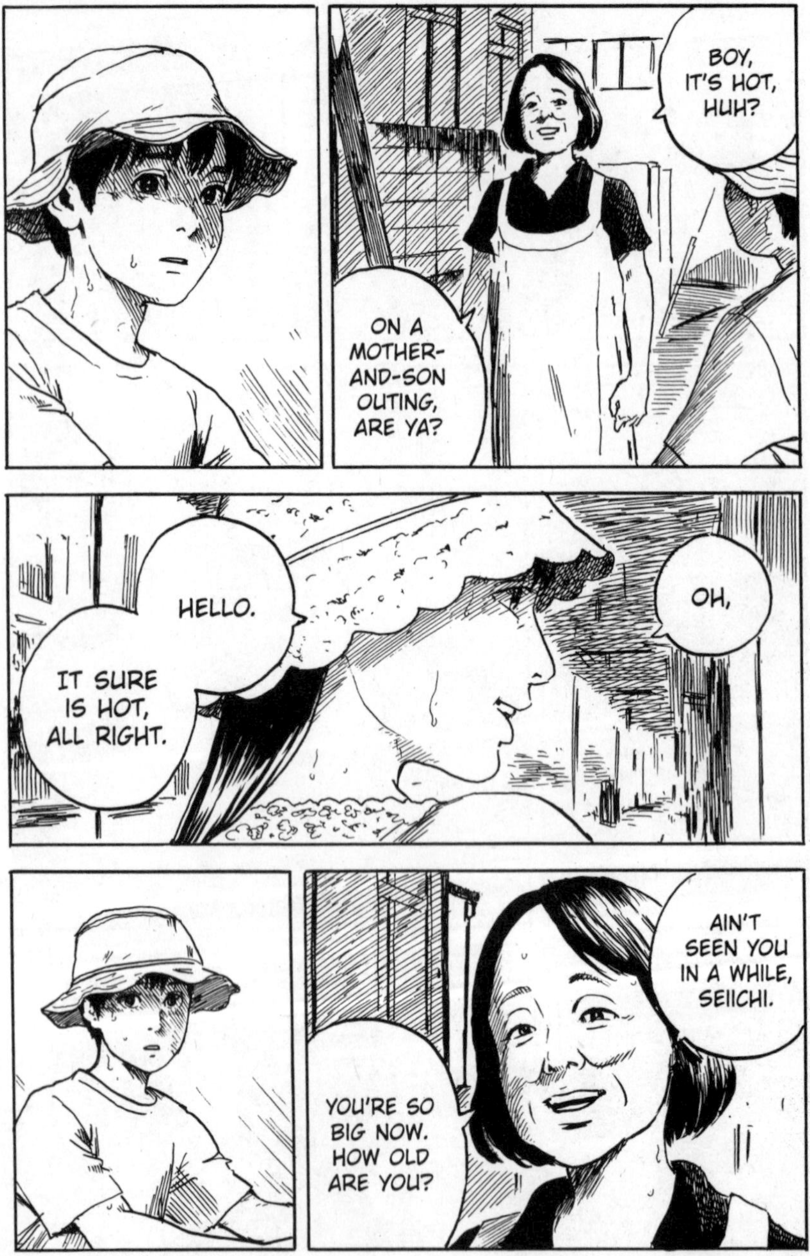
BOY, IT'S HOT, HUH?
ON A MOTHER-AND-SON OUTING, ARE YA?
OH,
HELLO.
IT SURE IS HOT, ALL RIGHT.
AIN'T SEEN YOU IN A WHILE, SEIICHI.
YOU'RE SO BIG NOW. HOW OLD ARE YOU?

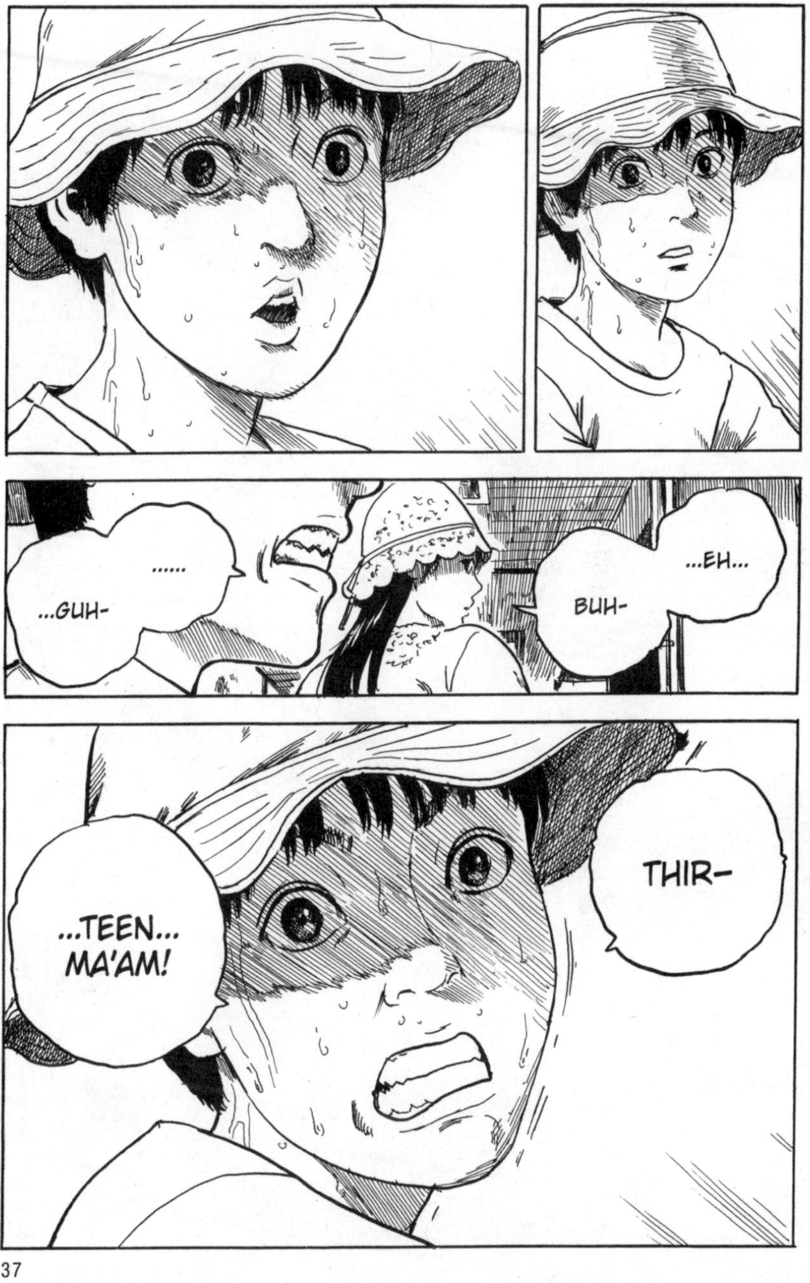
...EH...
BUH-
......
...GUH-
THIR-
...TEEN... MA'AM!

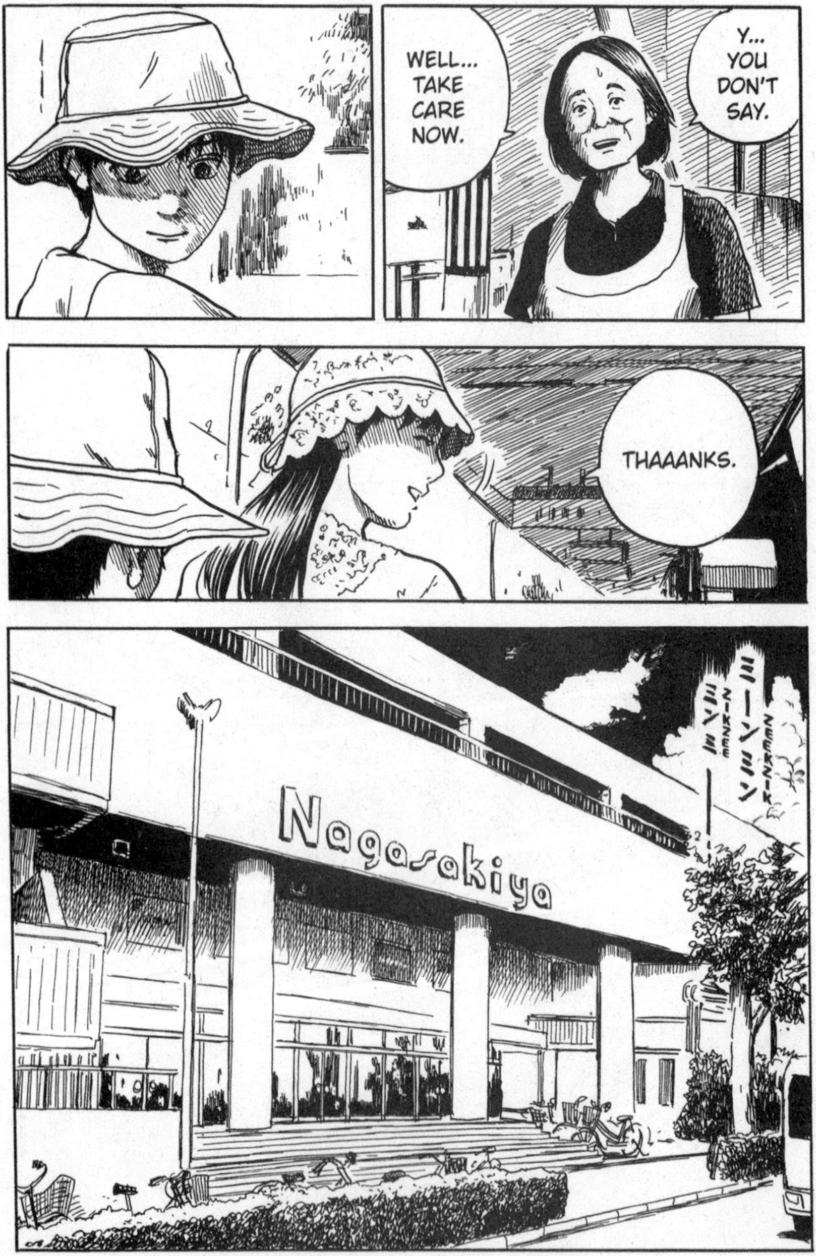
Y... YOU DON'T SAY.
WELL... TAKE CARE NOW.
THAAANKS.
ミーンミン
ZEEKZIK
ミンミーー
ZIKZEE
Nagasakiya

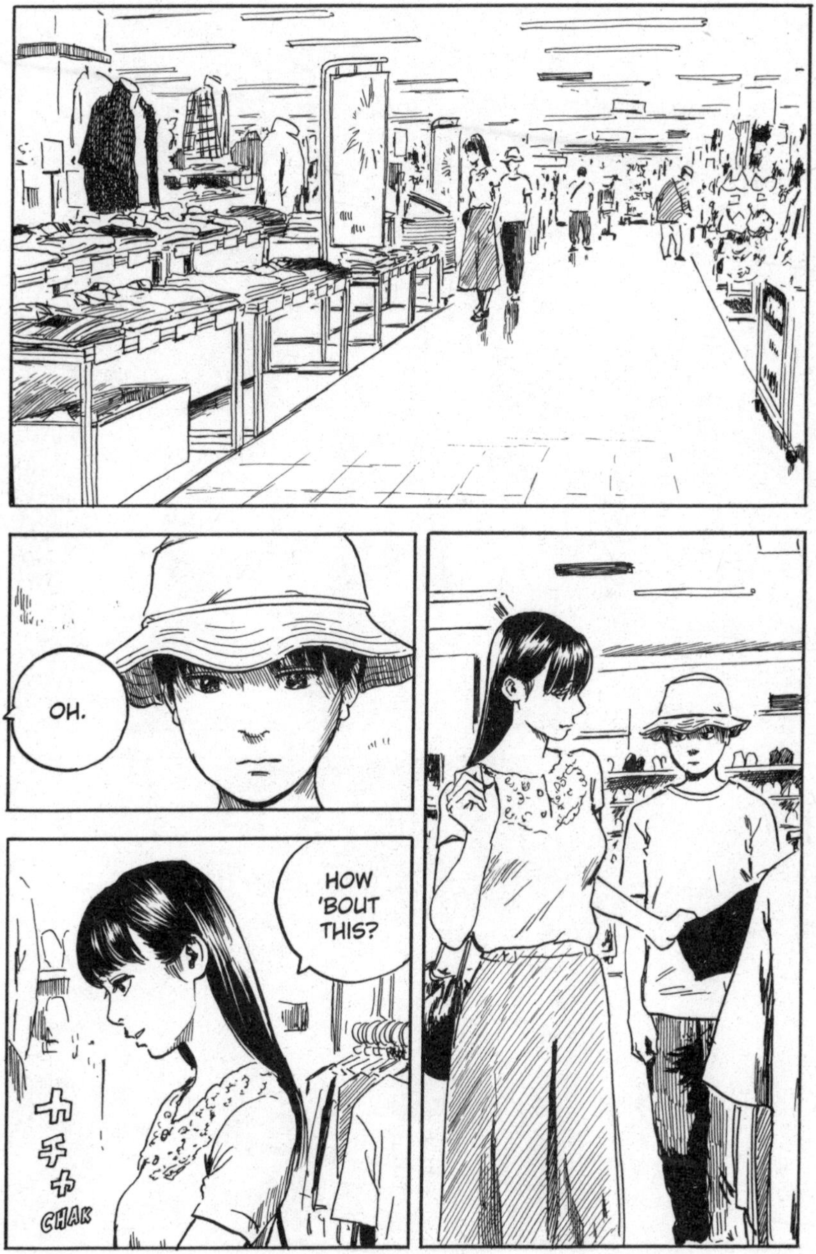
OH.
HOW 'BOUT THIS?
カチャ
CHAK

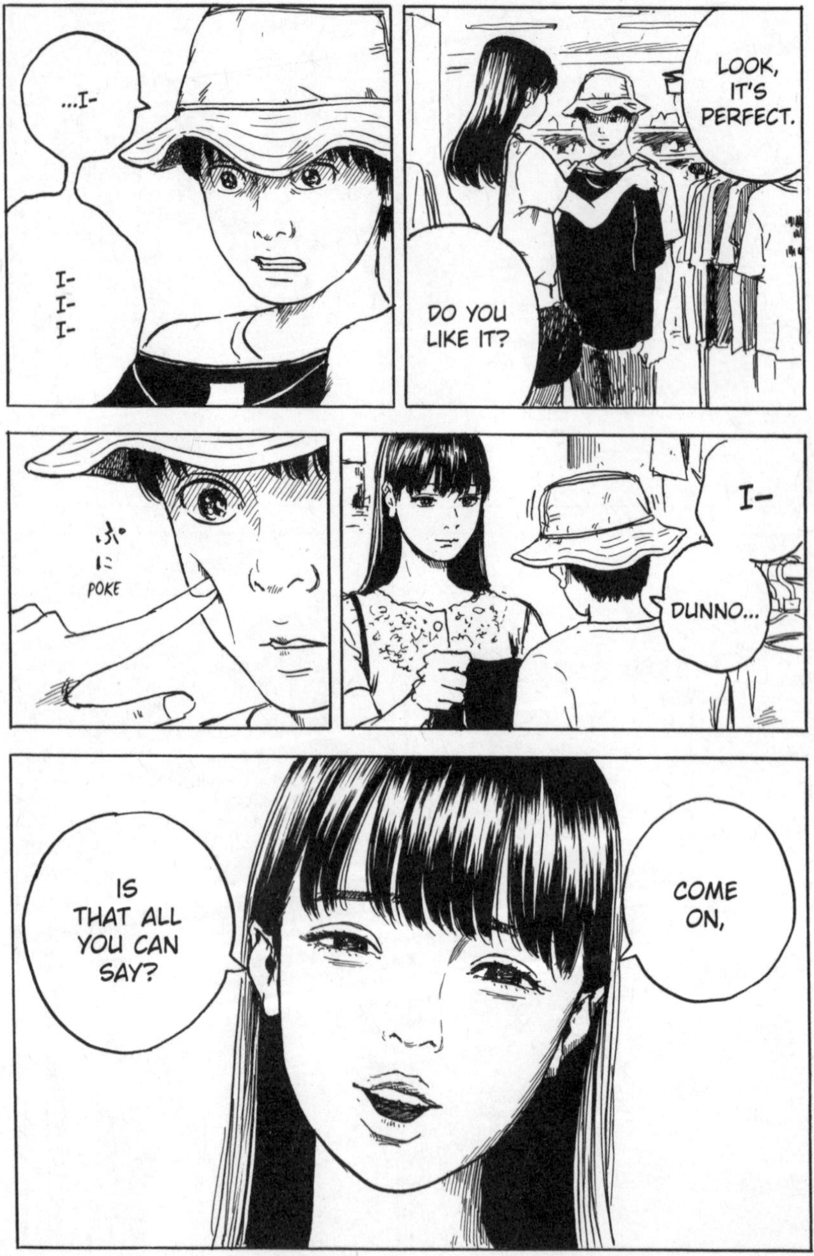
LOOK, IT'S PERFECT.
DO YOU LIKE IT?
...I-
I- I- I-
I-
DUNNO...
ぷに
POKE
COME ON,
IS THAT ALL YOU CAN SAY?

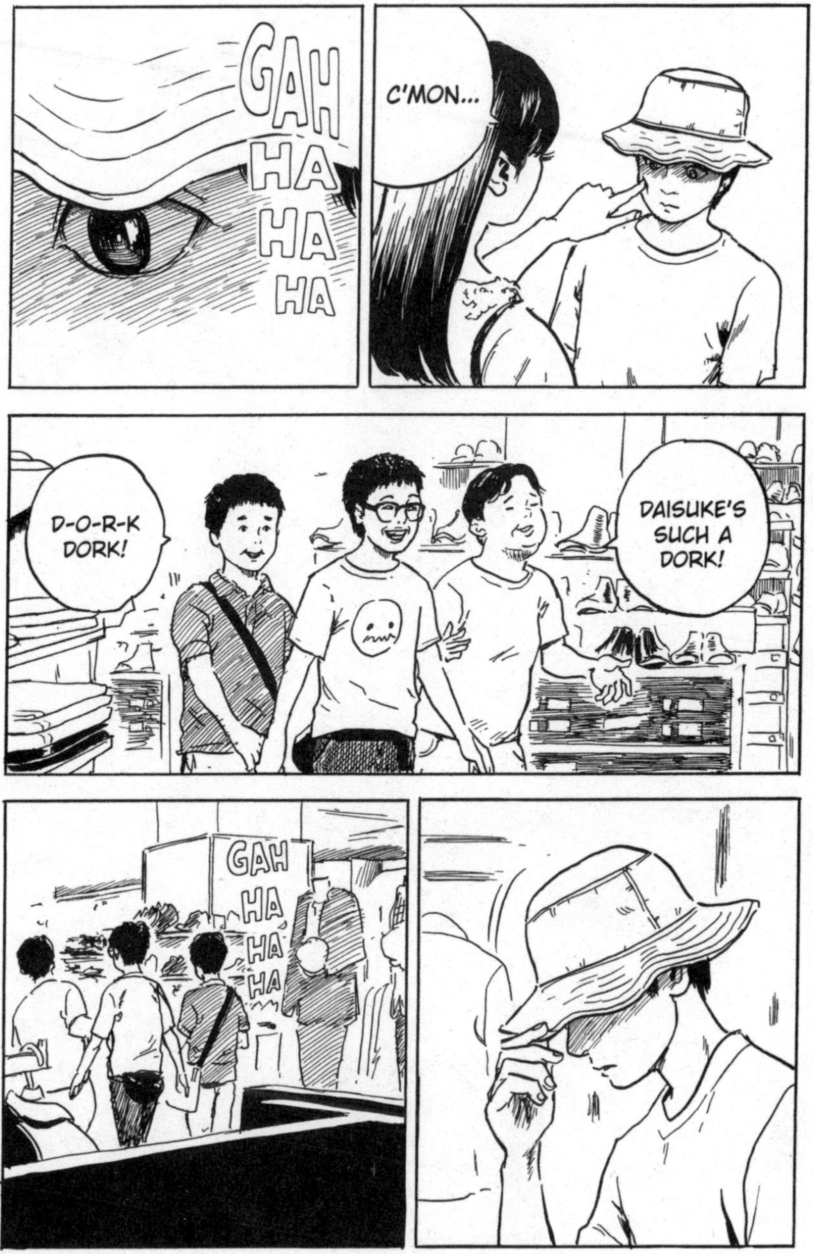
C'MON...
GAH HA HA HA
DAISUKE'S SUCH A DORK!
D-O-R-K DORK!
GAH HA HA HA

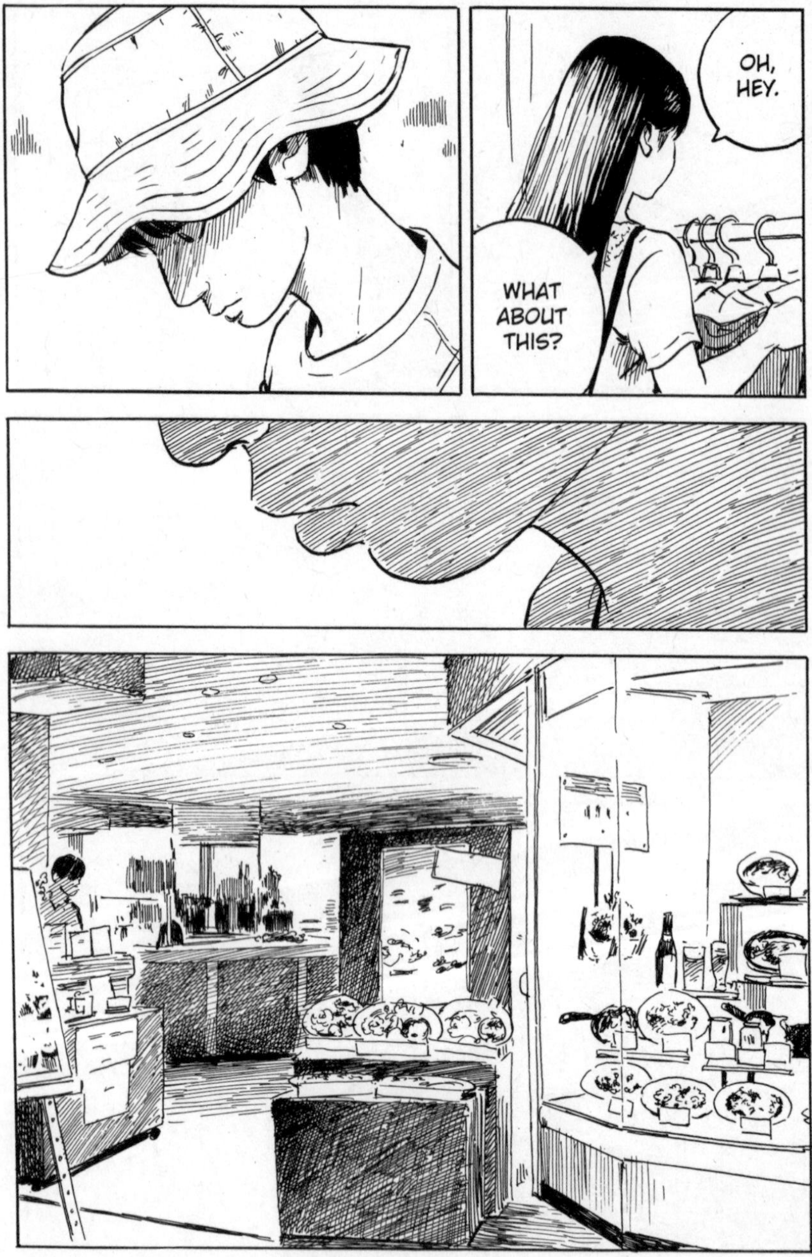
OH, HEY.
WHAT ABOUT THIS?

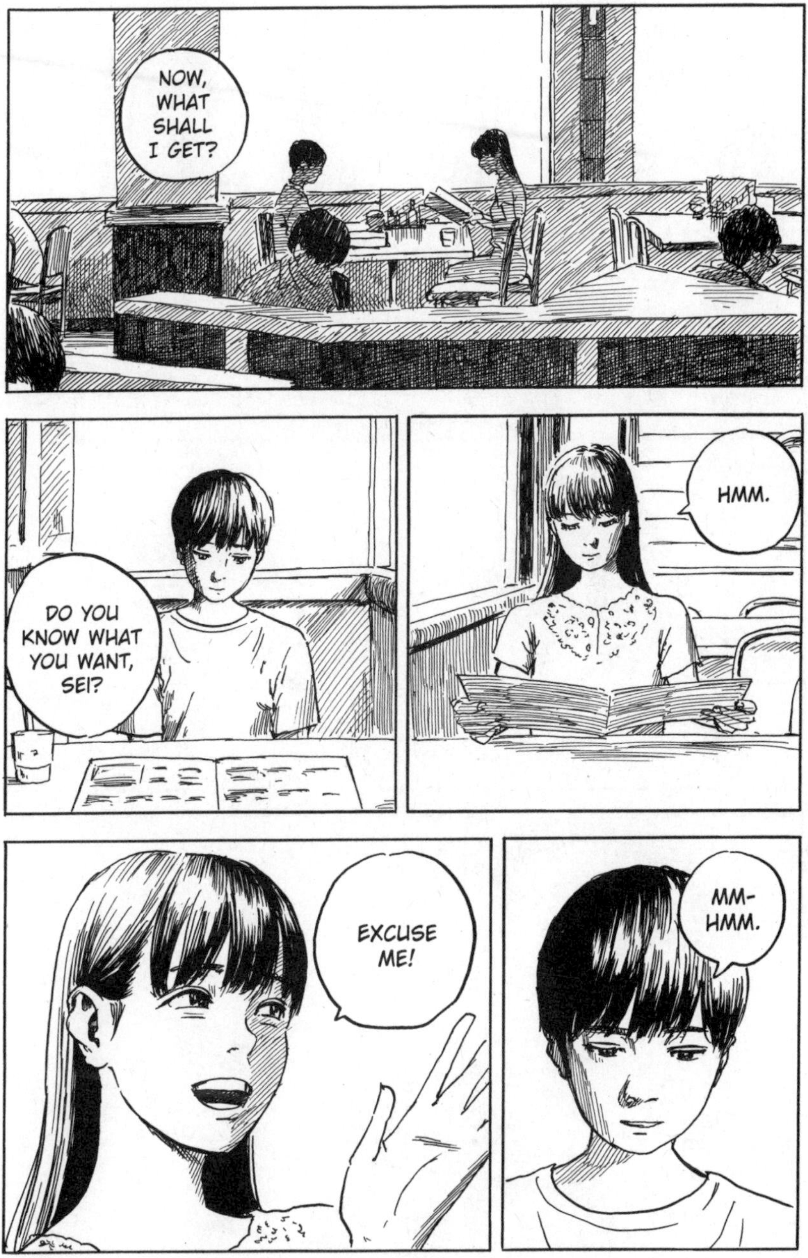
NOW, WHAT SHALL I GET?
HMM.
DO YOU KNOW WHAT YOU WANT, SEI?
MM-HMM.
EXCUSE ME!

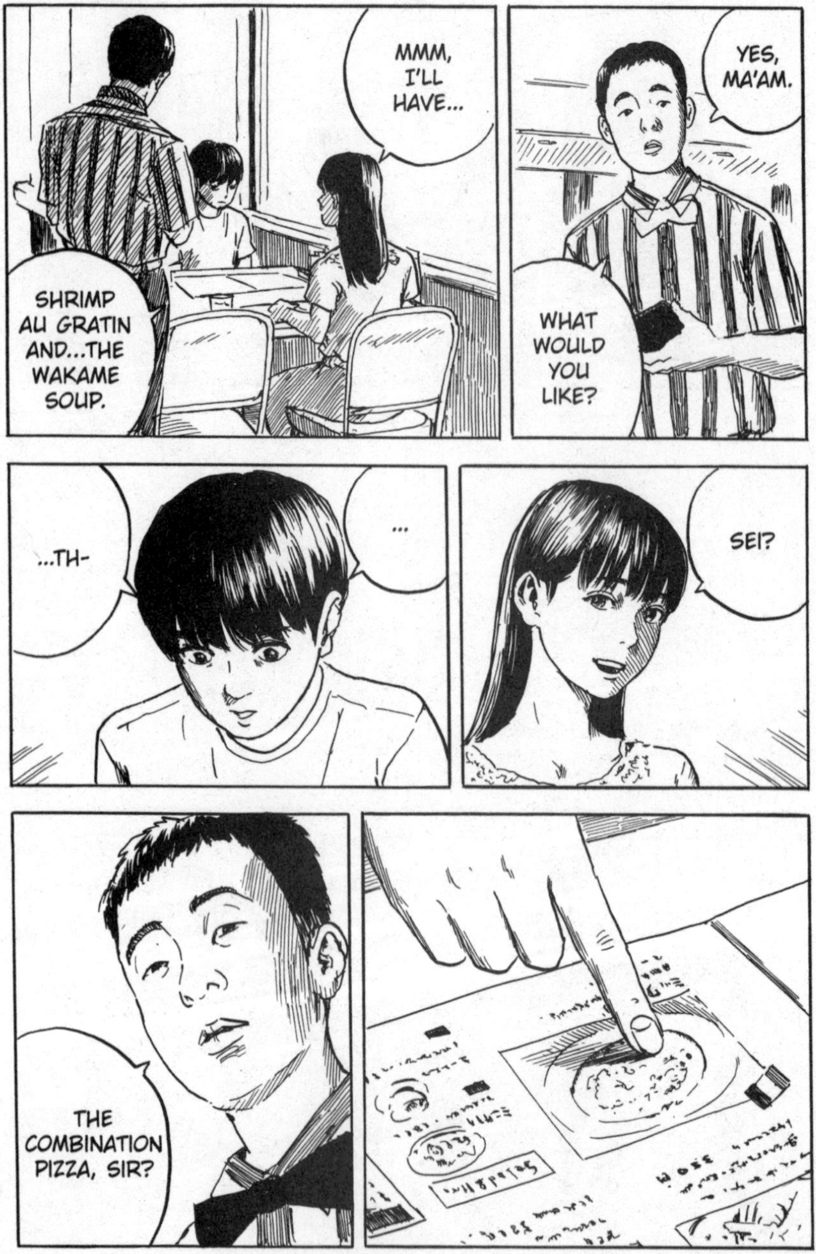
YES, MA'AM.
WHAT WOULD YOU LIKE?
MMM, I'LL HAVE...
SHRIMP AU GRATIN AND...THE WAKAME SOUP.
SEI?
...
...TH-
THE COMBINATION PIZZA, SIR?

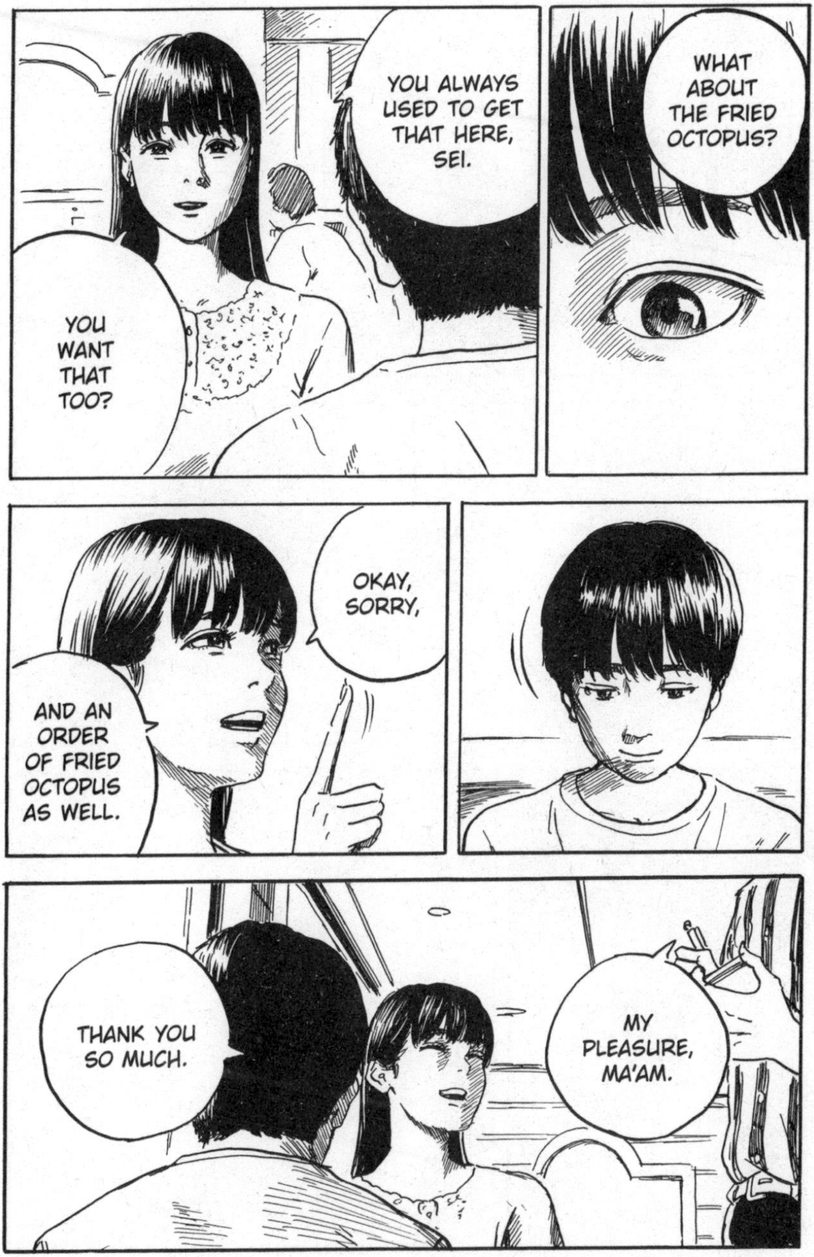
WHAT ABOUT THE FRIED OCTOPUS?
YOU ALWAYS USED TO GET THAT HERE, SEI.
YOU WANT THAT TOO?
OKAY, SORRY,
AND AN ORDER OF FRIED OCTOPUS AS WELL.
MY PLEASURE, MA'AM.
THANK YOU SO MUCH.

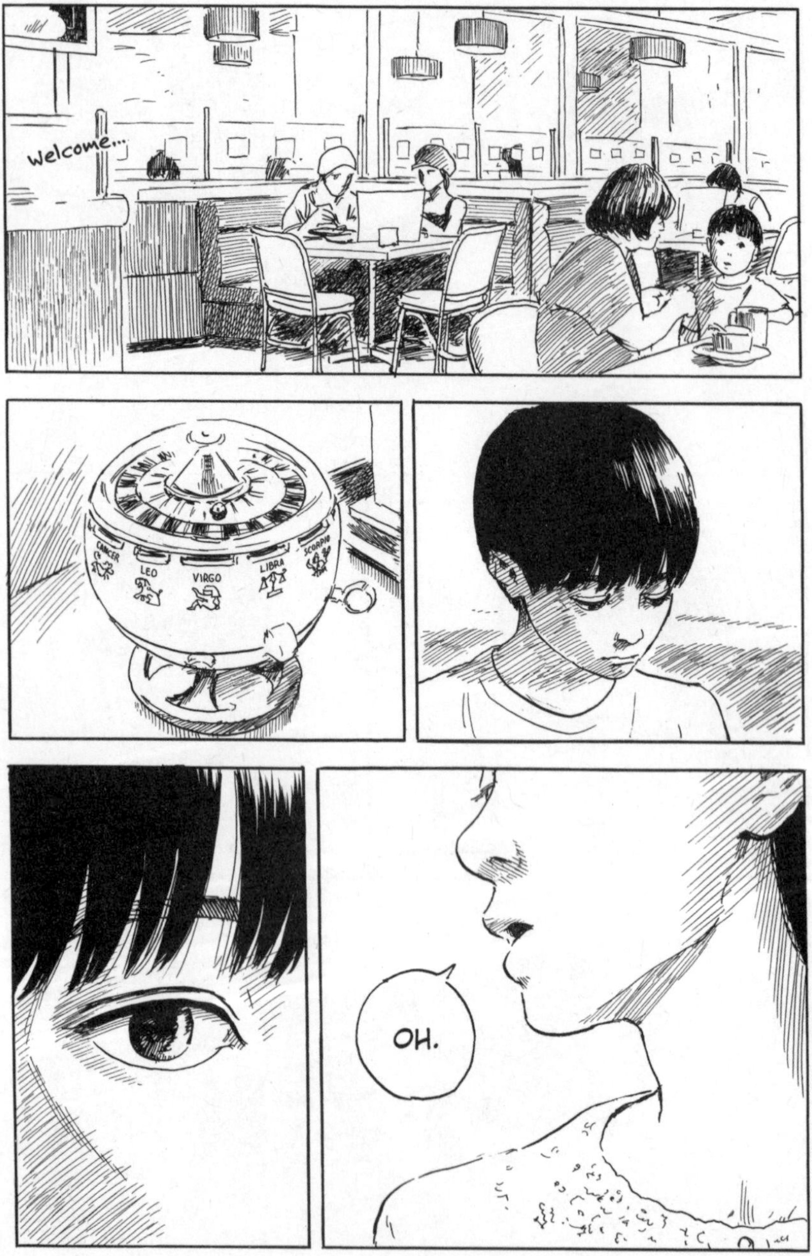
welcome...
CANCER
LEO
VIRGO
LIBRA
SCORPIO
OH.

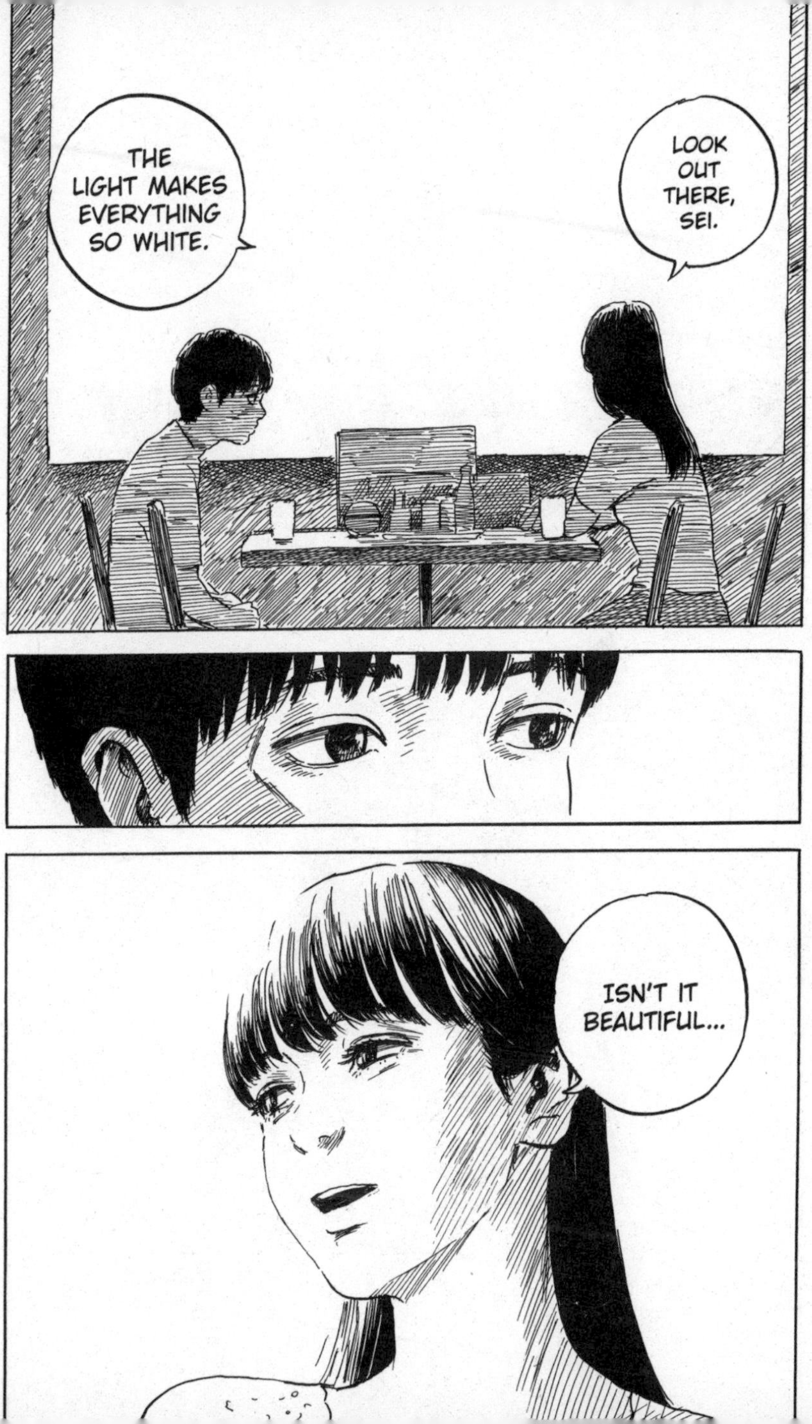
LOOK OUT THERE, SEI.
THE LIGHT MAKES EVERYTHING SO WHITE.
ISN'T IT BEAUTIFUL...

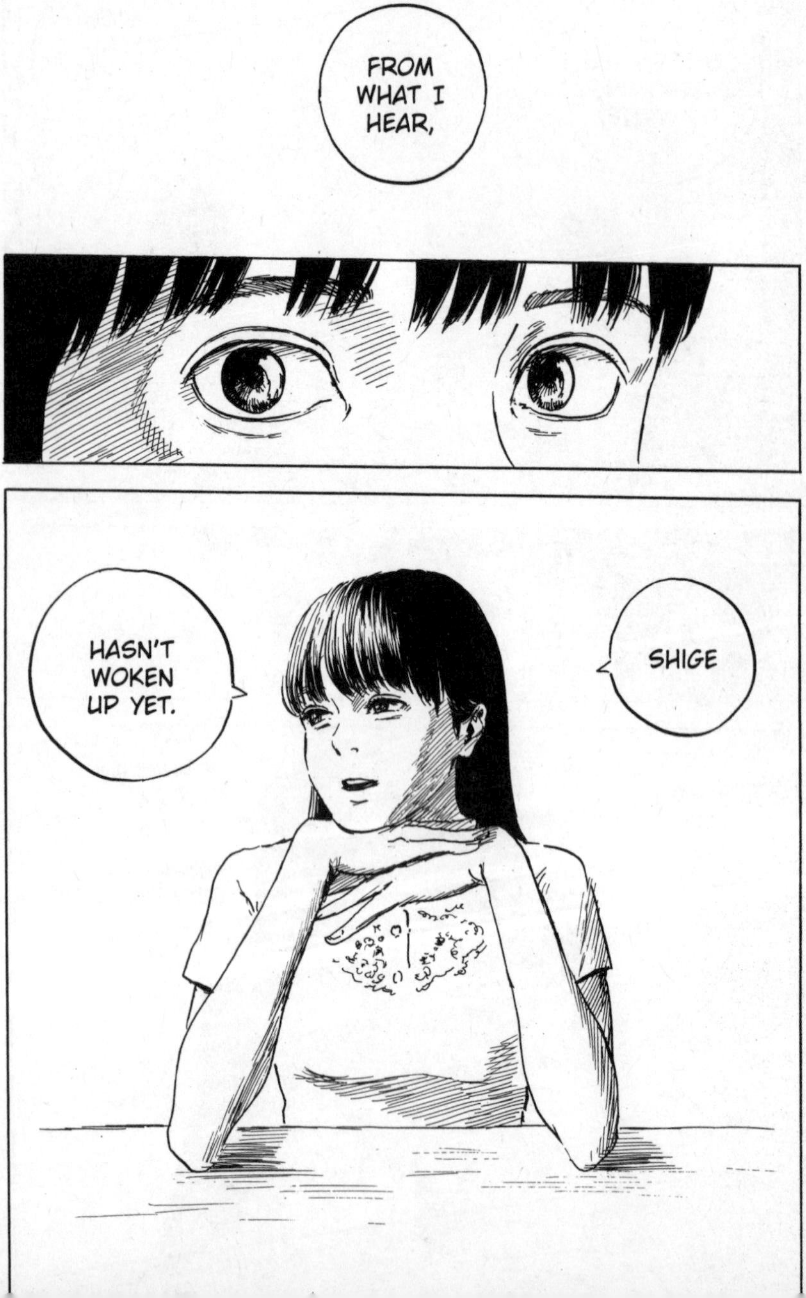
FROM WHAT I HEAR,
SHIGE
HASN'T WOKEN UP YET.

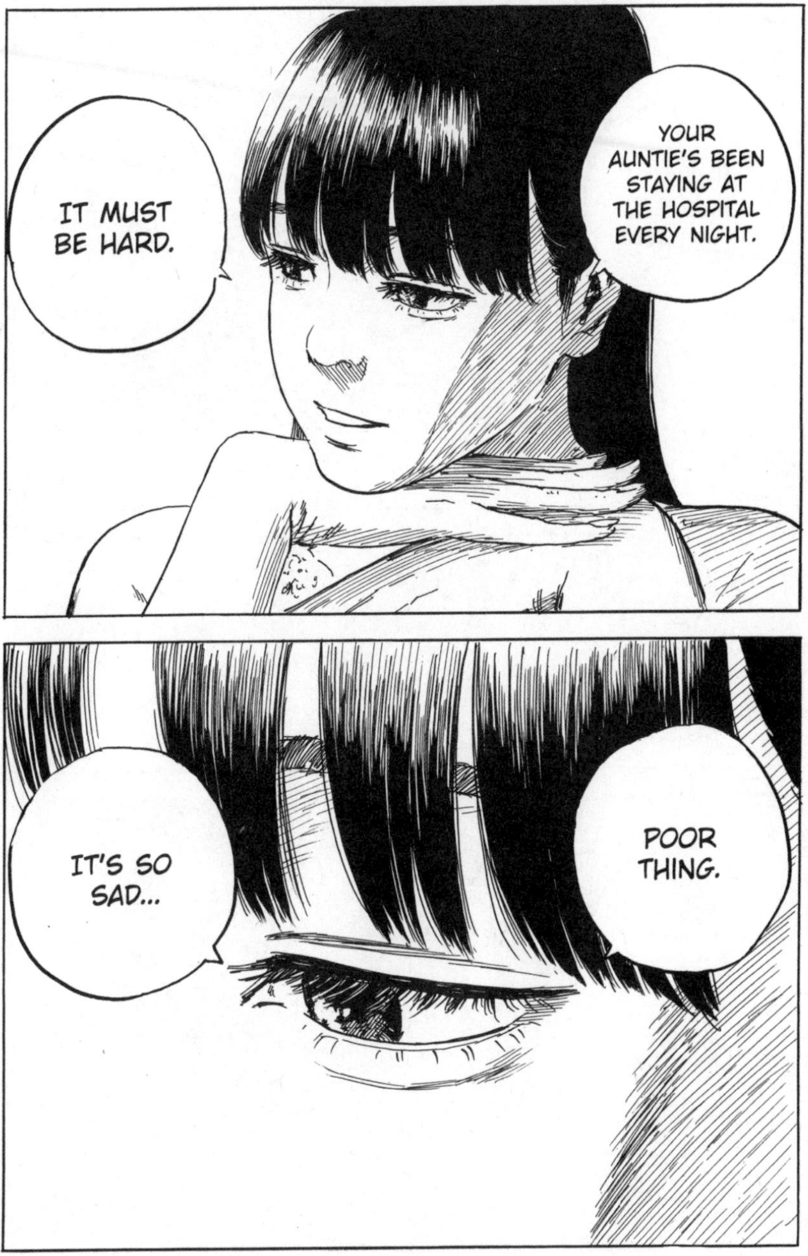

YOUR AUNTIE'S BEEN STAYING AT THE HOSPITAL EVERY NIGHT.
IT MUST BE HARD.
POOR THING.
IT'S SO SAD...

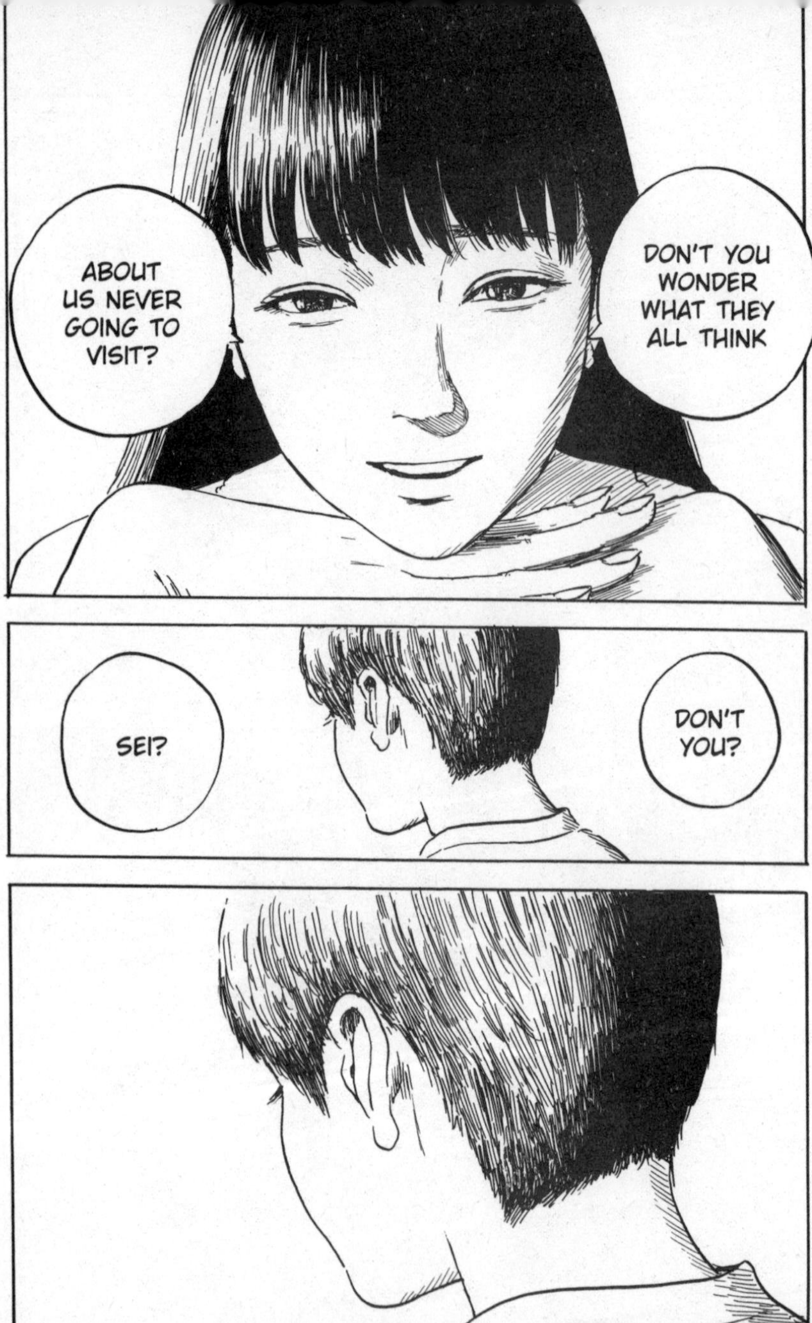
DON'T YOU WONDER WHAT THEY ALL THINK
ABOUT US NEVER GOING TO VISIT?
DON'T YOU?
SEI?

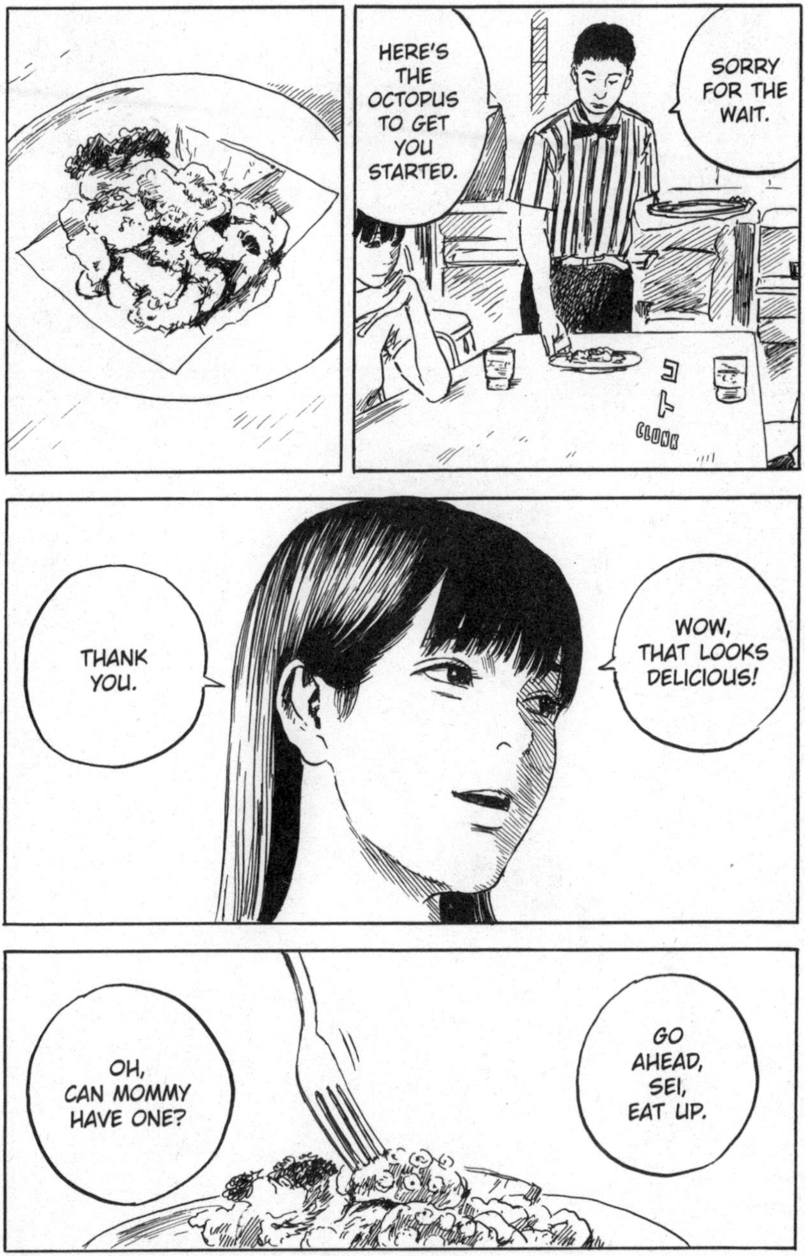
SORRY FOR THE WAIT.
HERE'S THE OCTOPUS TO GET YOU STARTED.
コト
CLUNK
WOW, THAT LOOKS DELICIOUS!
THANK YOU.
GO AHEAD, SEI, EAT UP.
OH, CAN MOMMY HAVE ONE?

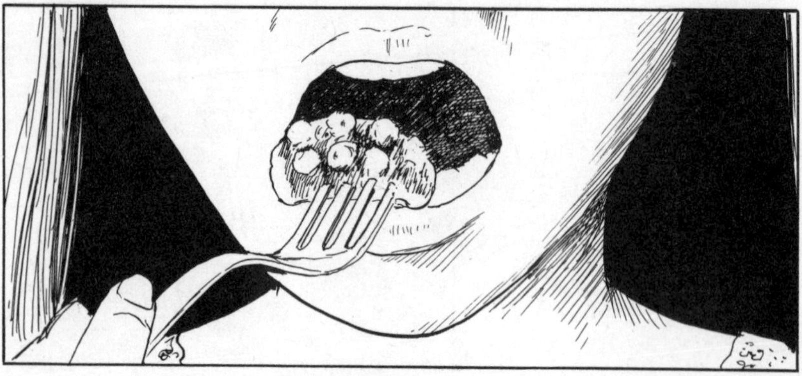

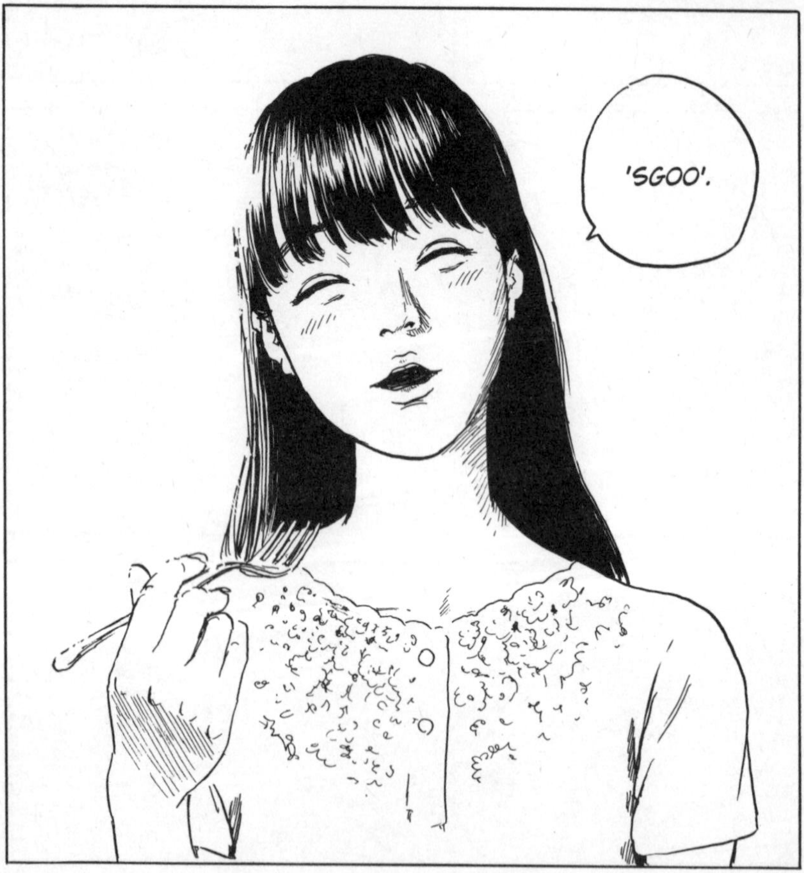
'SGOO'.

CHAPTER 18 Long Day

SEI...

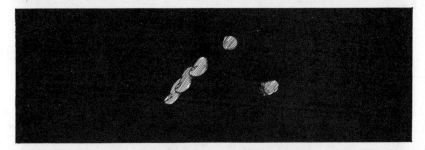

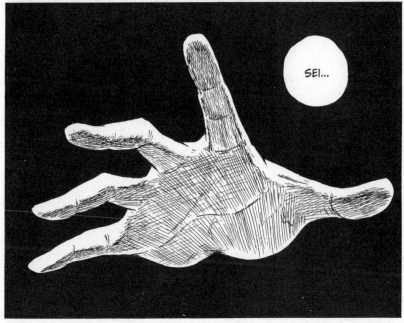

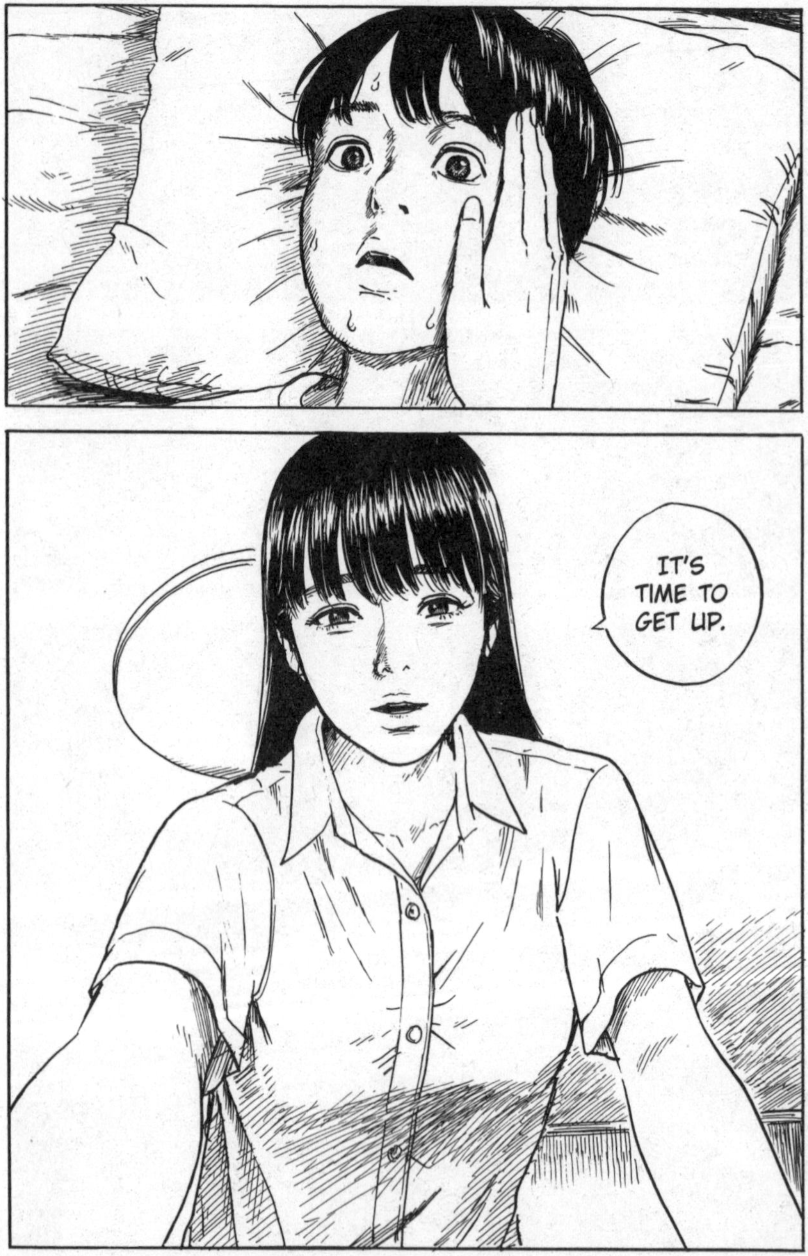
IT'S TIME TO GET UP.

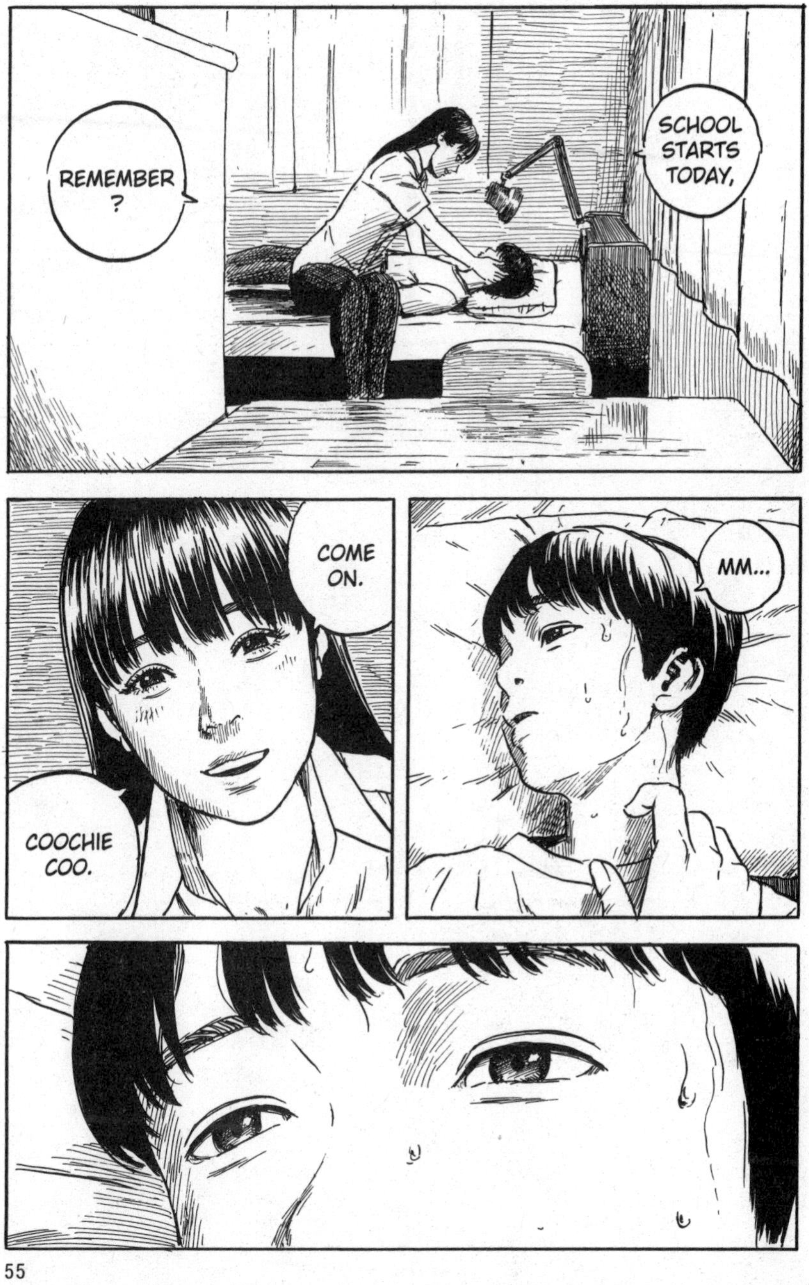
SCHOOL STARTS TODAY,
REMEMBER?
MM...
COME ON.
COOCHIE COO.

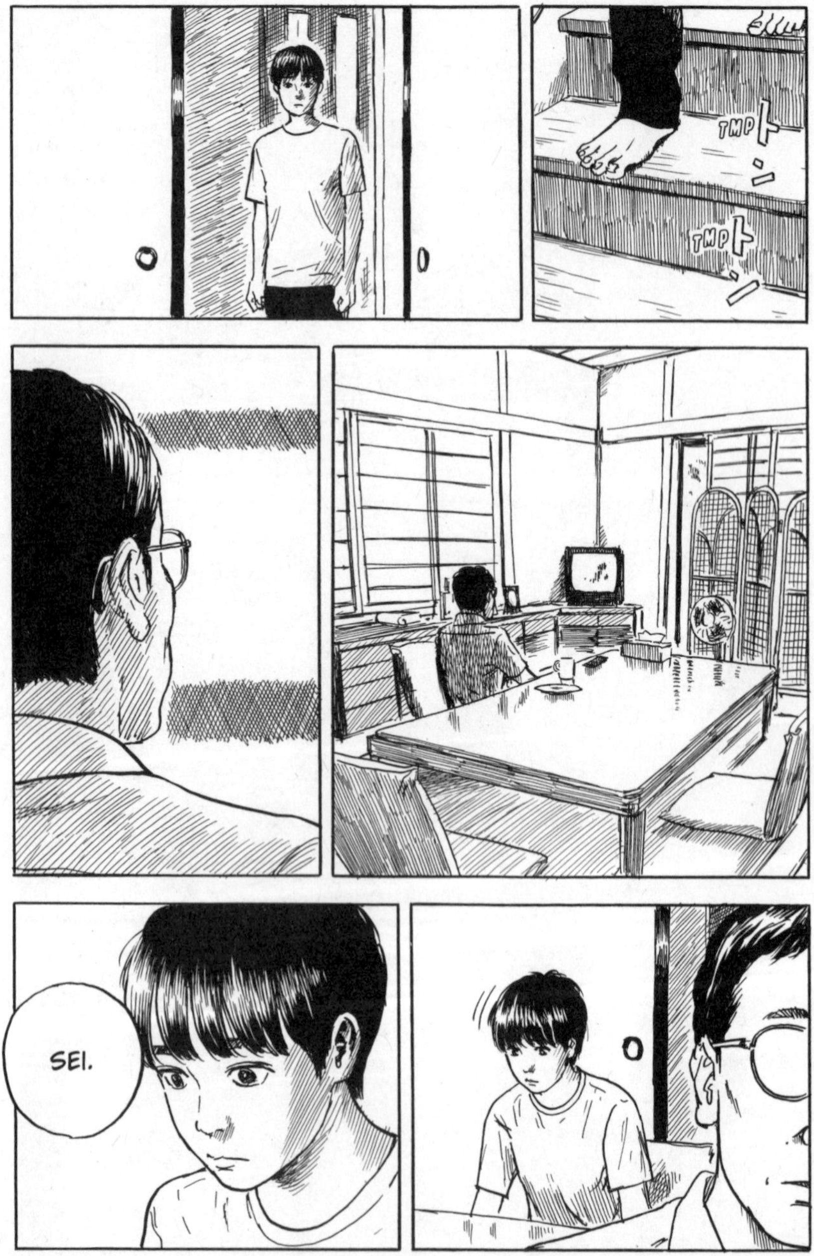
TMP トン
TMP トン
SEI.

WHICH DO YOU WANT,

A PORK BUN OR A RED BEAN BUN?

R—

...ER...

...R—

R...

R—

ERH—

ER...

GUH—

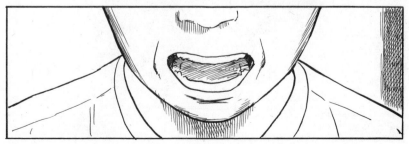

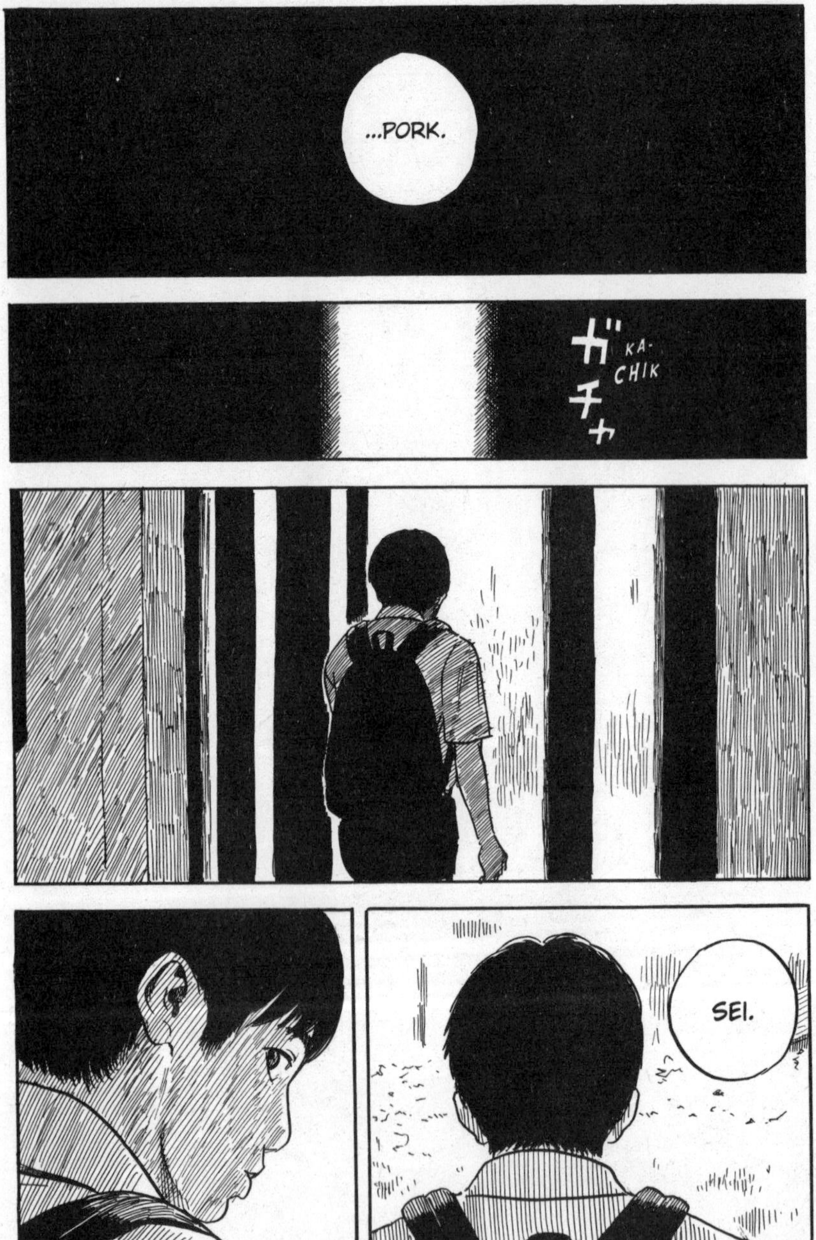
...PORK.
ガチャ
KA-CHIK
SEI.

IT'LL BE FINE.

BE CAREFUL.

ミーンミーン
ミーン
ZEEKZIK
ZIKZEE

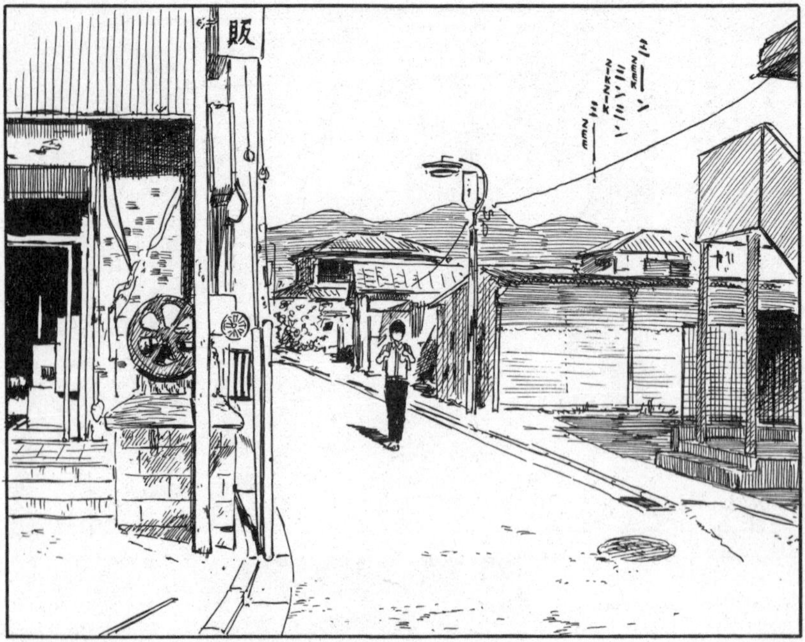
ミーン
MMMN
ミンミンミン
MIN-MIN
ミー
MMMN

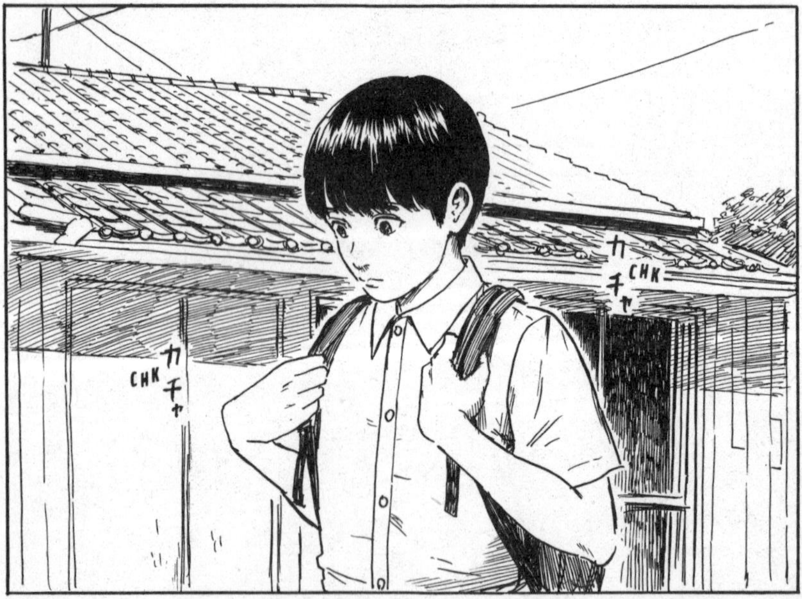
カチャ
CHK
カチャ
CHK

CHK
カチャ
CHK
カチャ
CHK
カチャ
CHK
カチャ
CHK
カチャ
CHK
カチャ
死後
you will be judged IN THE AFTERLIFE
CHK
カチャ
CHK
カチャ

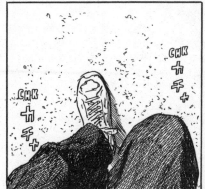

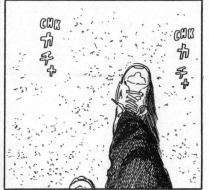

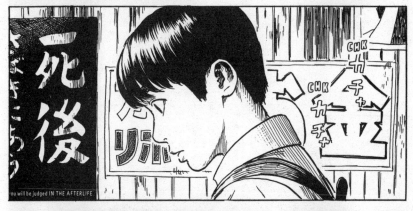

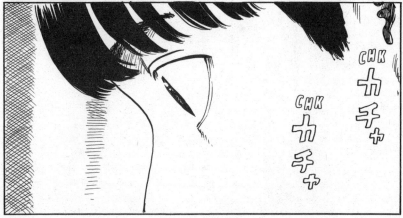

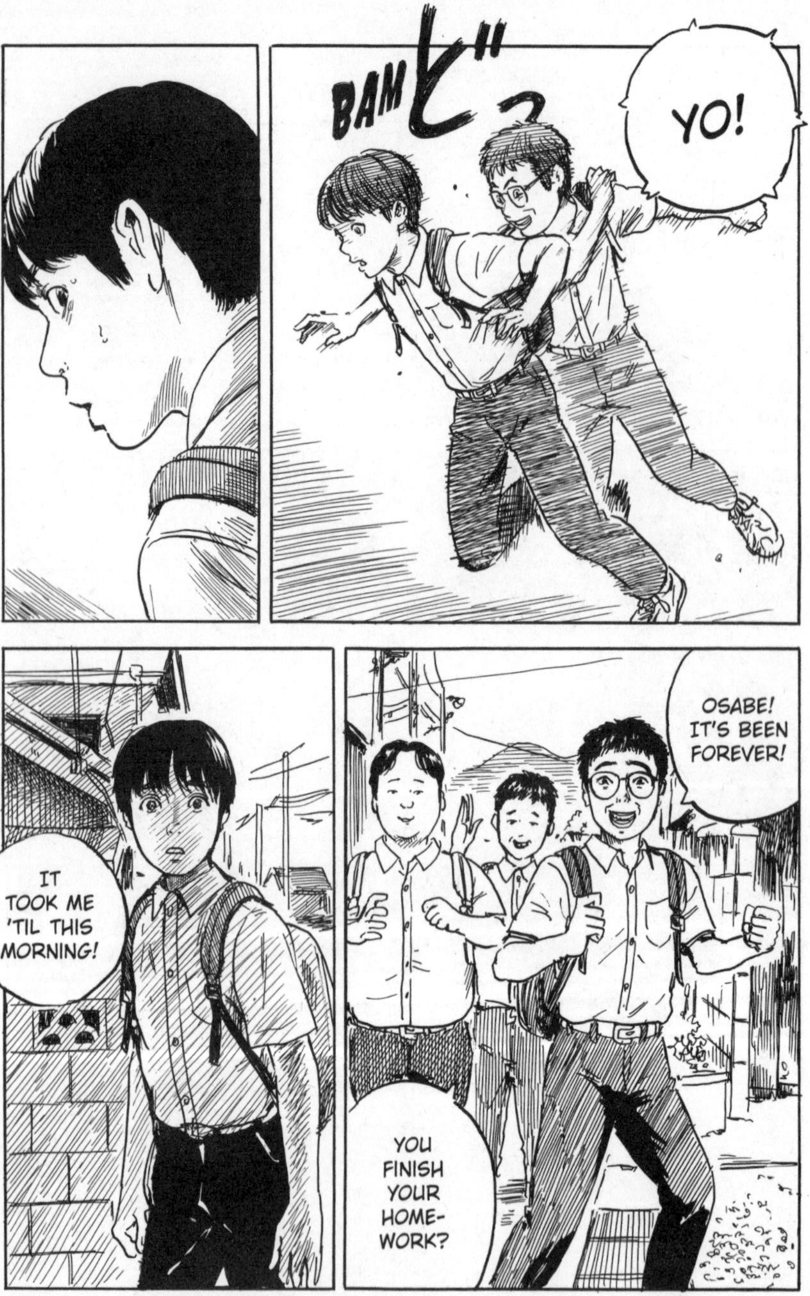
YO!
BAM どっ
OSABE! IT'S BEEN FOREVER!
YOU FINISH YOUR HOME-WORK?
IT TOOK ME 'TIL THIS MORNING!

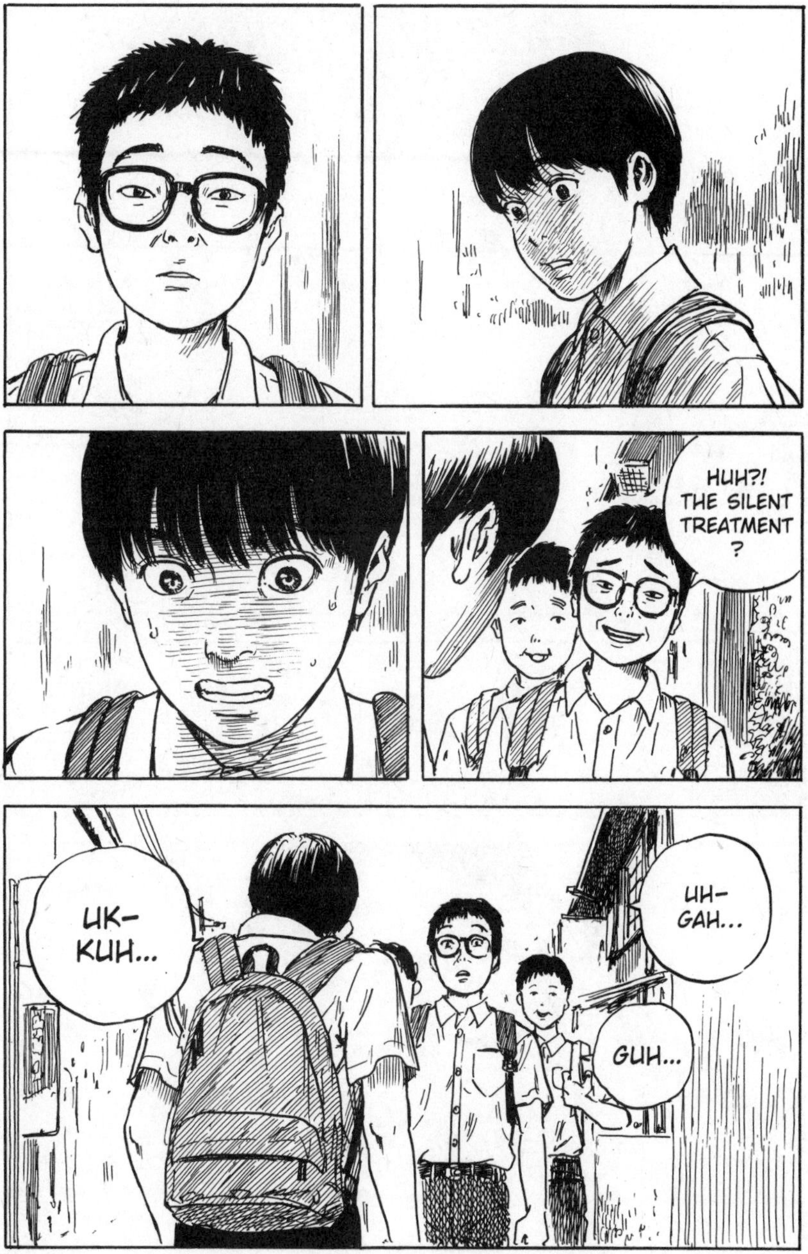
HUH?! THE SILENT TREATMENT ?
UH-GAH...
GUH...
UK-KUH...

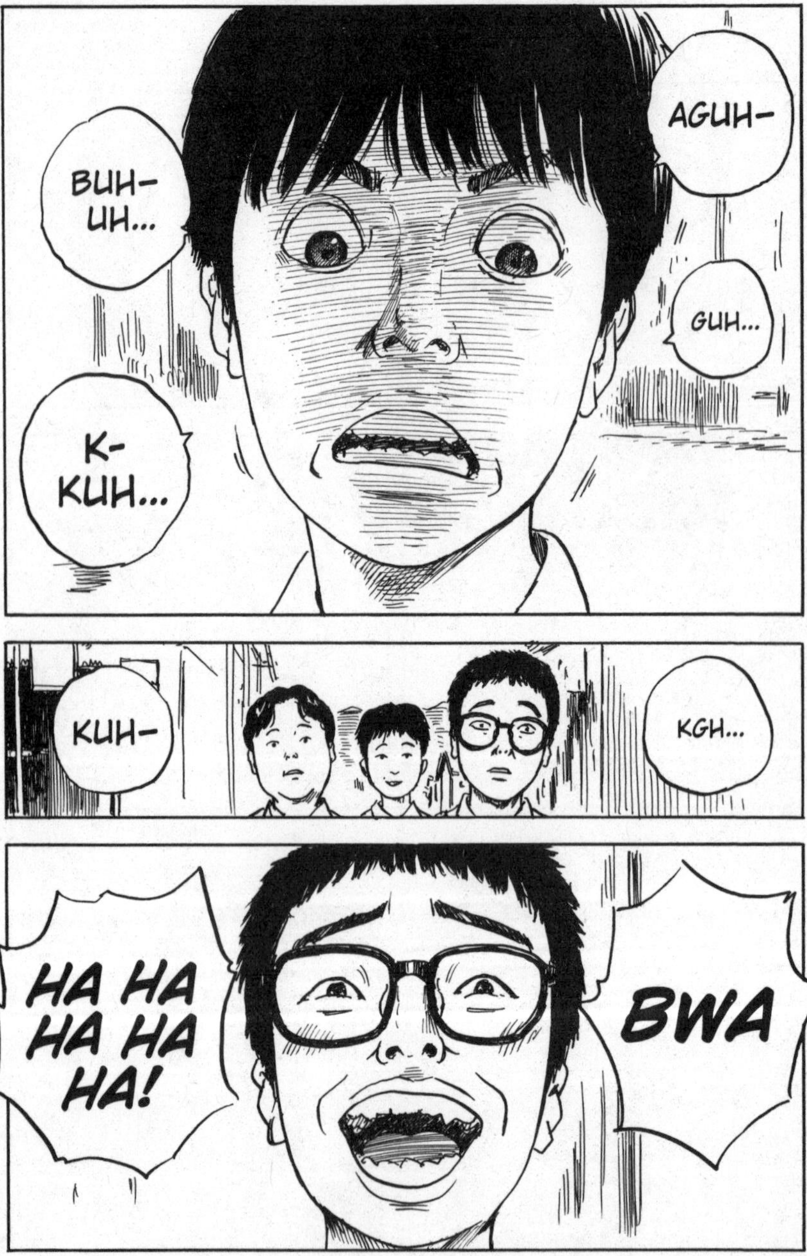
AGUH-
BUH-UH...
GUH...
K-KUH...
KGH...
KUH-
BWA
HA HA HA HA HA!

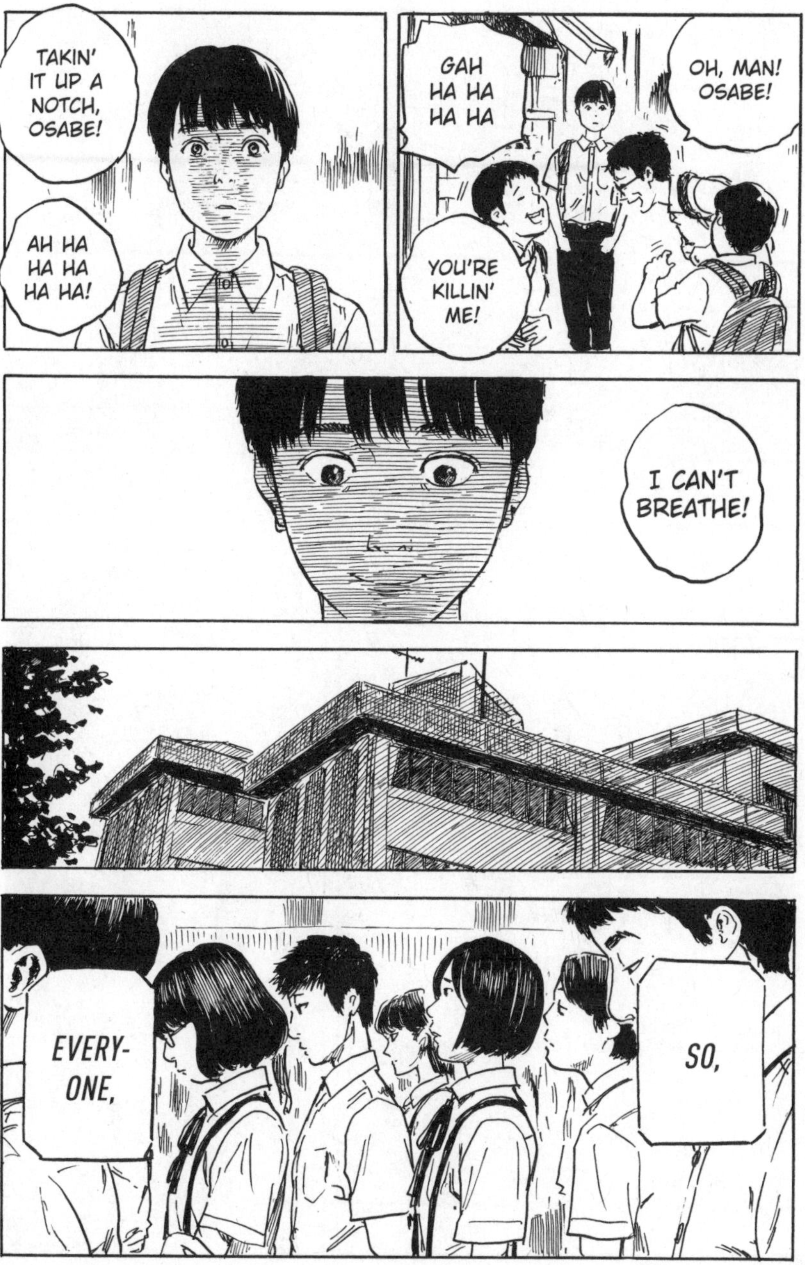
OH, MAN! OSABE!
GAH HA HA HA HA
YOU'RE KILLIN' ME!
TAKIN' IT UP A NOTCH, OSABE!
AH HA HA HA HA HA!
I CAN'T BREATHE!
SO,
EVERY-ONE,

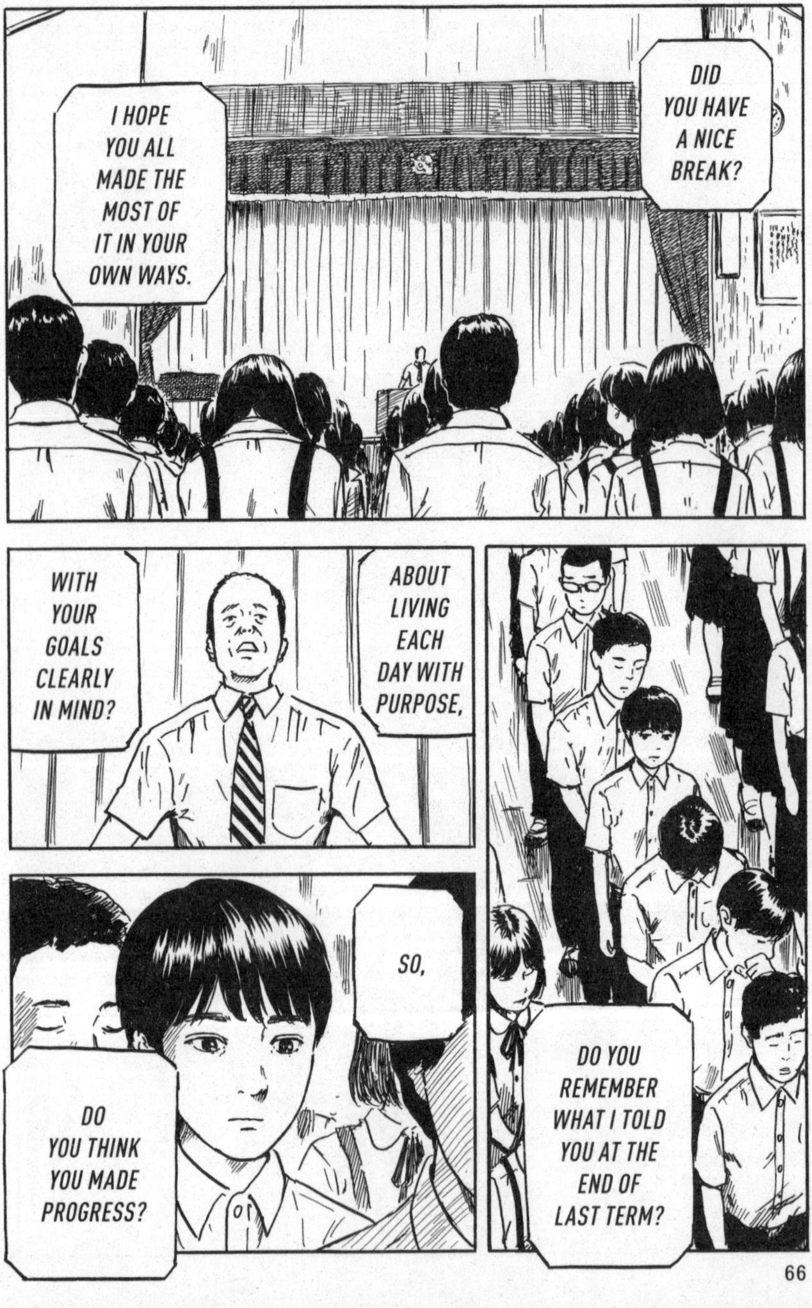
DID YOU HAVE A NICE BREAK?
I HOPE YOU ALL MADE THE MOST OF IT IN YOUR OWN WAYS.
DO YOU REMEMBER WHAT I TOLD YOU AT THE END OF LAST TERM?
ABOUT LIVING EACH DAY WITH PURPOSE,
WITH YOUR GOALS CLEARLY IN MIND?
SO,
DO YOU THINK YOU MADE PROGRESS?

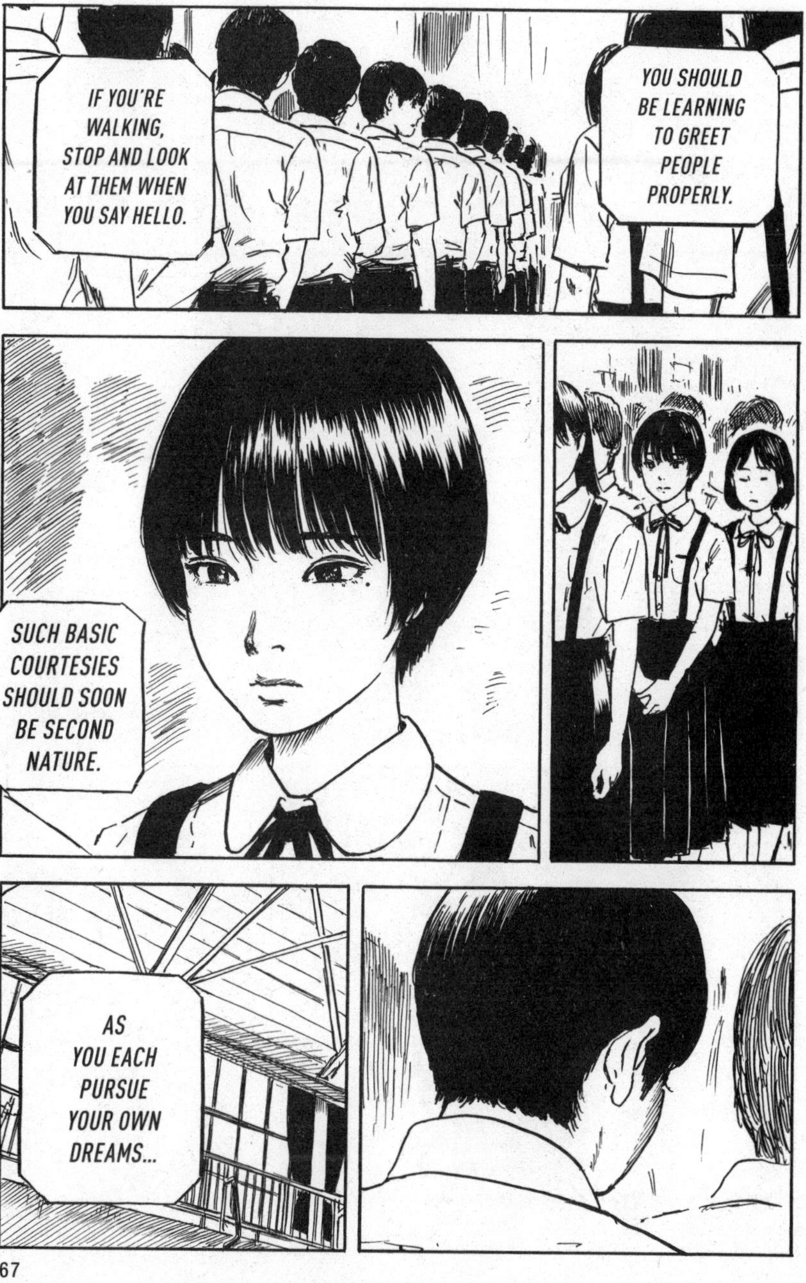
YOU SHOULD BE LEARNING TO GREET PEOPLE PROPERLY.
IF YOU'RE WALKING, STOP AND LOOK AT THEM WHEN YOU SAY HELLO.
SUCH BASIC COURTESIES SHOULD SOON BE SECOND NATURE.
AS YOU EACH PURSUE YOUR OWN DREAMS...

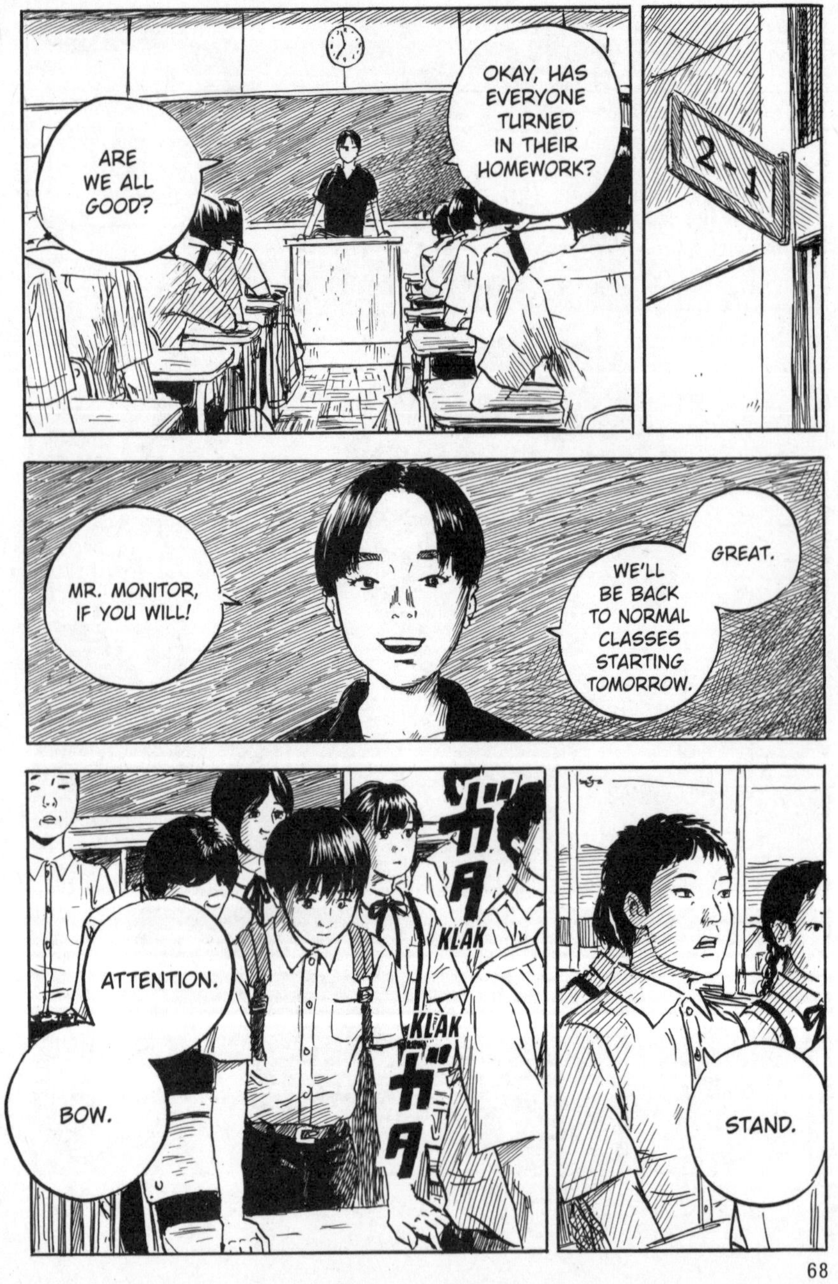
OKAY, HAS EVERYONE TURNED IN THEIR HOMEWORK?
ARE WE ALL GOOD?
GREAT.
WE'LL BE BACK TO NORMAL CLASSES STARTING TOMORROW.
MR. MONITOR, IF YOU WILL!
STAND.
ガタ
KLAK
KLAK
ガタ
ATTENTION.
BOW.

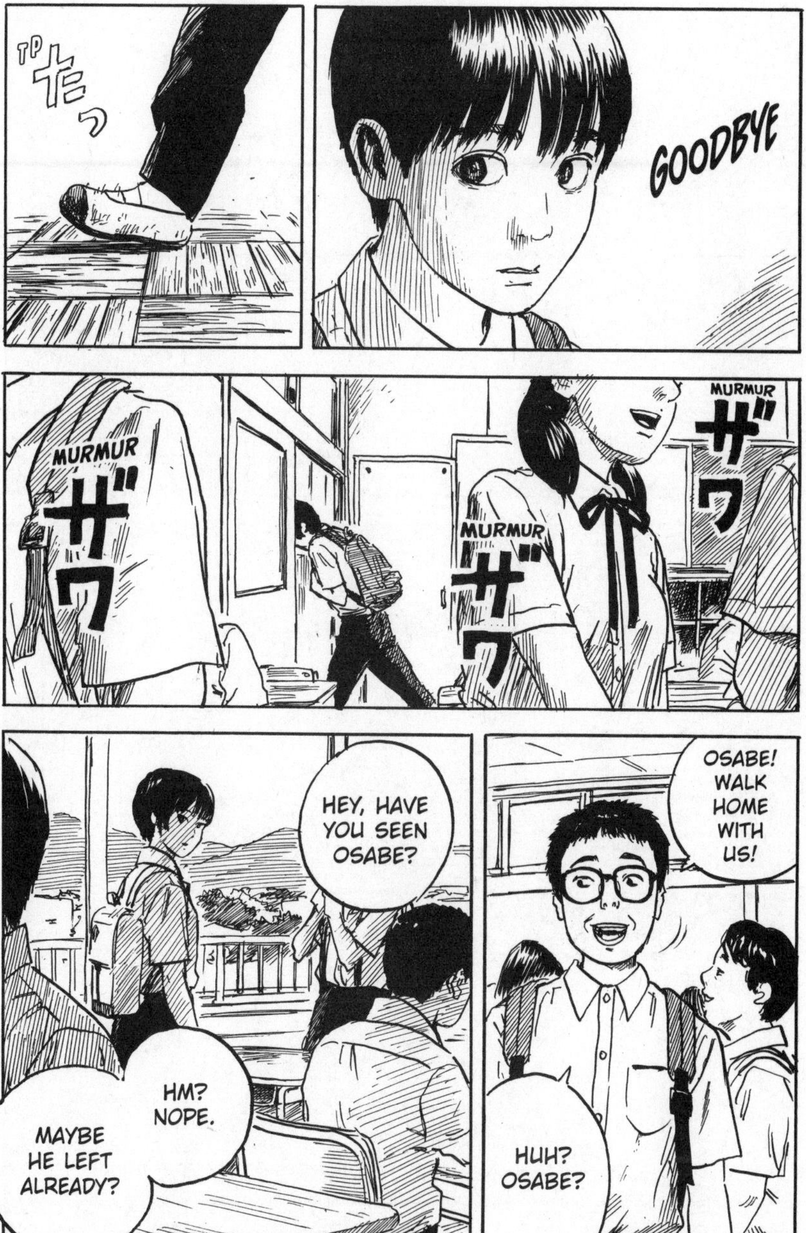
GOODBYE
TP
たっ
MURMUR
ザワ
MURMUR
ザワ
MURMUR
ザワ
OSABE! WALK HOME WITH US!
HUH? OSABE?
HEY, HAVE YOU SEEN OSABE?
HM? NOPE.
MAYBE HE LEFT ALREADY?

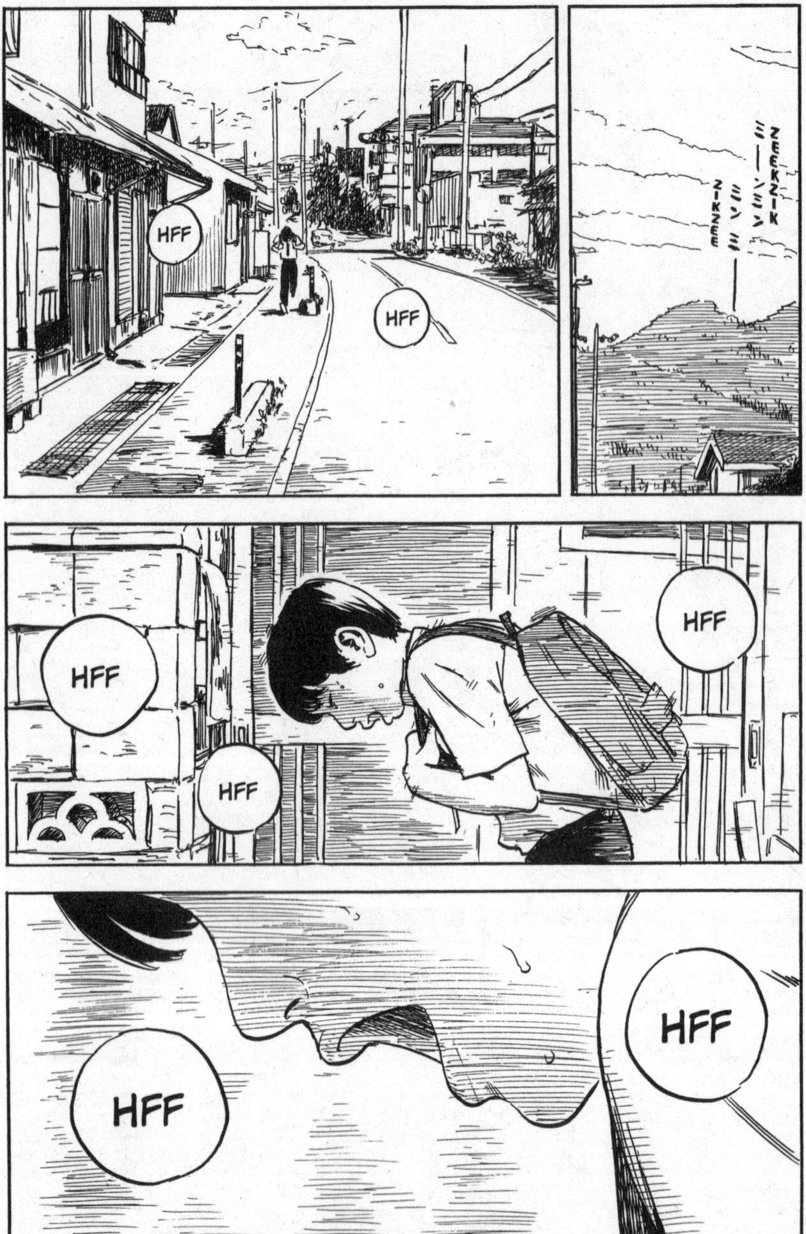
ZEEKZIK
ミーンミン
ミンミー
ZIKZEE
HFF
HFF
HFF
HFF
HFF
HFF
HFF

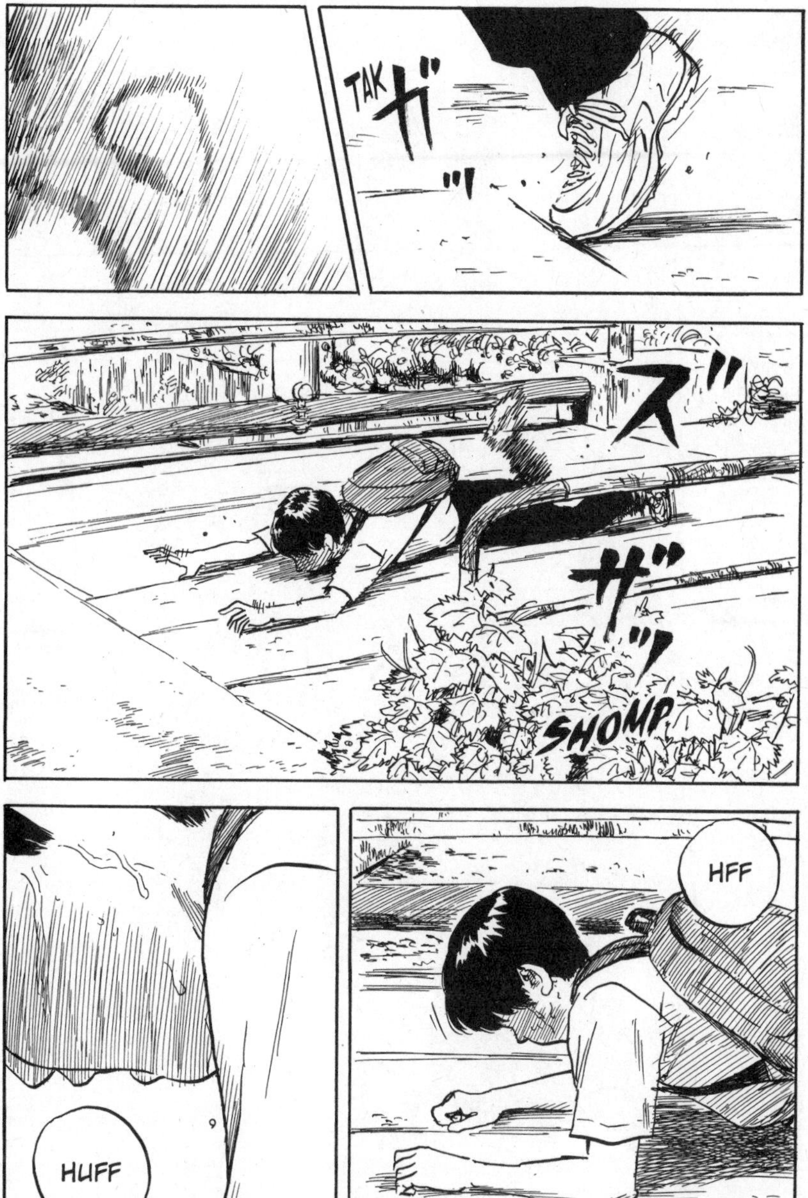
TAK
ガッ
ズ
ザッ
SHOMP
HFF
HUFF

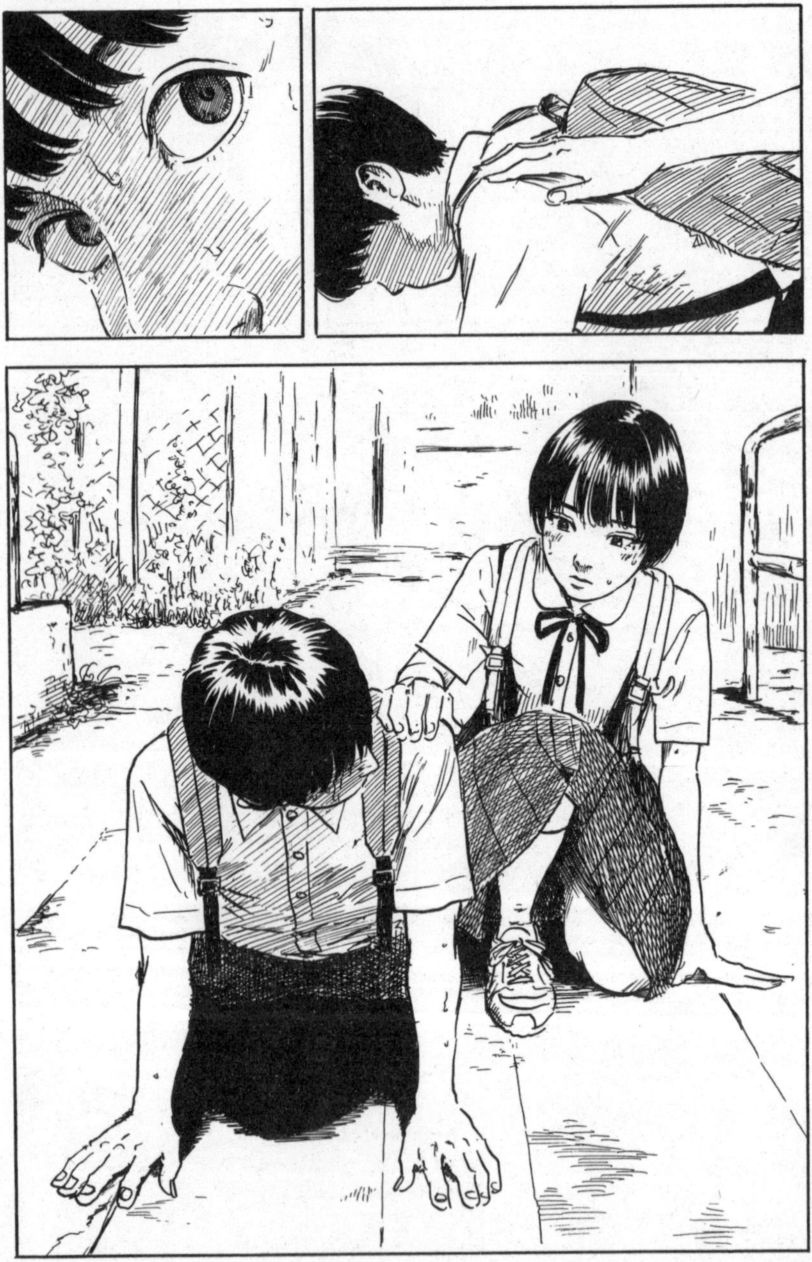

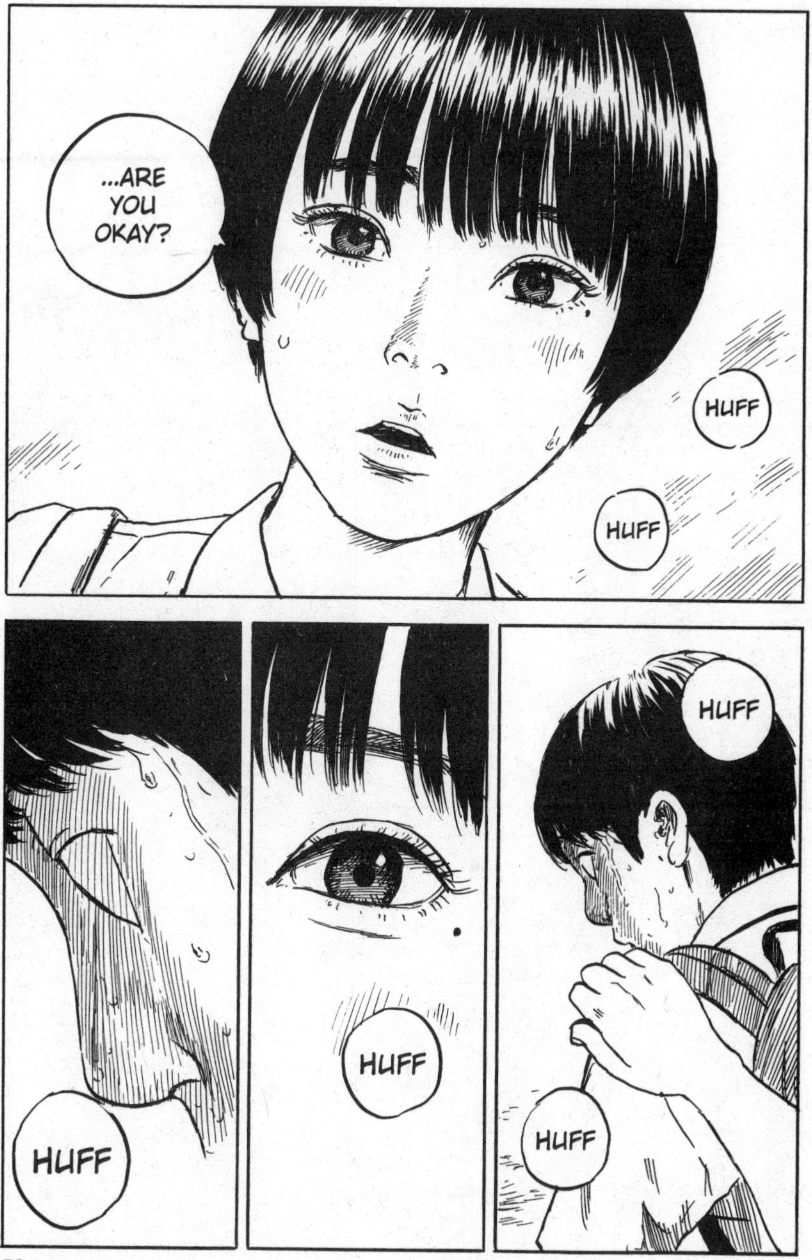
...ARE YOU OKAY?
HUFF
HUFF
HUFF
HUFF
HUFF
HUFF

HUH...

ARE YOU BLEEDING?

LET ME SEE YOUR KNEE.

THAT LOOKS PAINFUL...

OH, MAN!

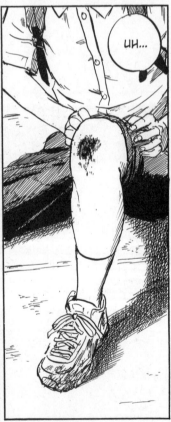

UH...

RUSTLE

HOLD ON.

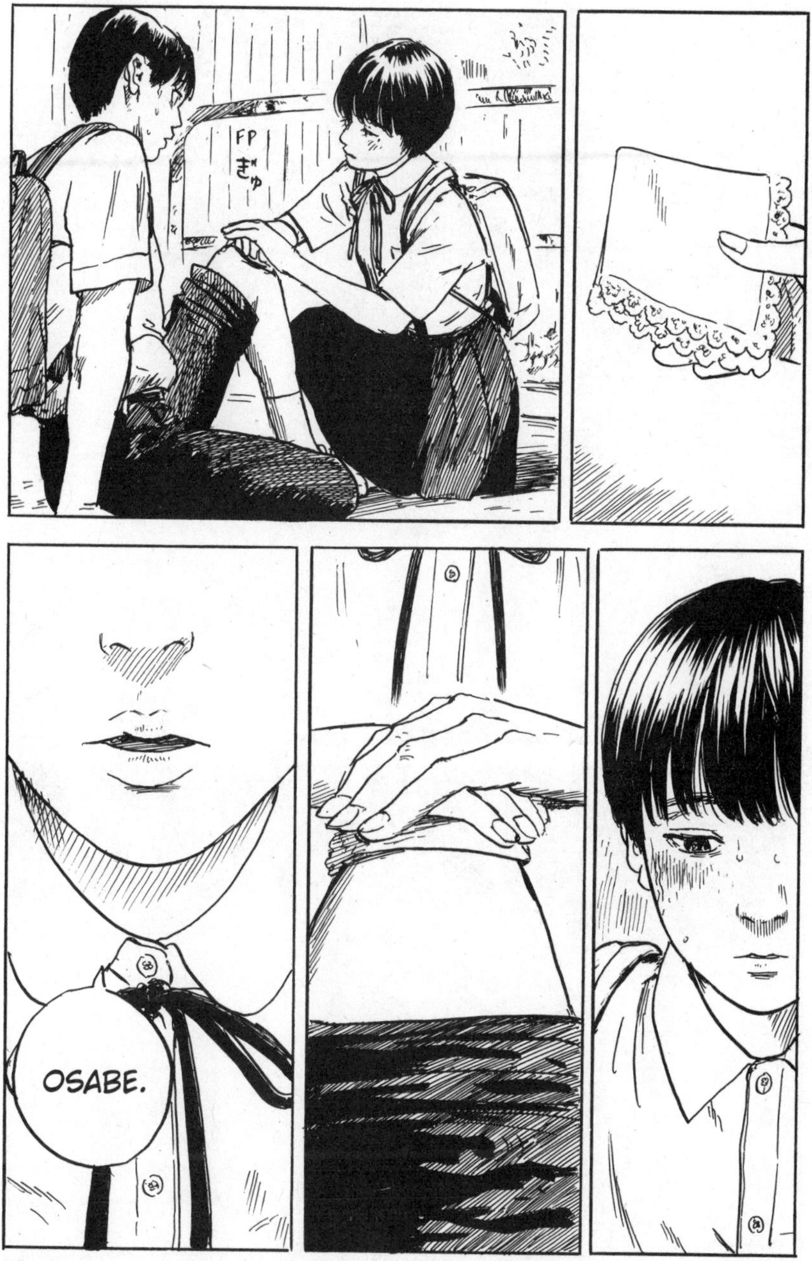
FP
ぎゅ
OSABE.

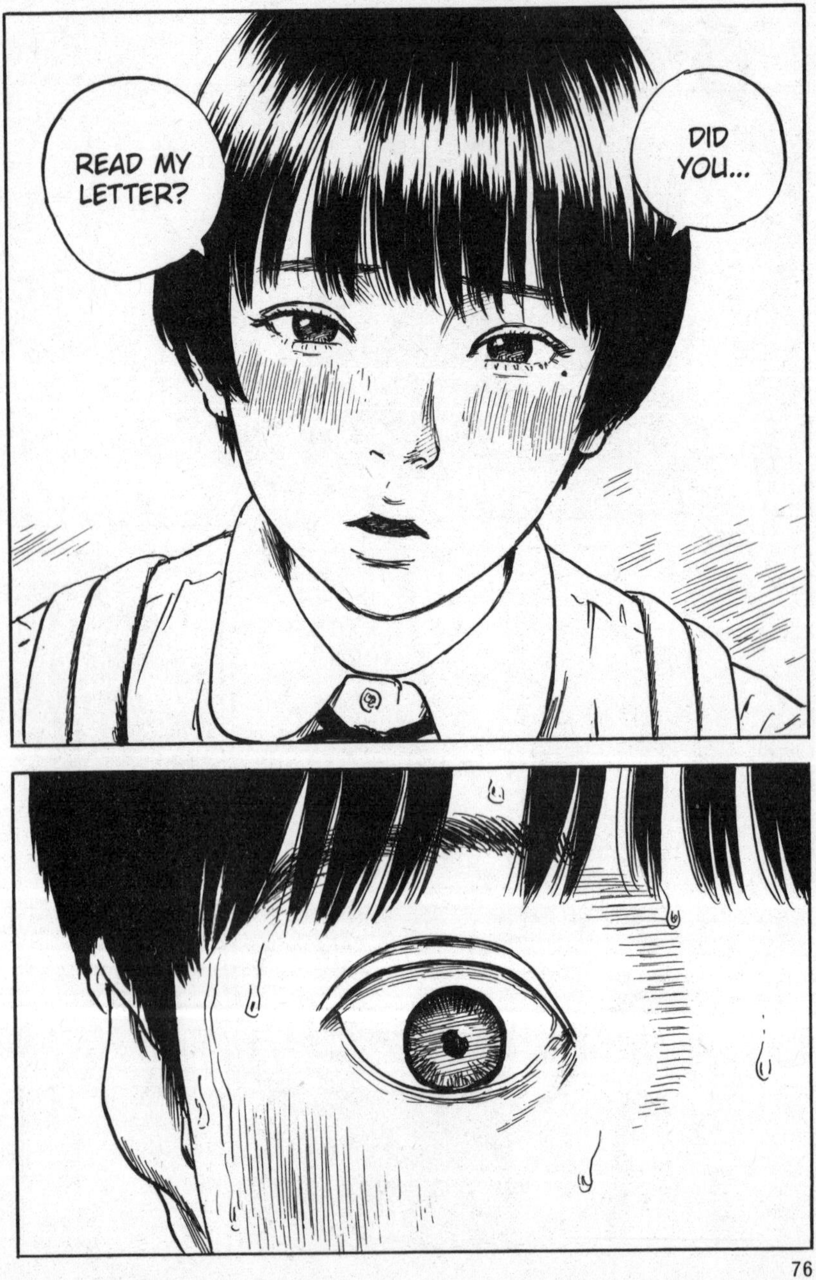
DID YOU...
READ MY LETTER?

CHAPTER 19 Answer

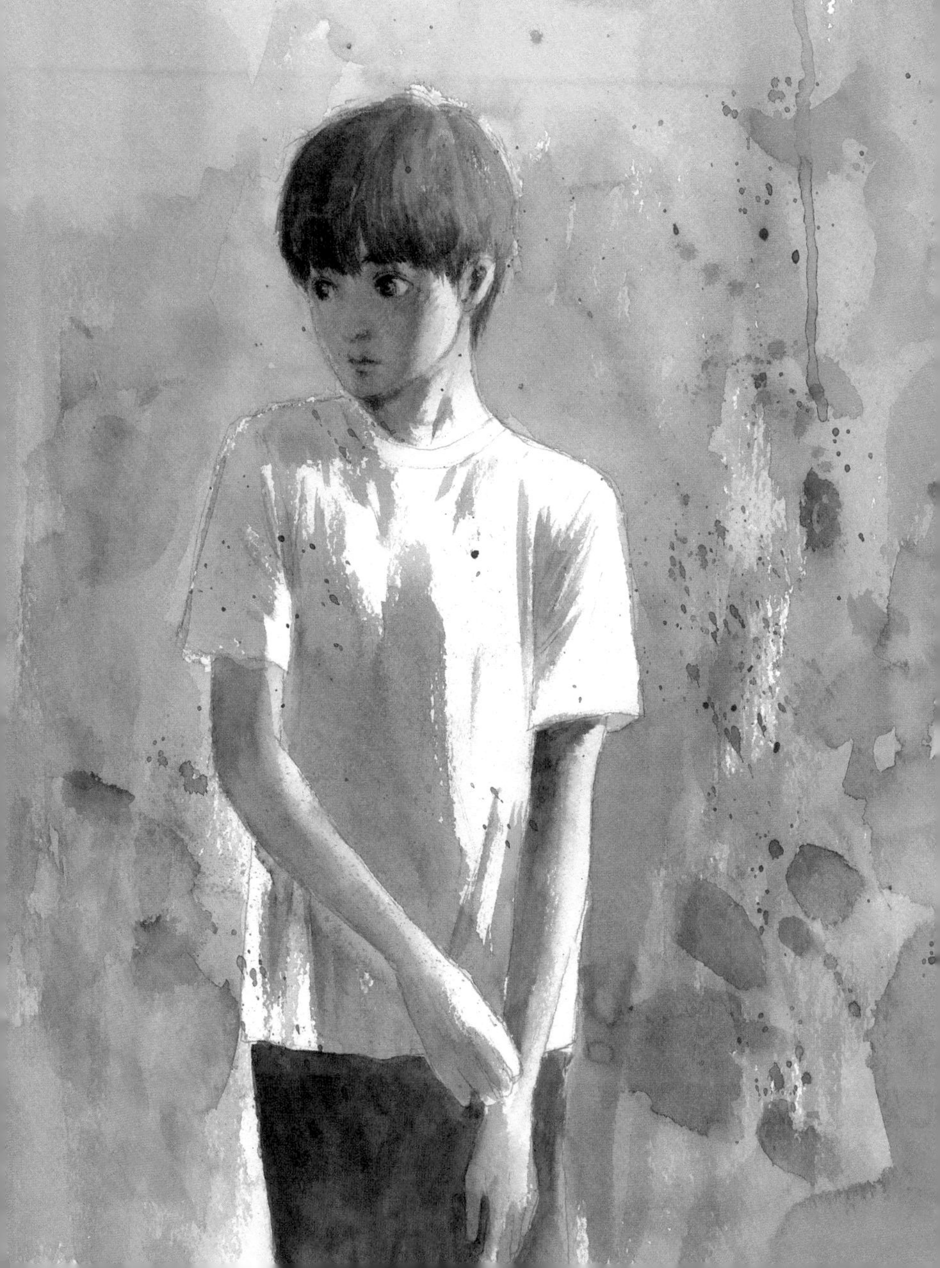

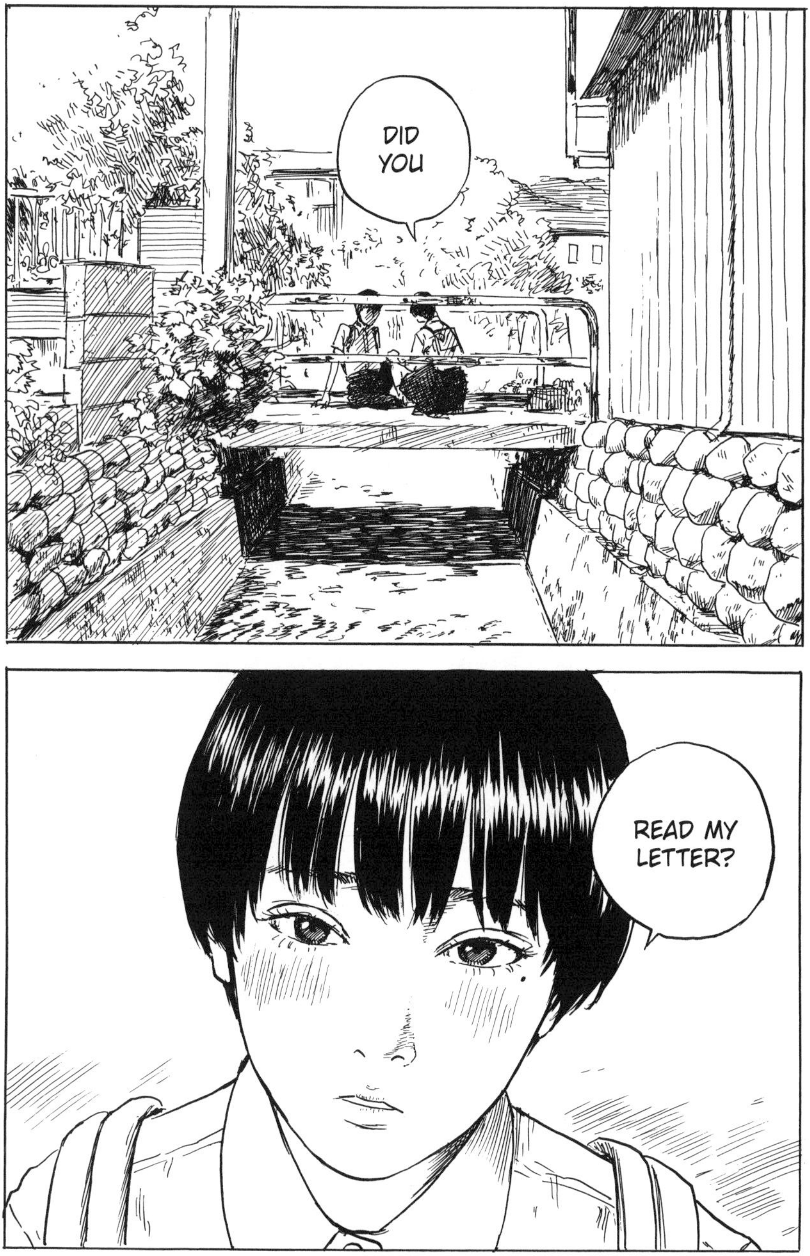
DID YOU
READ MY LETTER?

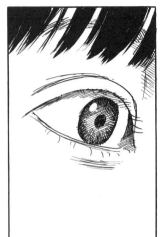

EAH.

...Y-

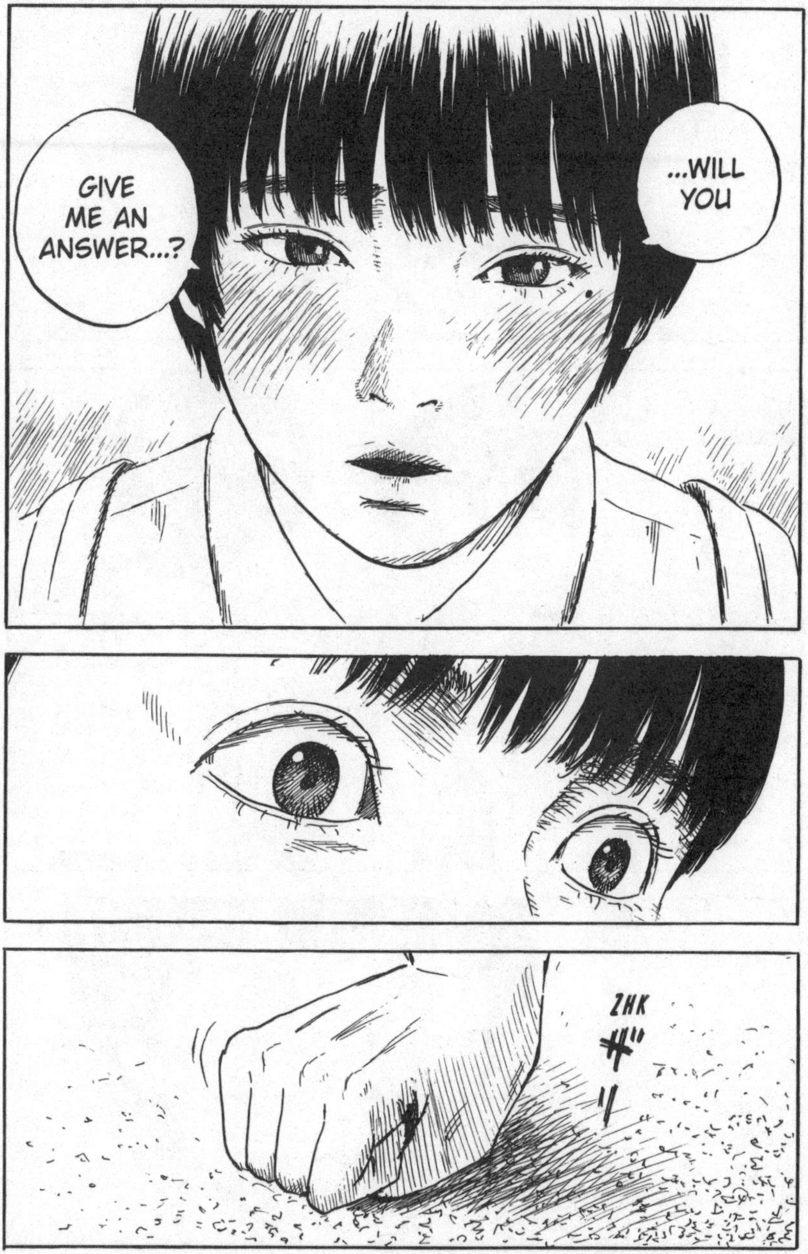
...WILL YOU
GIVE ME AN ANSWER...?
ZHK
ザッ

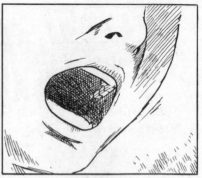

S–

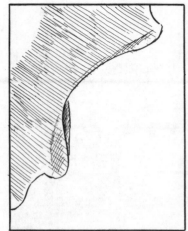

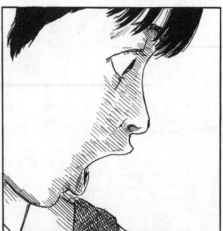

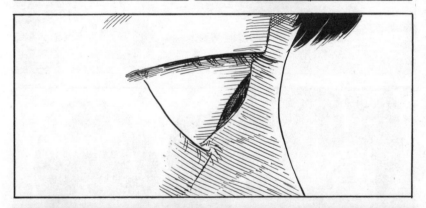

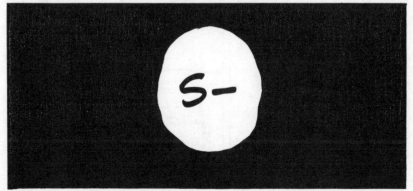

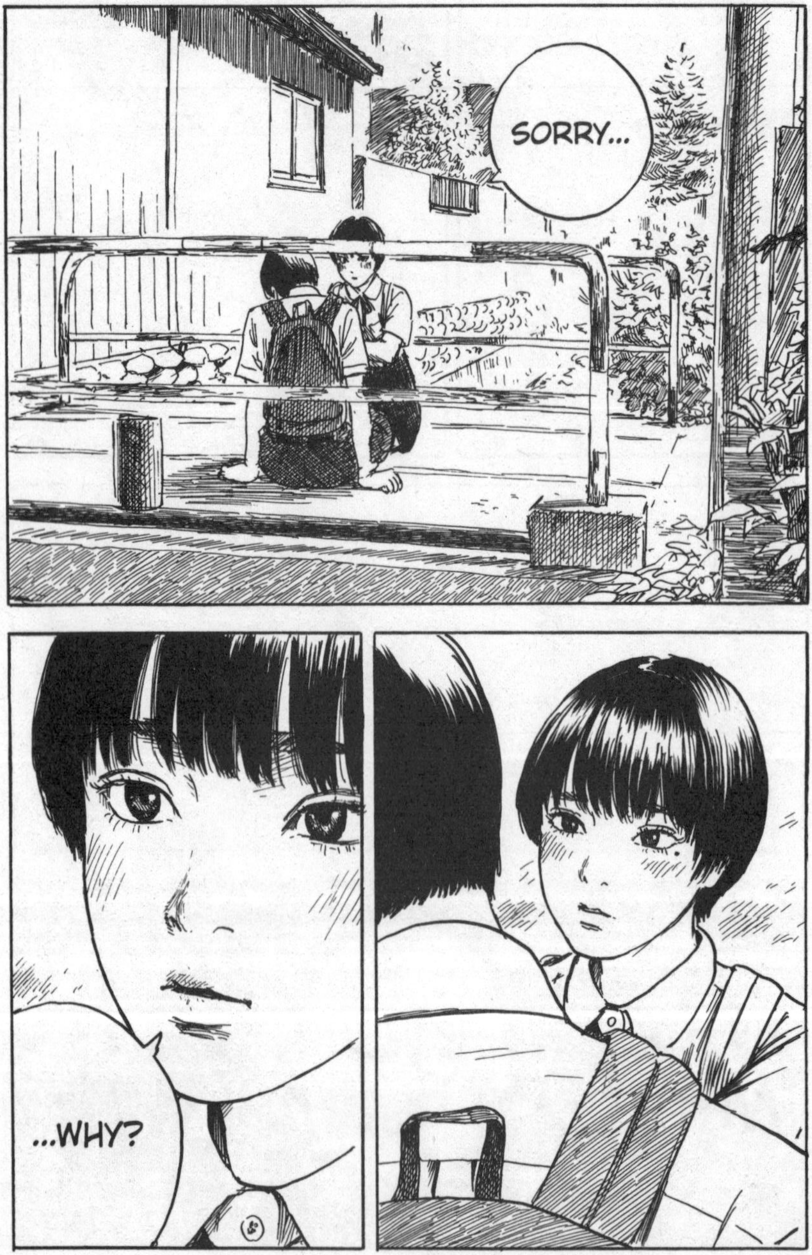
SORRY...
...WHY?

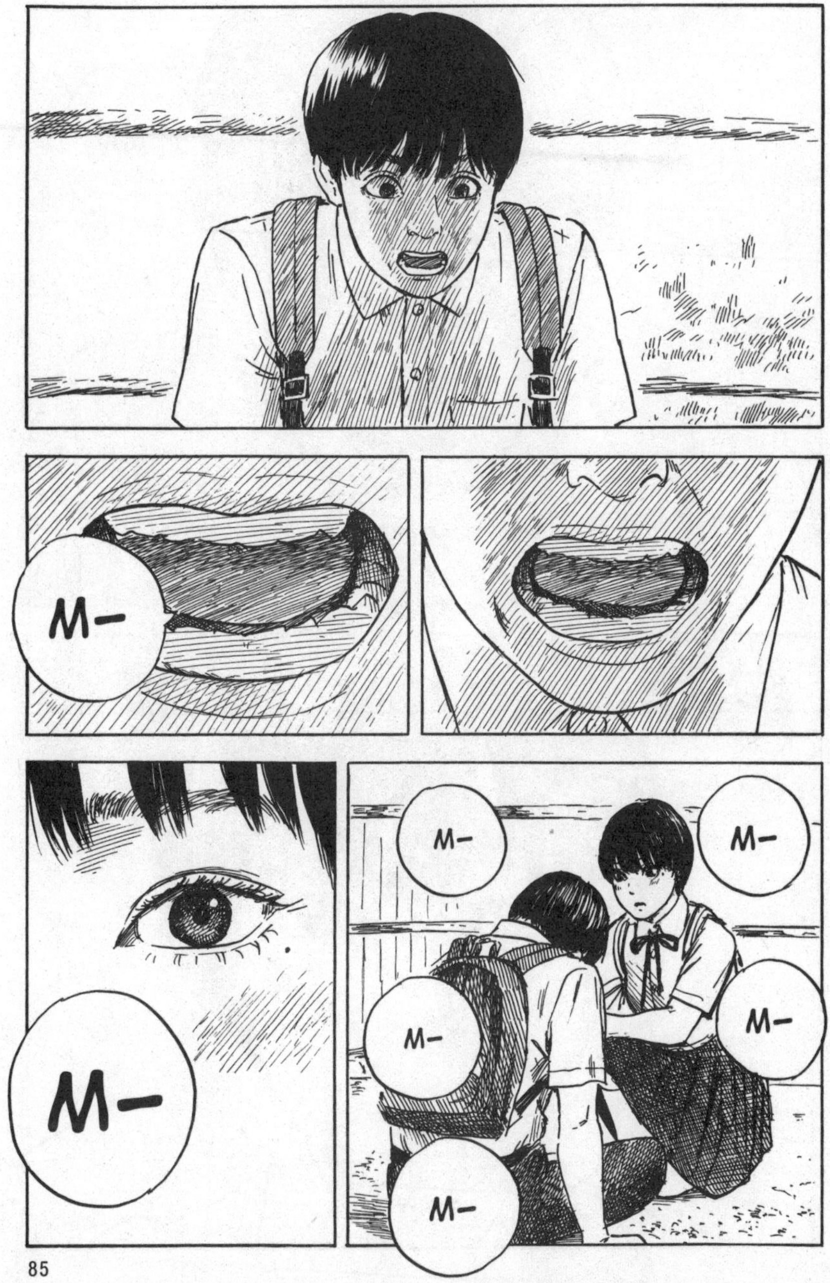
M–
M–
M–
M–
M–
M–
M–

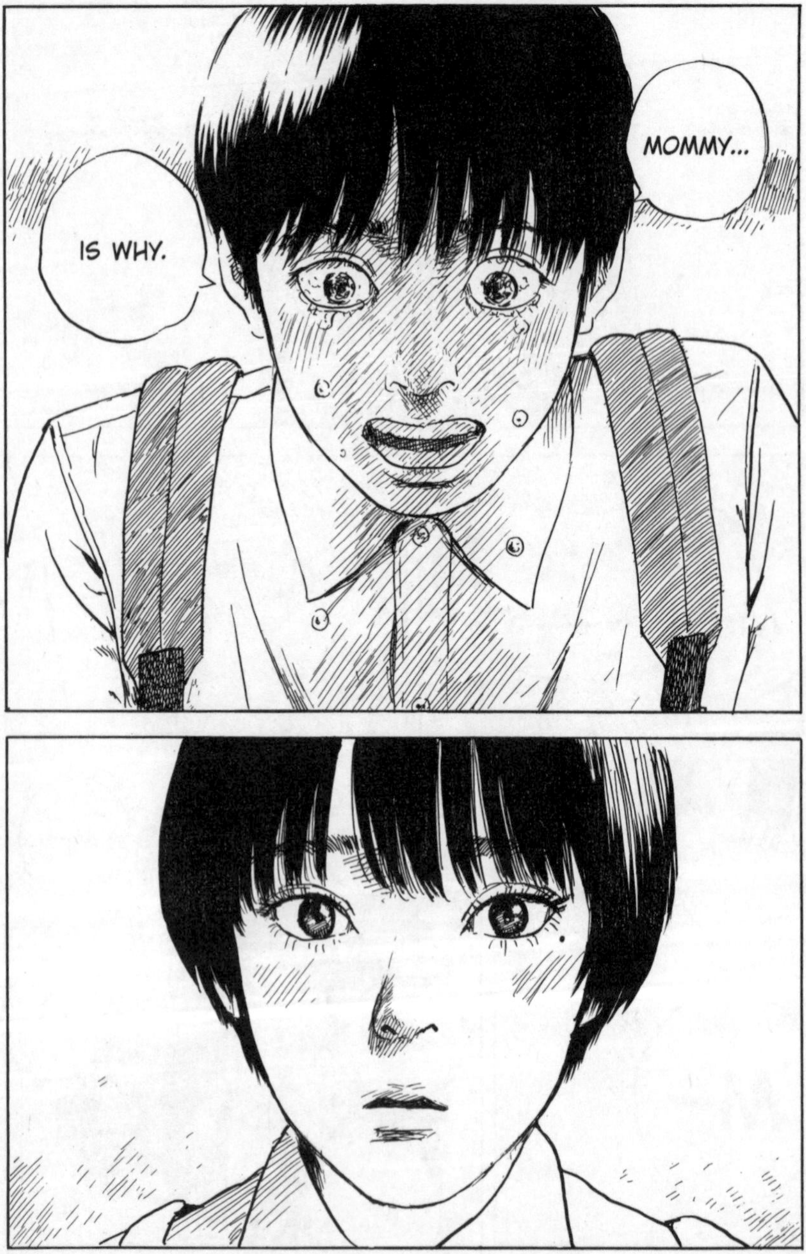
MOMMY...
IS WHY.

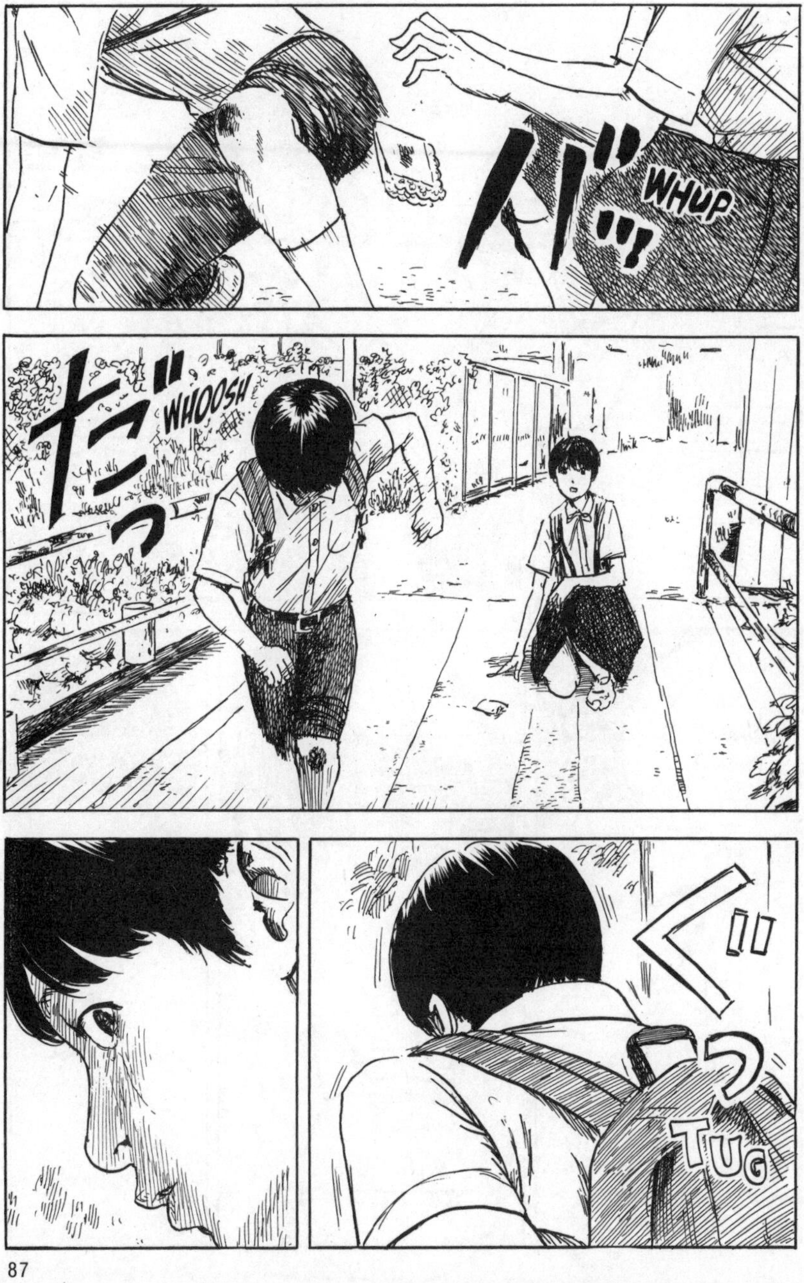
WHUP
WHOOSH
TUG

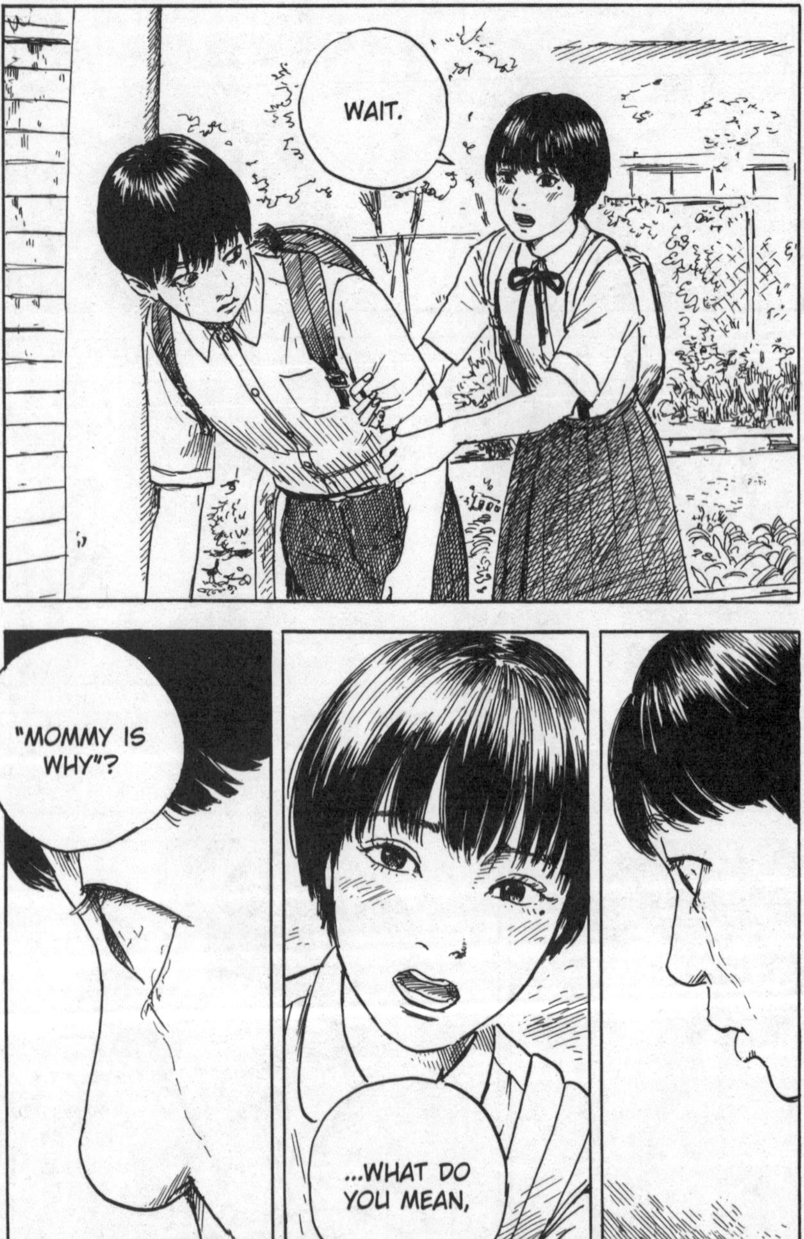
WAIT.
...WHAT DO YOU MEAN,
"MOMMY IS WHY"?

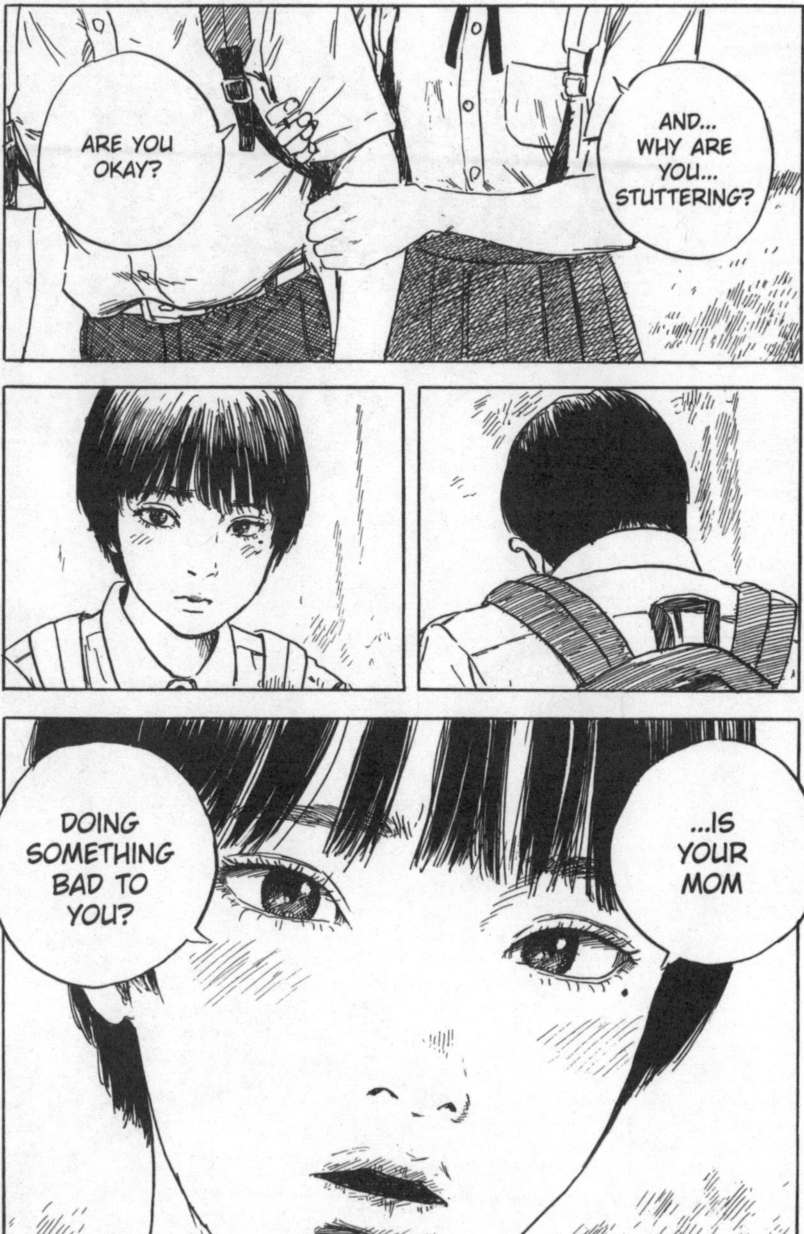
AND... WHY ARE YOU... STUTTERING?
ARE YOU OKAY?
...IS YOUR MOM
DOING SOMETHING BAD TO YOU?

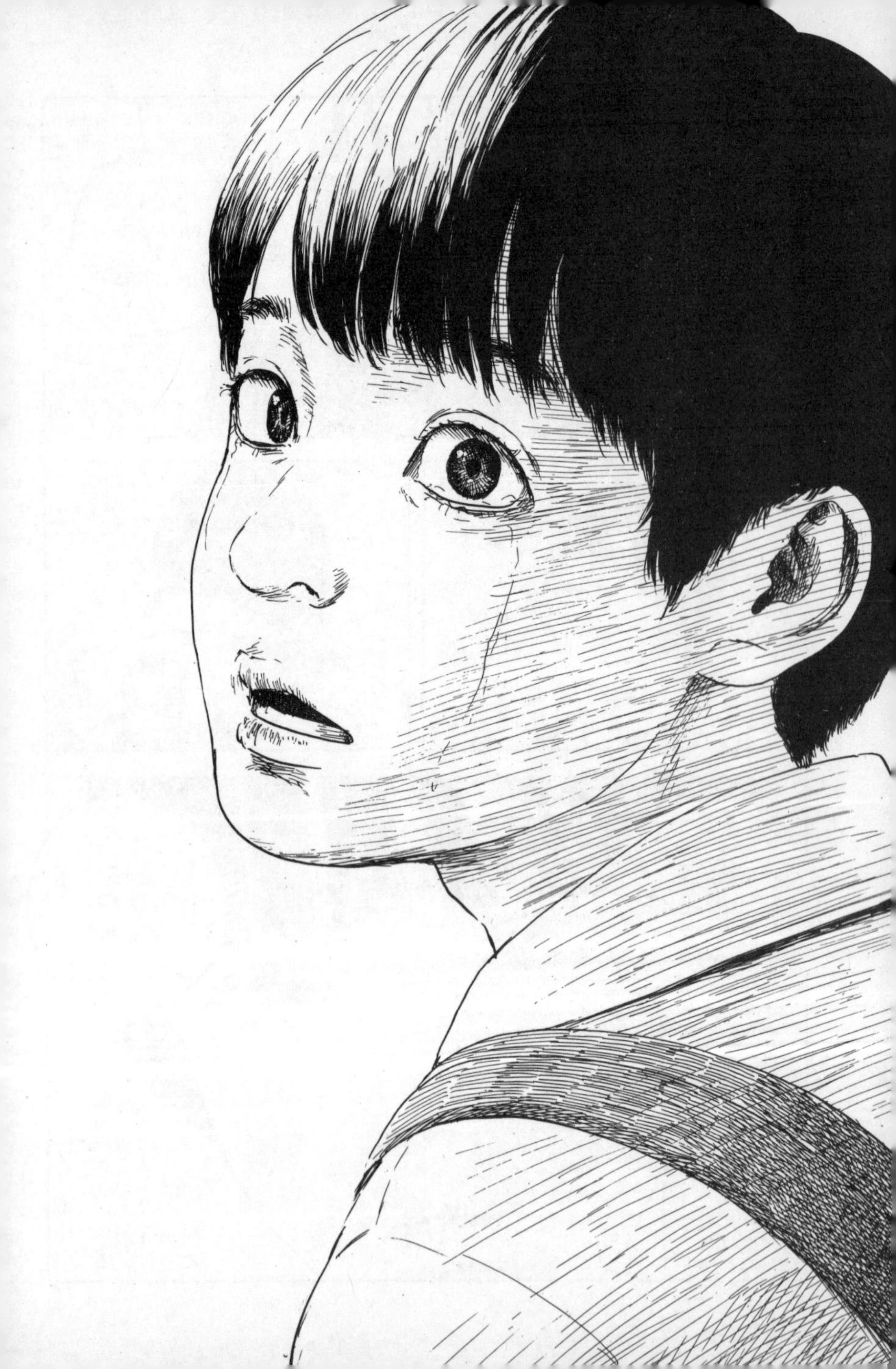

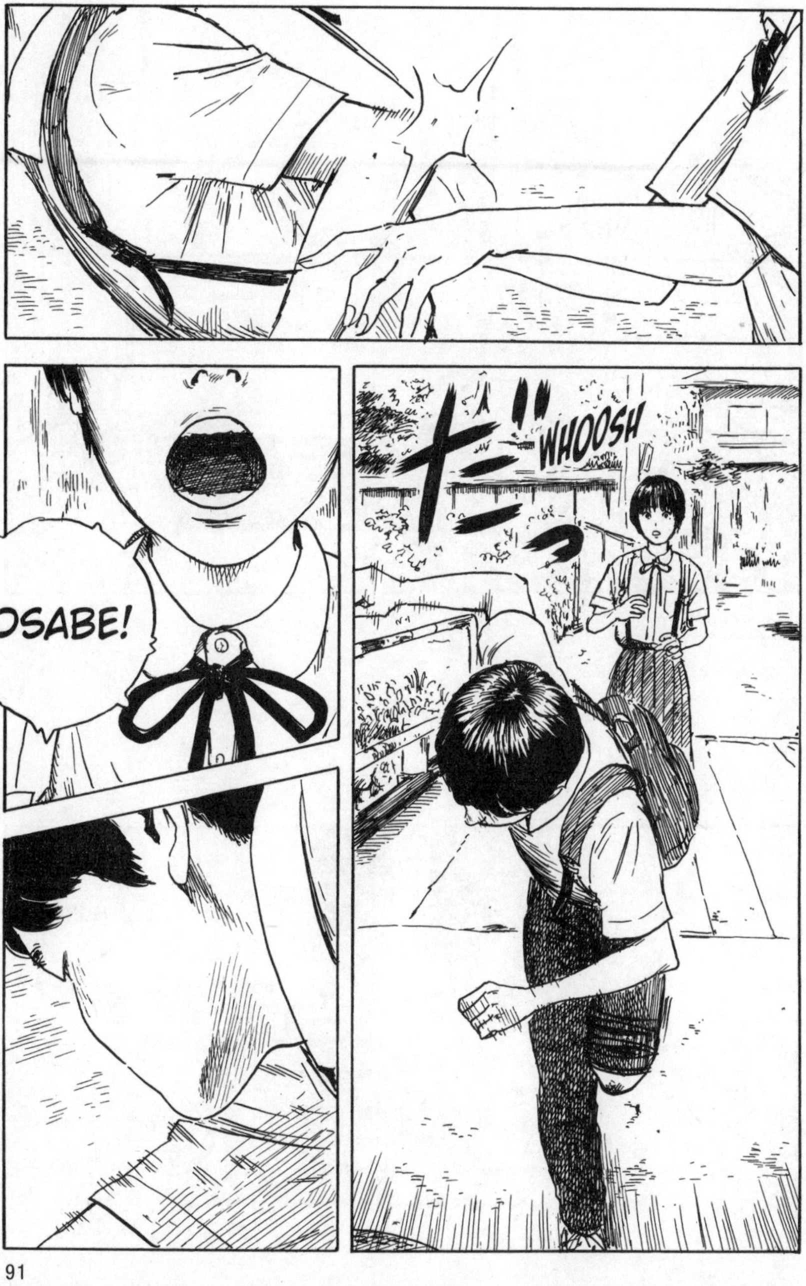
WHOOSH
OSABE!

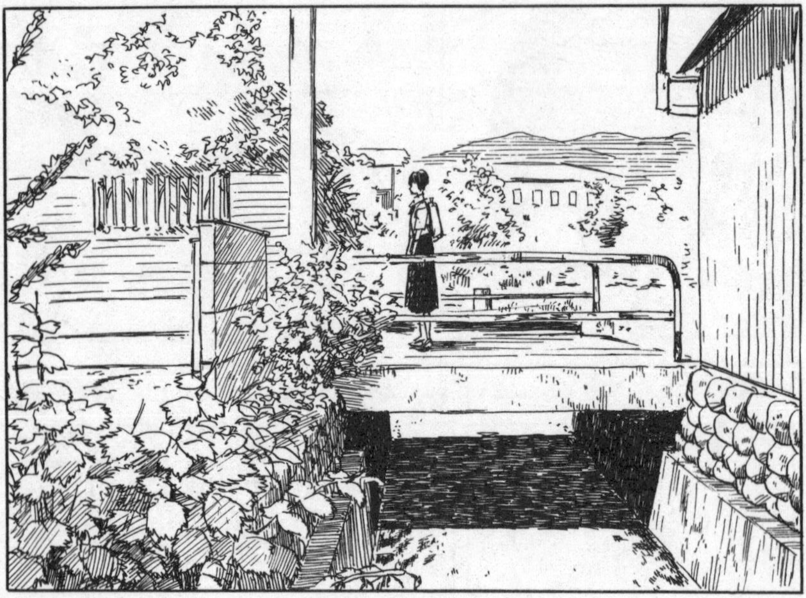

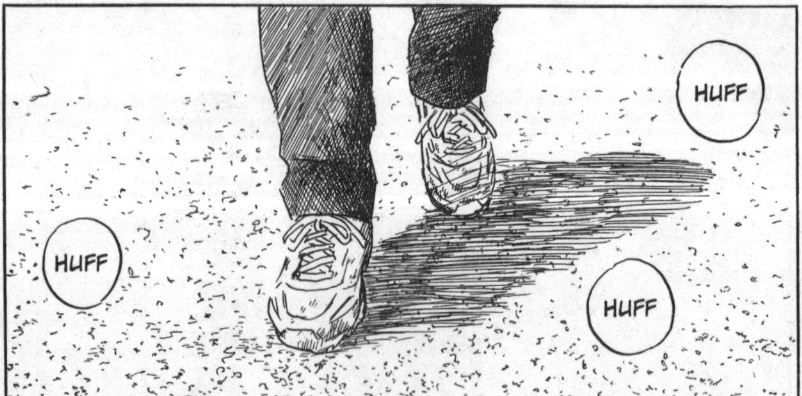
HUFF
HUFF
HUFF

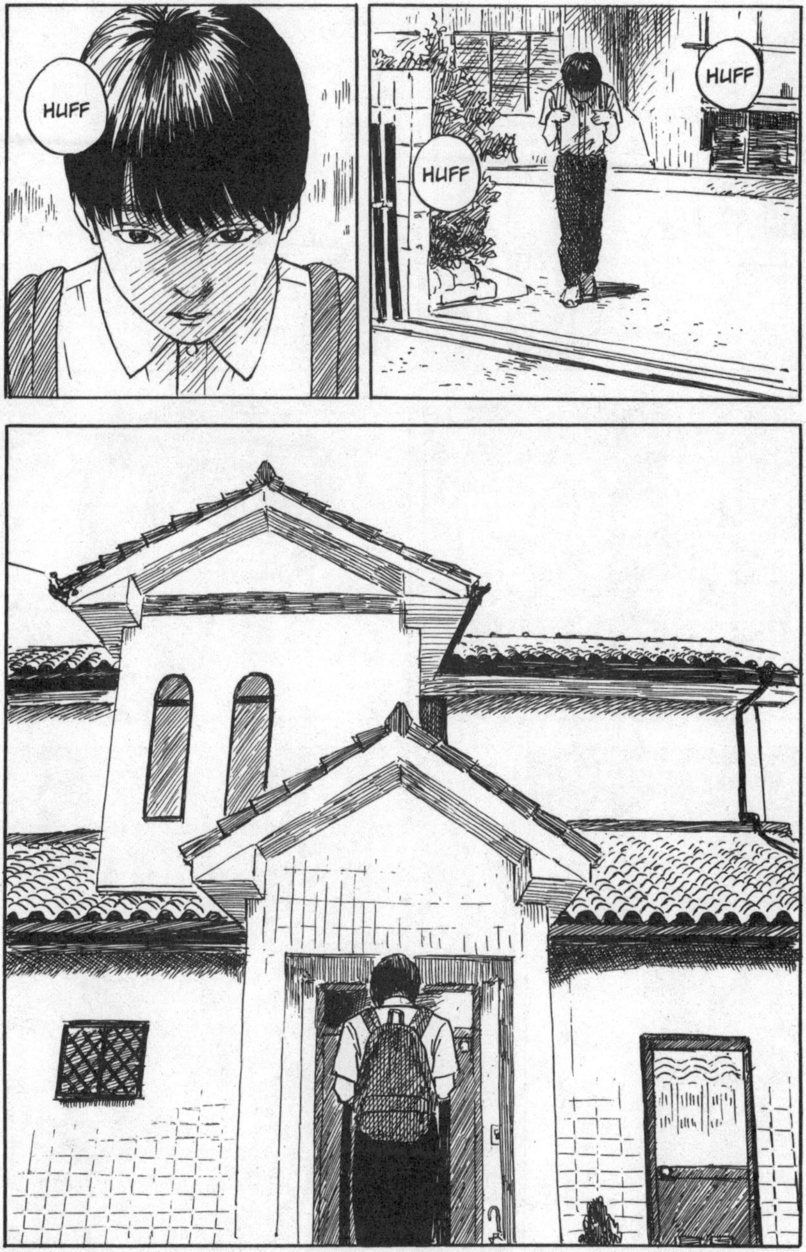
HUFF
HUFF
HUFF

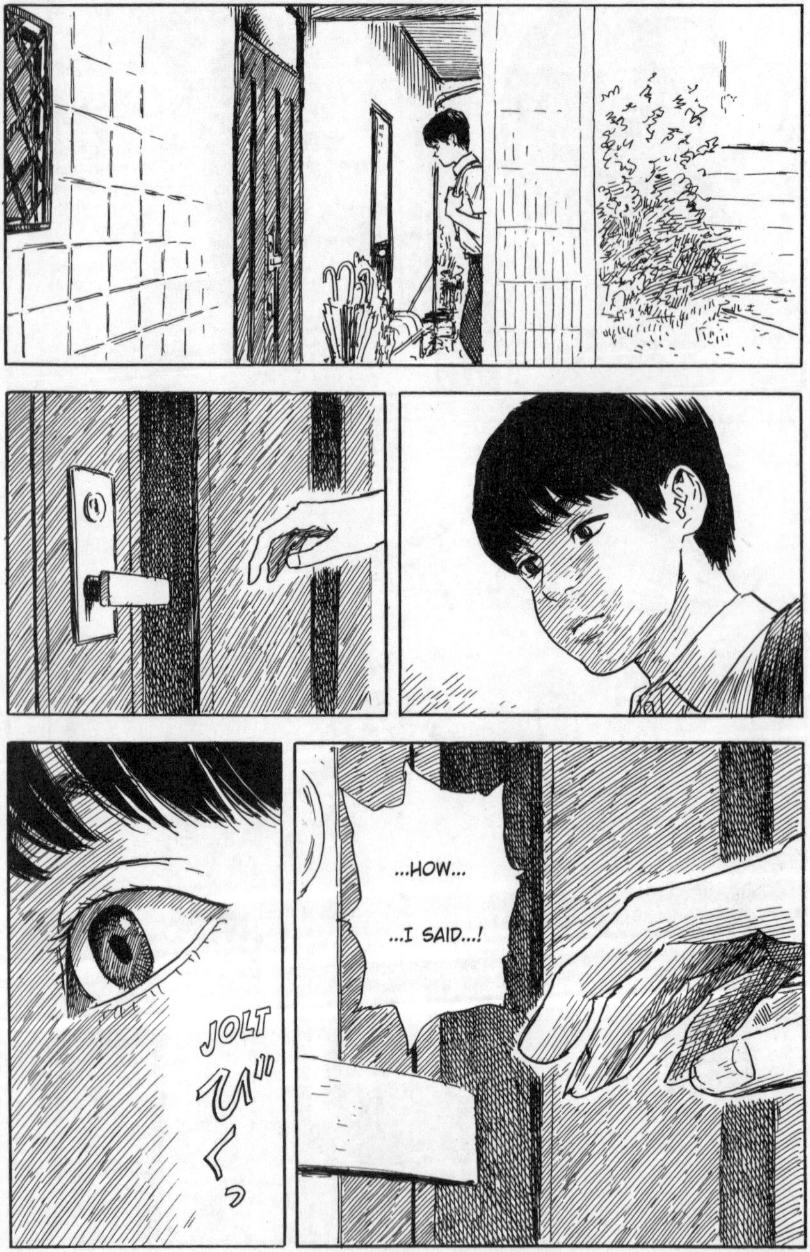
...HOW...
...I SAID...!
JOLT
びくっ

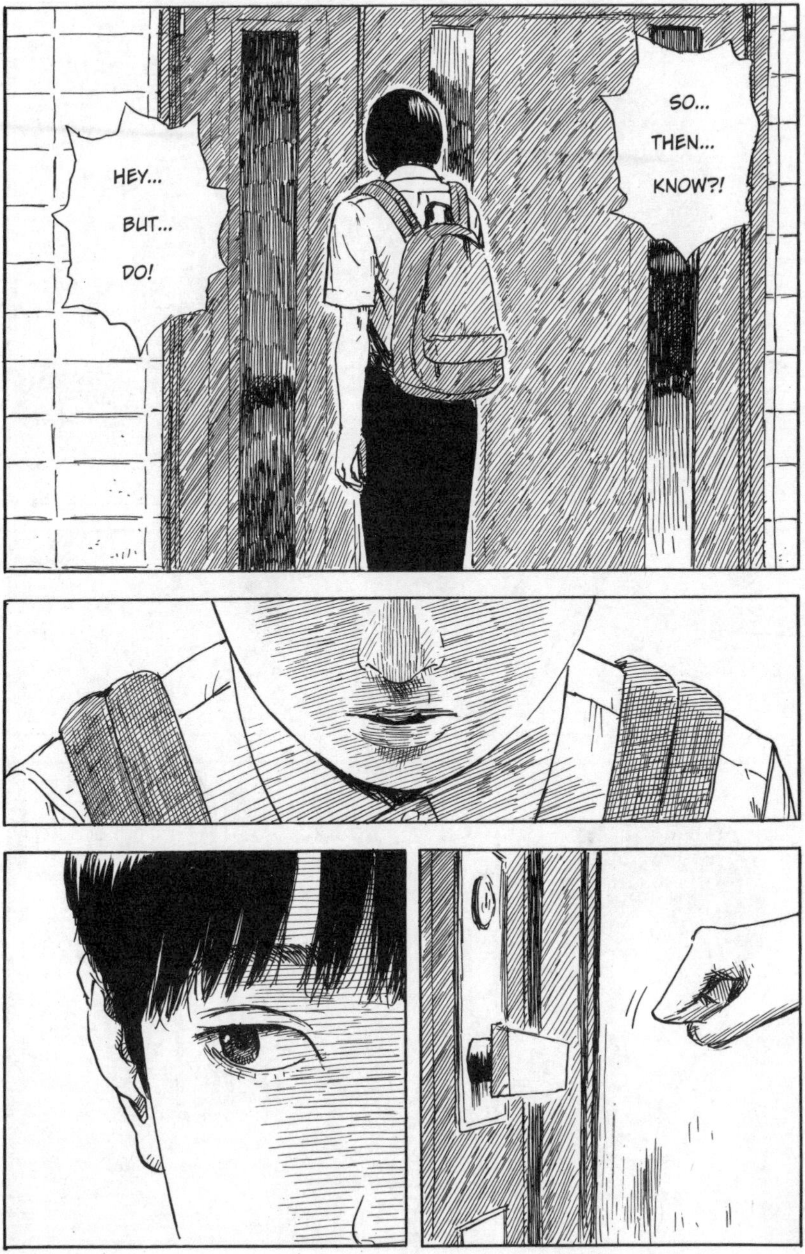
SO... THEN... KNOW?!
HEY... BUT... DO!

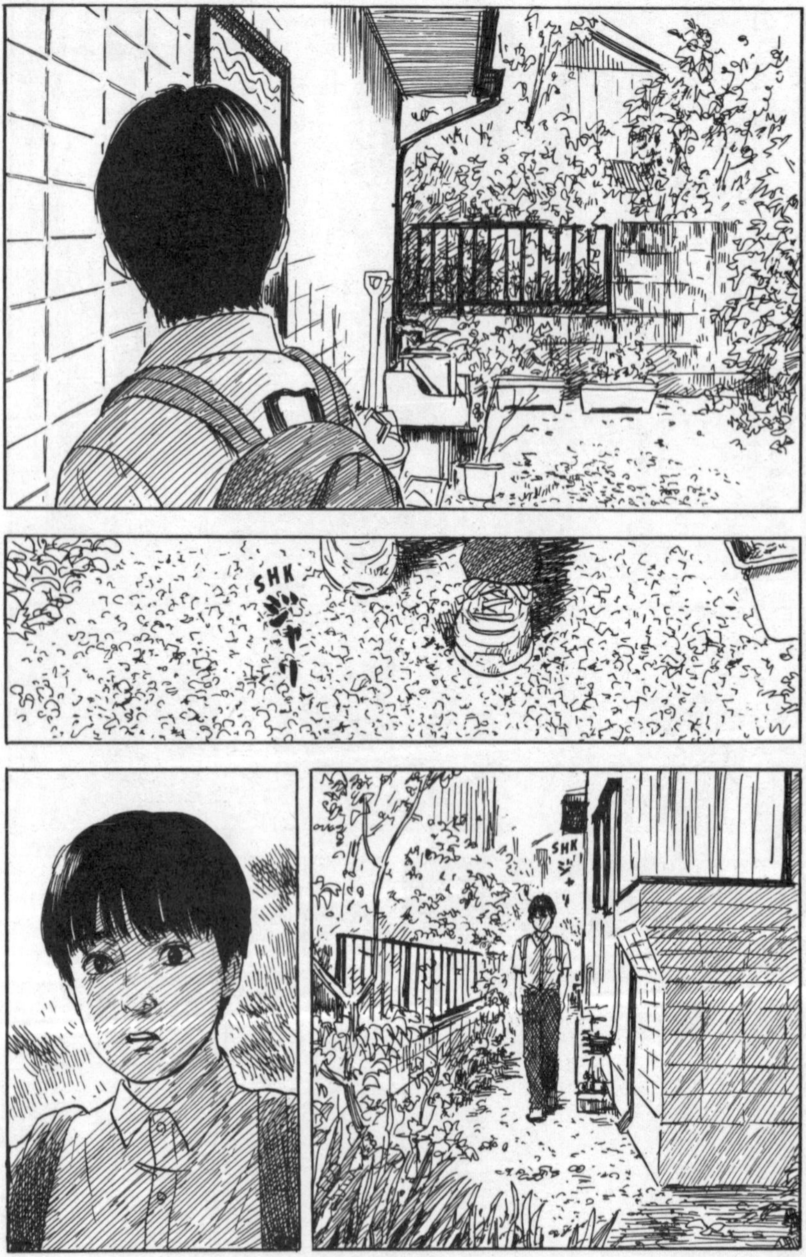
SHK
ジャリ
SHK
ジャリ

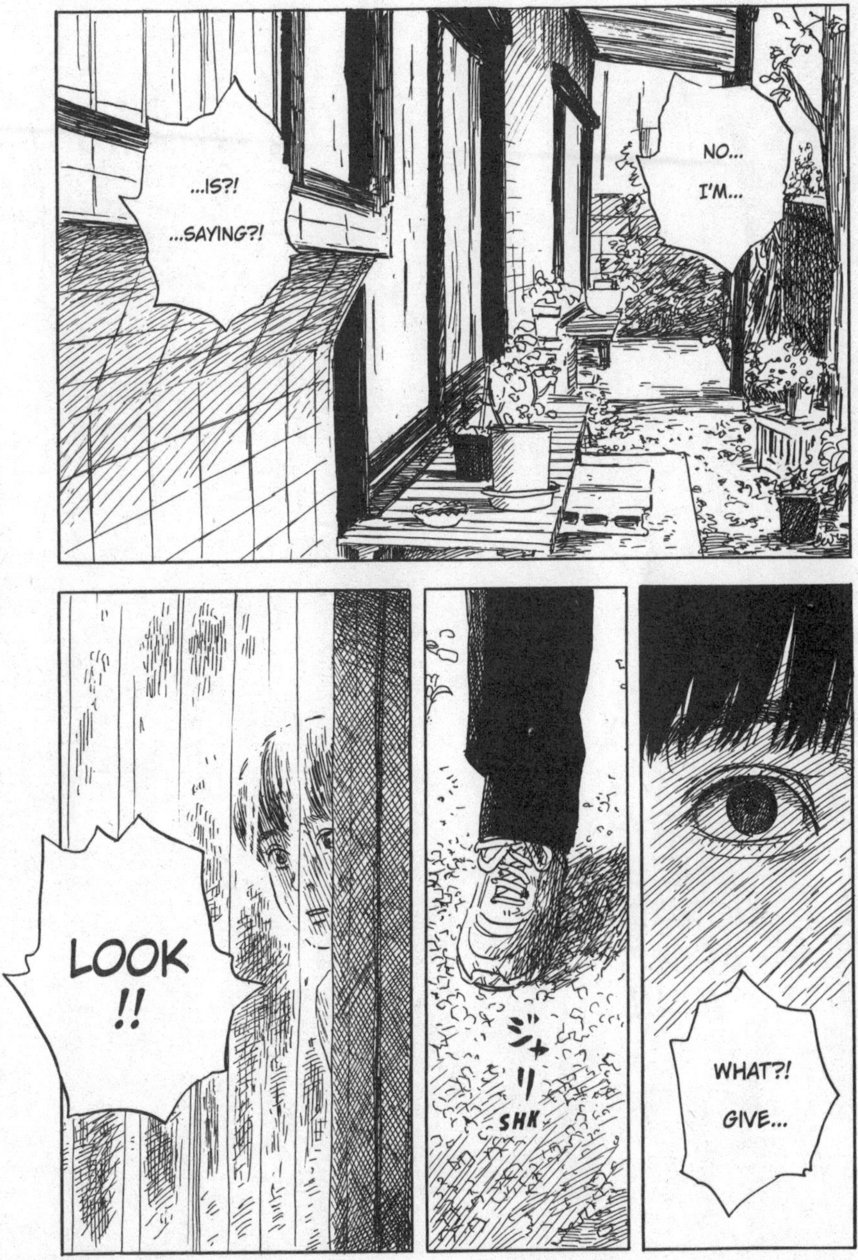
NO... I'M...
...IS?! ...SAYING?!
WHAT?! GIVE...
ジャリ
SHK
LOOK !!

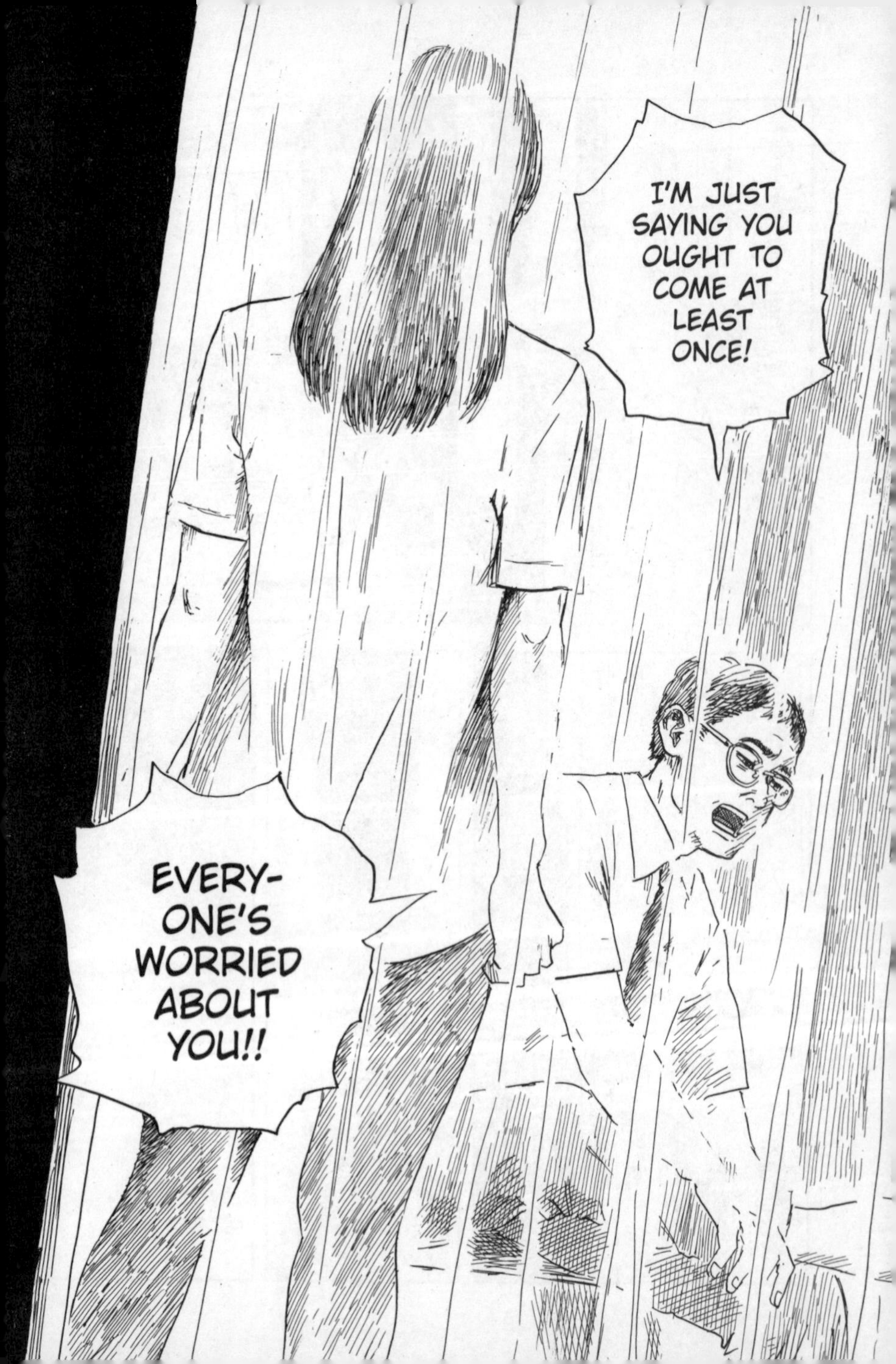
I'M JUST SAYING YOU OUGHT TO COME AT LEAST ONCE!
EVERY-ONE'S WORRIED ABOUT YOU!!

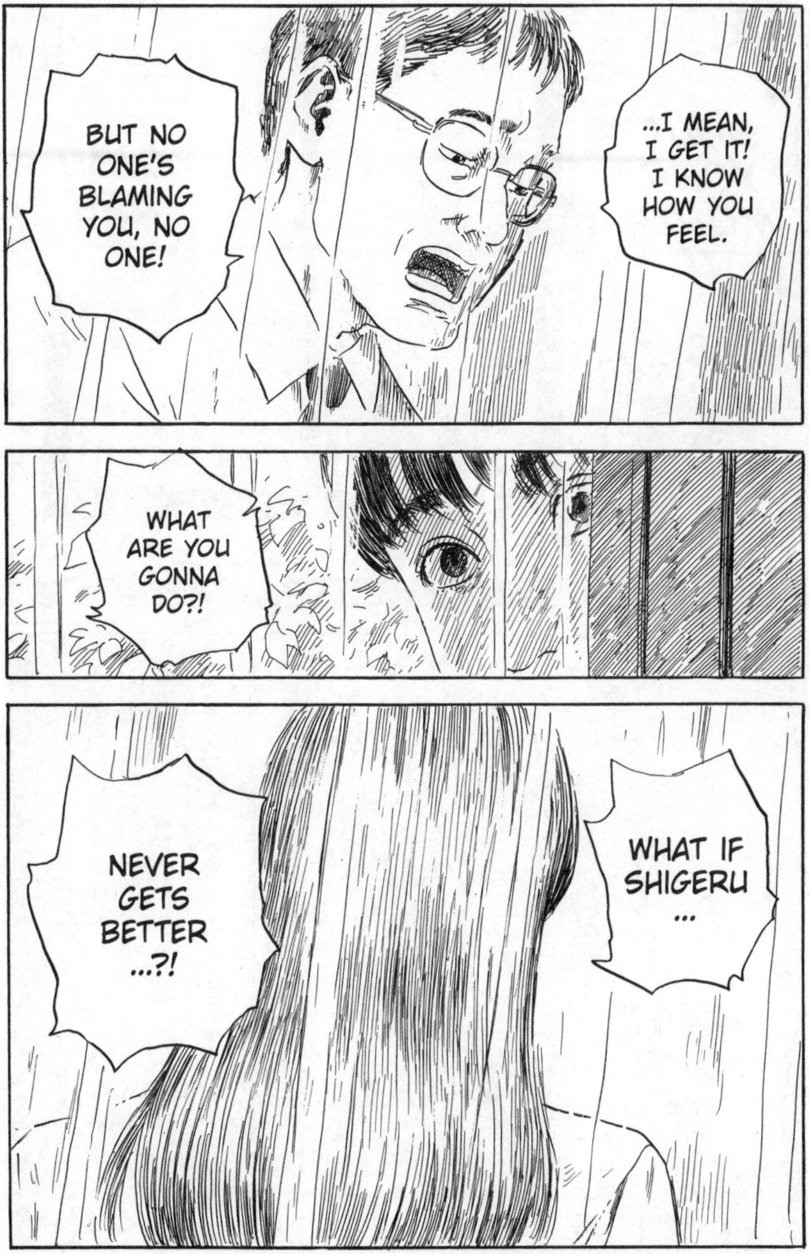
...I MEAN, I GET IT! I KNOW HOW YOU FEEL.
BUT NO ONE'S BLAMING YOU, NO ONE!
WHAT ARE YOU GONNA DO?!
WHAT IF SHIGERU ...
NEVER GETS BETTER ...?!

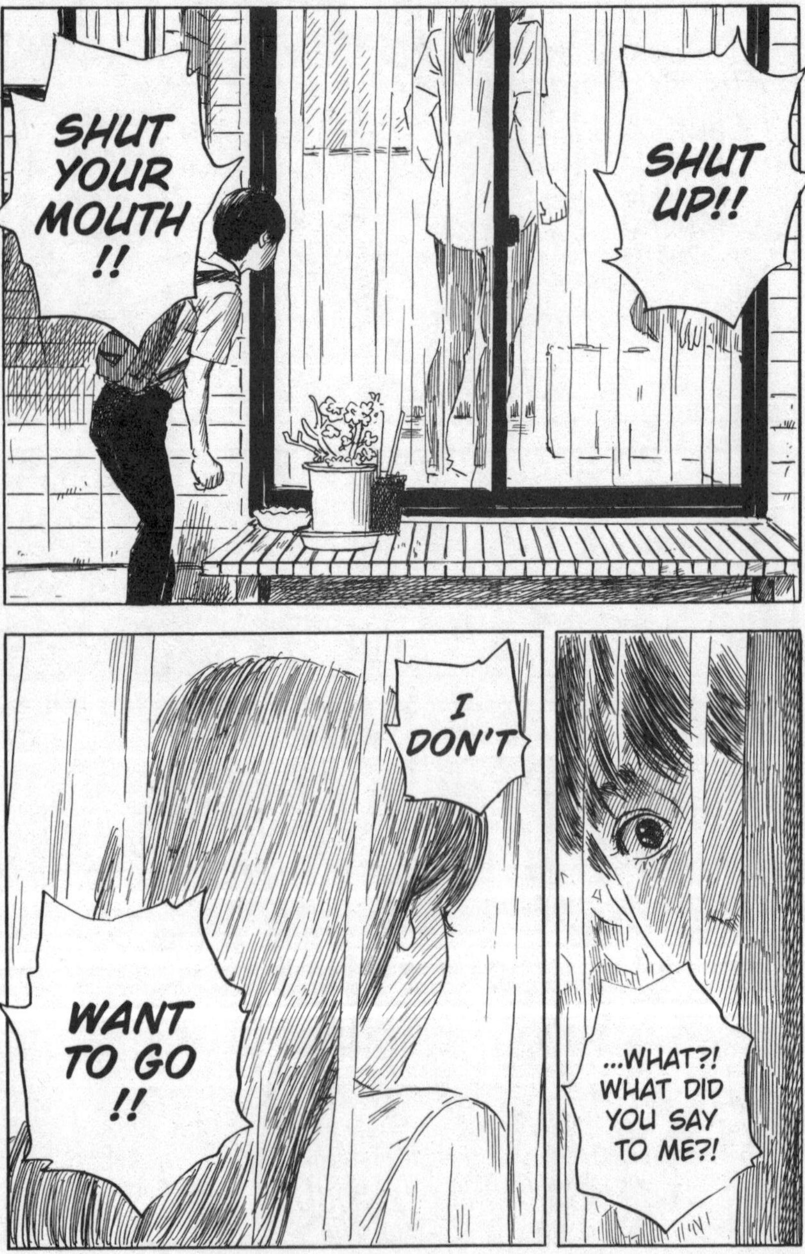
SHUT UP!!
SHUT YOUR MOUTH!!
...WHAT?! WHAT DID YOU SAY TO ME?!
I DON'T
WANT TO GO!!

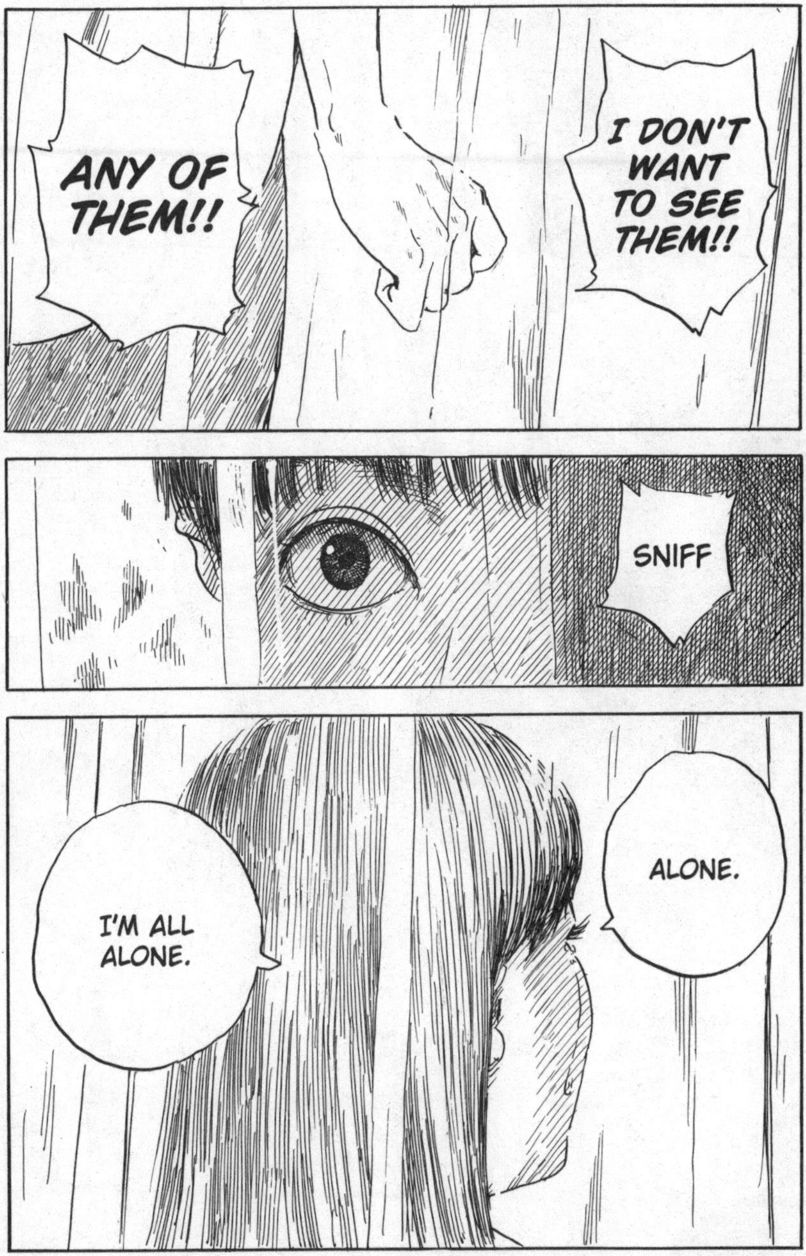
I DON'T WANT TO SEE THEM!!
ANY OF THEM!!
SNIFF
ALONE.
I'M ALL ALONE.

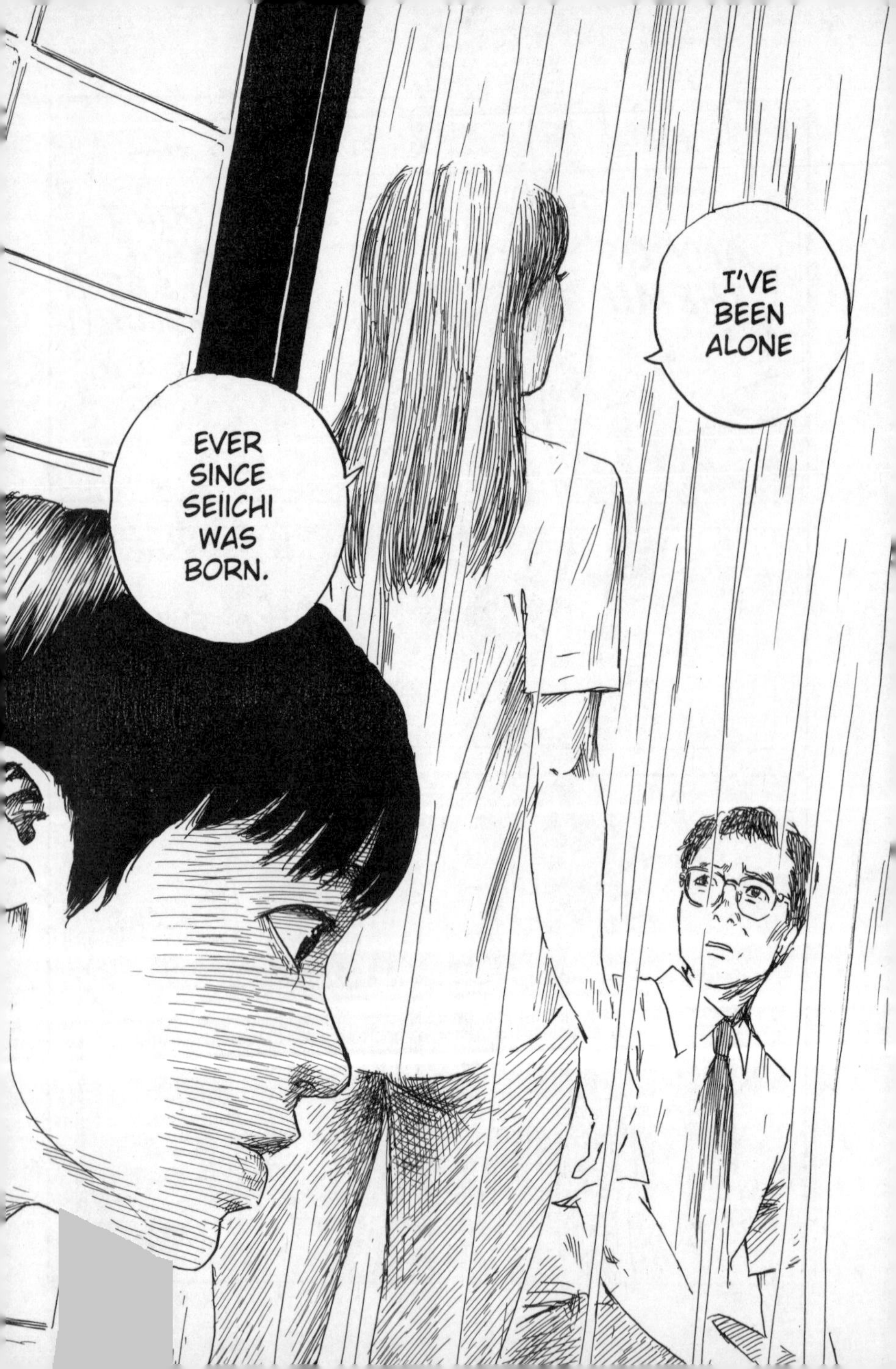
I'VE BEEN ALONE
EVER SINCE SEIICHI WAS BORN.

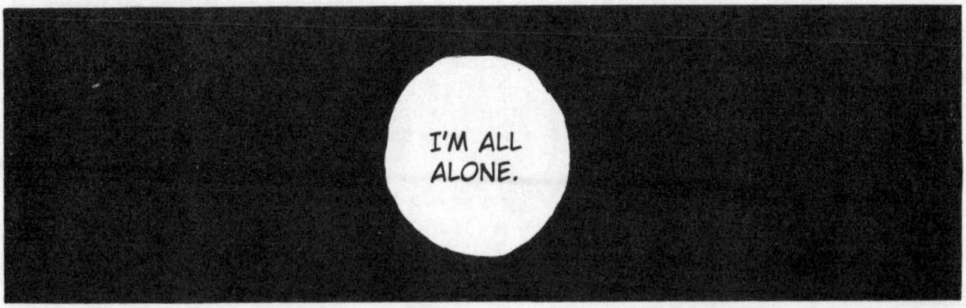
I'M ALL ALONE.

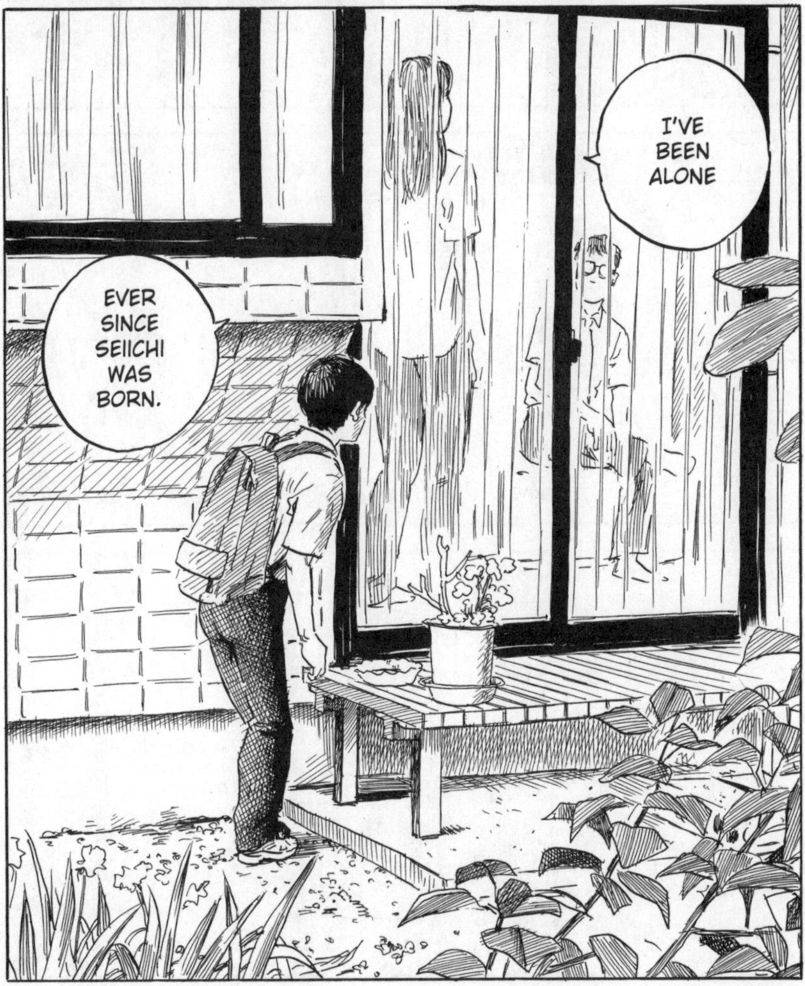
I'VE BEEN ALONE
EVER SINCE SEIICHI WAS BORN.

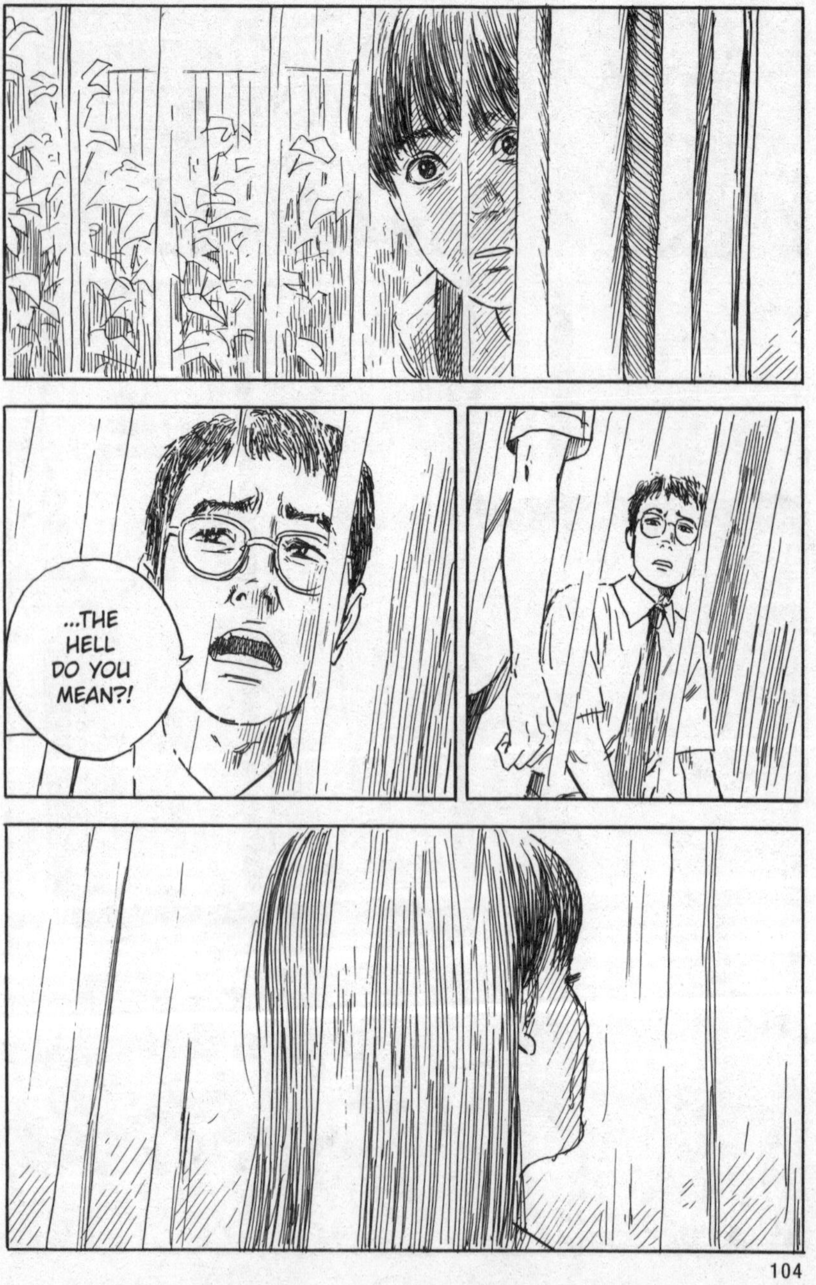
...THE HELL DO YOU MEAN?!

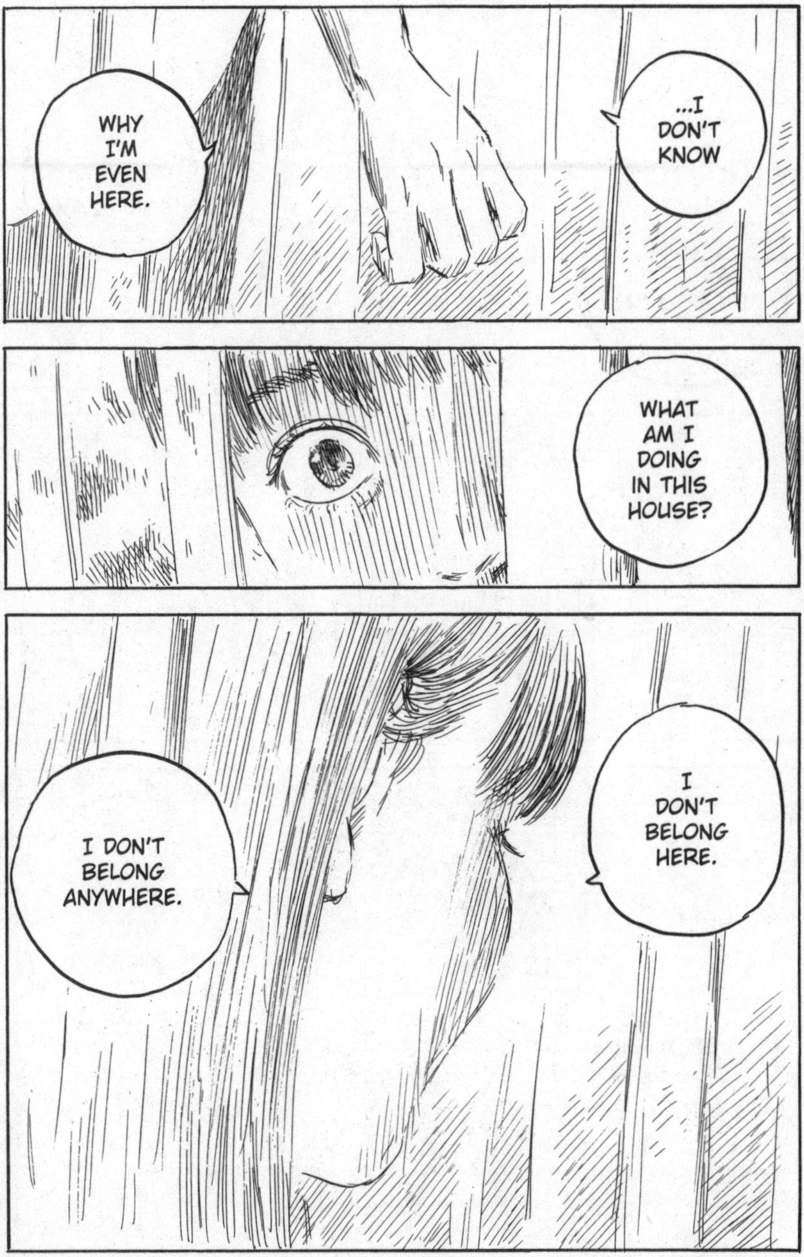
...I DON'T KNOW
WHY I'M EVEN HERE.
WHAT AM I DOING IN THIS HOUSE?
I DON'T BELONG HERE.
I DON'T BELONG ANYWHERE.

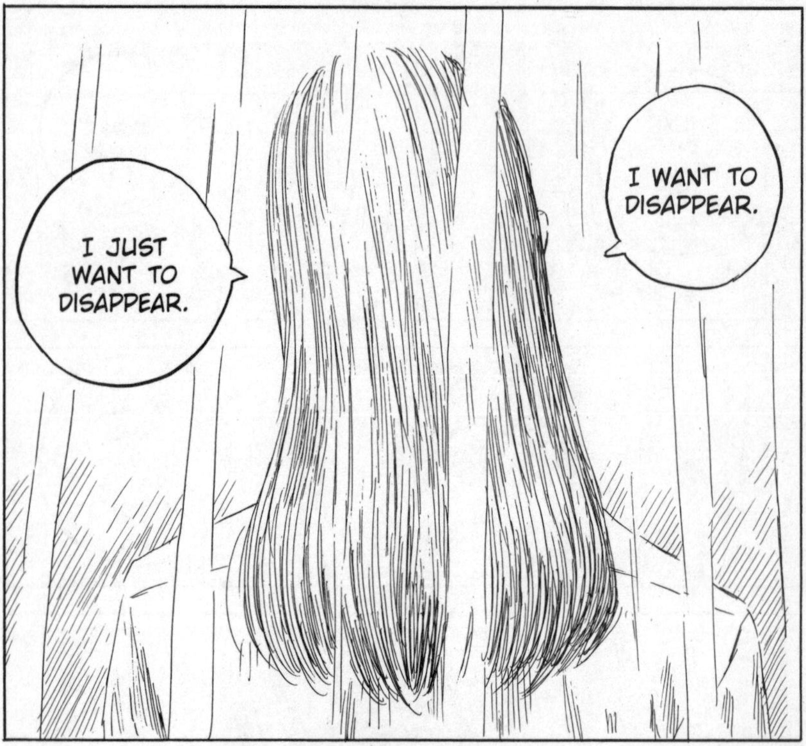
I WANT TO DISAPPEAR.
I JUST WANT TO DISAPPEAR.

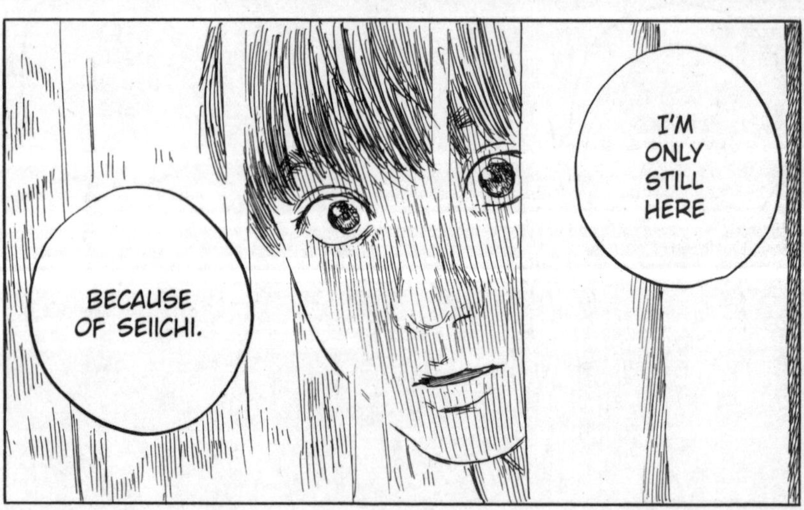
I'M ONLY STILL HERE
BECAUSE OF SEIICHI.

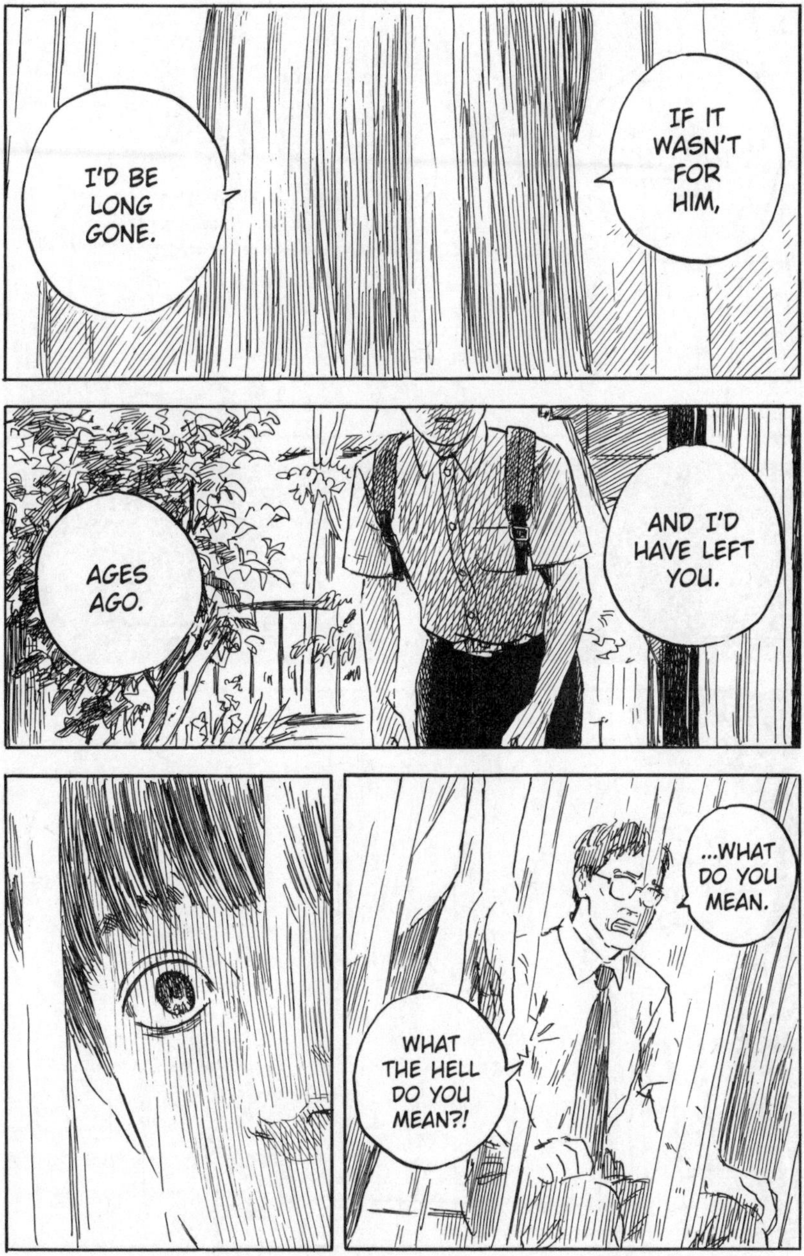
IF IT WASN'T FOR HIM,
I'D BE LONG GONE.
AND I'D HAVE LEFT YOU.
AGES AGO.
...WHAT DO YOU MEAN.
WHAT THE HELL DO YOU MEAN?!

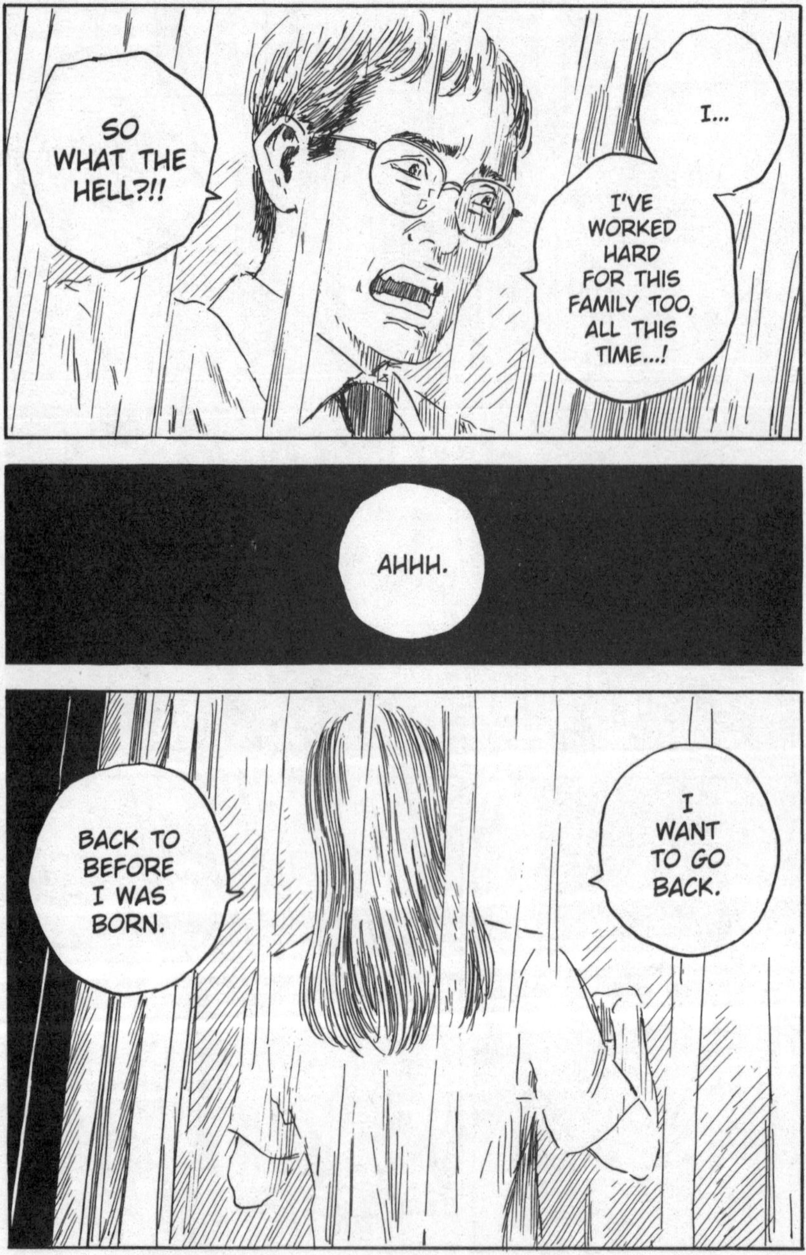
I...
I'VE WORKED HARD FOR THIS FAMILY TOO, ALL THIS TIME...!
SO WHAT THE HELL?!!
AHHH.
I WANT TO GO BACK.
BACK TO BEFORE I WAS BORN.

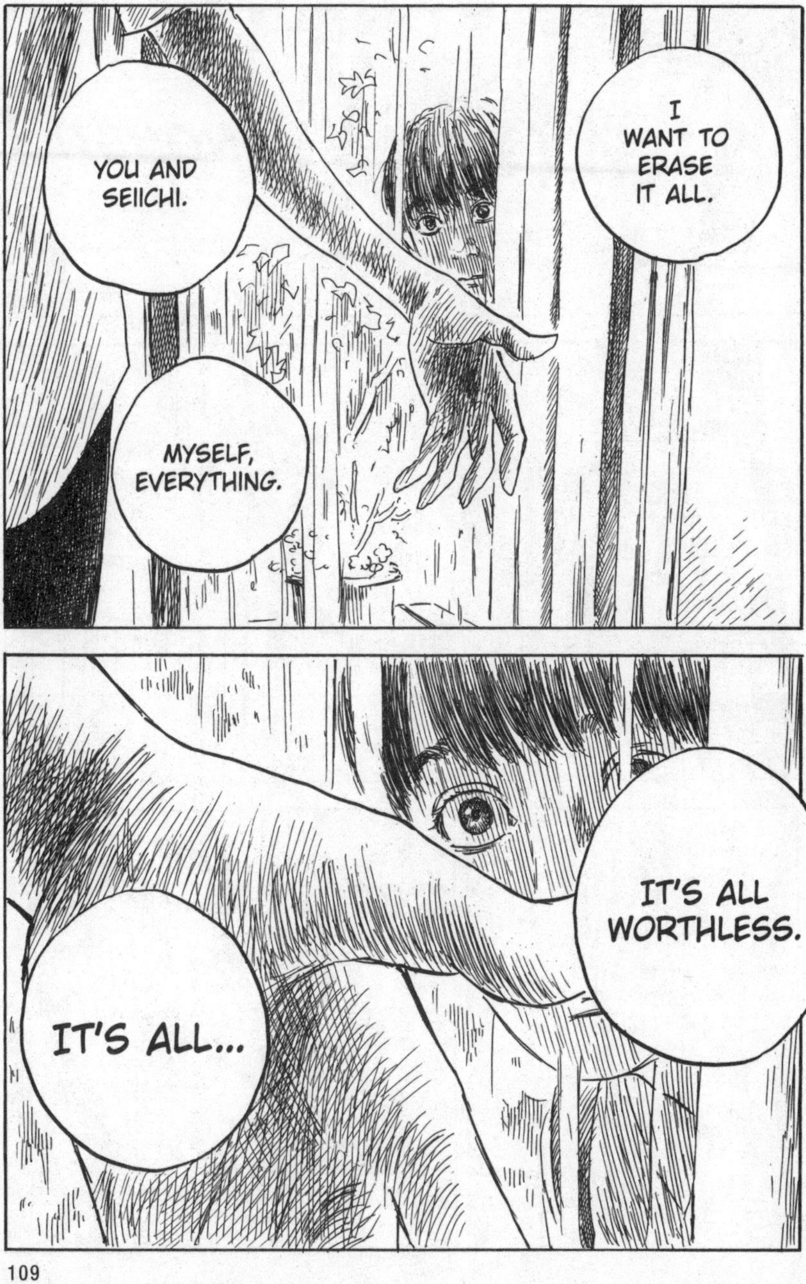
I WANT TO ERASE IT ALL.
YOU AND SEIICHI.
MYSELF, EVERYTHING.
IT'S ALL WORTHLESS.
IT'S ALL...

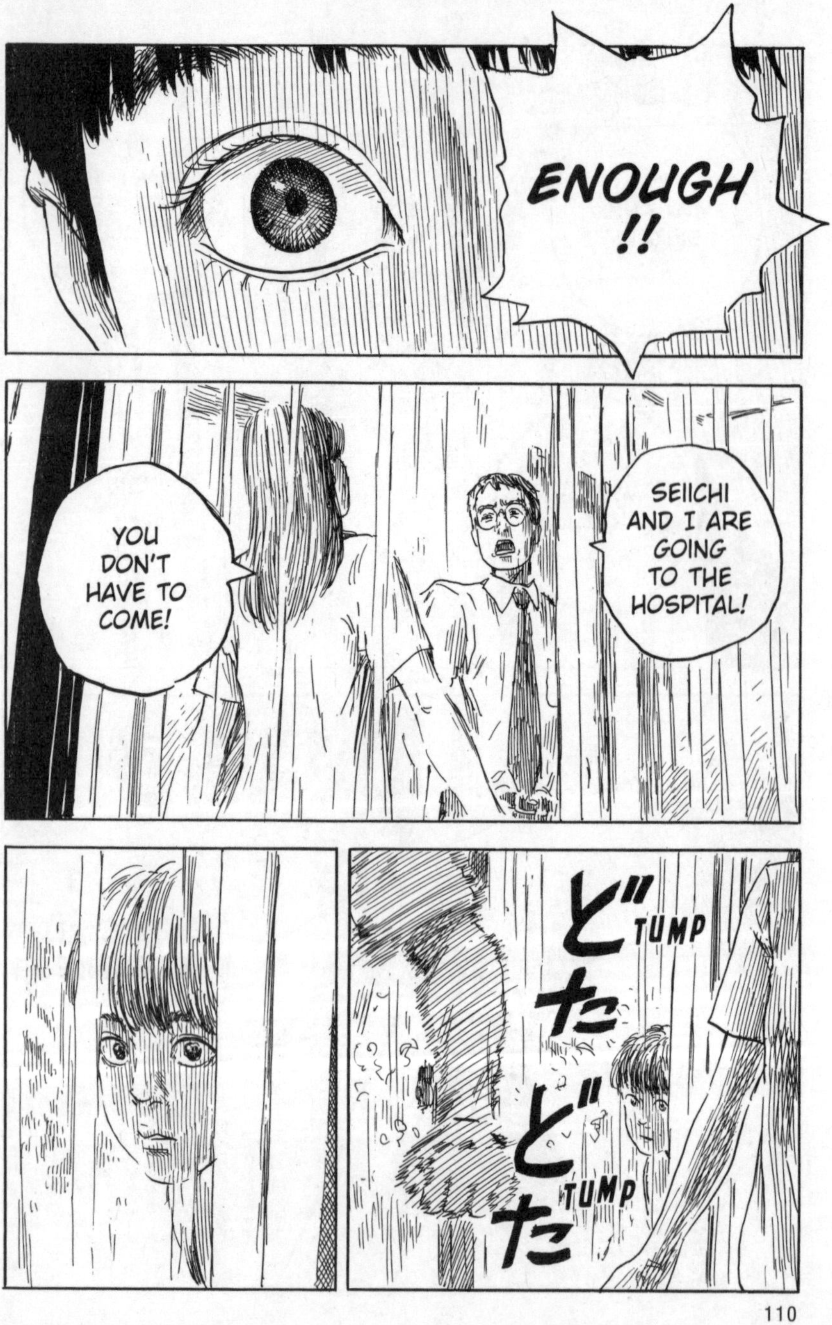
ENOUGH!!
SEIICHI AND I ARE GOING TO THE HOSPITAL!
YOU DON'T HAVE TO COME!
どた TUMP
どた TUMP

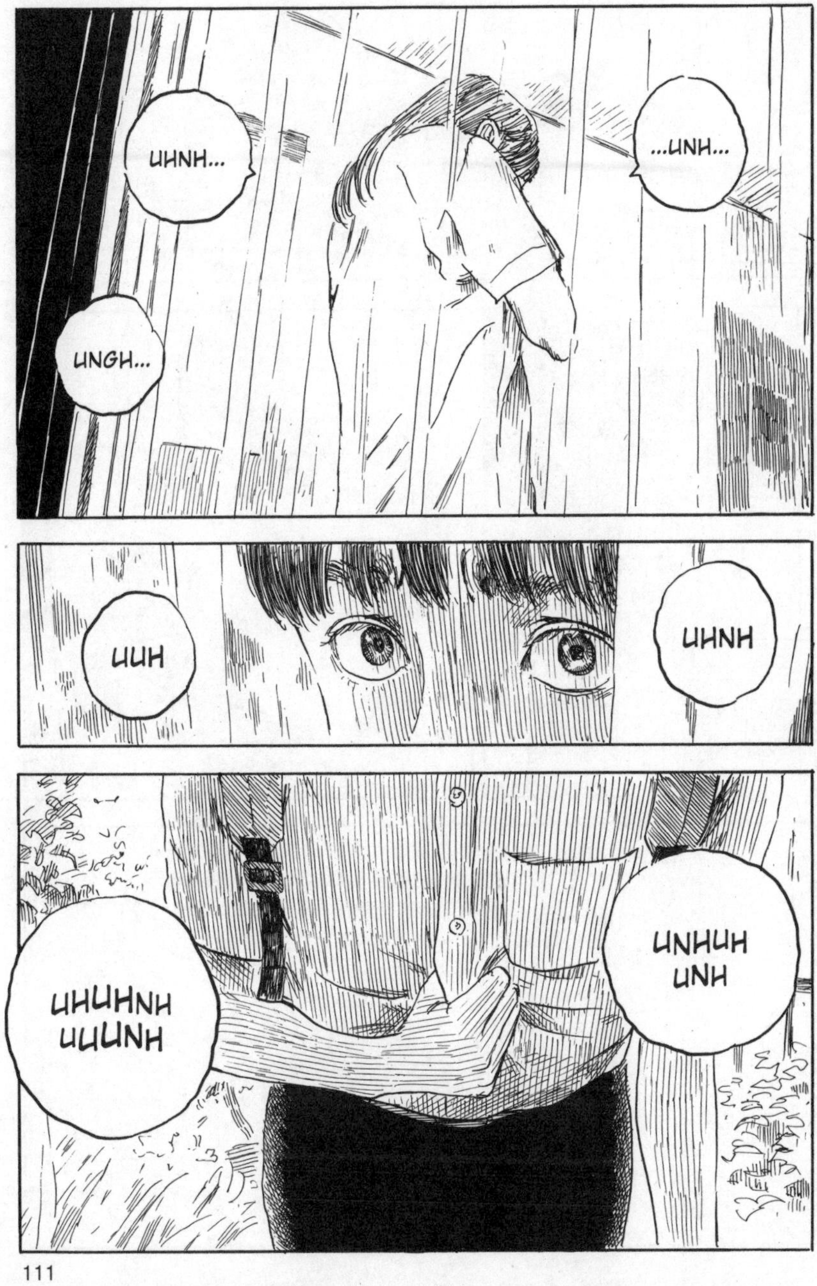
...UNH...
UHNH...
UNGH...
UHNH
UUH
UNHUH UNH
UHUHNH UUUNH

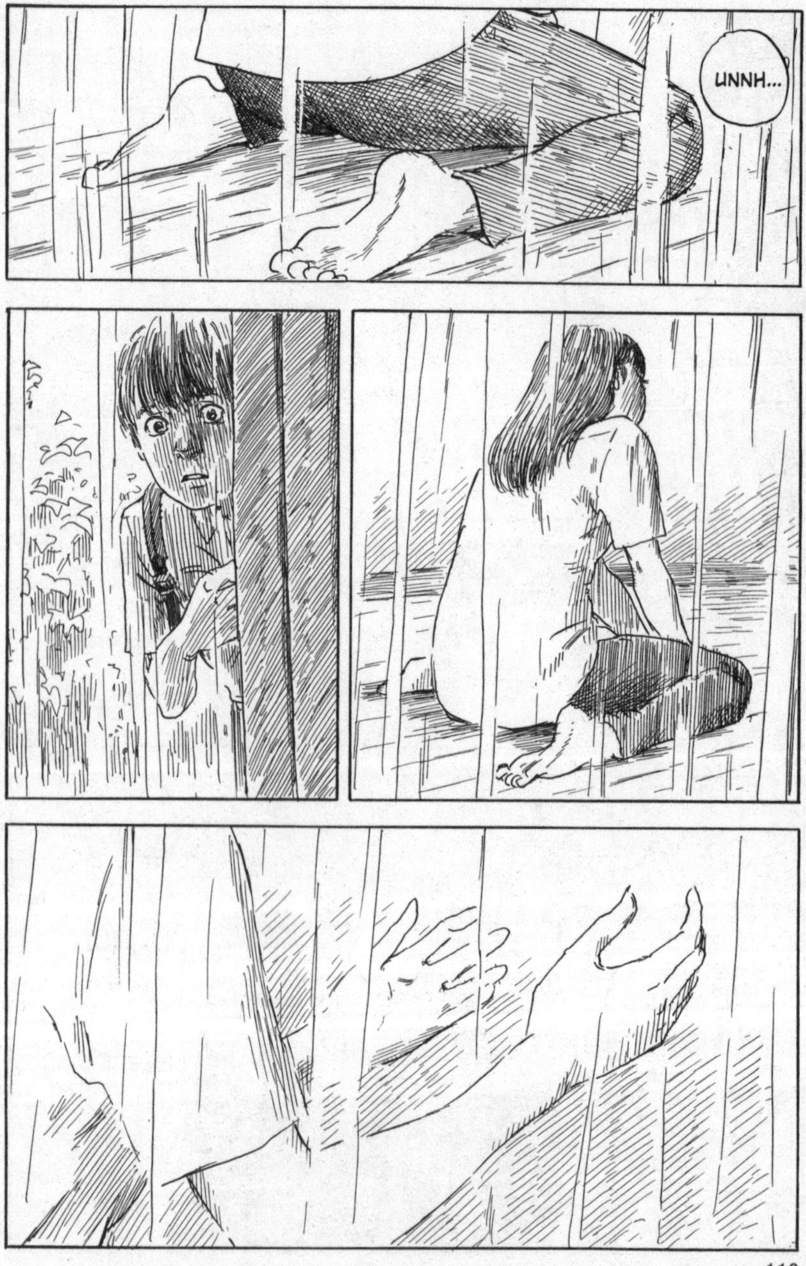
UNNH...

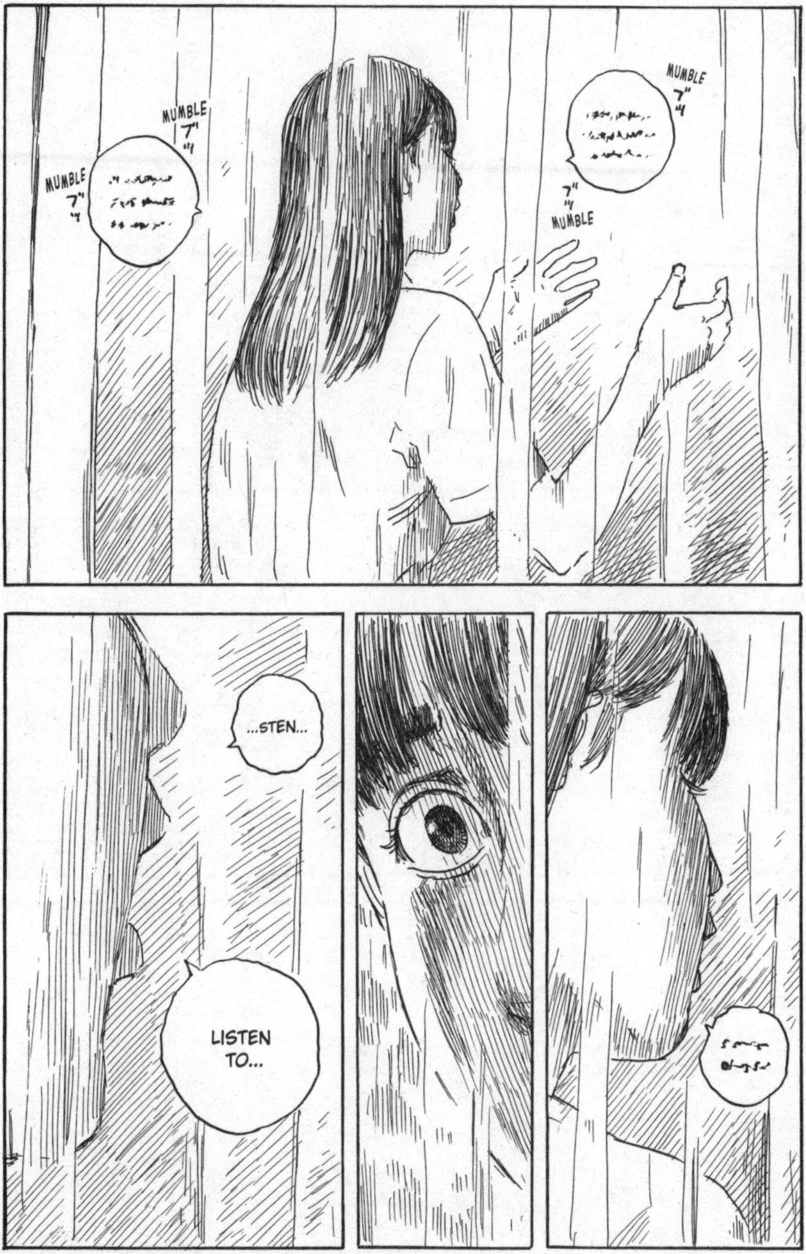
MUMBLE
MUMBLE
MUMBLE
MUMBLE
...STEN...
LISTEN TO...

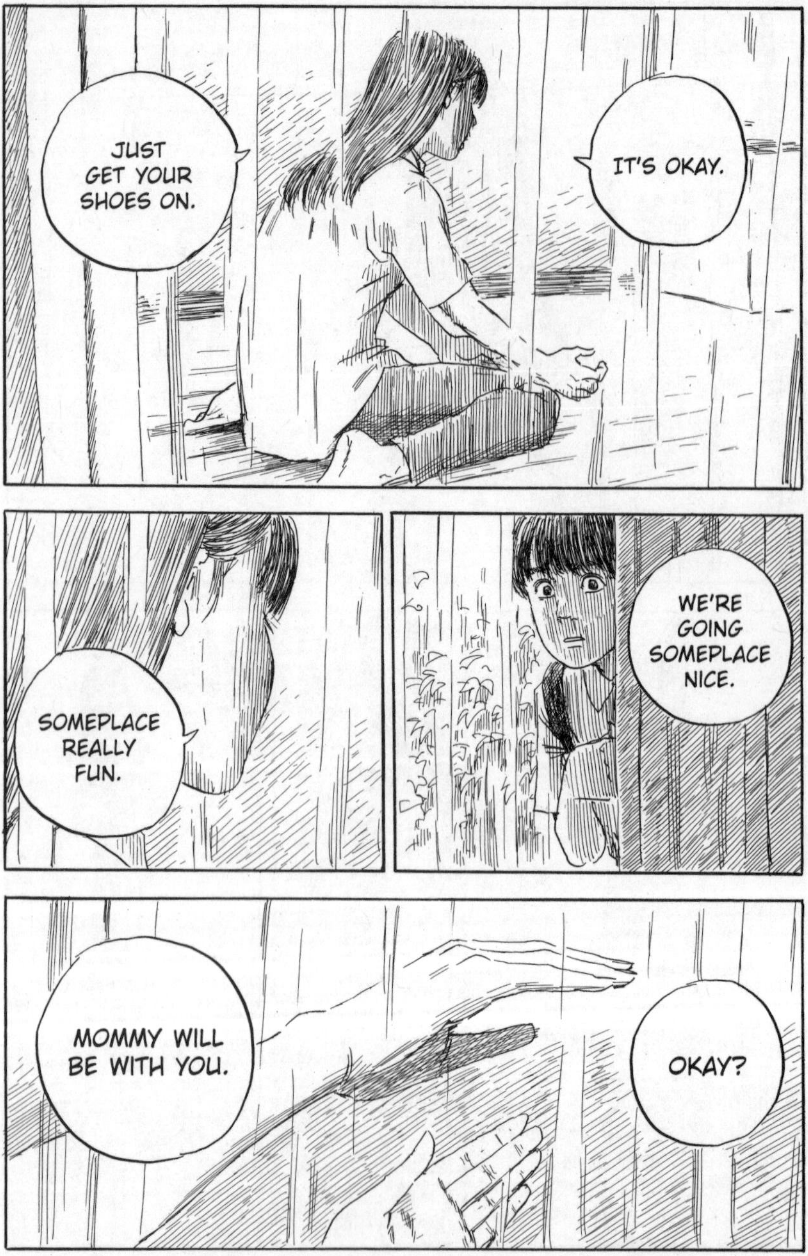
IT'S OKAY.
JUST GET YOUR SHOES ON.
WE'RE GOING SOMEPLACE NICE.
SOMEPLACE REALLY FUN.
MOMMY WILL BE WITH YOU.
OKAY?

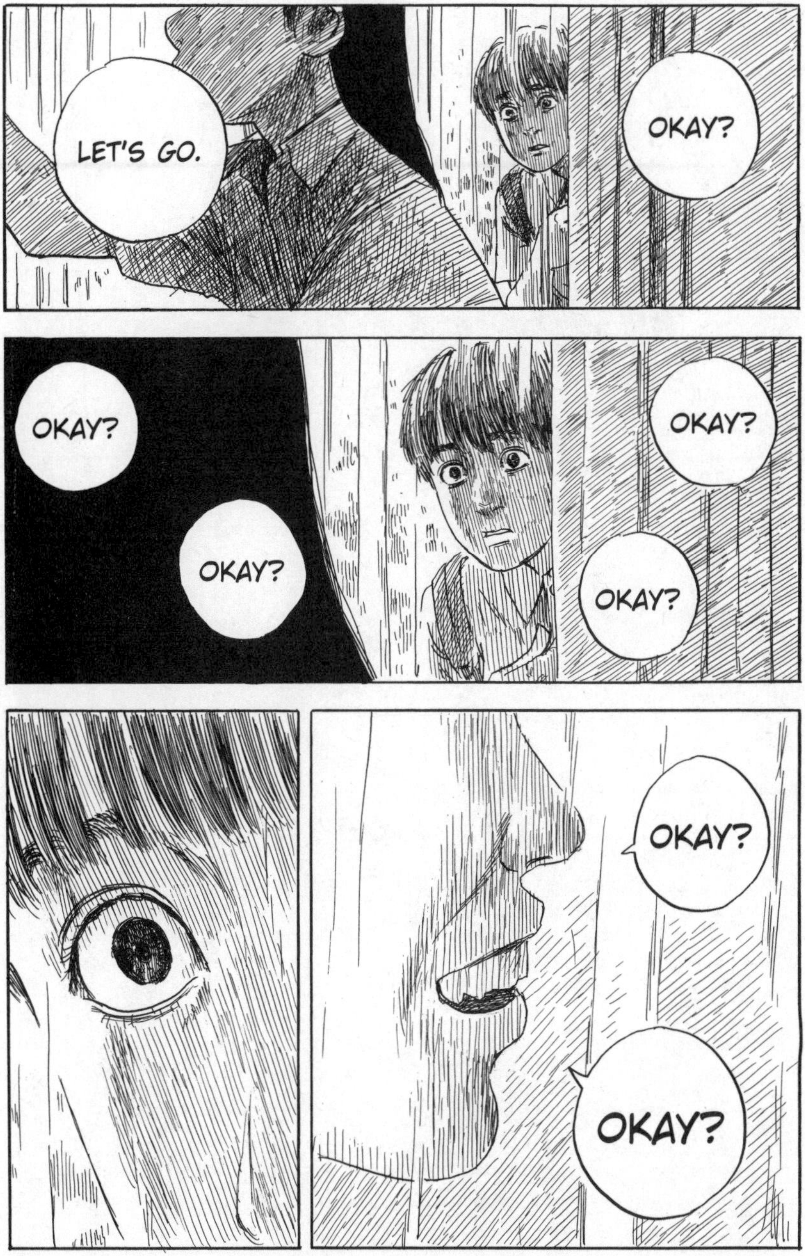
OKAY?
LET'S GO.
OKAY?
OKAY?
OKAY?
OKAY?
OKAY?
OKAY?

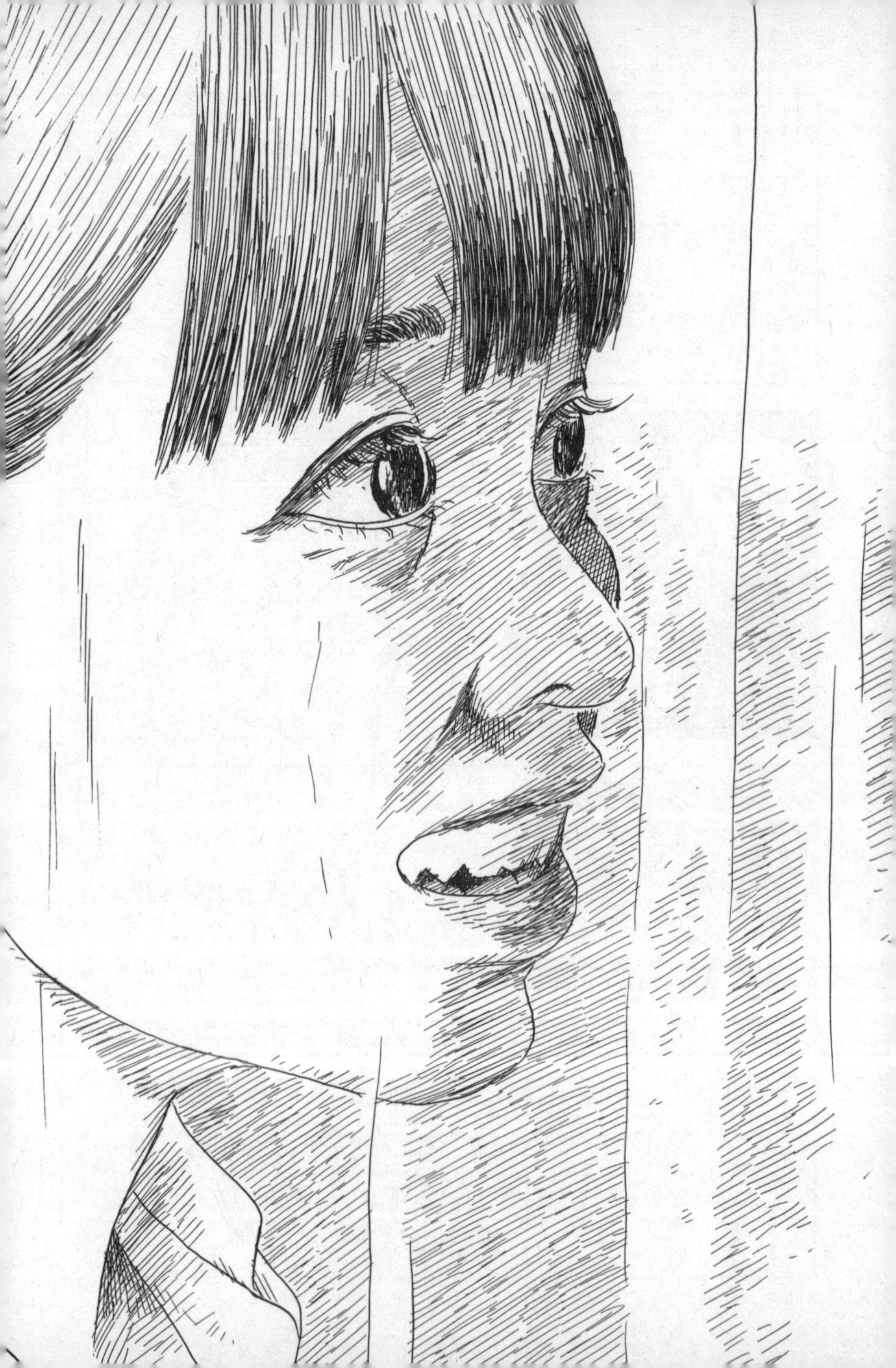

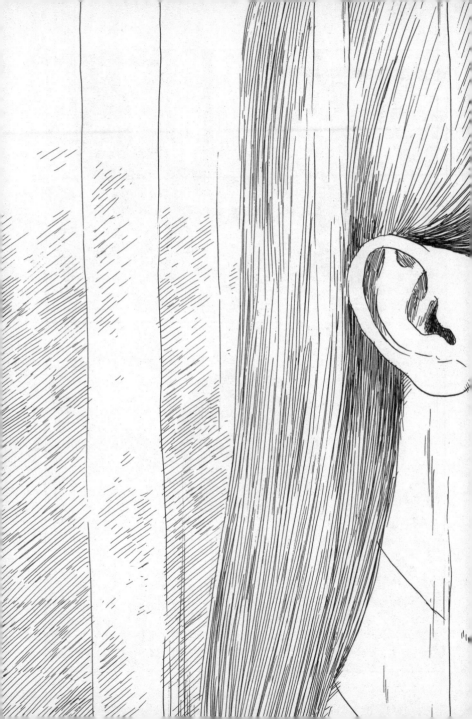

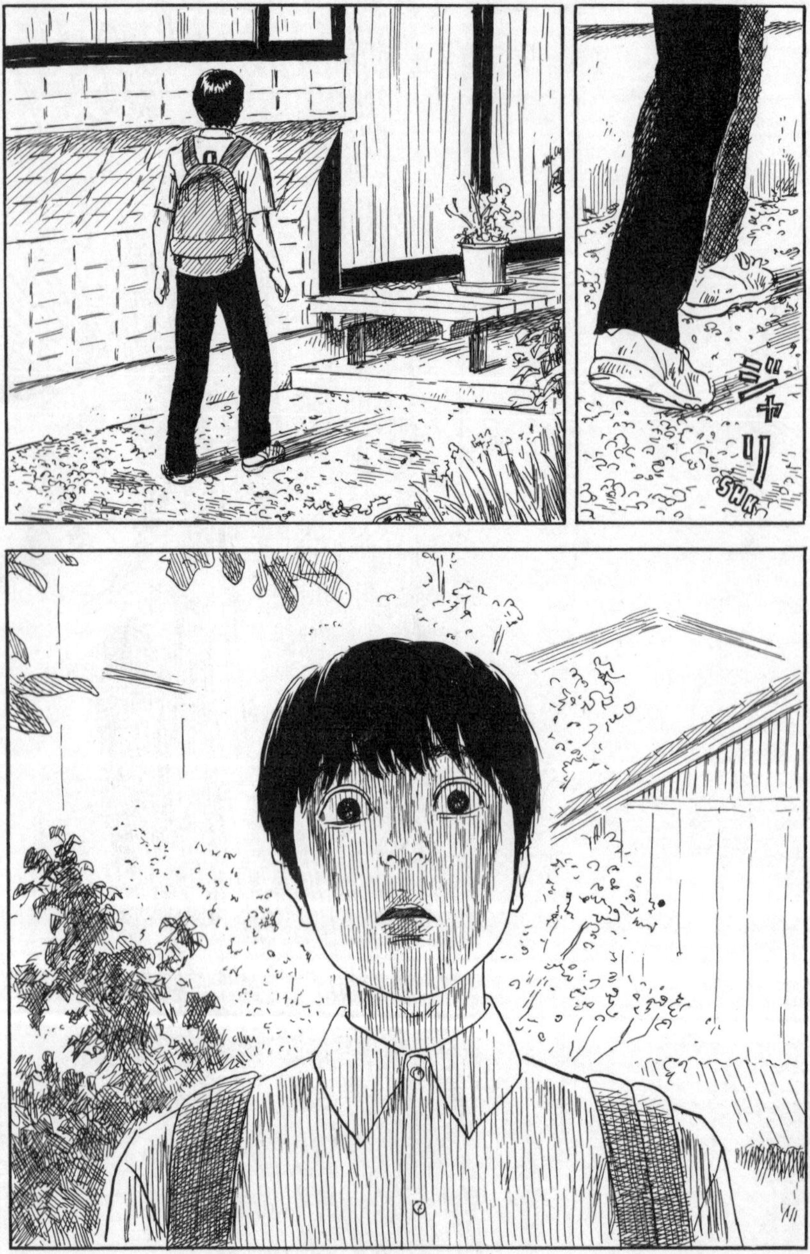
ジャリ
SHK

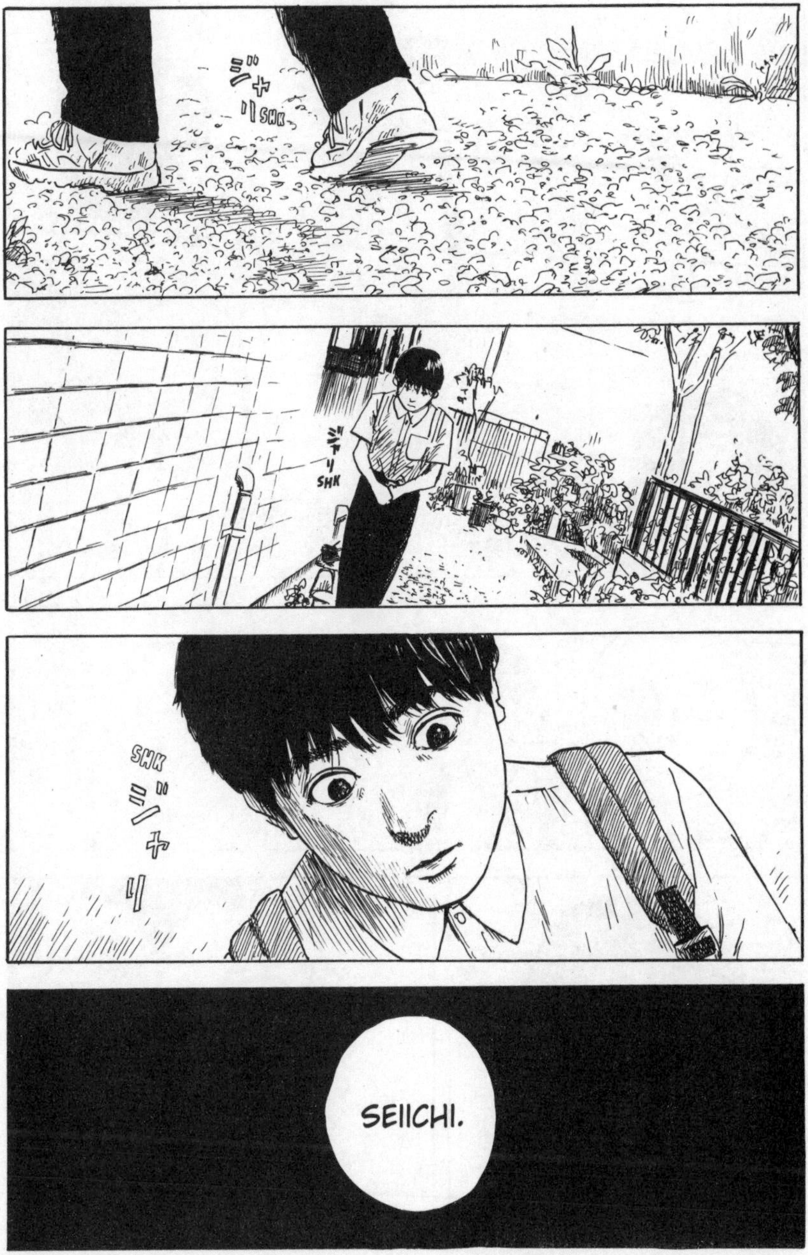
ジャリ
SHK
ジャリ
SHK
SHK
ジャリ
SEIICHI.

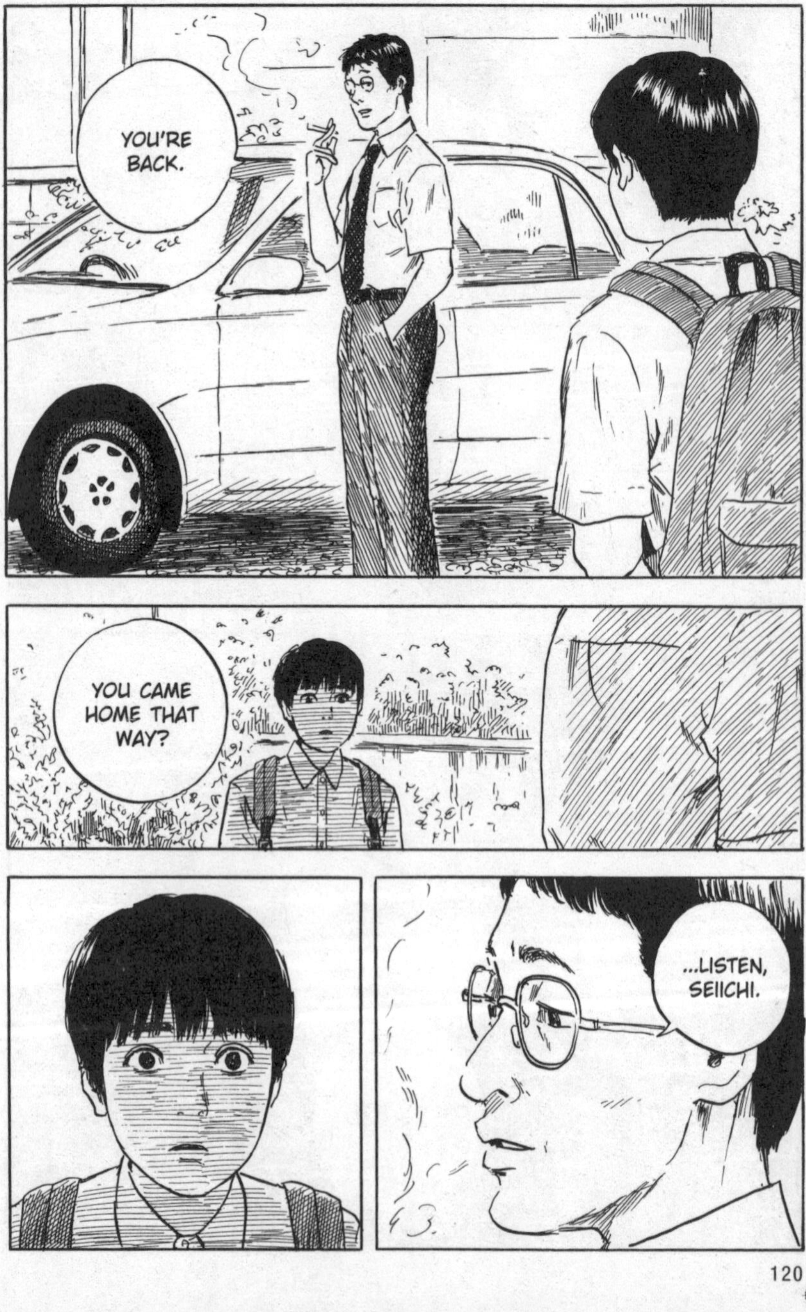
YOU'RE BACK.
YOU CAME HOME THAT WAY?
...LISTEN, SEIICHI.

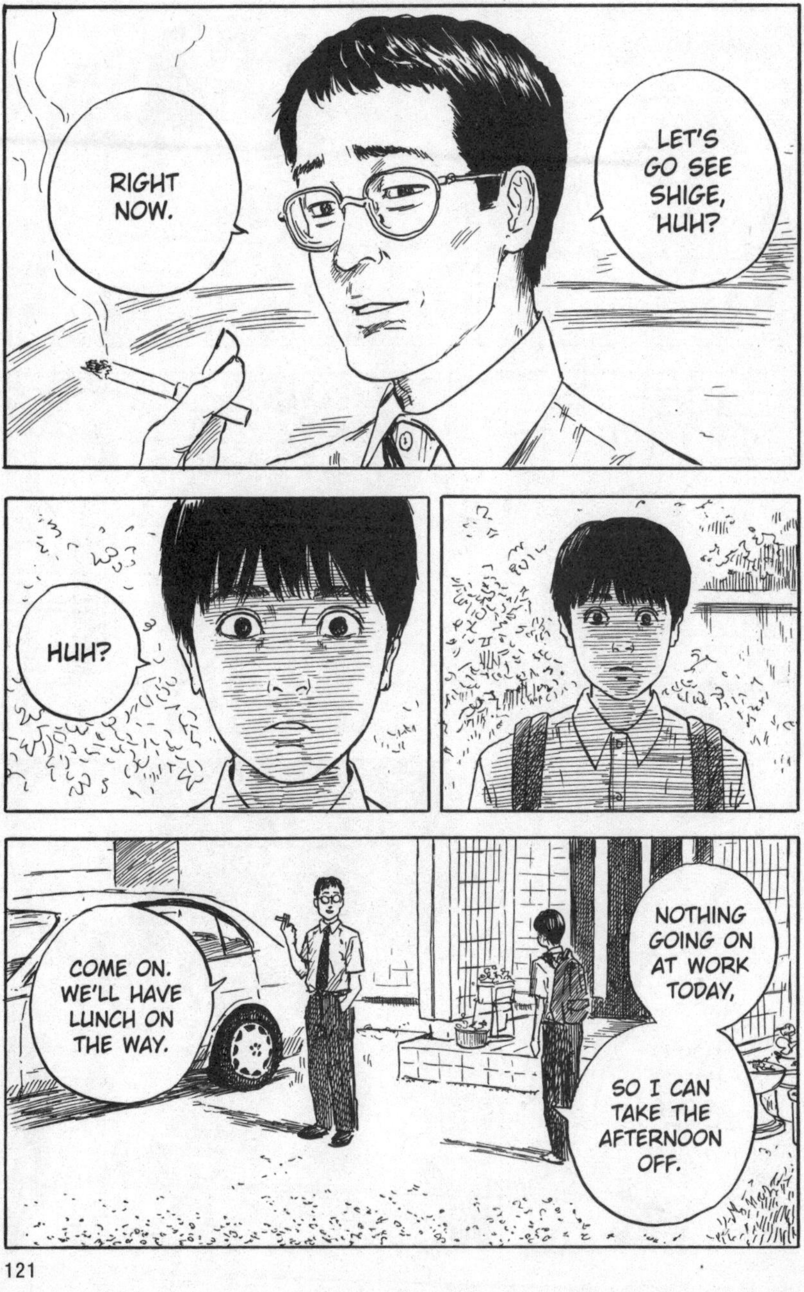
LET'S GO SEE SHIGE, HUH?
RIGHT NOW.
HUH?
NOTHING GOING ON AT WORK TODAY,
SO I CAN TAKE THE AFTERNOON OFF.
COME ON. WE'LL HAVE LUNCH ON THE WAY.

M-
M-
M-
M-
M-
M-
DON'T WORRY ABOUT YOUR MOM.

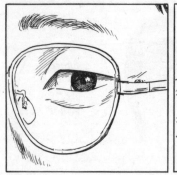

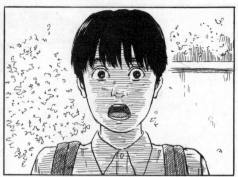

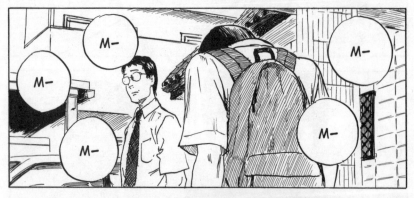

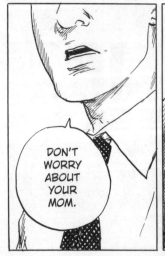

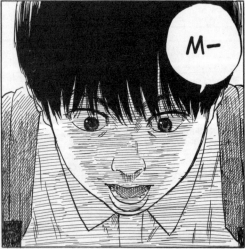

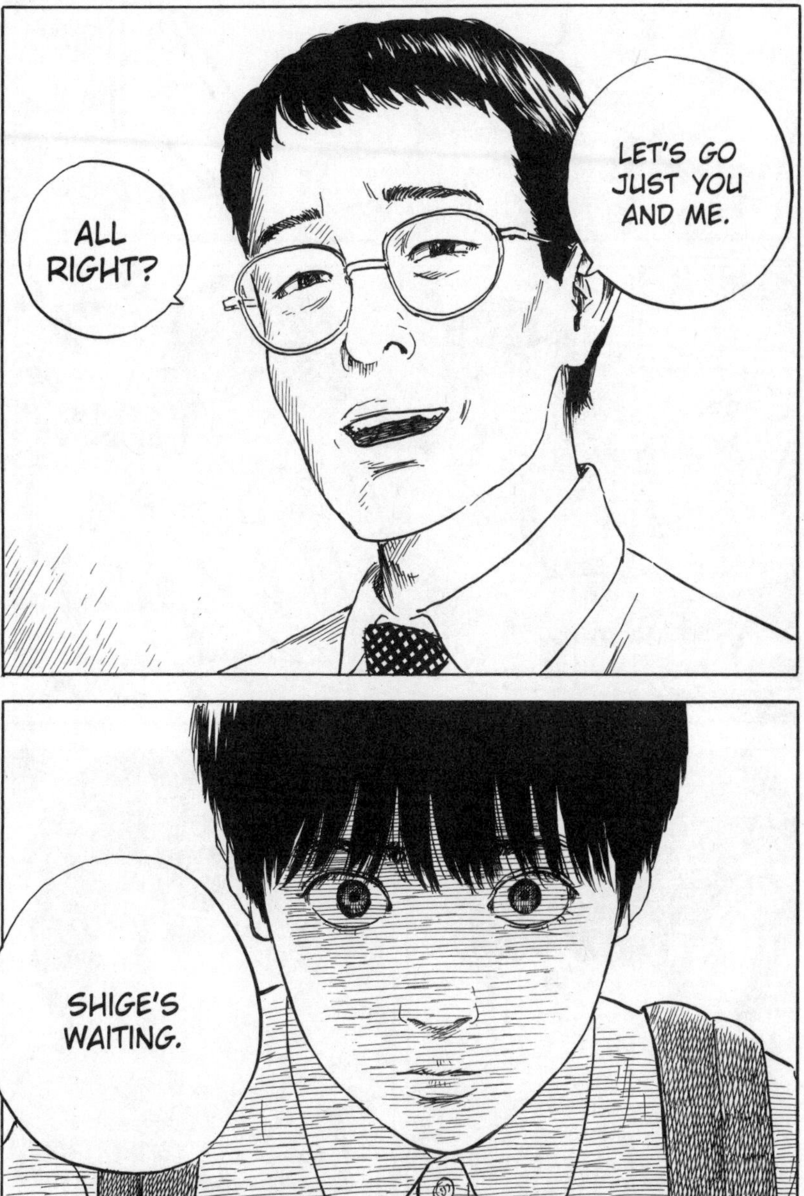
LET'S GO JUST YOU AND ME.
ALL RIGHT?
SHIGE'S WAITING.

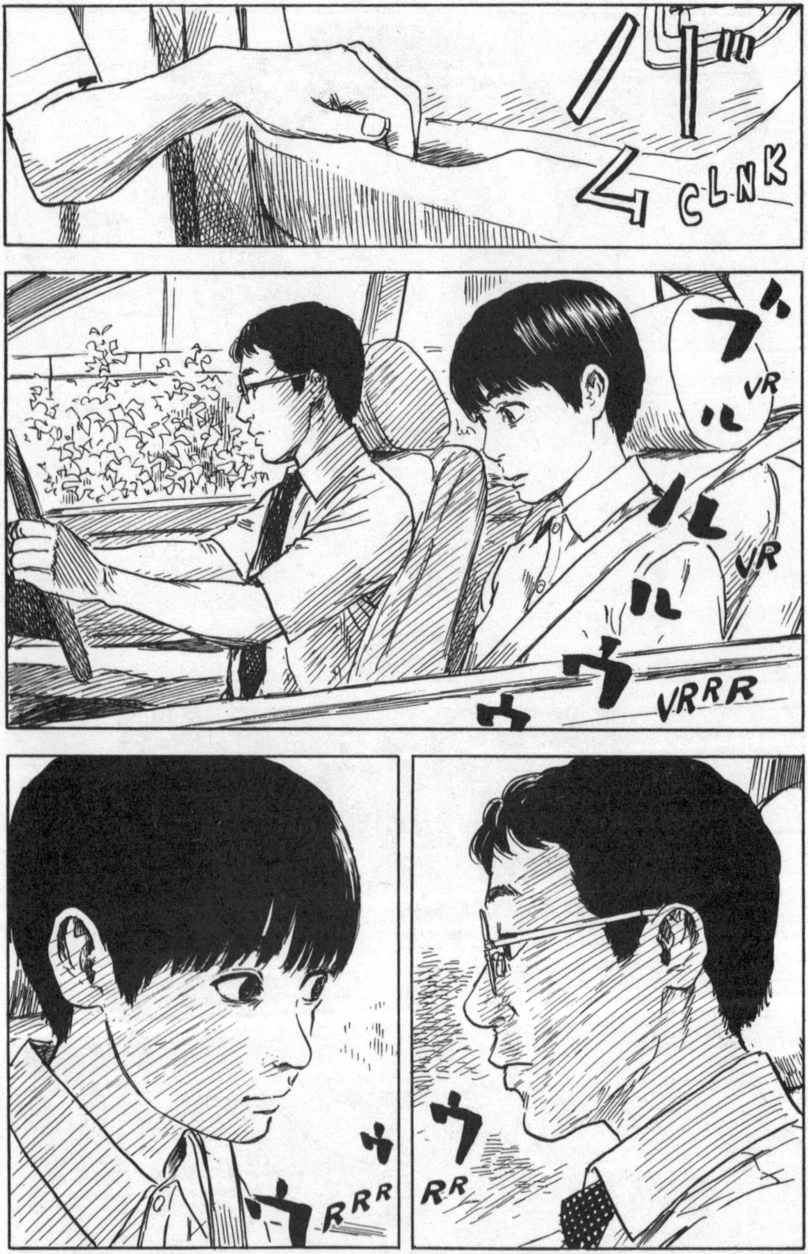
CLNK
VR
VR
VRRR
RR
RRR

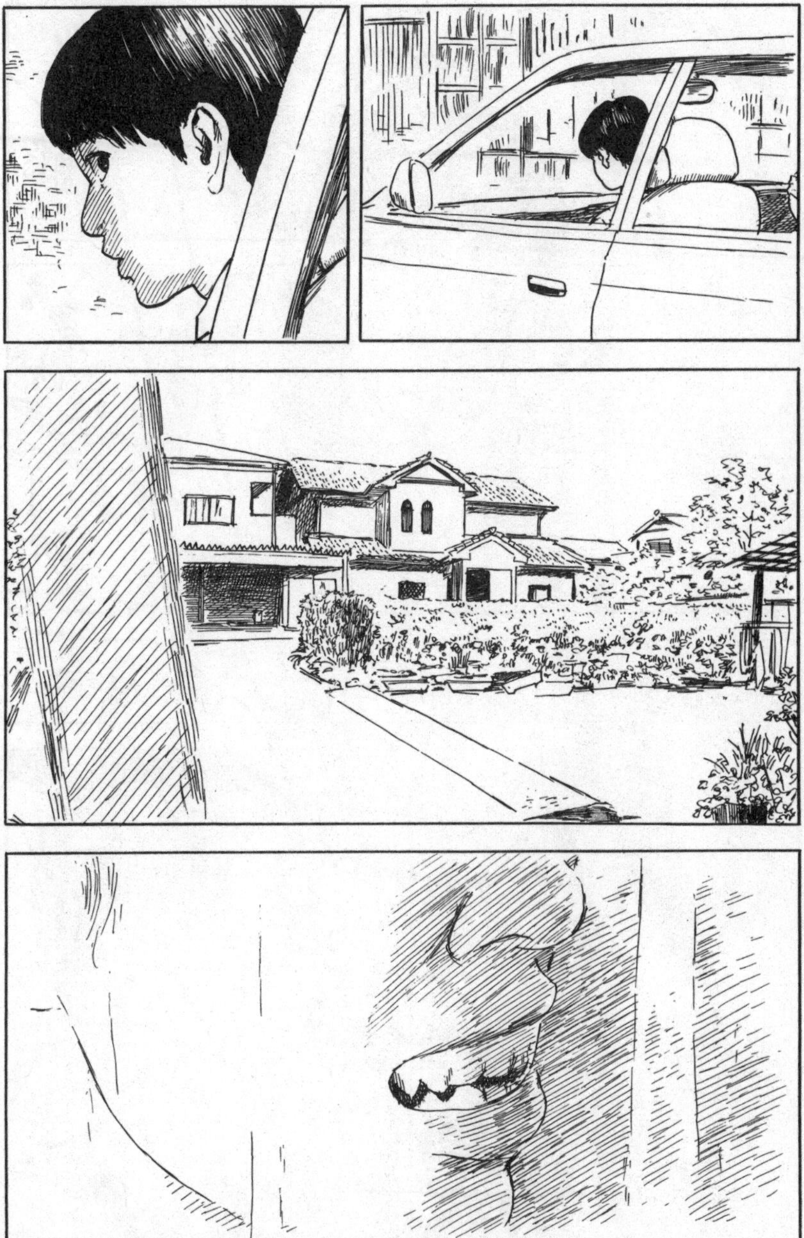

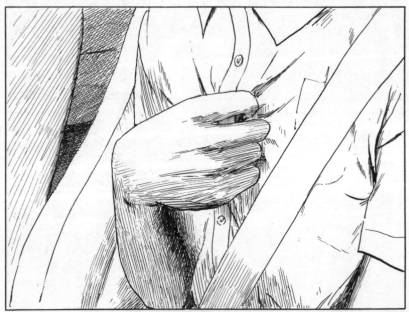

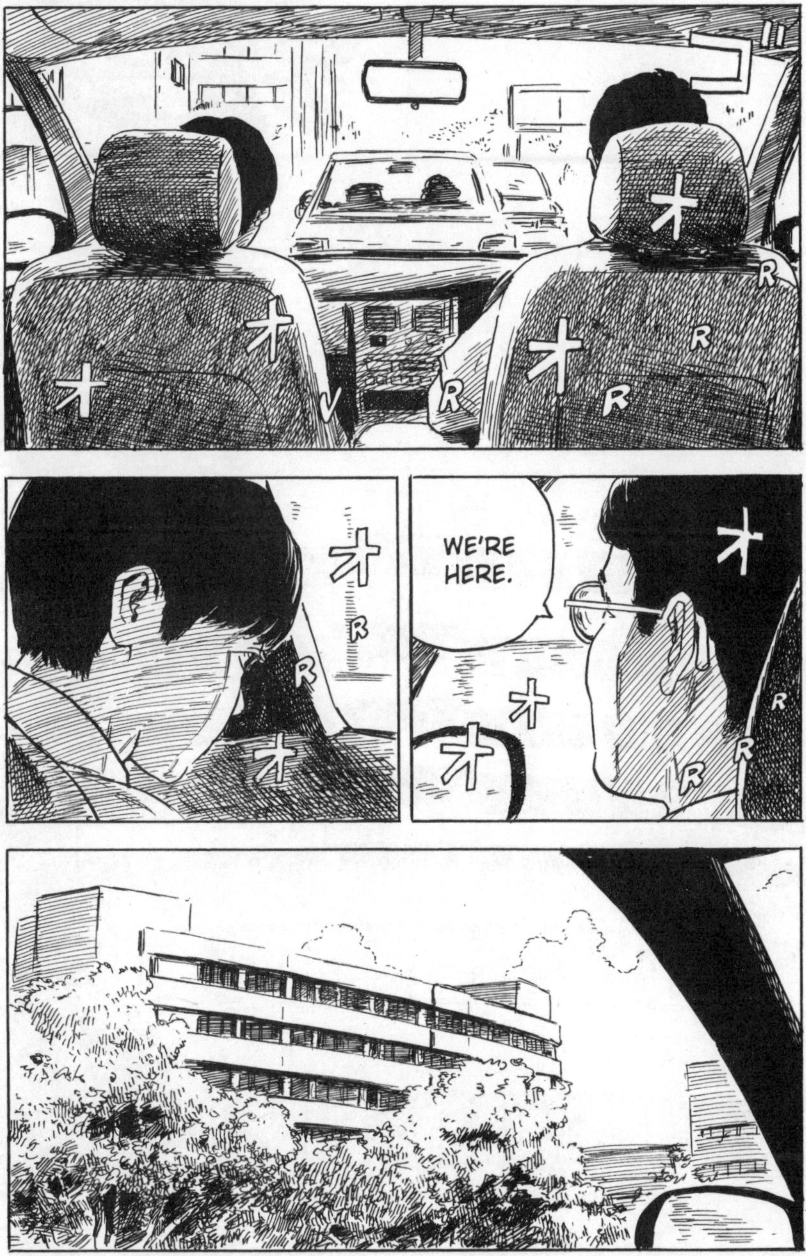
ゴ
オ
R
R
R
R
オ
オ
オ
WE'RE HERE.
オ
R
R
R
オ
オ
オ
R
R
オ

CHAPTER 21 Confrontation

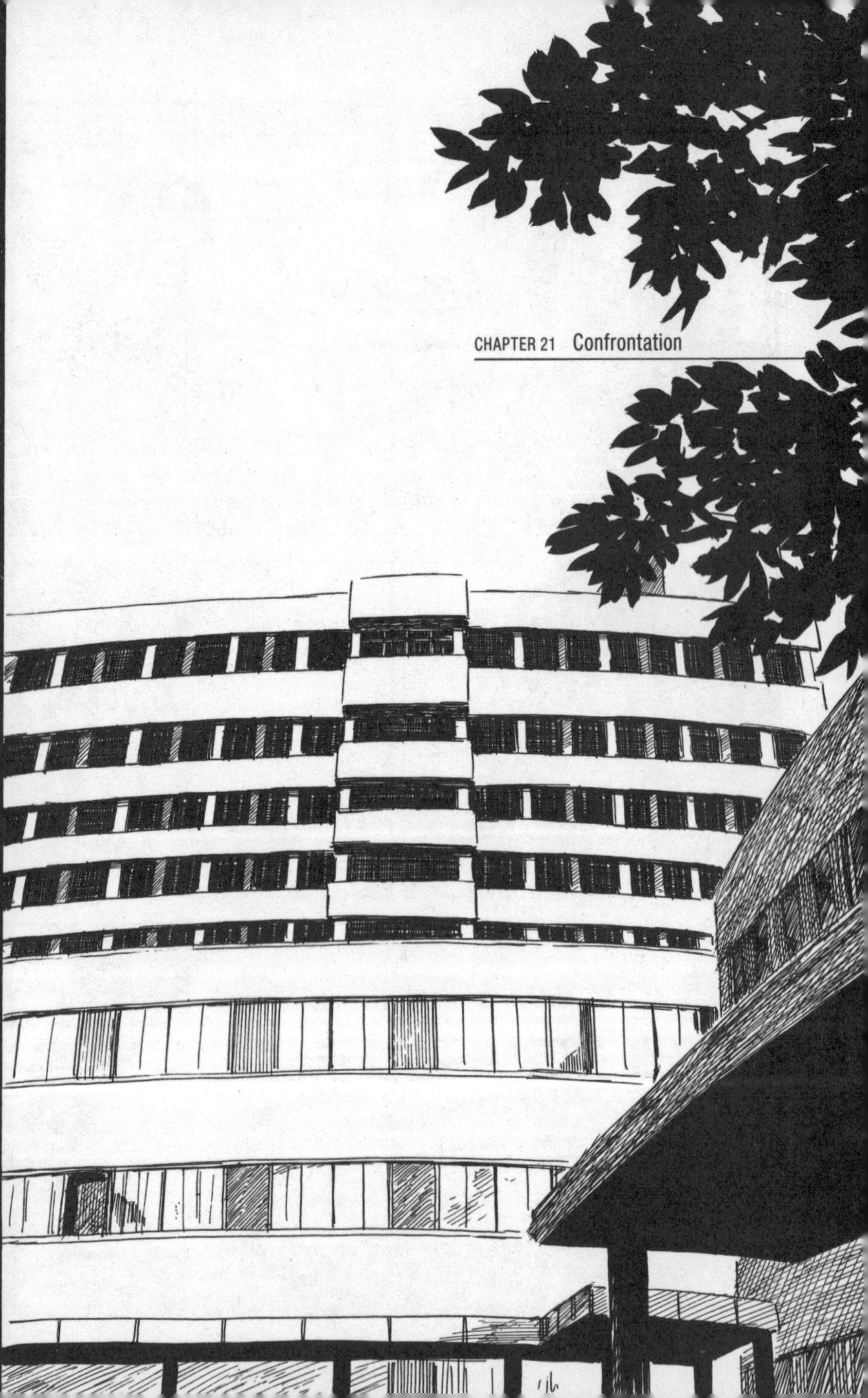

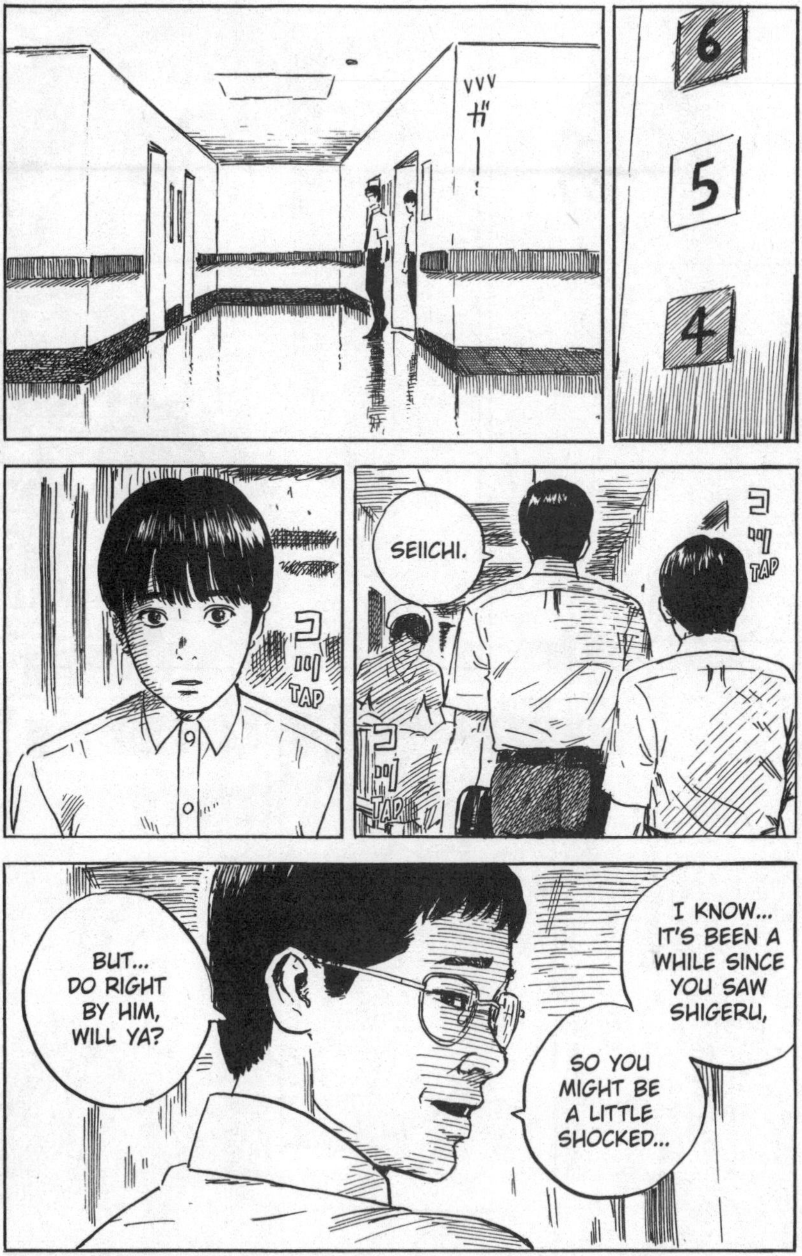
6
5
4
VVV
ガ
SEIICHI.
コツ
TAP
コツ
TAP
コツ
TAP
I KNOW... IT'S BEEN A WHILE SINCE YOU SAW SHIGERU,
SO YOU MIGHT BE A LITTLE SHOCKED...
BUT... DO RIGHT BY HIM, WILL YA?

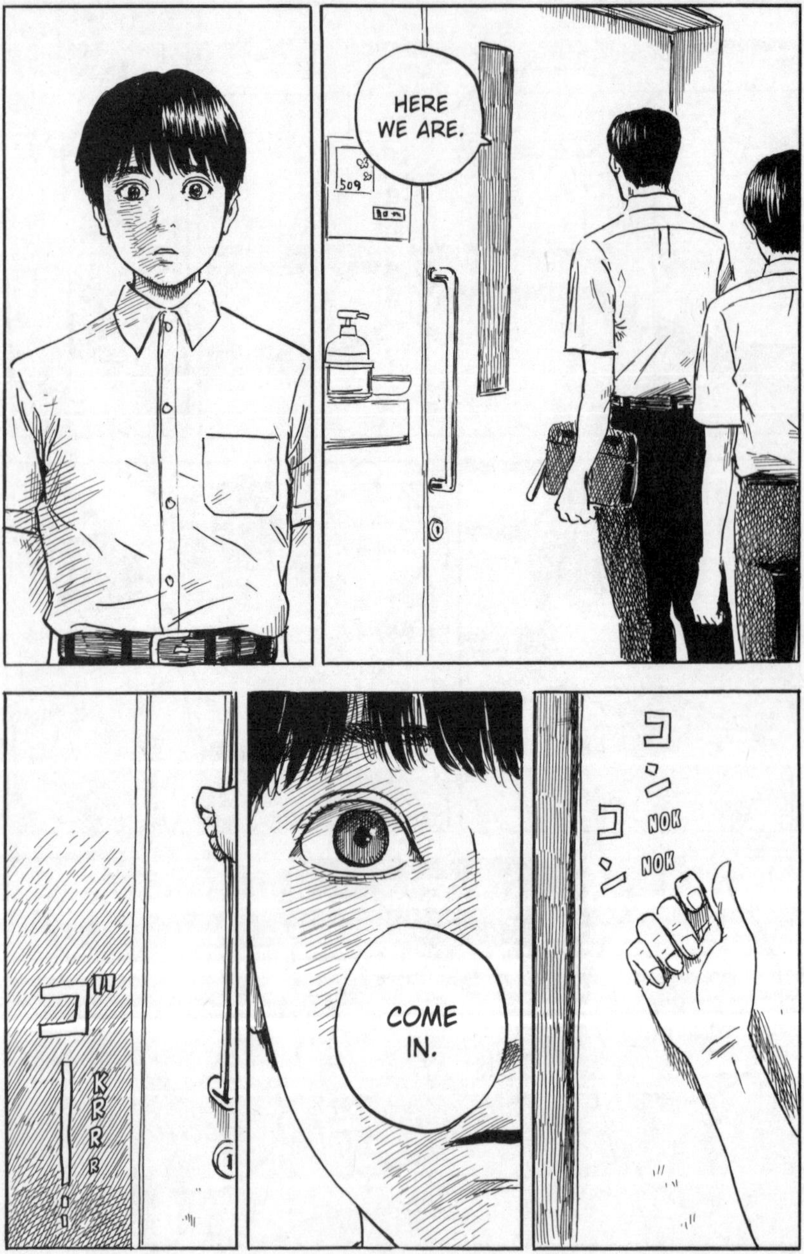
HERE WE ARE.
コン
NOK
コン
NOK
COME IN.
ゴー
KRRR

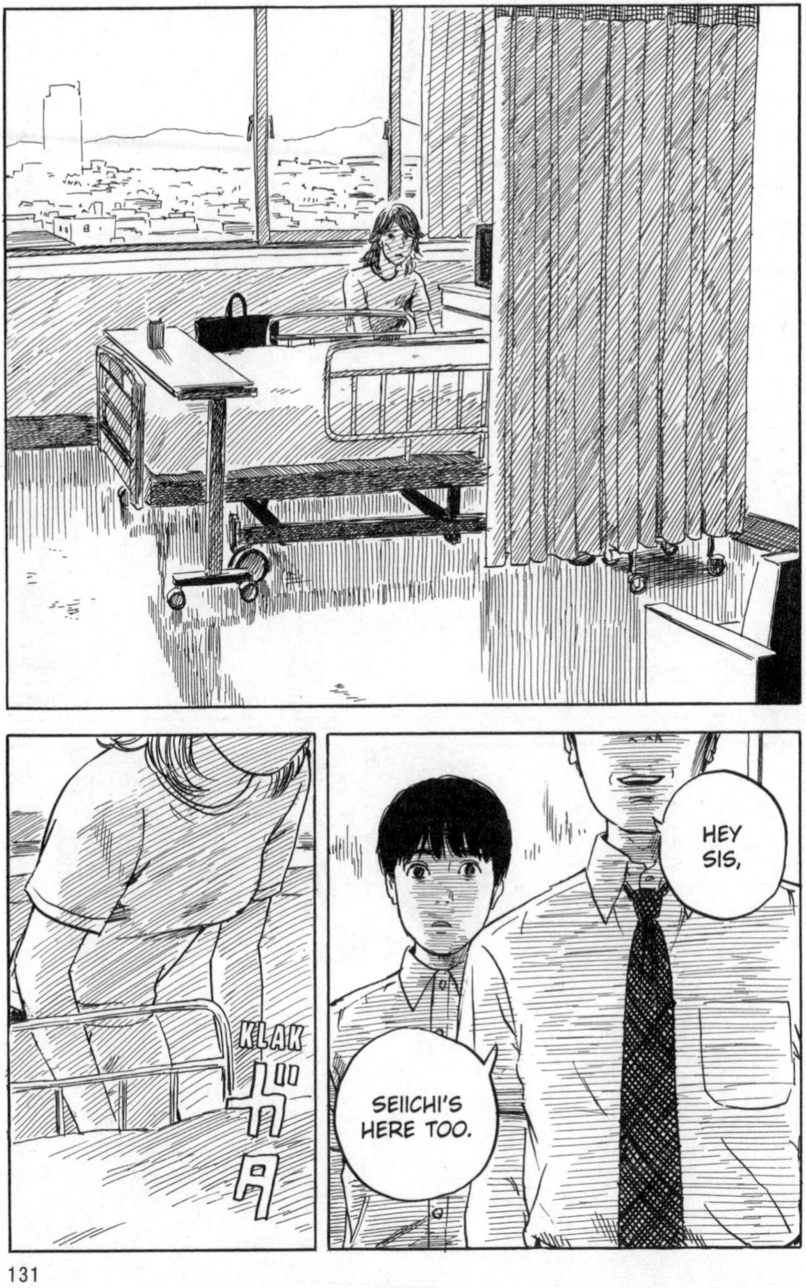
HEY SIS,
SEIICHI'S HERE TOO.
KLAK
ガラ

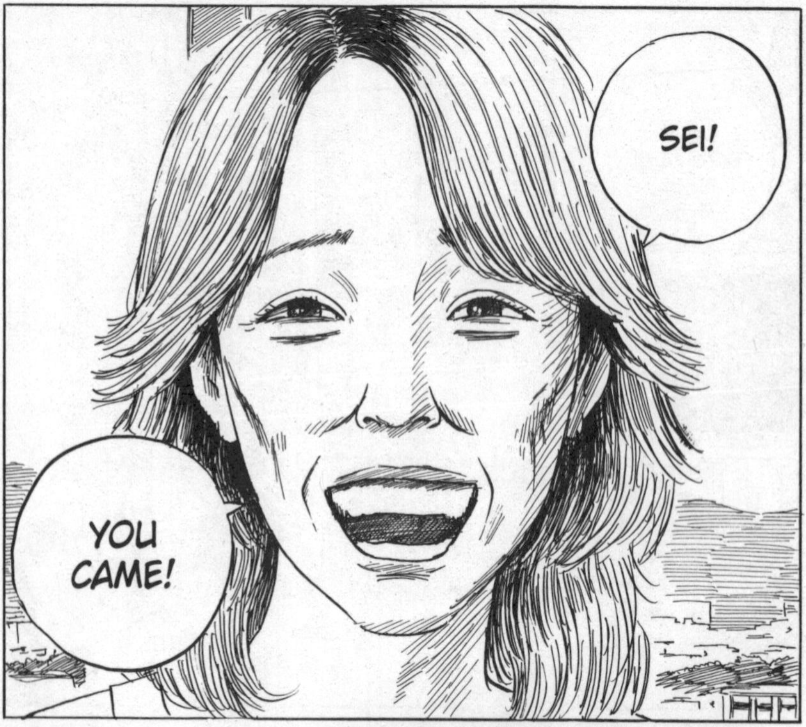
SEI!
YOU CAME!
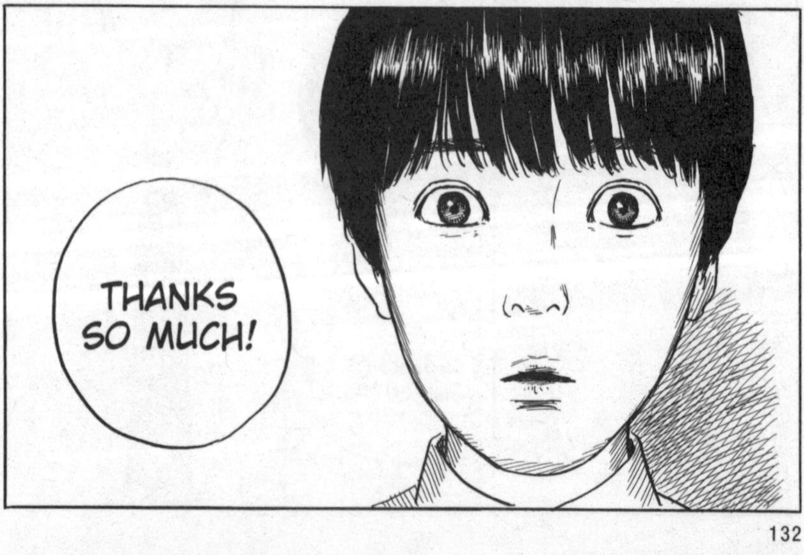
THANKS SO MUCH!

SHIGERU.
LOOK, SEI'S HERE TO SEE YOU!
SEI,
COME ON! COME ON IN!
SHIGE-RU,
HE'S HERE.

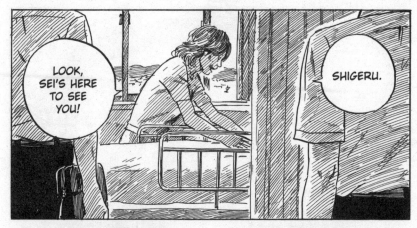

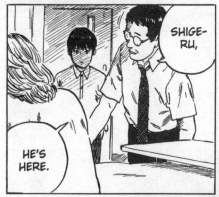

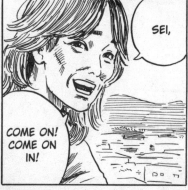

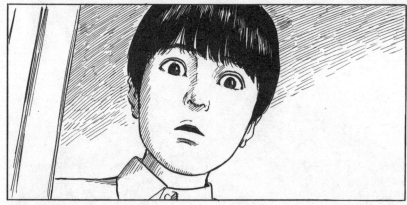

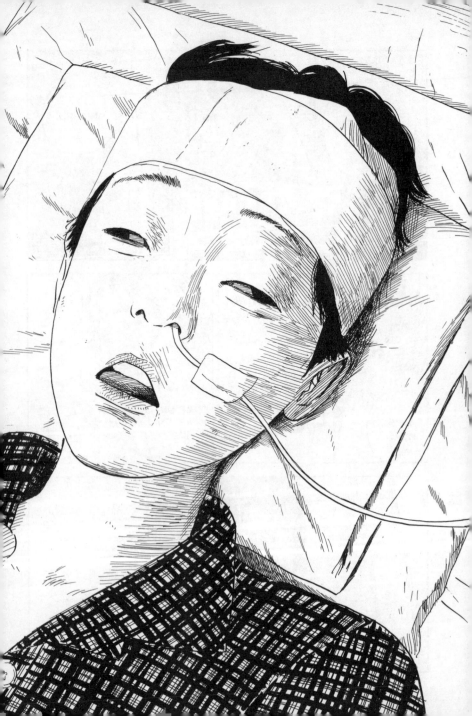

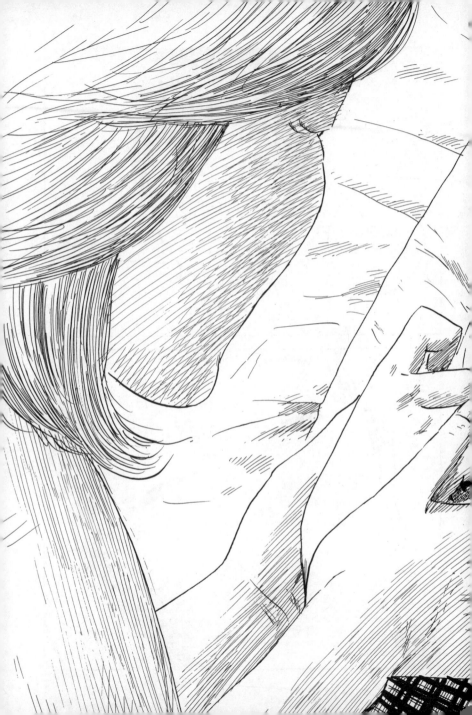

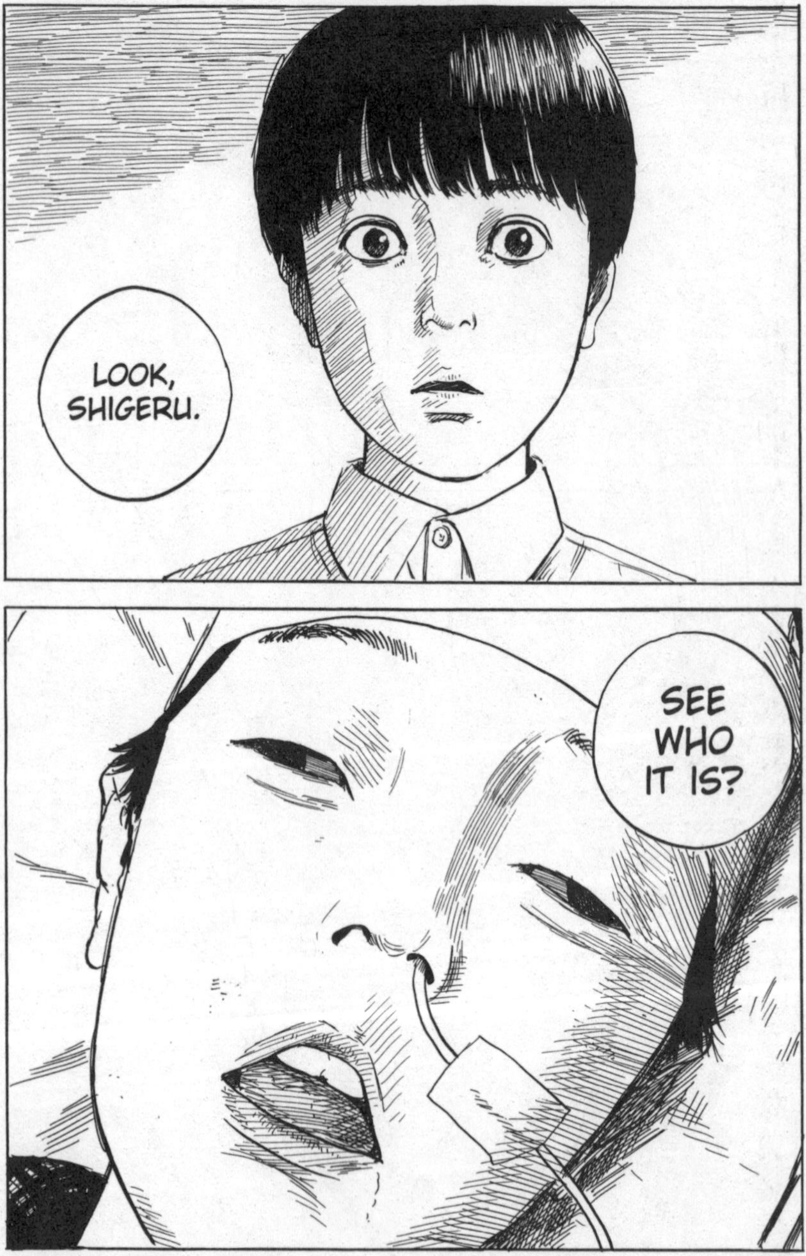
LOOK, SHIGERU.
SEE WHO IT IS?

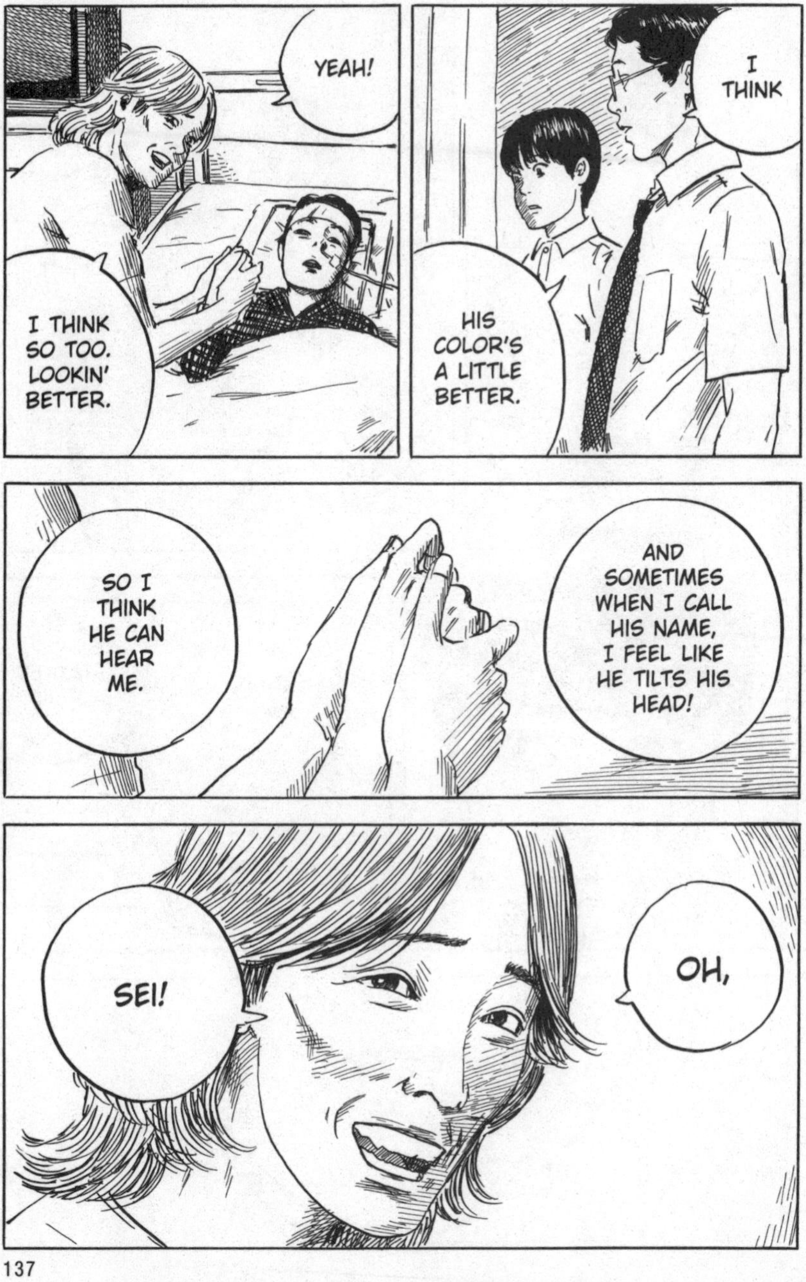
I THINK
HIS COLOR'S A LITTLE BETTER.
YEAH!
I THINK SO TOO. LOOKIN' BETTER.
AND SOMETIMES WHEN I CALL HIS NAME, I FEEL LIKE HE TILTS HIS HEAD!
SO I THINK HE CAN HEAR ME.
OH,
SEI!

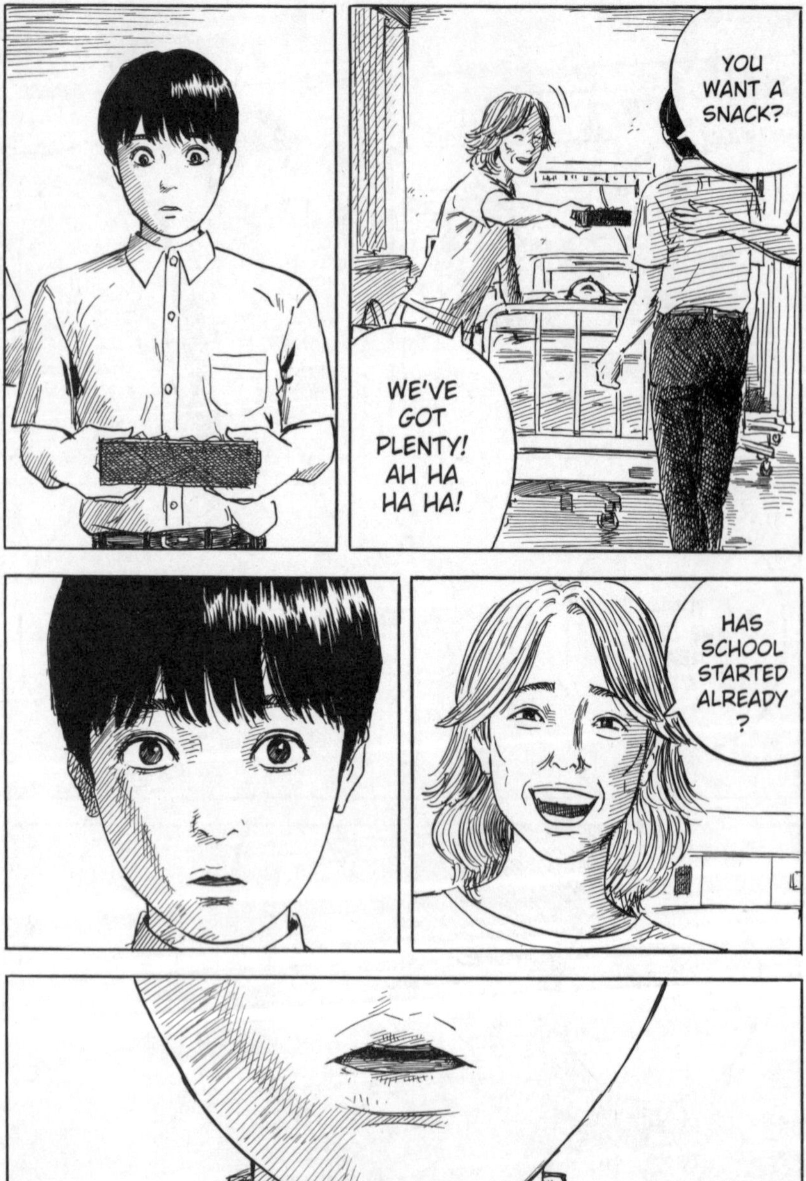
YOU WANT A SNACK?
WE'VE GOT PLENTY! AH HA HA HA!
HAS SCHOOL STARTED ALREADY?

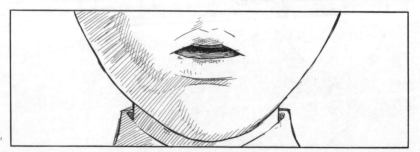

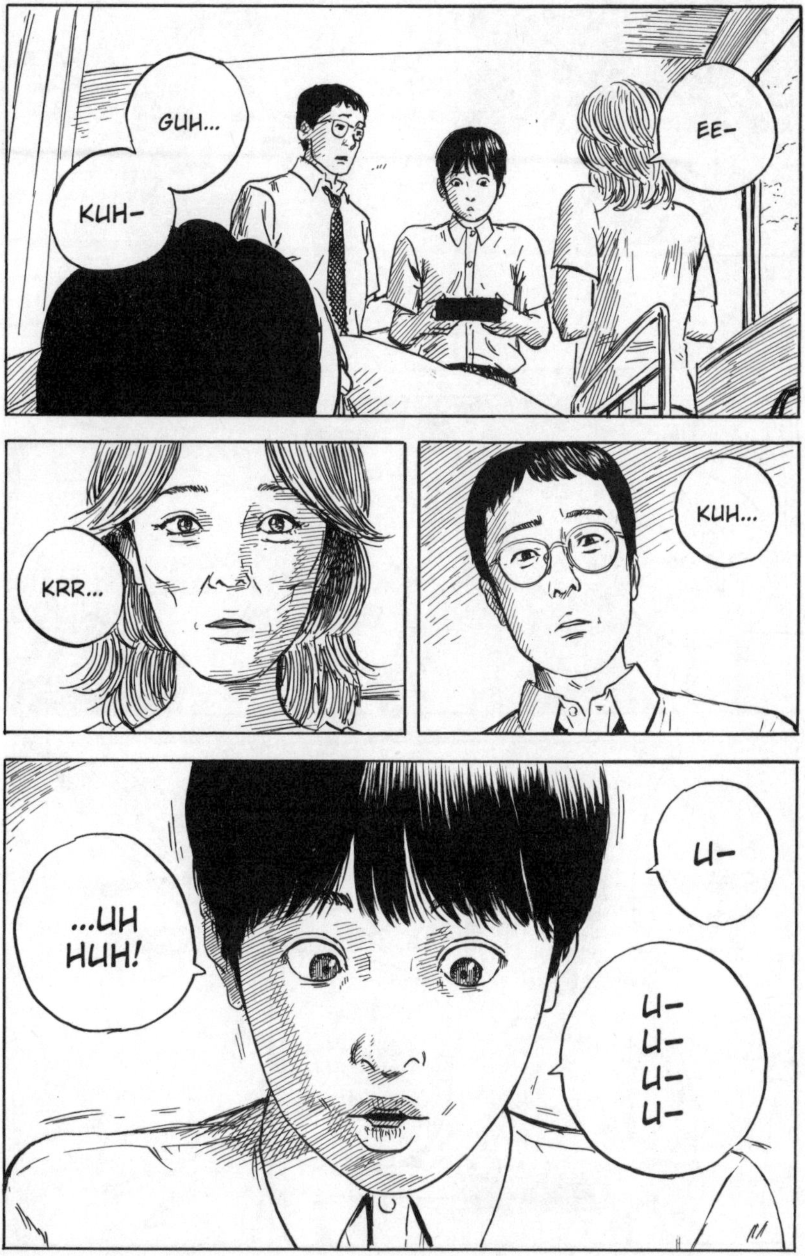
EE-
GUH...
KUH-
KUH...
KRR...
U-
U- U- U- U-
...UH HUH!

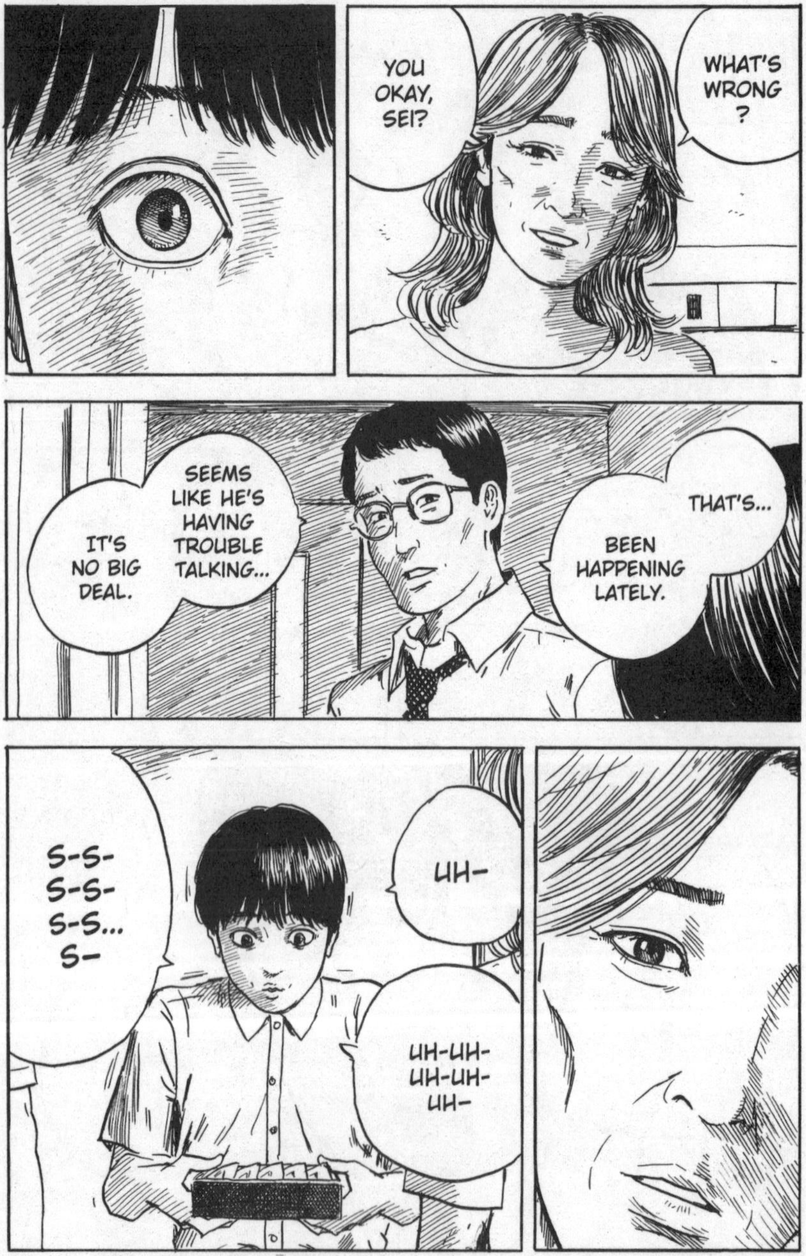
WHAT'S WRONG ?
YOU OKAY, SEI?
THAT'S...
BEEN HAPPENING LATELY.
SEEMS LIKE HE'S HAVING TROUBLE TALKING...
IT'S NO BIG DEAL.
UH-
UH-UH- UH-UH- UH-
S-S- S-S- S-S... S-

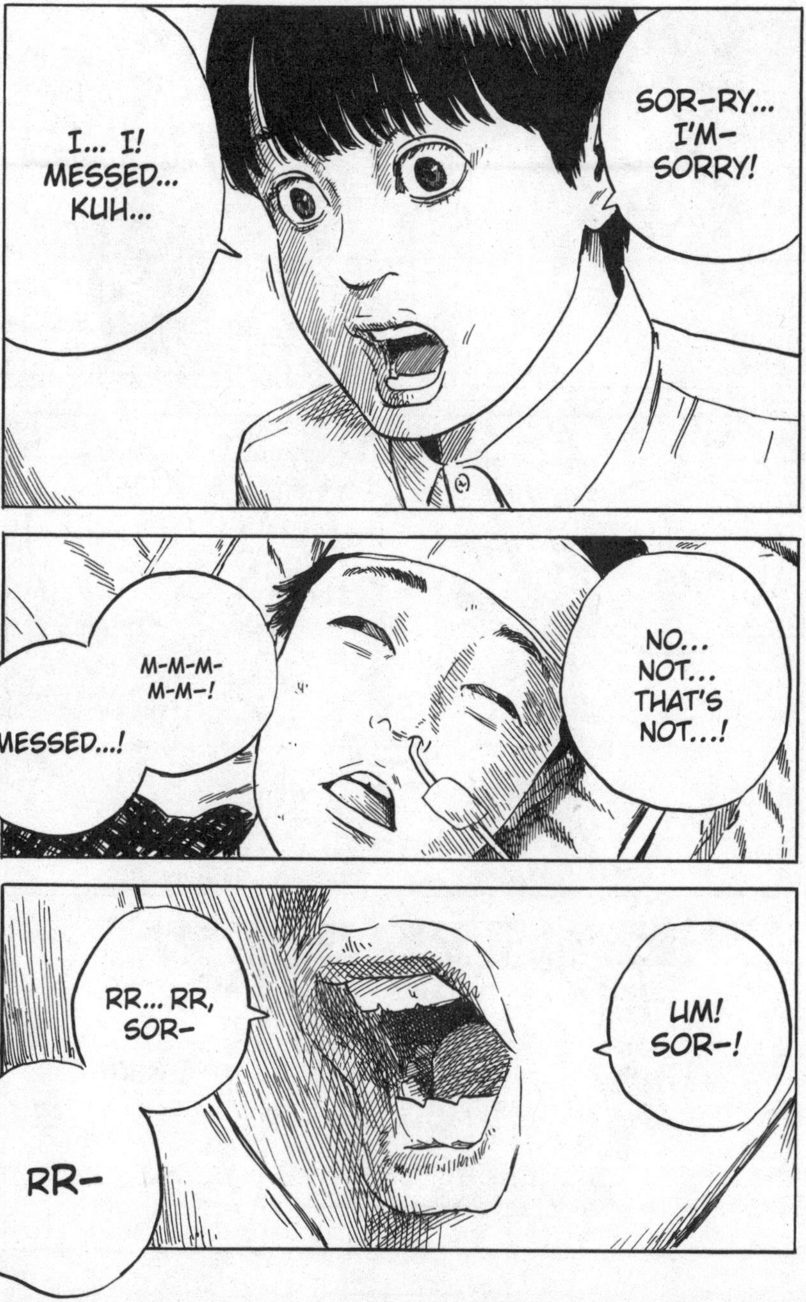
SOR-RY... I'M-SORRY!
I... I! MESSED... KUH...
NO... NOT... THAT'S NOT...!
M-M-M-M-M-! MESSED...!
UM! SOR-!
RR... RR, SOR-
RR-

THAT IS A BIG DEAL, ICHIRO!

I'M SORRY.

...SEI.

I KNOW...

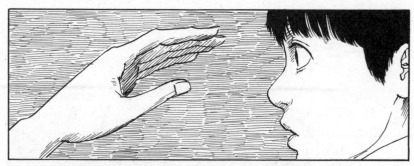

ALL OF THIS WITH SHIGERU

HAS BEEN HARD ON YOU, TOO.

I'M SORRY...

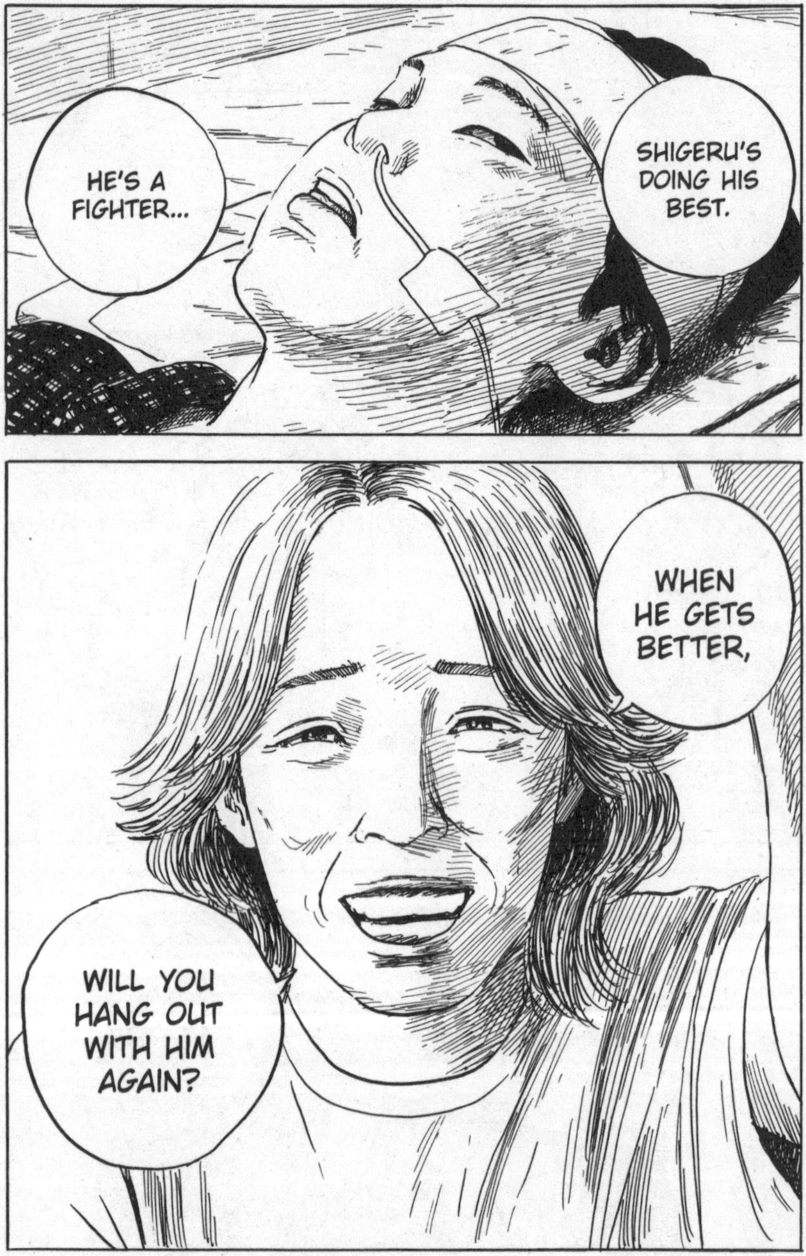
SHIGERU'S DOING HIS BEST.
HE'S A FIGHTER...
WHEN HE GETS BETTER,
WILL YOU HANG OUT WITH HIM AGAIN?

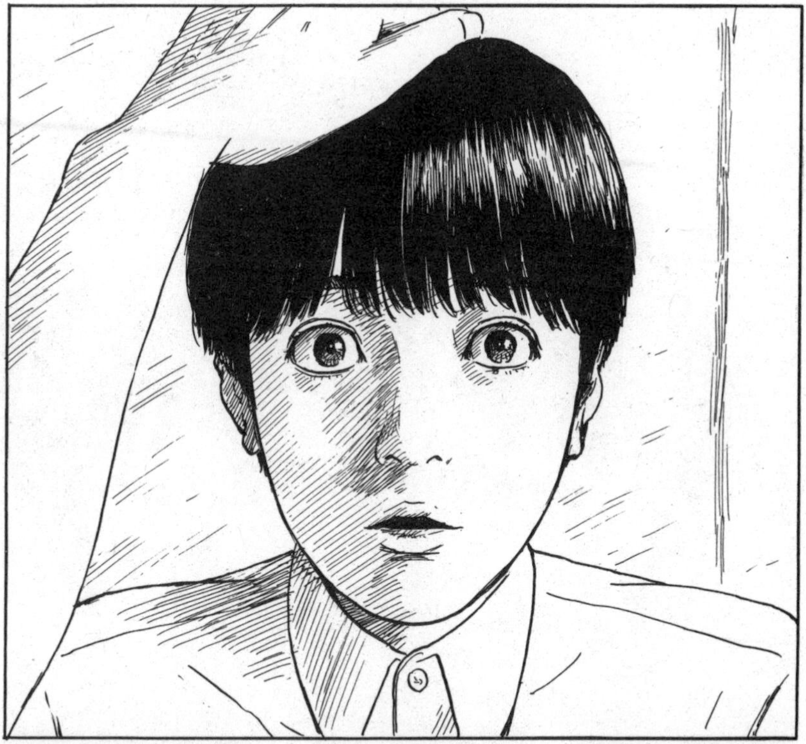
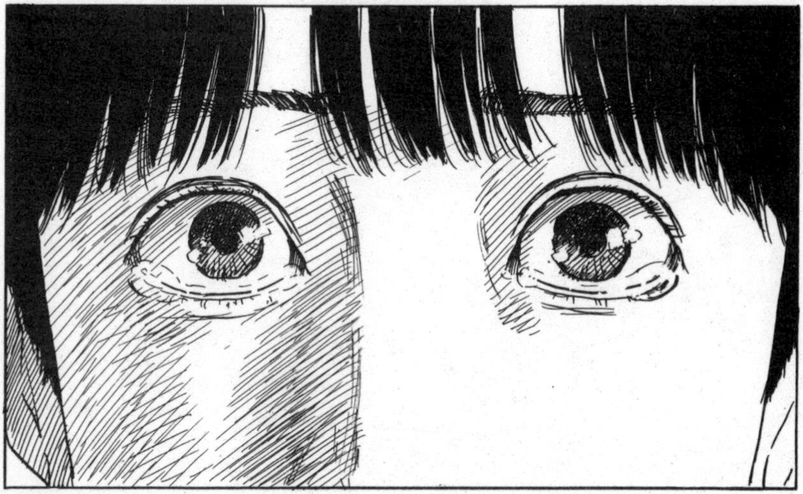

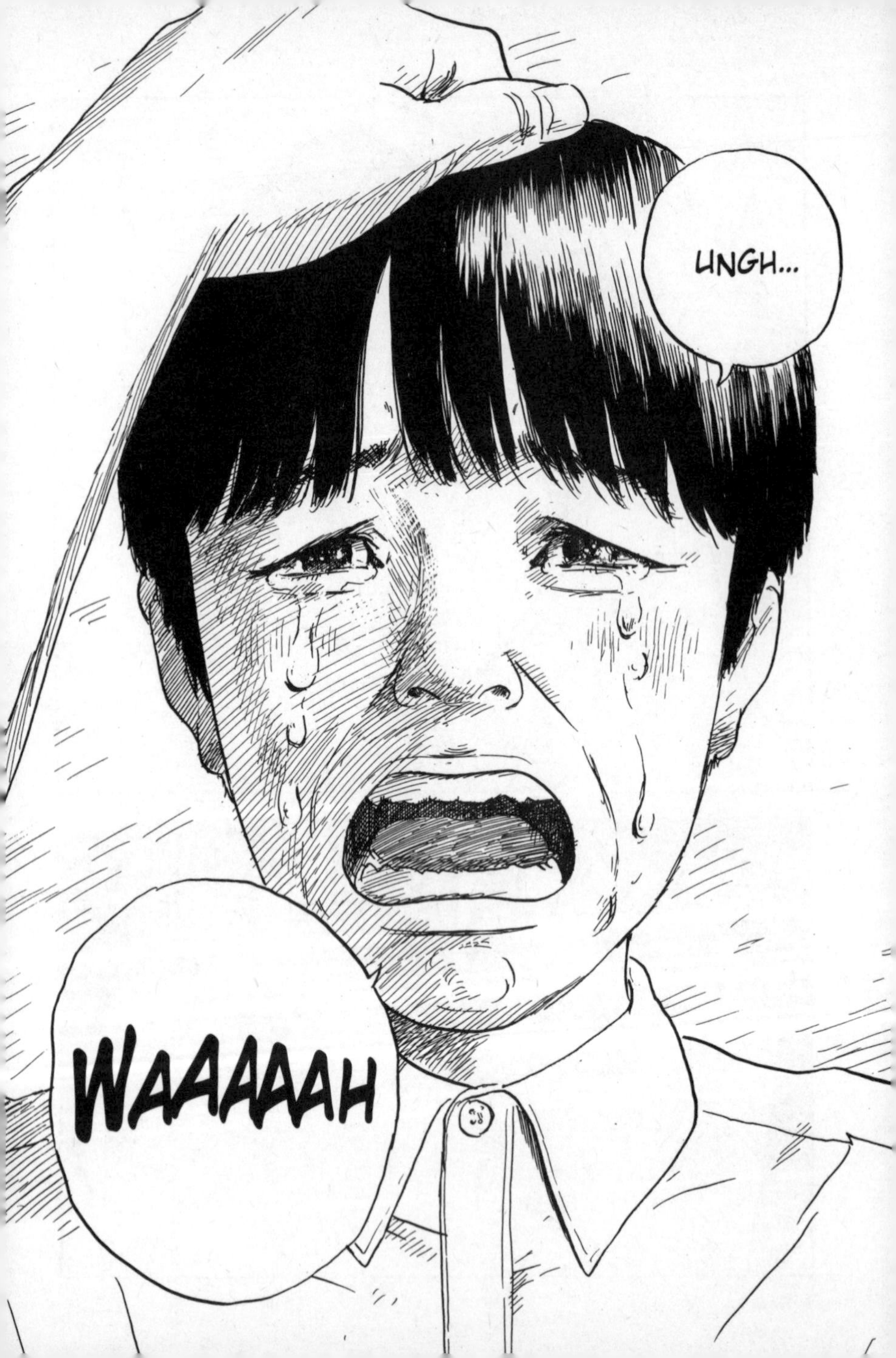
UNGH...
WAAAAAH

AAHH...
KHUH
UNH
WAAAAH
AGH... AAAAAH

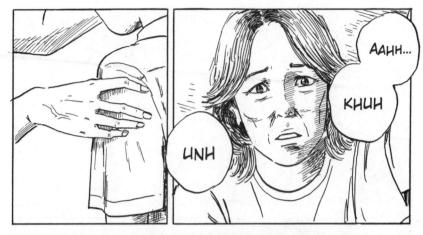

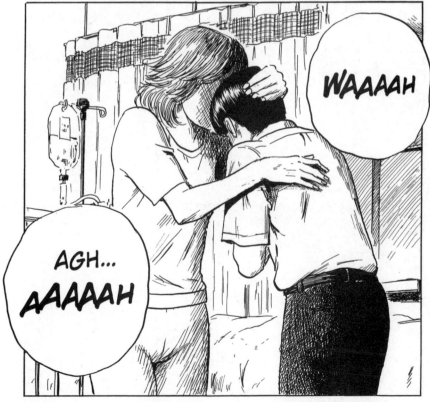

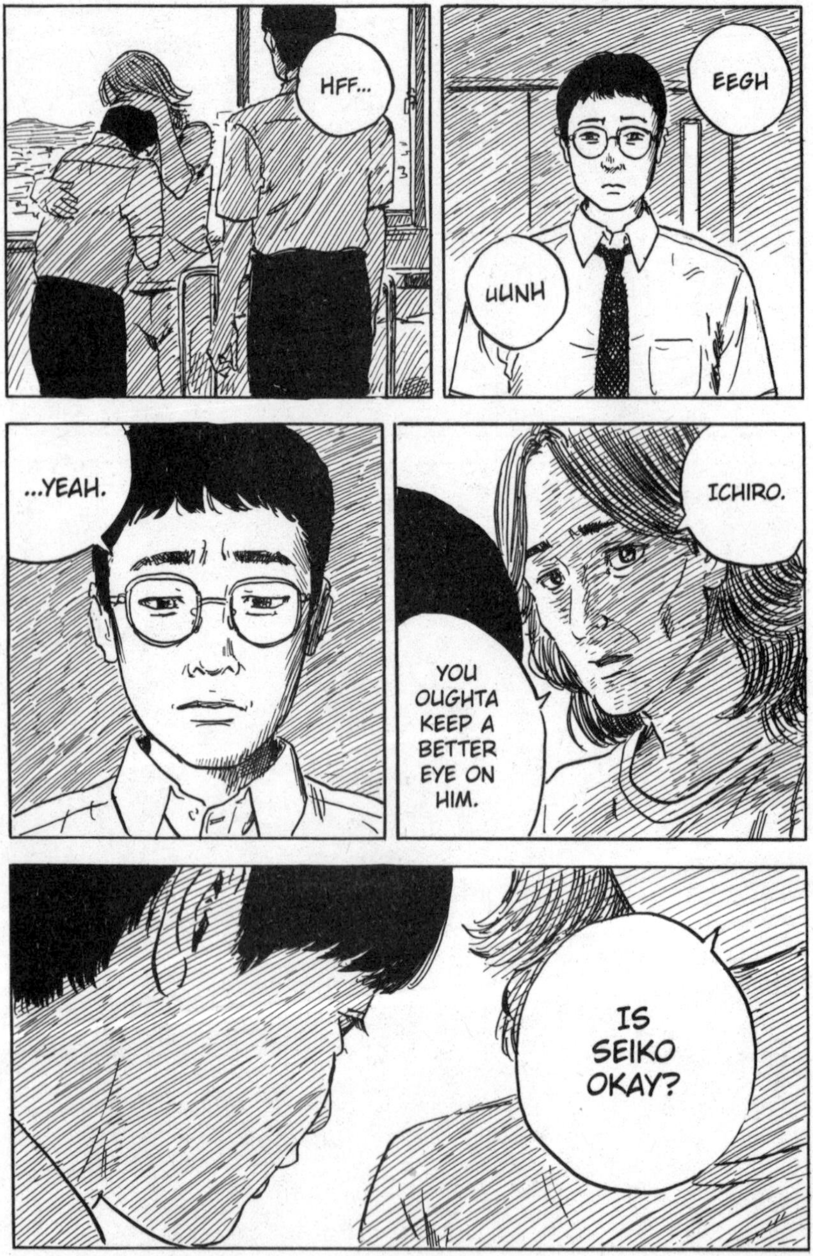
EEGH
UUNH
HFF...
ICHIRO.
YOU OUGHTA KEEP A BETTER EYE ON HIM.
...YEAH.
IS SEIKO OKAY?

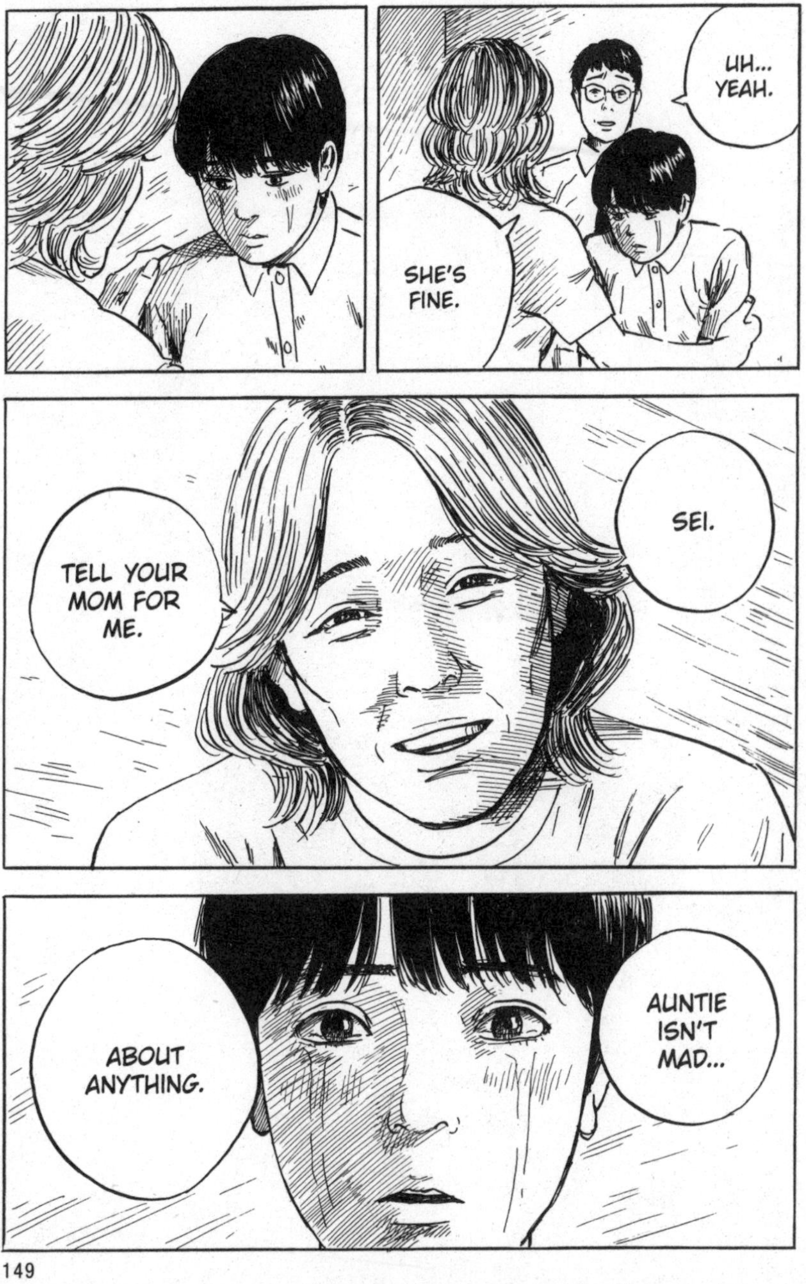
UH... YEAH.
SHE'S FINE.
SEI.
TELL YOUR MOM FOR ME.
AUNTIE ISN'T MAD...
ABOUT ANYTHING.

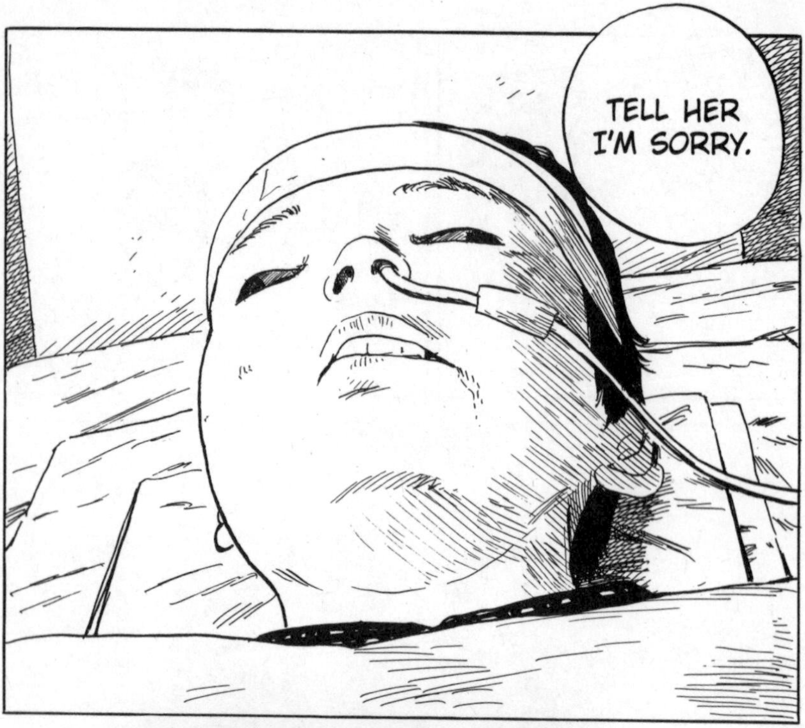
TELL HER I'M SORRY.

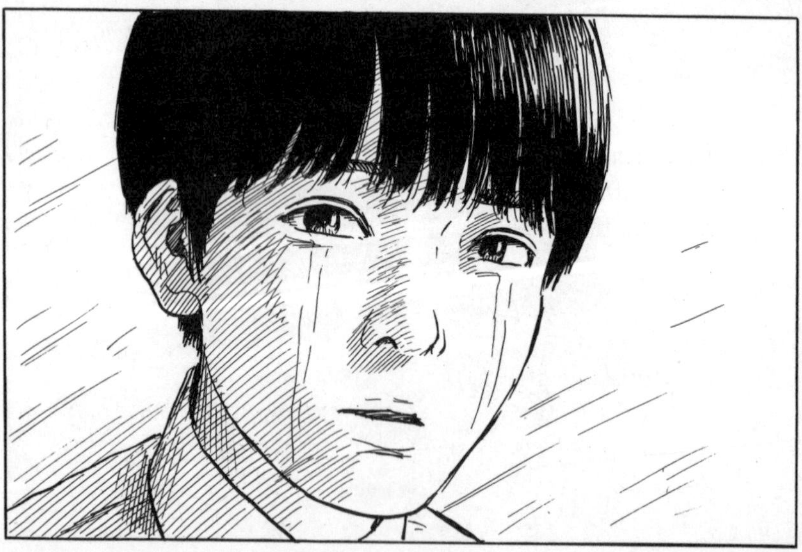

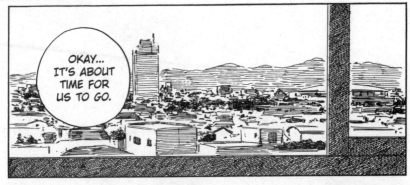

OKAY... IT'S ABOUT TIME FOR US TO GO.

UH...

SEI, TAKE THIS, WOULD YA?

IT'S SOME SWEETS.

YOU DON'T HAVE TO DO THAT, SIS.

FOR COMING.

THANKS SO MUCH.

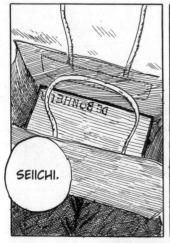

SEIICHI.
BEFORE WE HEAD HOME,
WHY DON'T YOU SAY SOMETHING TO SHIGERU?

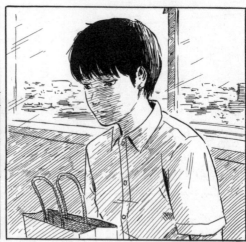

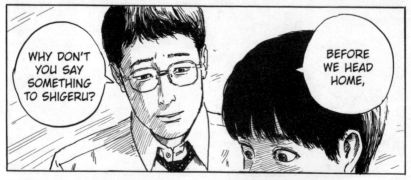

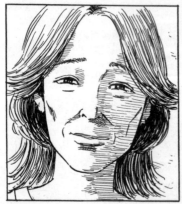

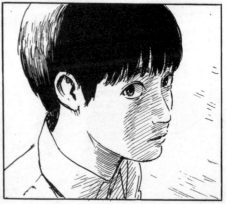

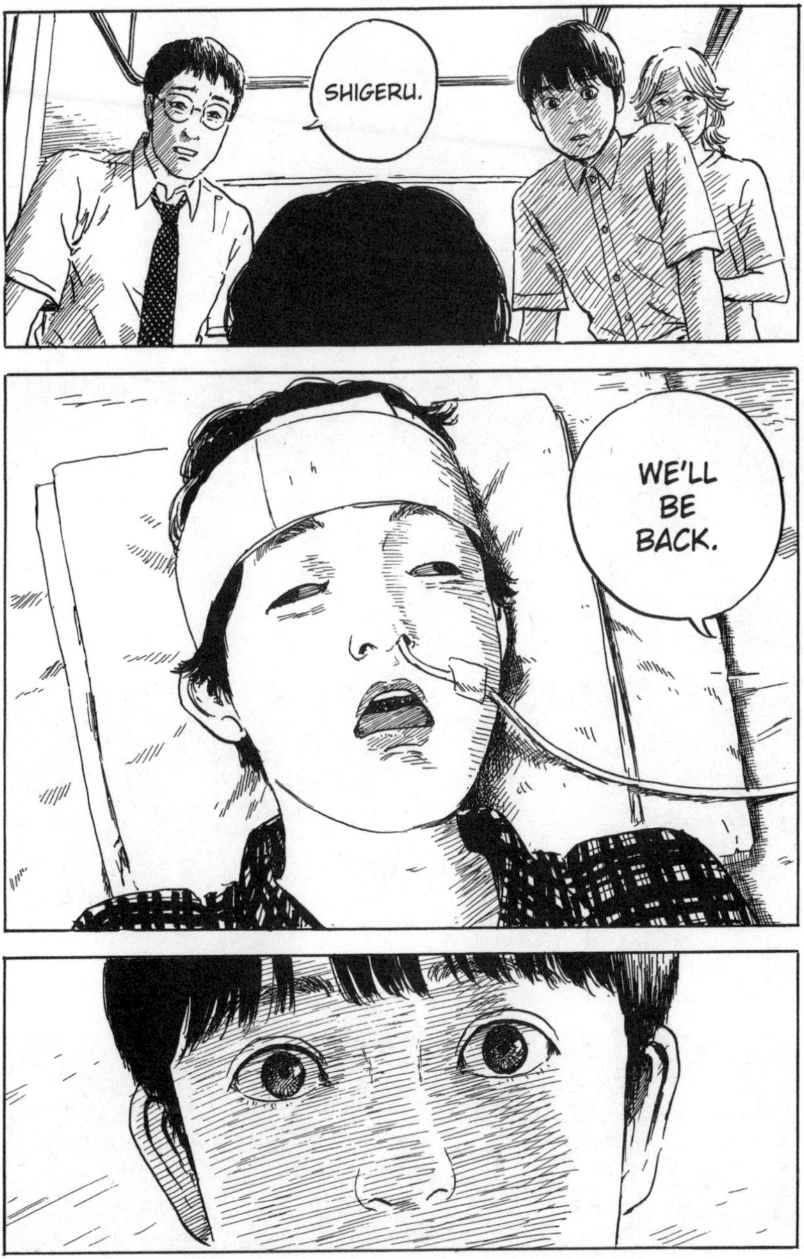
SHIGERU.
WE'LL BE BACK.

SEI,
HOLD HIS HAND, WOULD YA?

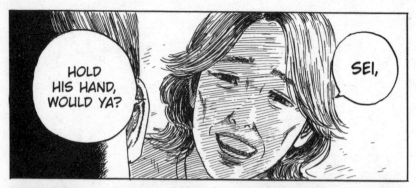

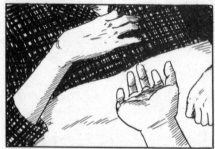

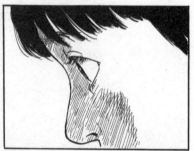

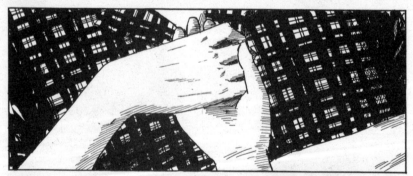

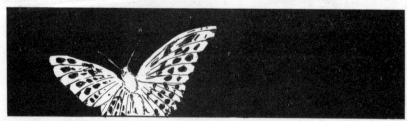

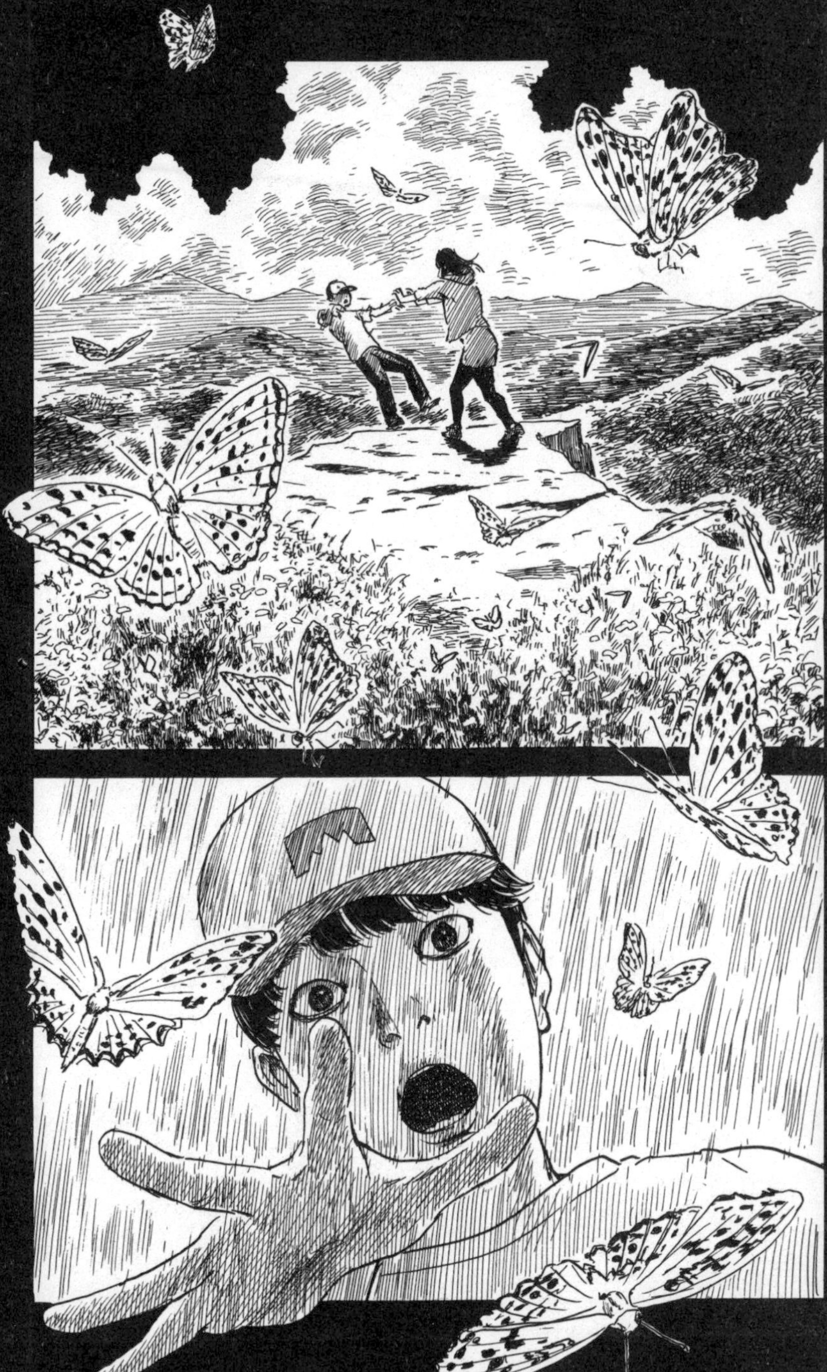

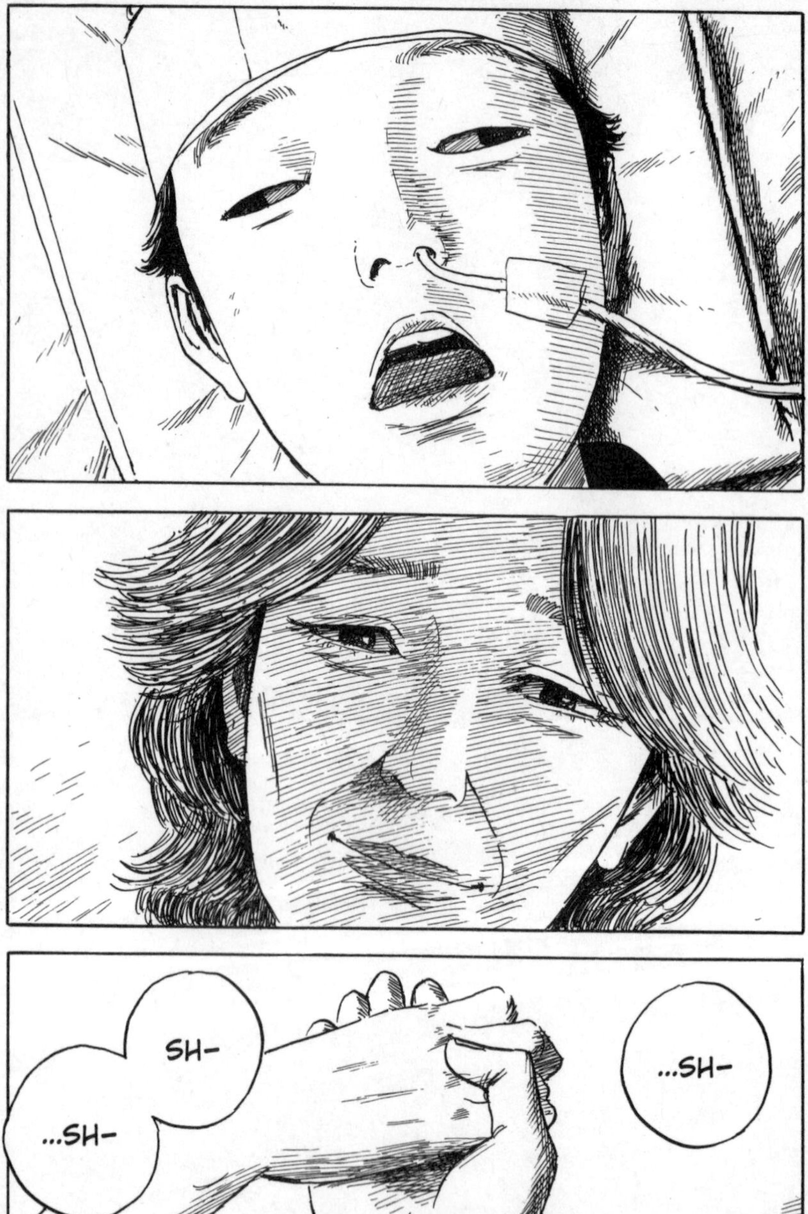
...SH-
SH-
...SH-

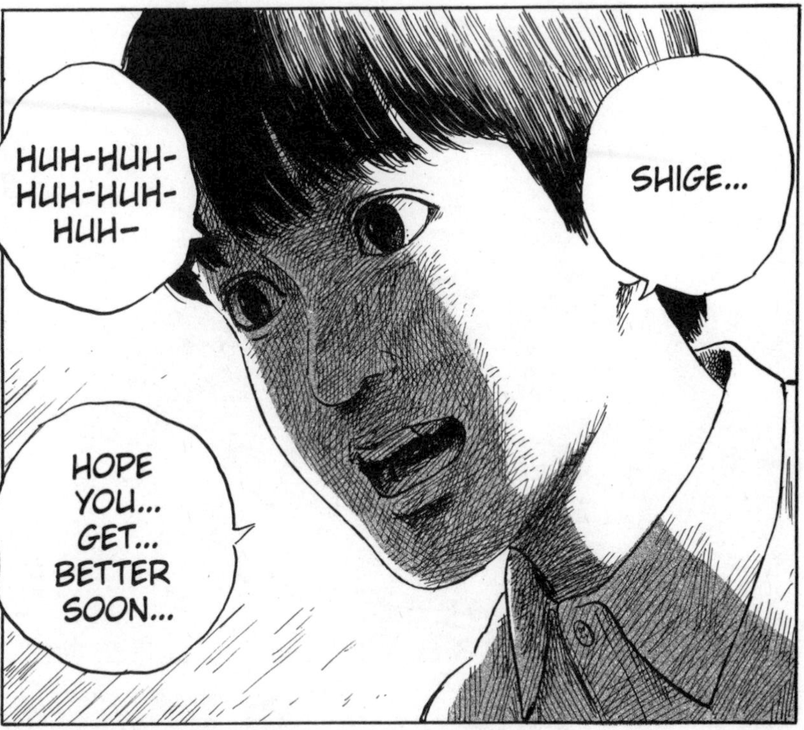
SHIGE...
HUH-HUH-HUH-HUH-HUH-
HOPE YOU... GET... BETTER SOON...

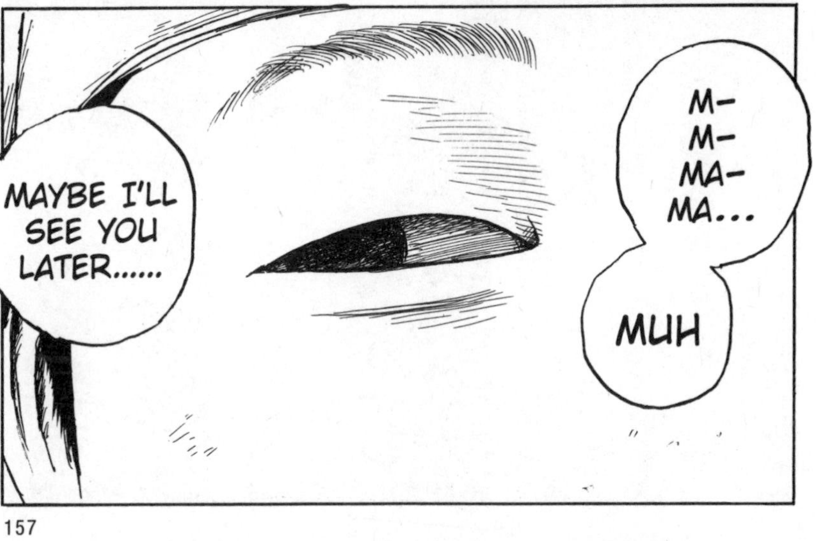
M-M-MA-MA...
MUH
MAYBE I'LL SEE YOU LATER......

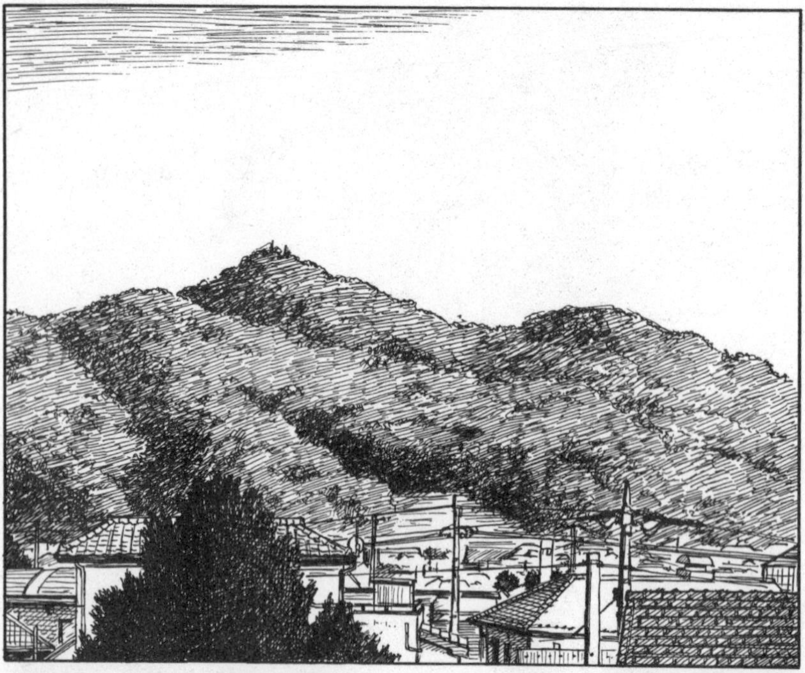

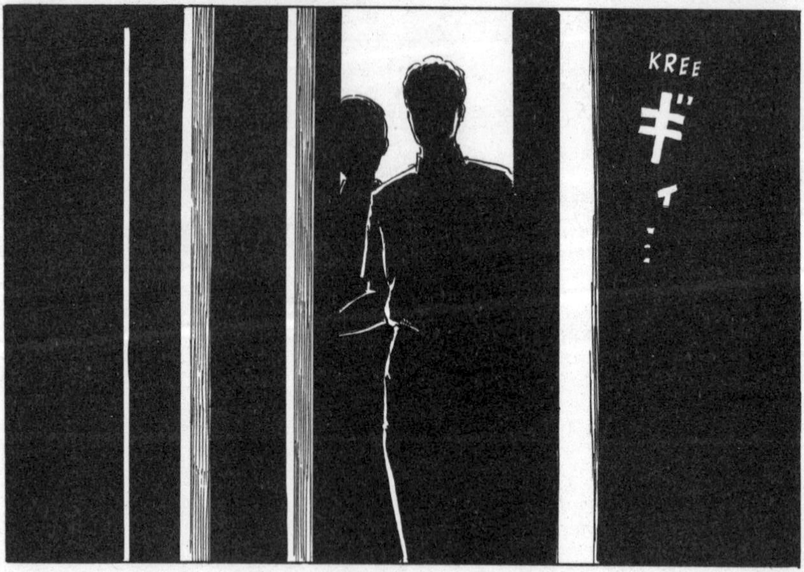
KREE
ギィ…

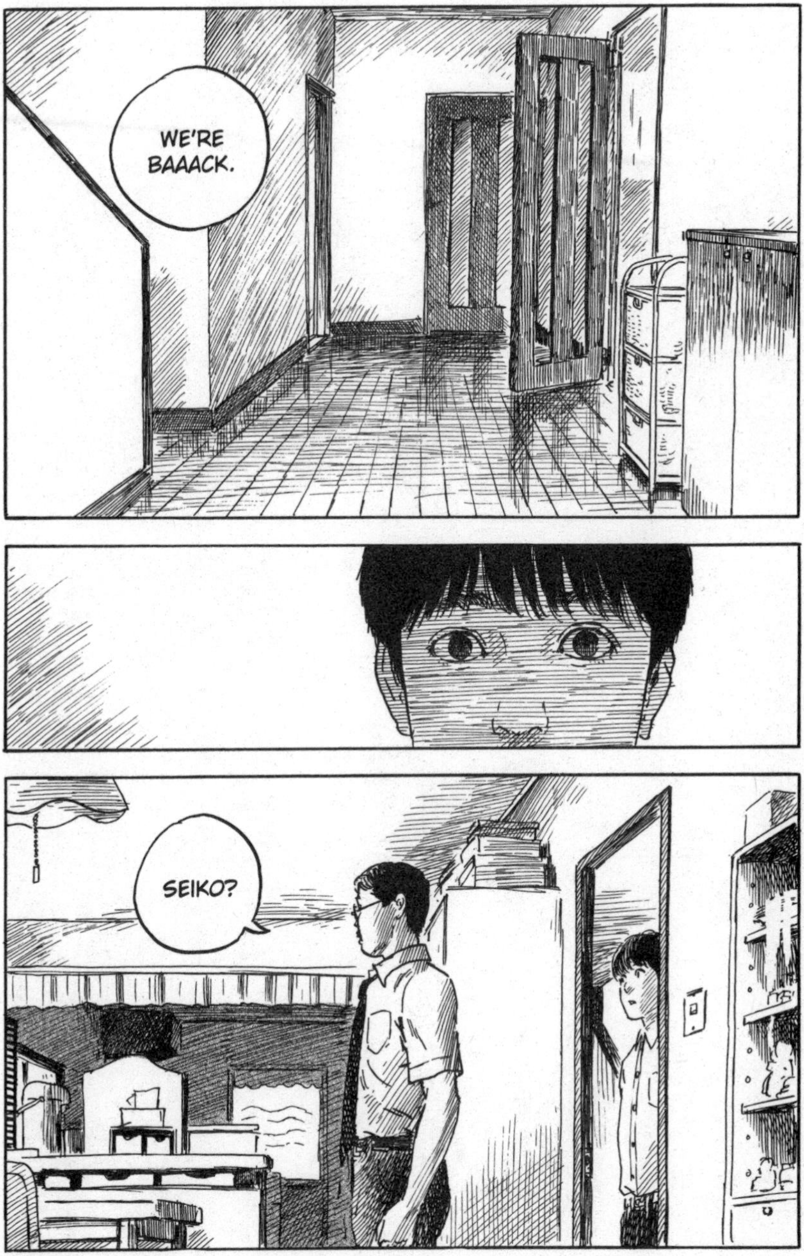
WE'RE BAAACK.
SEIKO?

SHE'S NOT HERE.
GUESS SHE MUST BE OUT SHOPPING.
カナ SHREE
カナ SHREE
カナ… SHREE

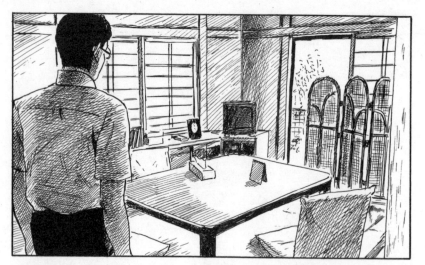

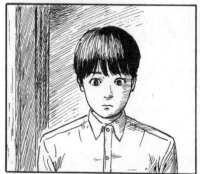

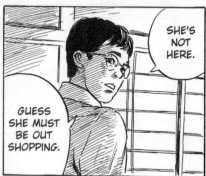

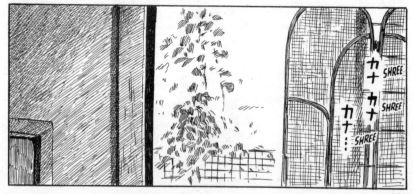

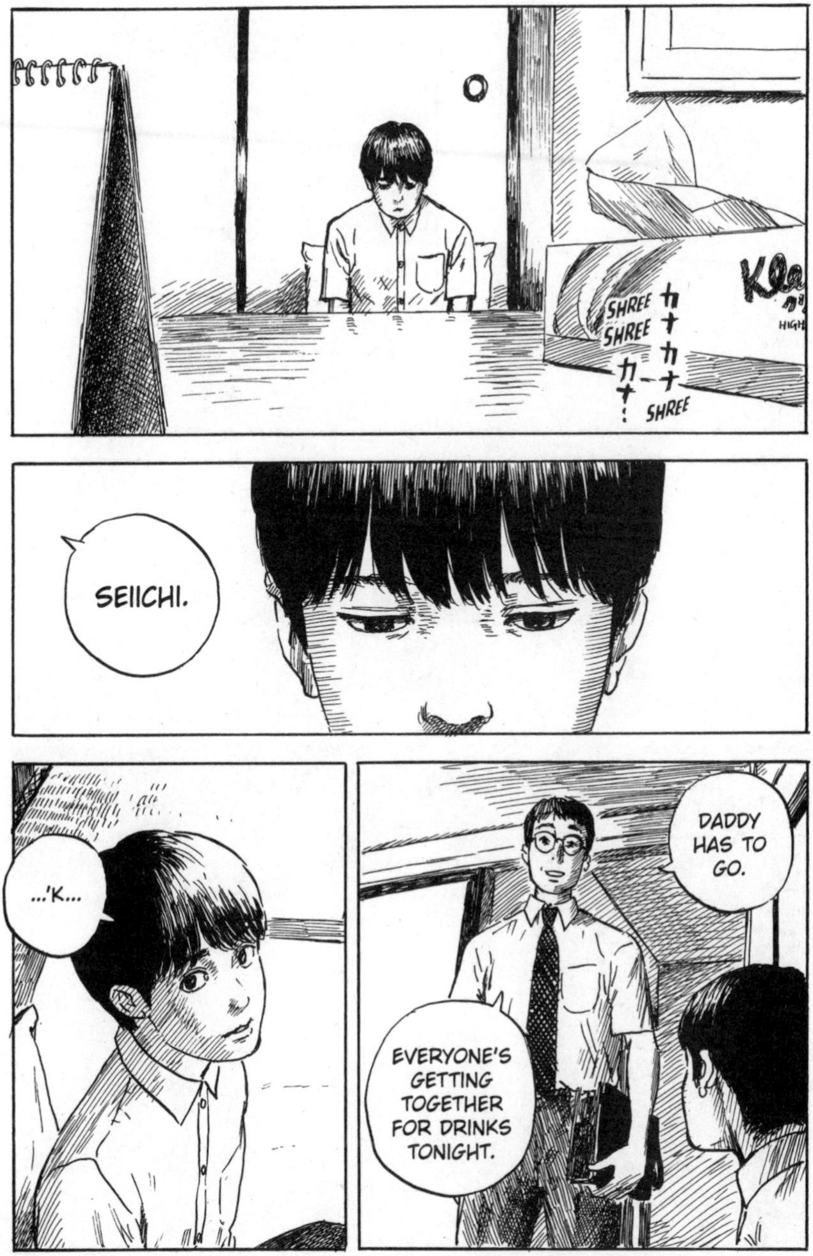
SHREE
SHREE
カナカナ
カナ!
SHREE
SEIICHI.
DADDY HAS TO GO.
EVERYONE'S GETTING TOGETHER FOR DRINKS TONIGHT.
...'K...

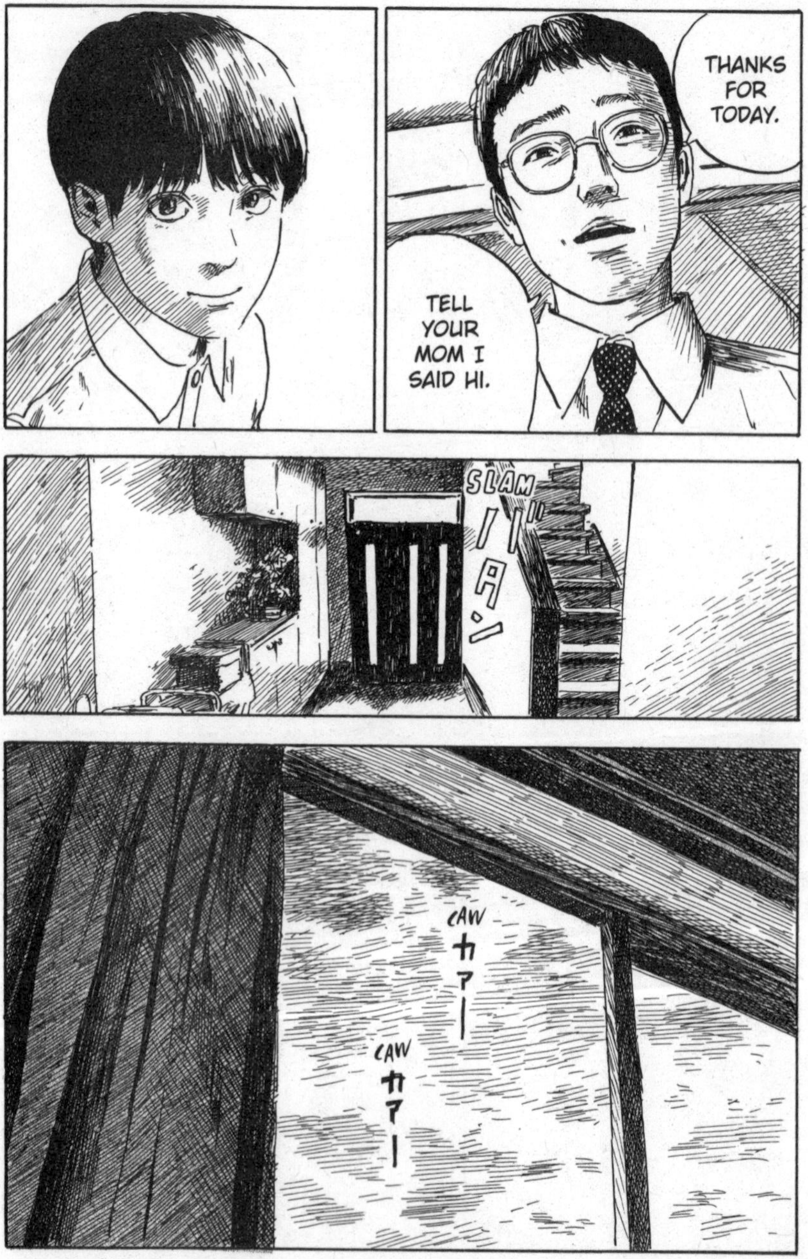
THANKS FOR TODAY.
TELL YOUR MOM I SAID HI.
SLAM
バタン
CAW
カァー
CAW
カァー

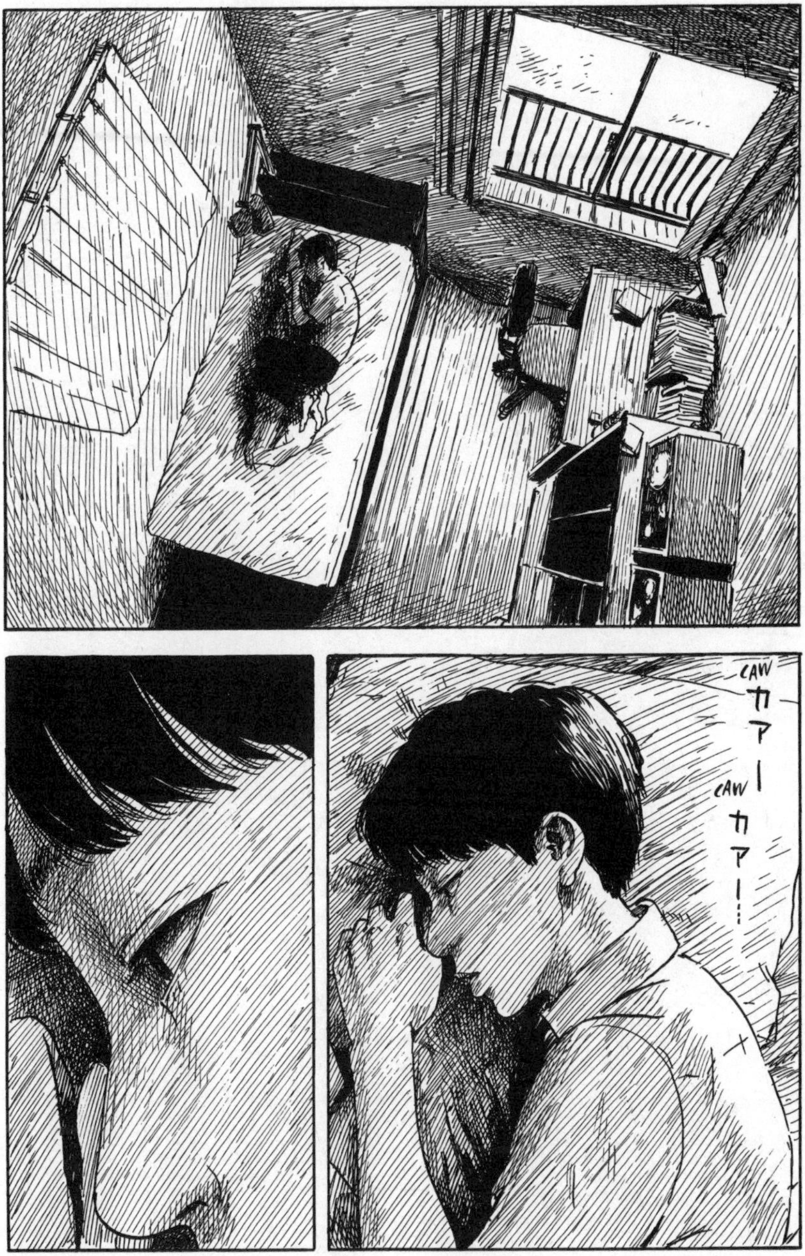
CAW
カアー
CAW
カアー…

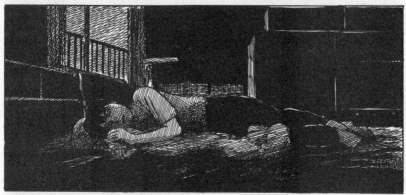

GRM...
TMP
トン
TMP
トン

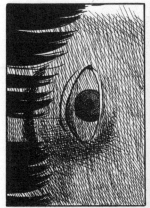

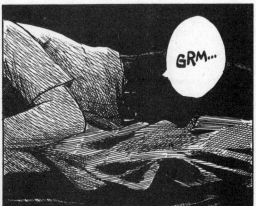

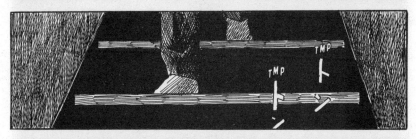

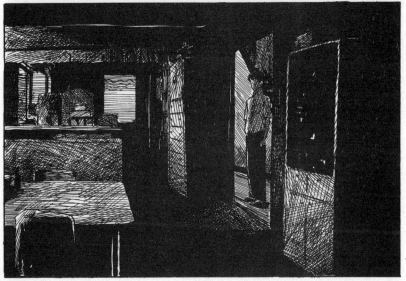

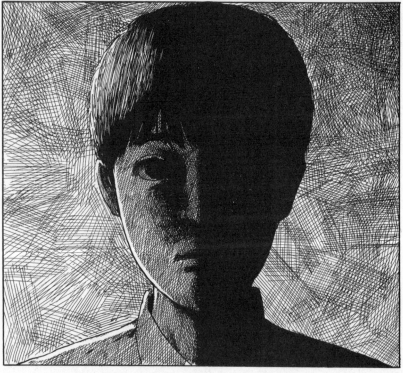

KA-CHIK
ガチャ
KREE
ギイ!

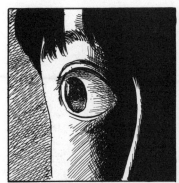

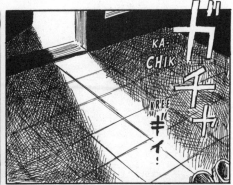

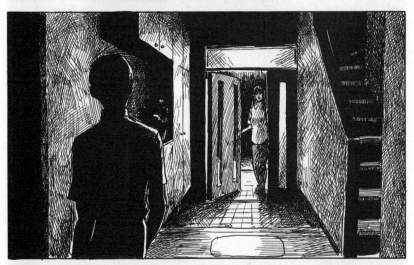

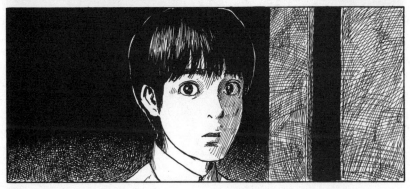

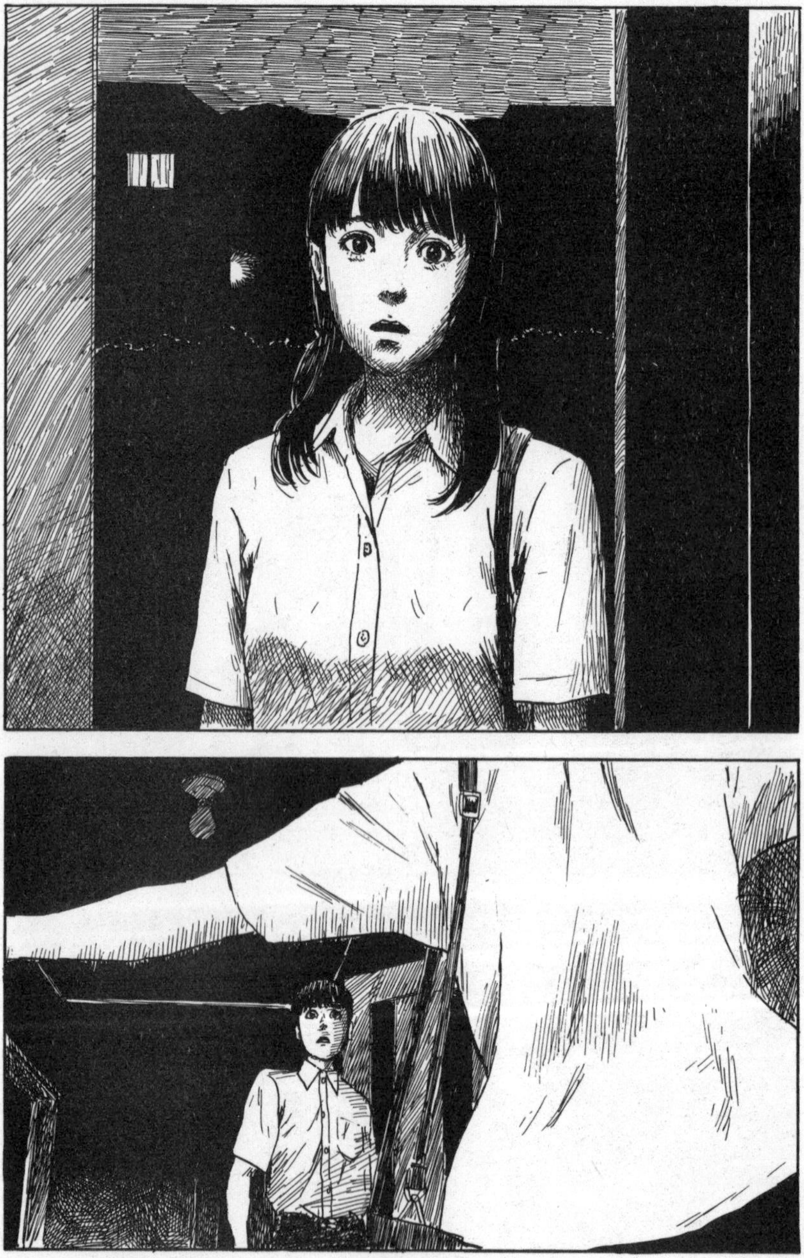

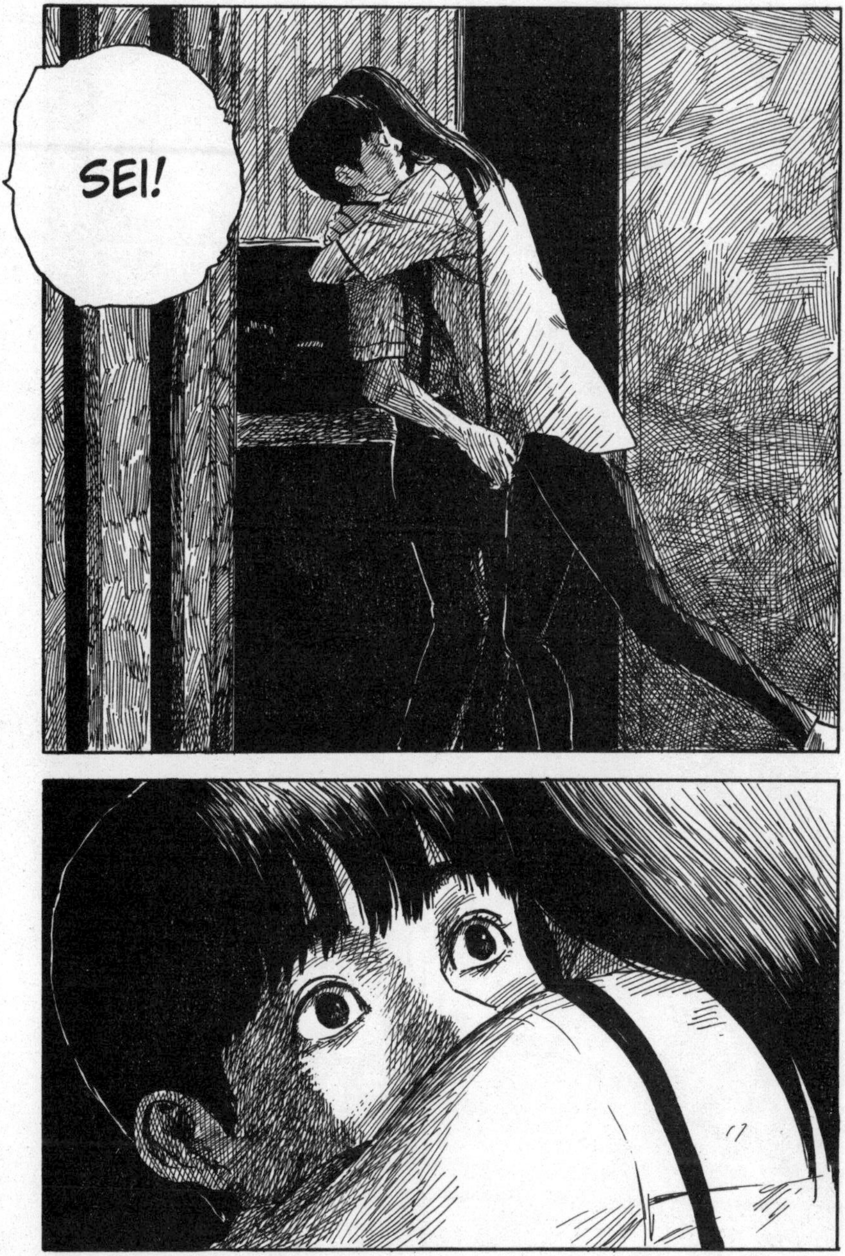
SEI!

THANK GOODNESS!
YOU NEVER CAME HOME FROM SCHOOL...
I'VE BEEN LOOKING FOR YOU ALL THIS TIME...!

WHERE
WERE YOU?

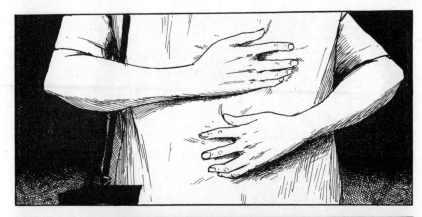

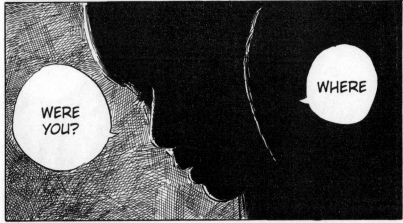

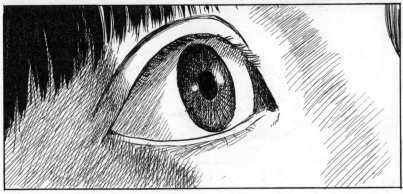

UH...
UM...
D-
...D-
......D-
D-
DADDY-

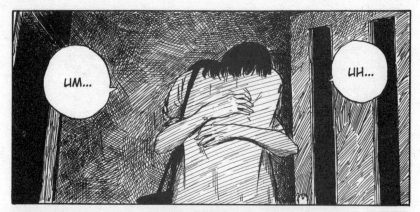

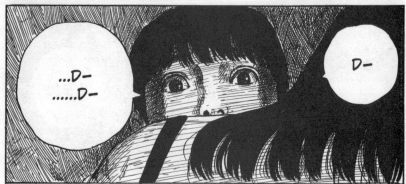

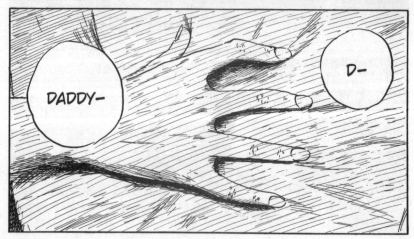

...NO...
YOU... WENT TO SEE SHIGE?

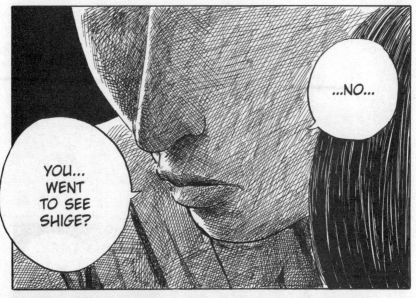

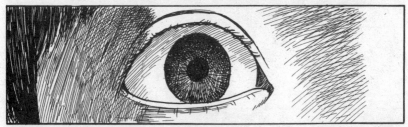

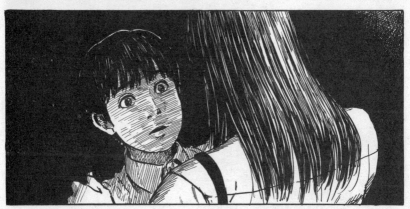

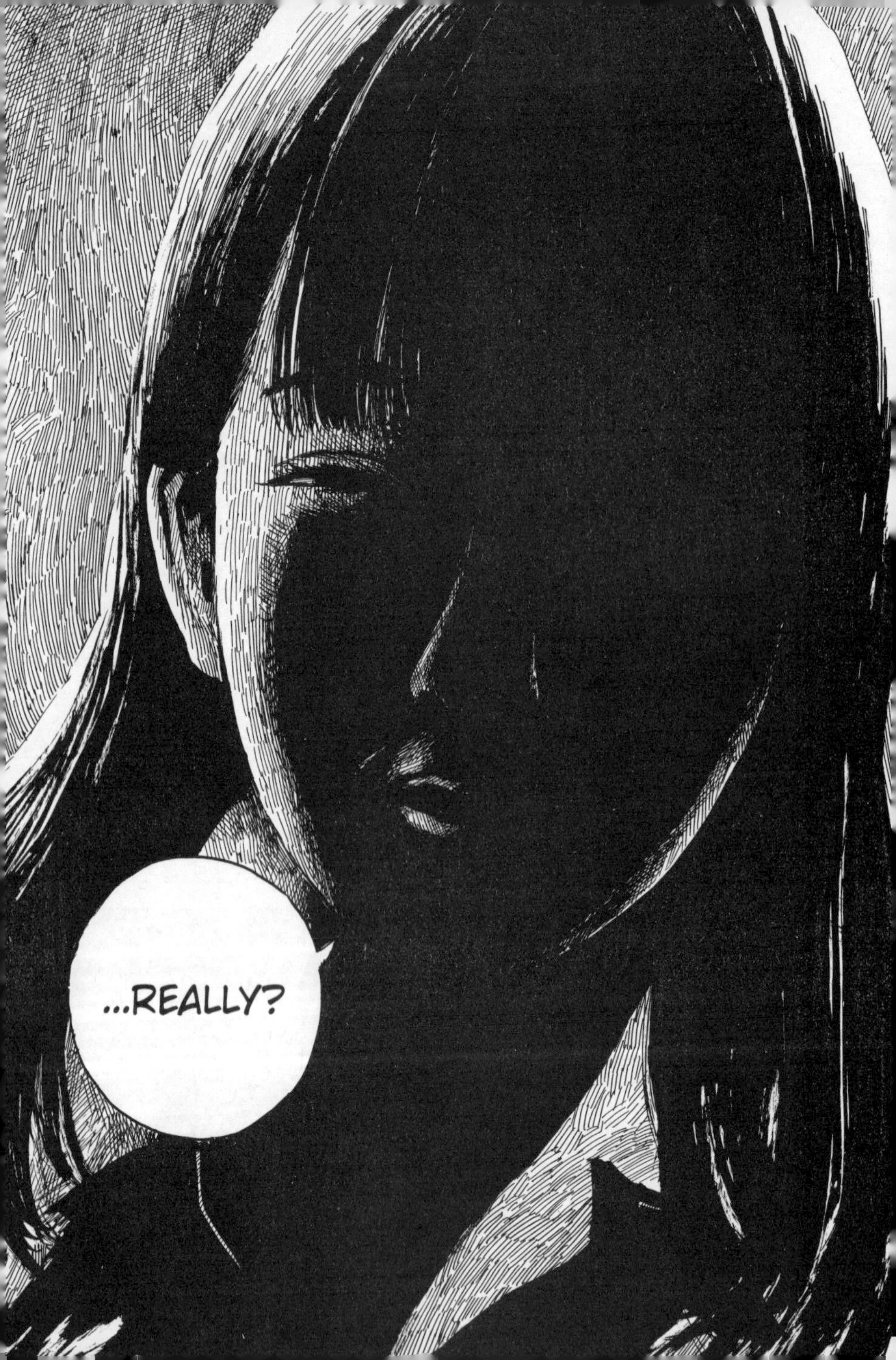
...REALLY?

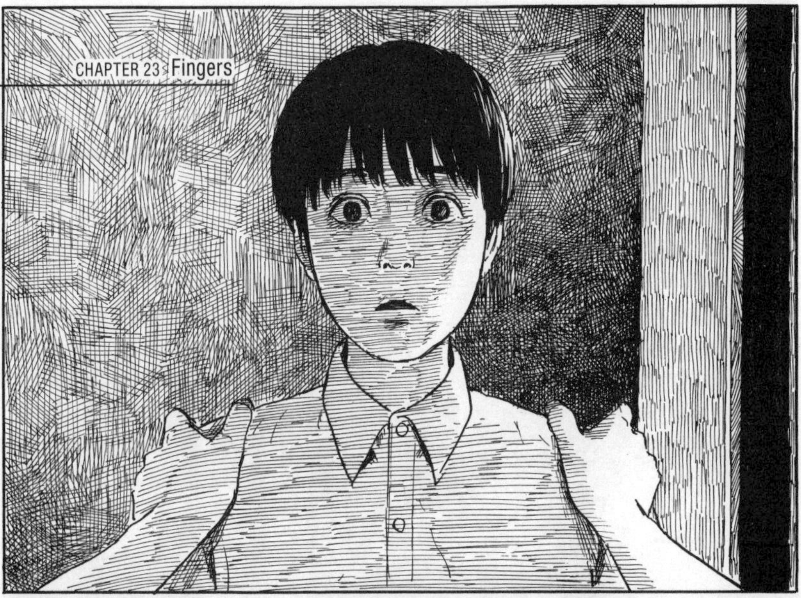
CHAPTER 23 Fingers
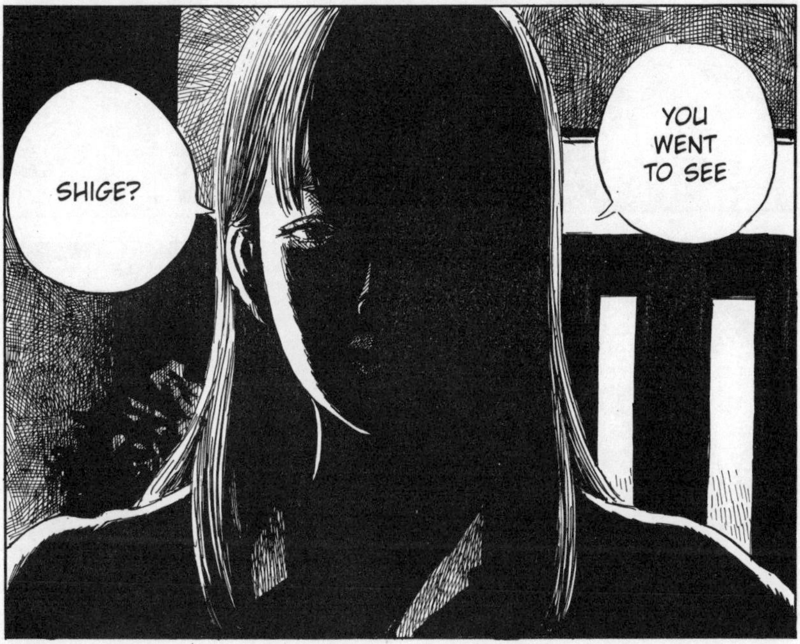
YOU WENT TO SEE
SHIGE?

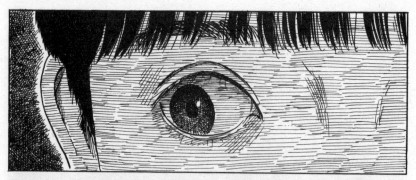

OH...

...NN—

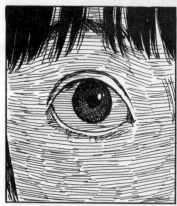

......

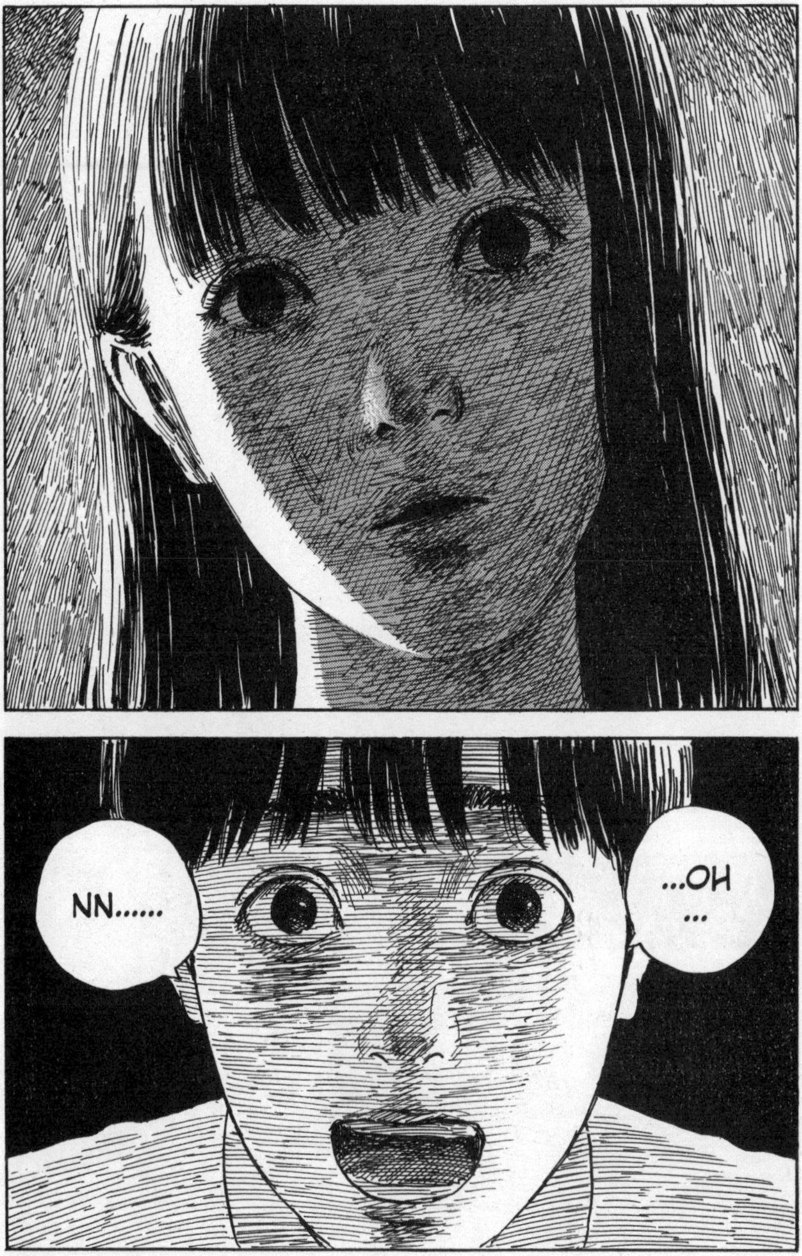
...OH ...
NN......

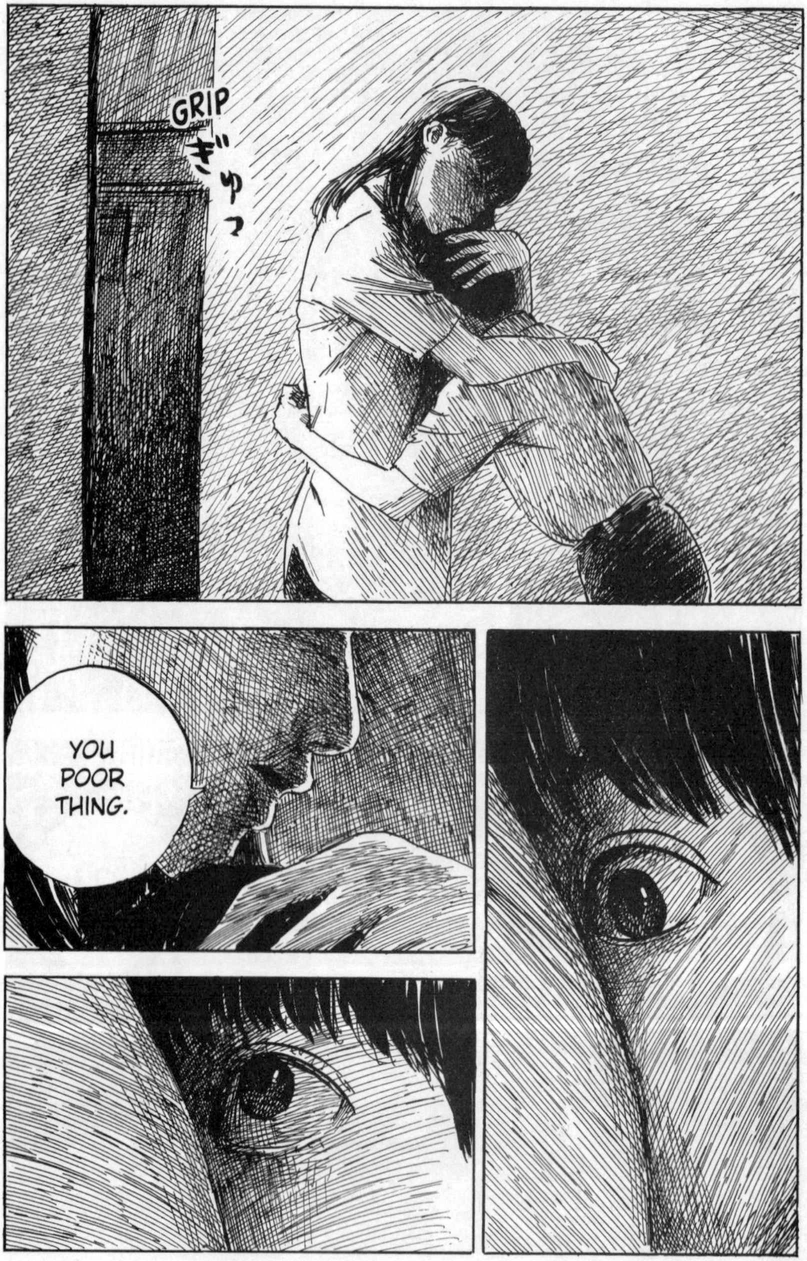
GRIP
ぎゅっ
YOU POOR THING.

YOU DIDN'T WANT TO, DID YOU?
IT MUST HAVE BEEN AWFUL!
YOU DIDN'T WANT TO,
BUT DADDY FORCED YOU TO GO, DIDN'T HE?!
ぎゅうう
SQUEEZE

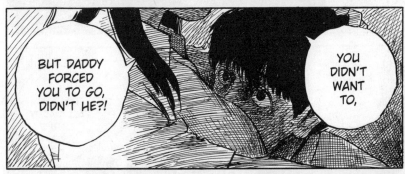

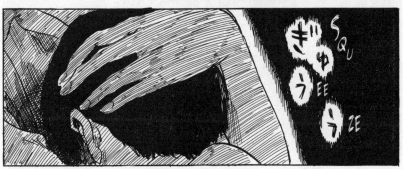

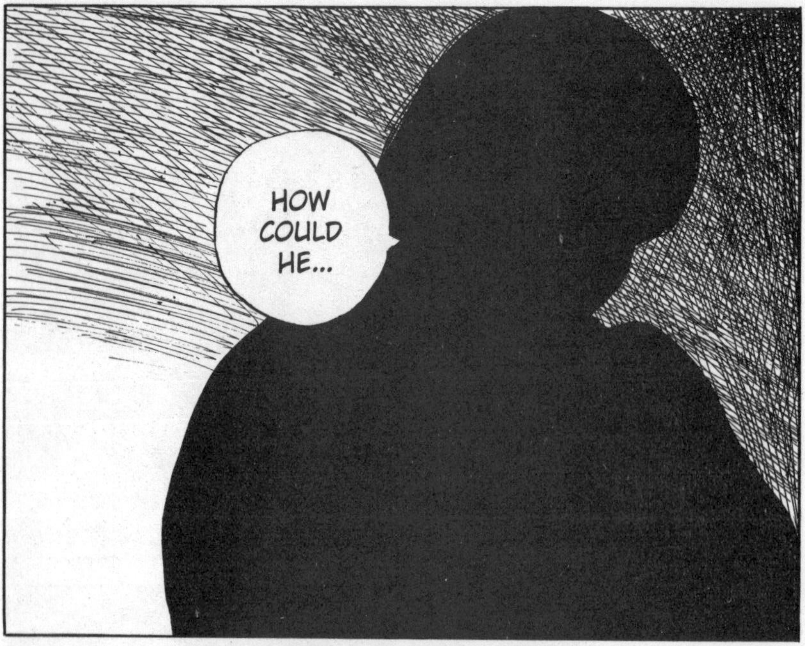
HOW COULD HE...

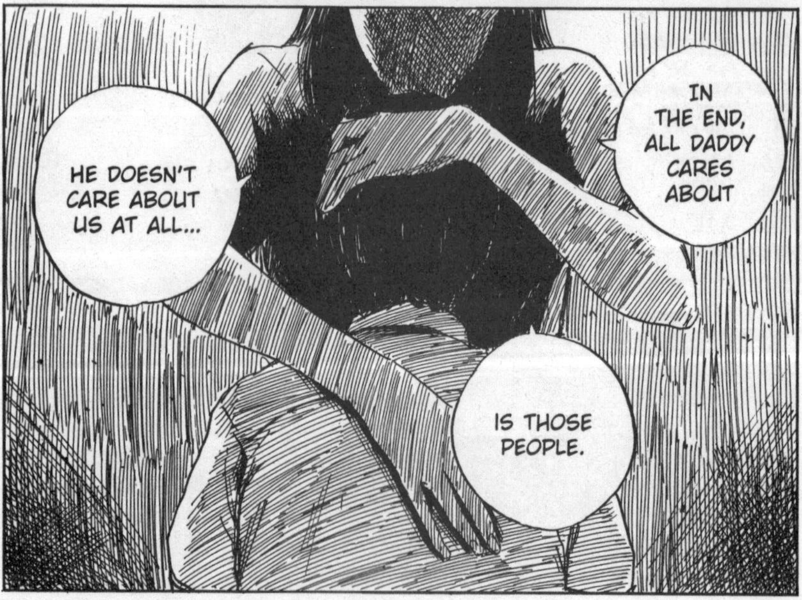
IN THE END, ALL DADDY CARES ABOUT
IS THOSE PEOPLE.
HE DOESN'T CARE ABOUT US AT ALL...

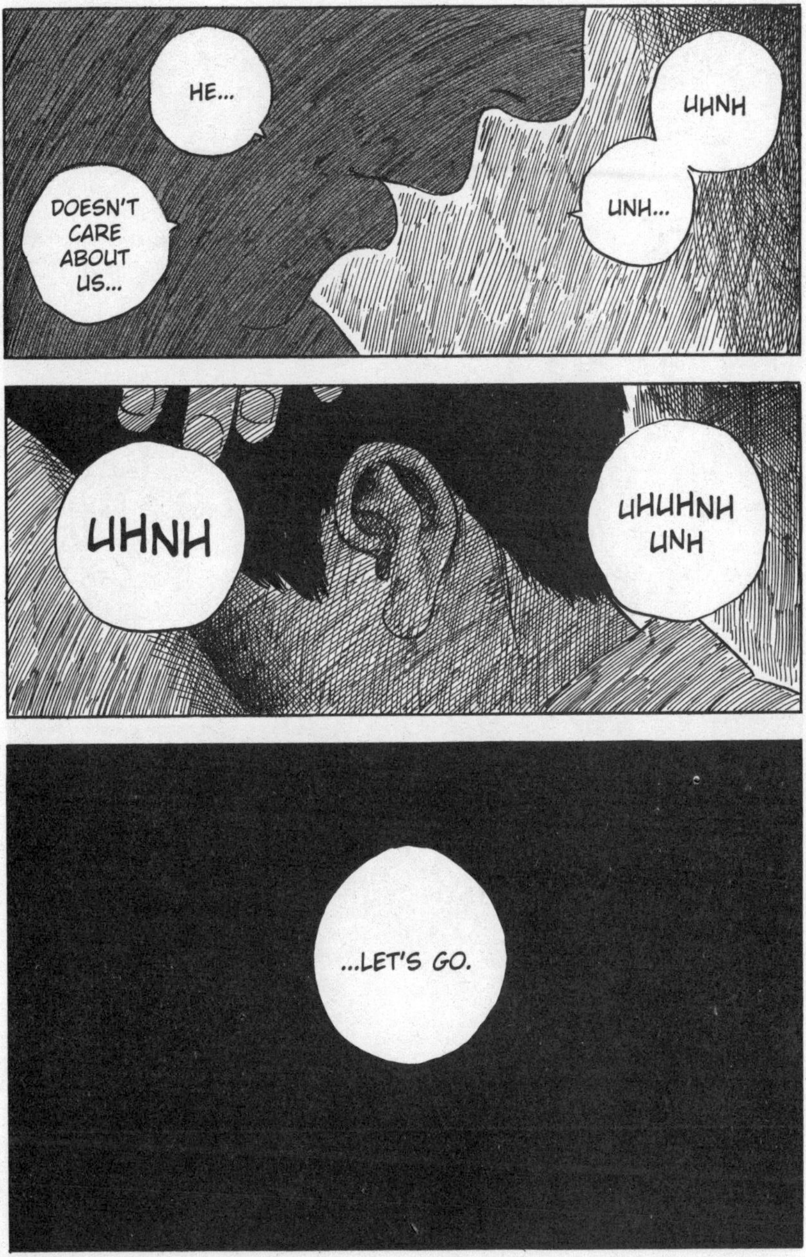
UHNH
UNH...
HE...
DOESN'T CARE ABOUT US...
UHUHNH UNH
UHNH
...LET'S GO.

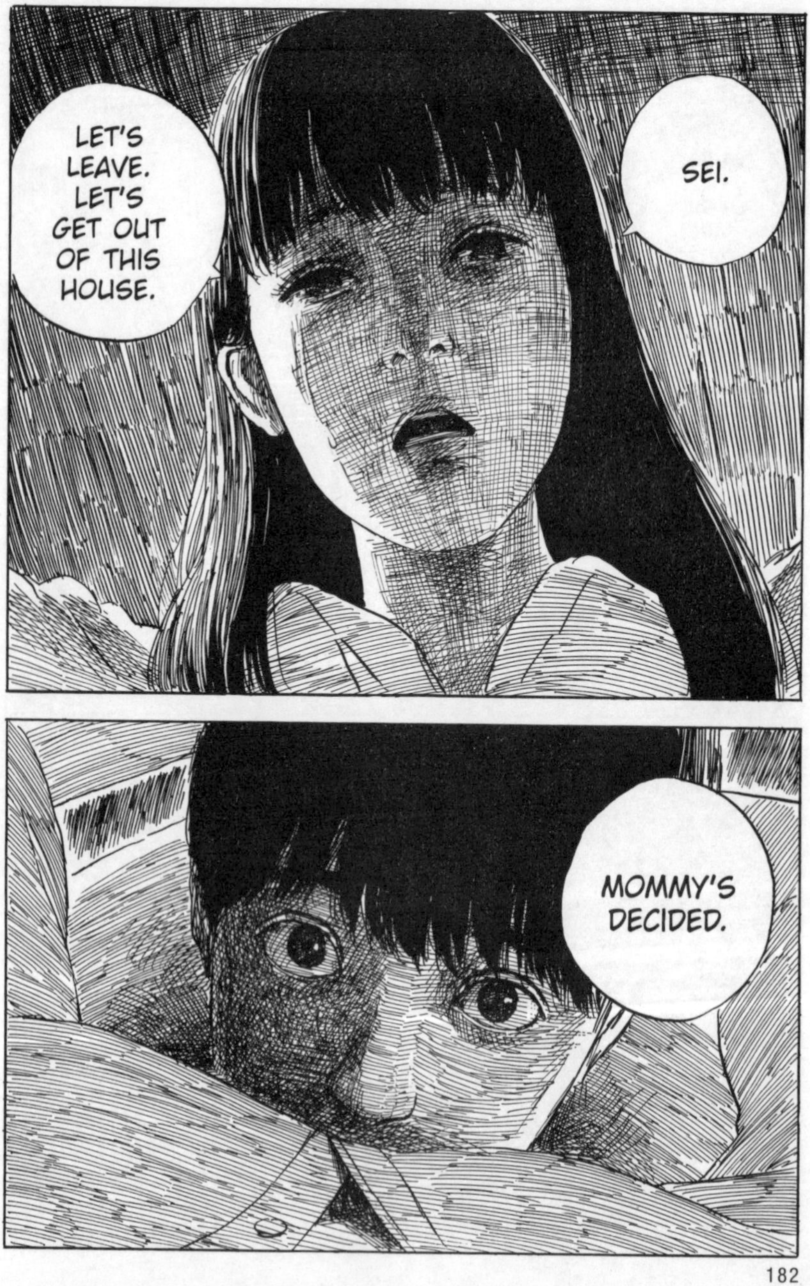
SEI.
LET'S LEAVE. LET'S GET OUT OF THIS HOUSE.
MOMMY'S DECIDED.

WHEN THE TIME COMES,
WILL YOU COME WITH ME?

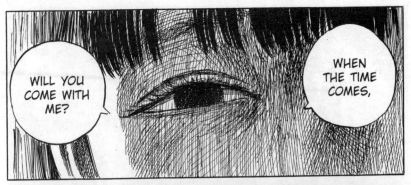

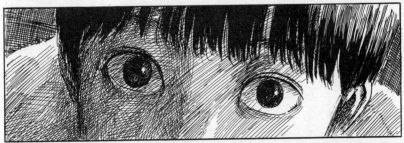

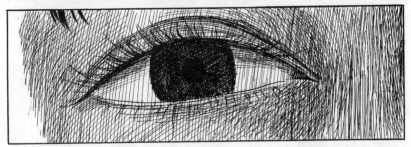

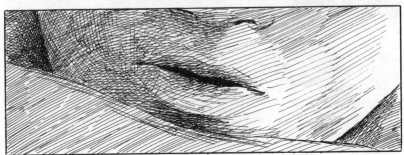

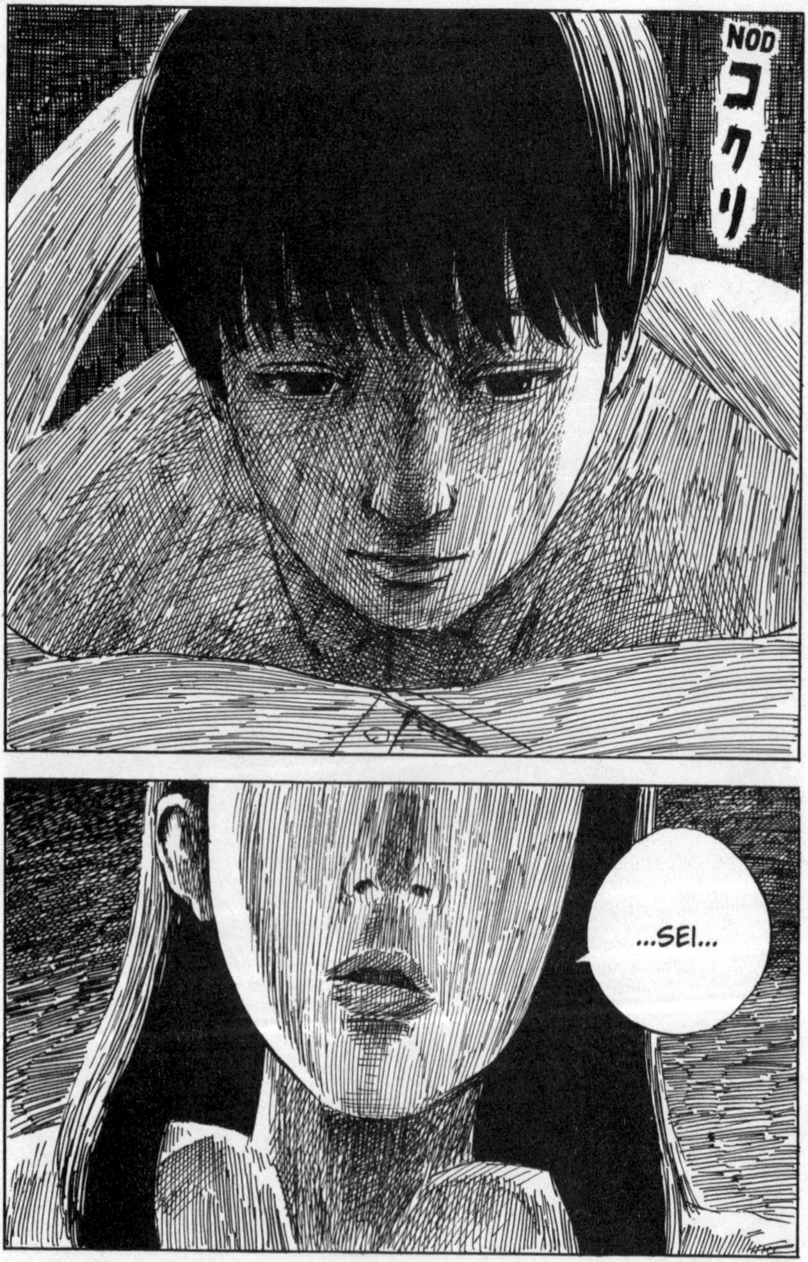
NOD
コクリ
...SEI...

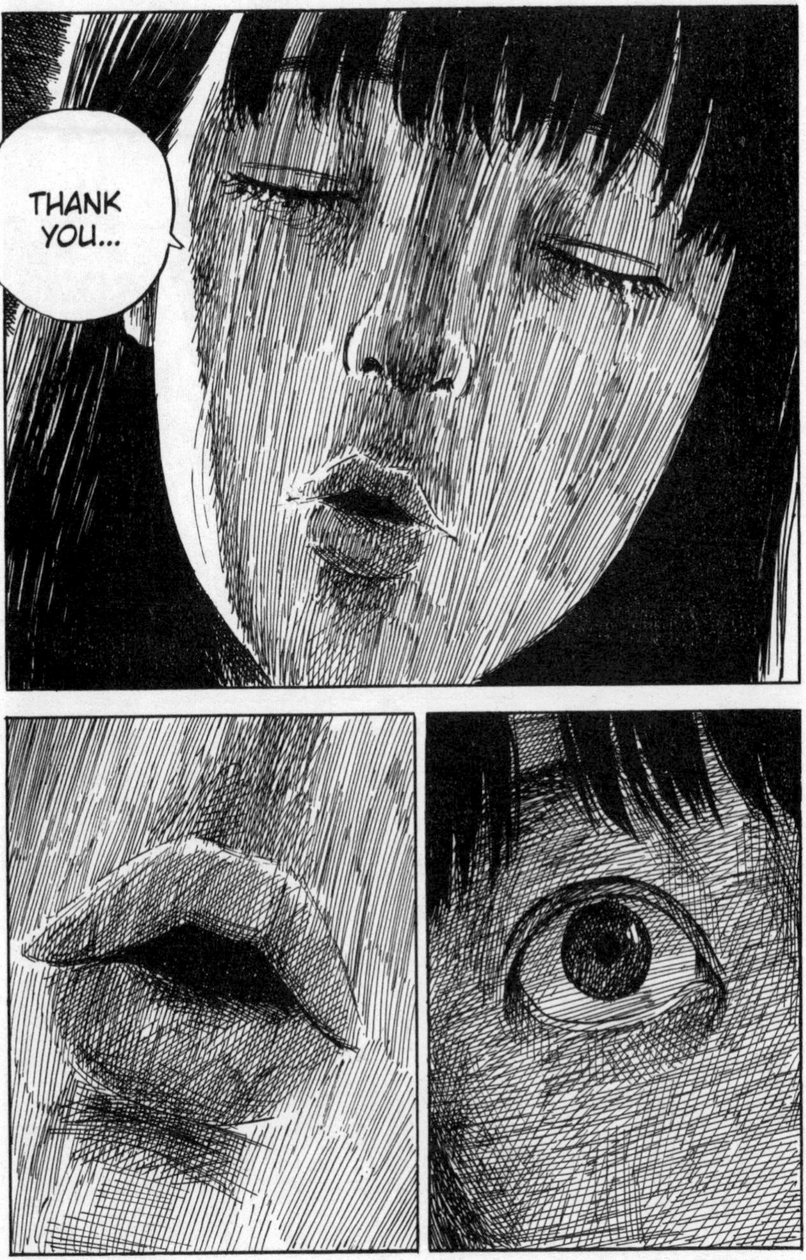
THANK YOU...

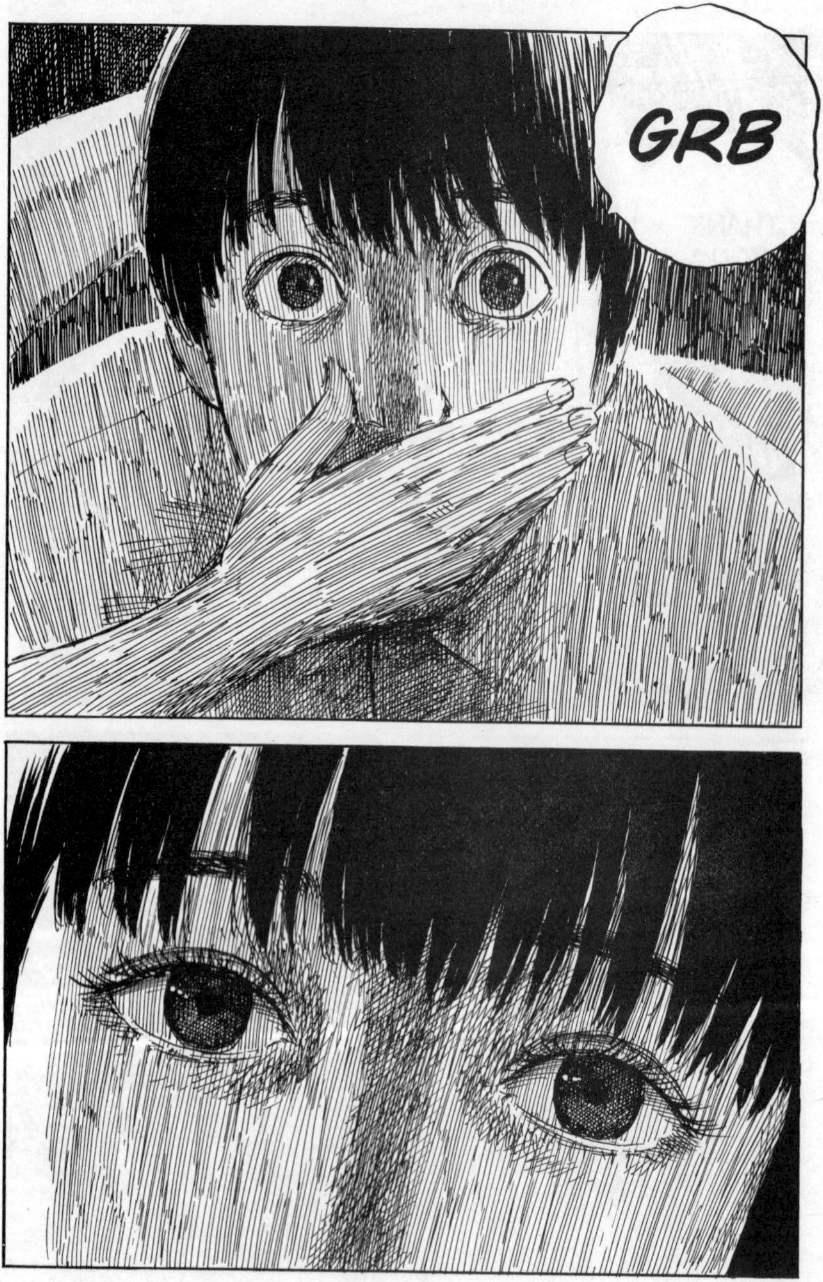
GRB

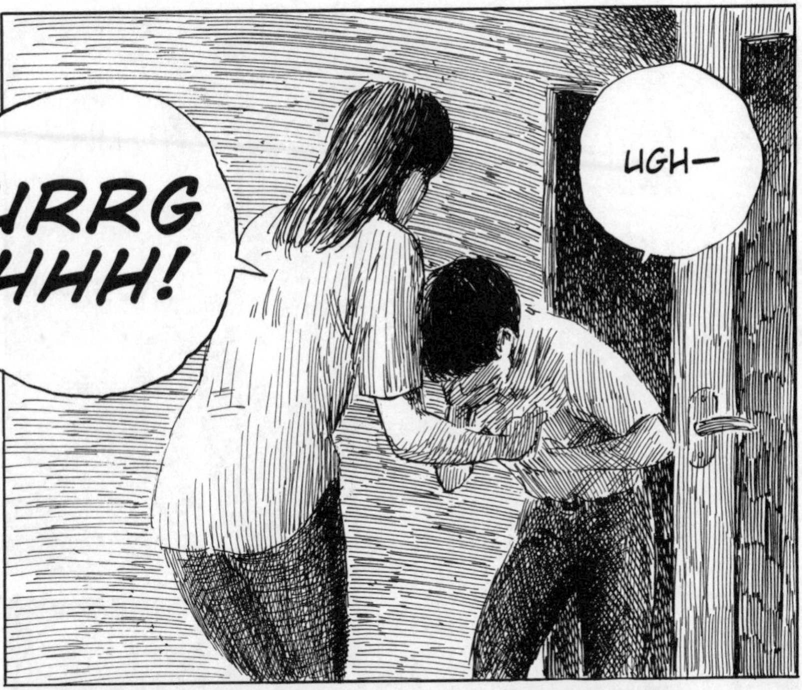
UGH—
URRG HHH!

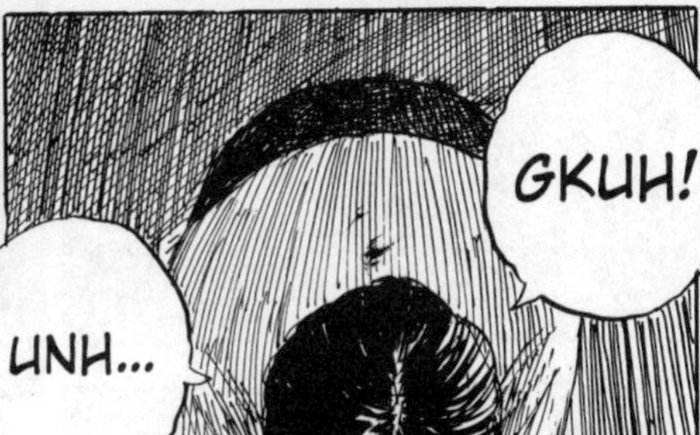
GKUH!
UNH...
GUGHH!

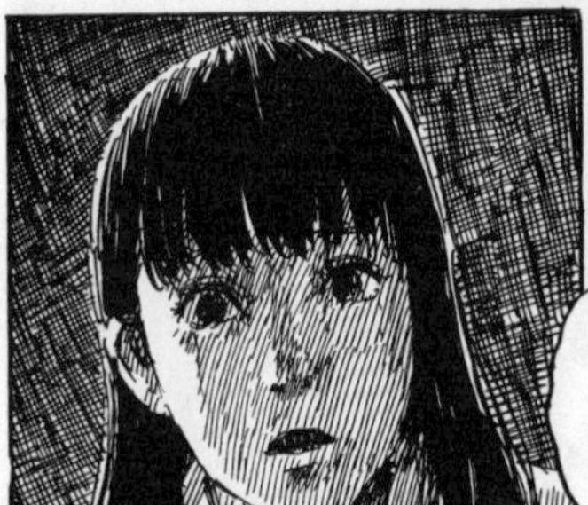

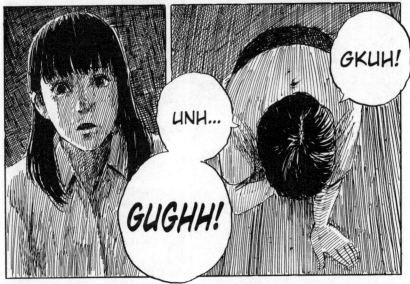

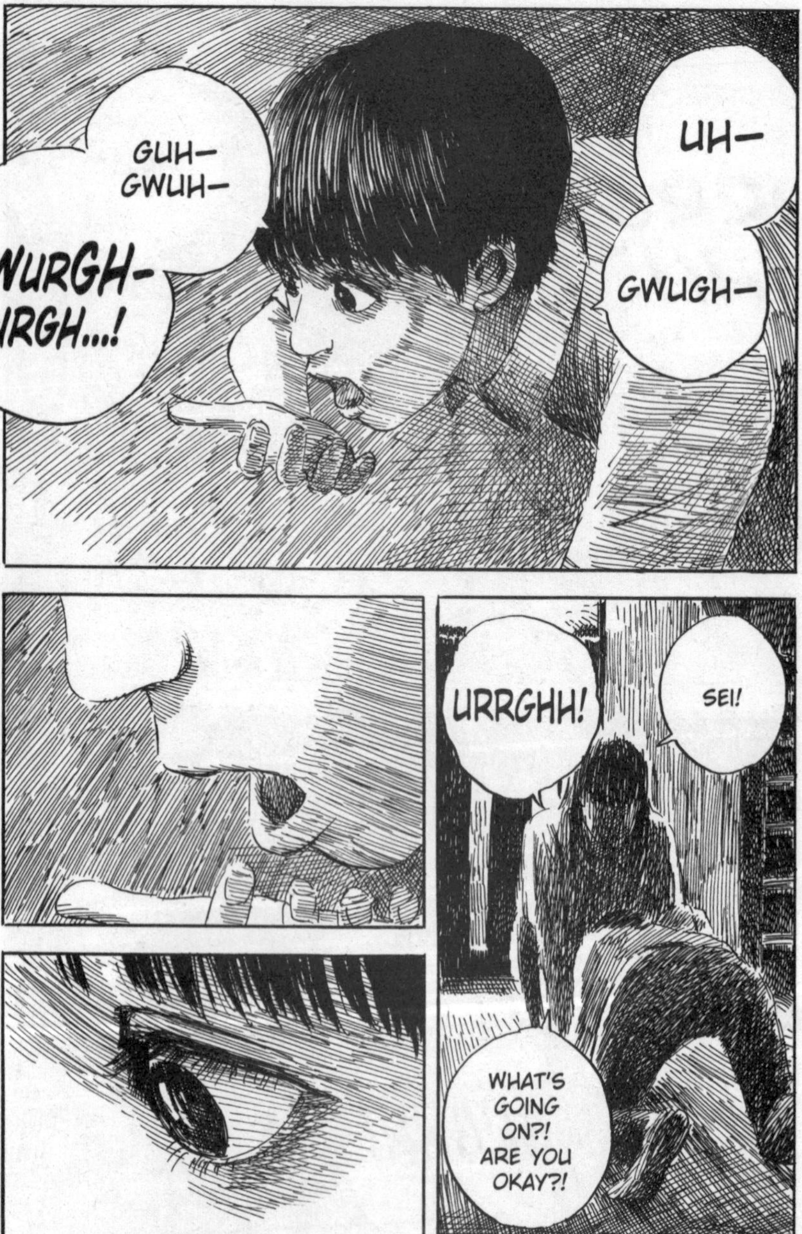
UH-
GWUGH-
GUH-
GWUH-
GWURGH-
URGH...!
SEI!
URRGHH!
WHAT'S
GOING
ON?!
ARE YOU
OKAY?!

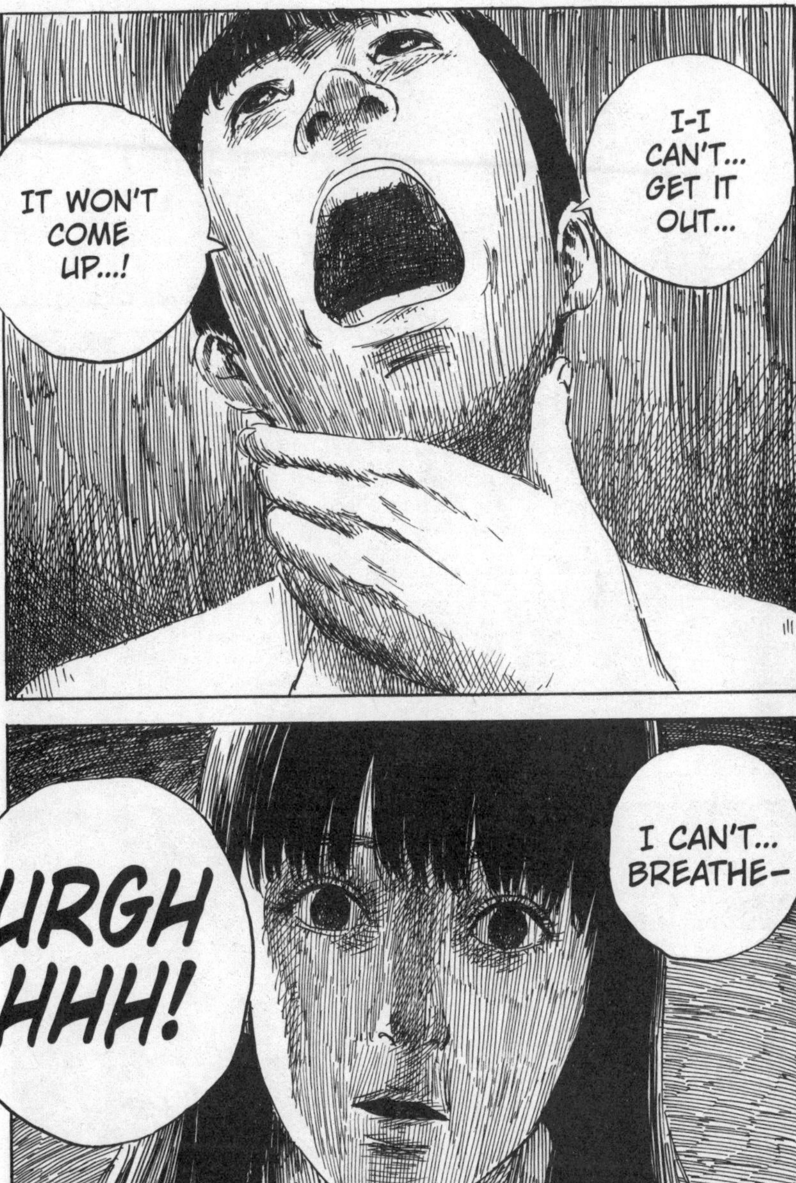
I-I CAN'T... GET IT OUT...
IT WON'T COME UP...!
I CAN'T... BREATHE-
URGH HHH!

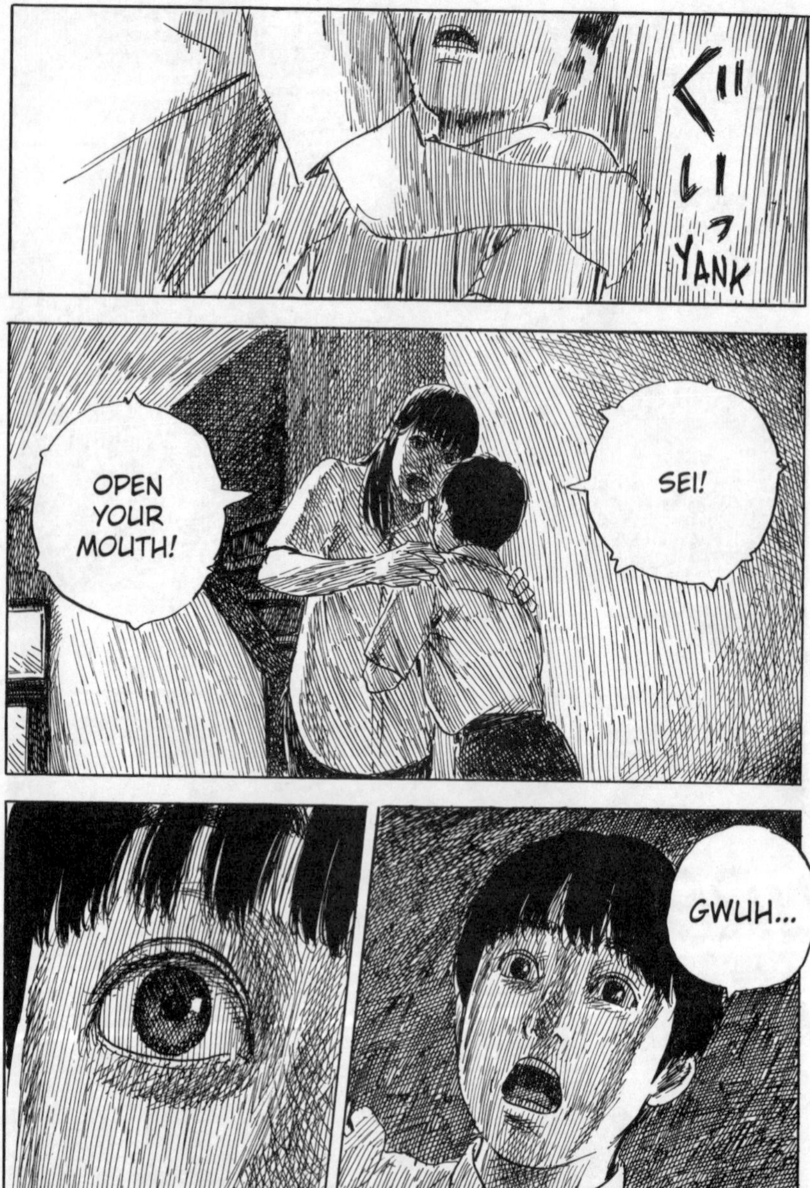
ぐいっ
YANK
SEI!
OPEN YOUR MOUTH!
GWUH...

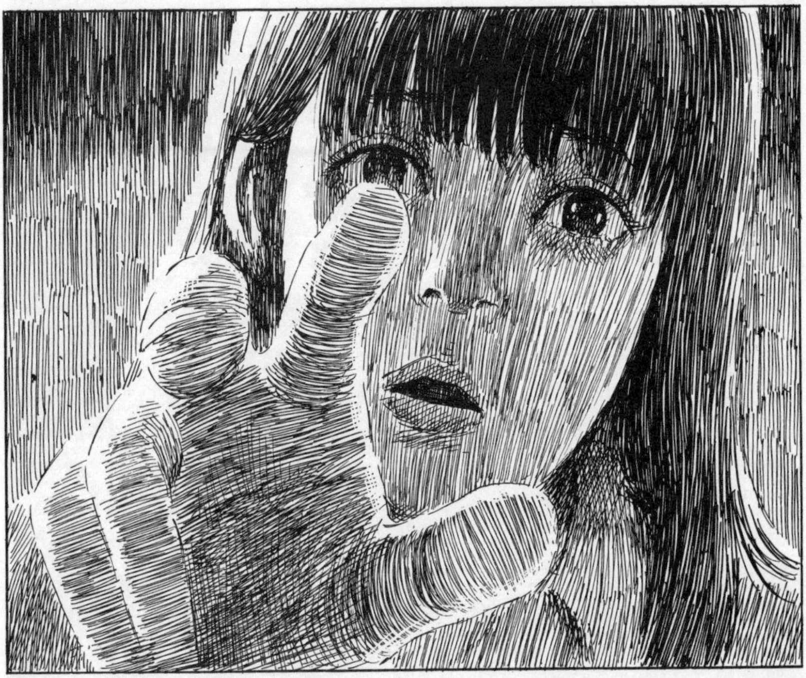

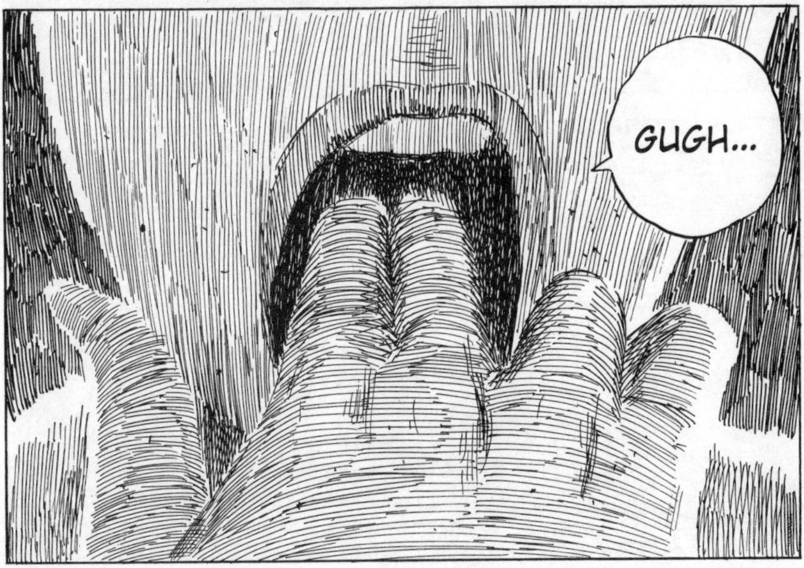
GUGH...

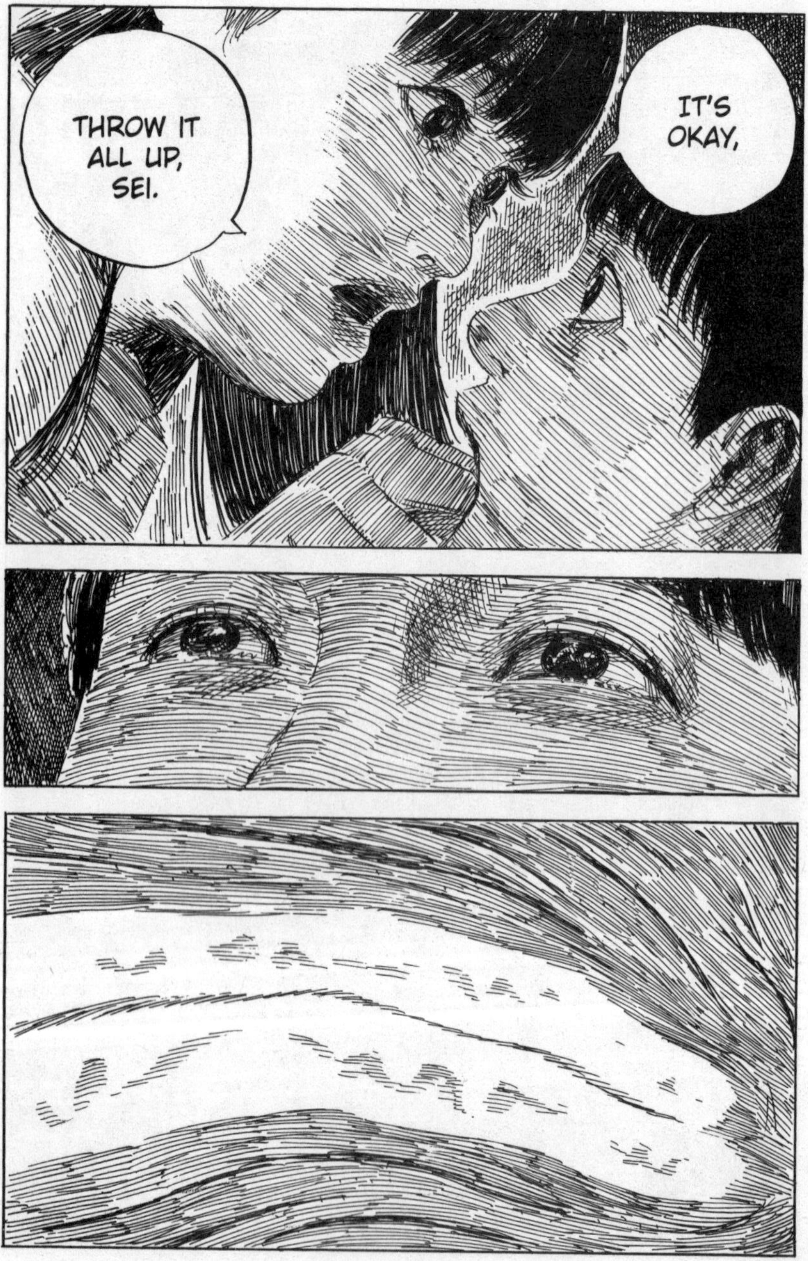
IT'S OKAY,
THROW IT ALL UP, SEI.

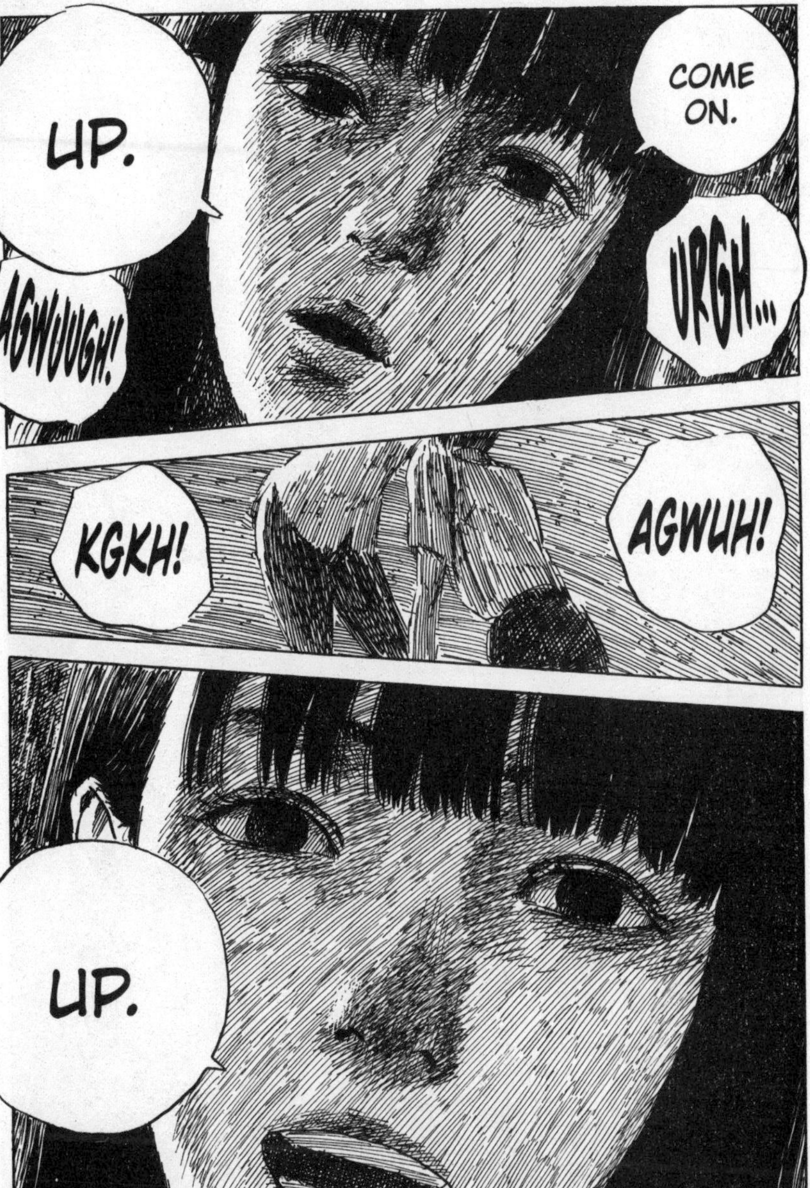
COME ON.
UP.
URGH...
AGWUUGH!
AGWUH!
KGKH!
UP.

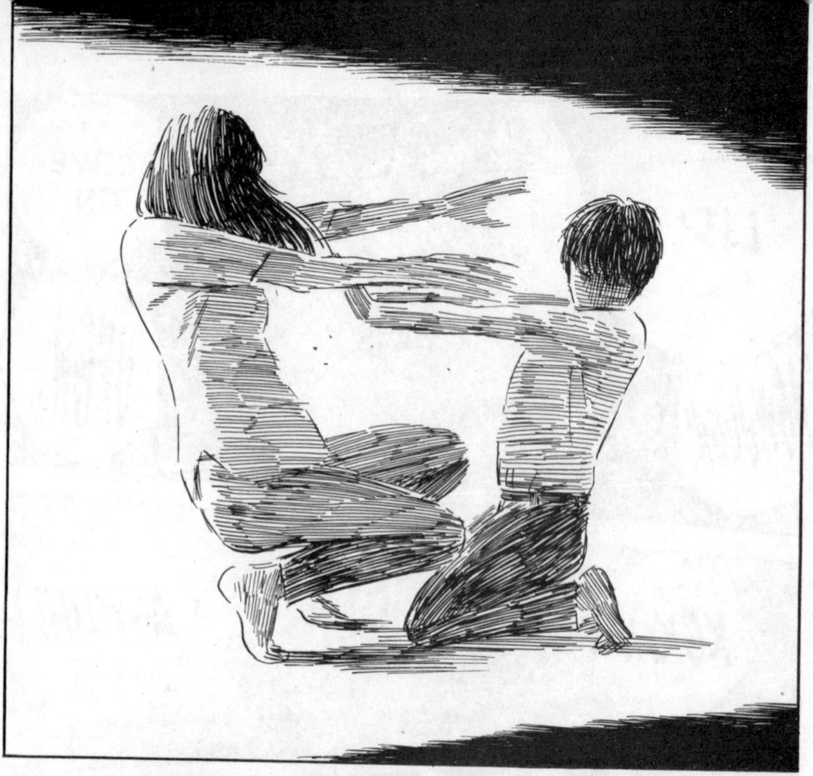

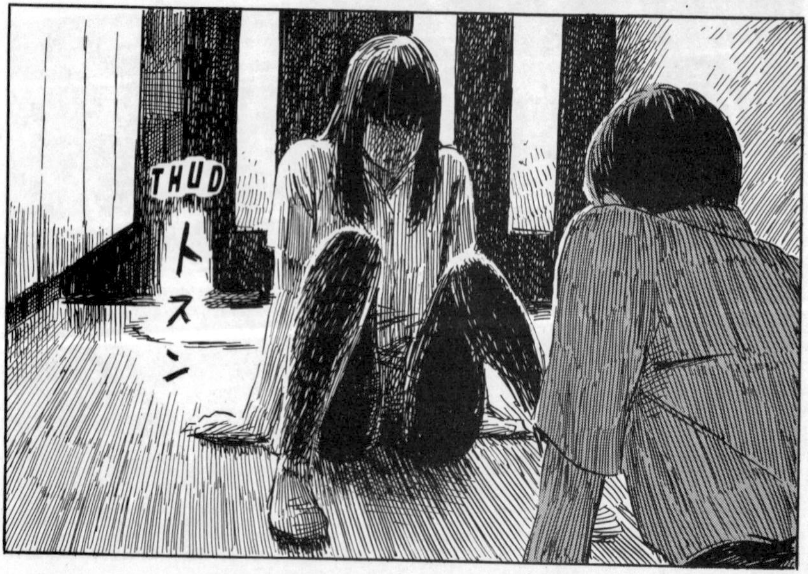
THUD
トスン

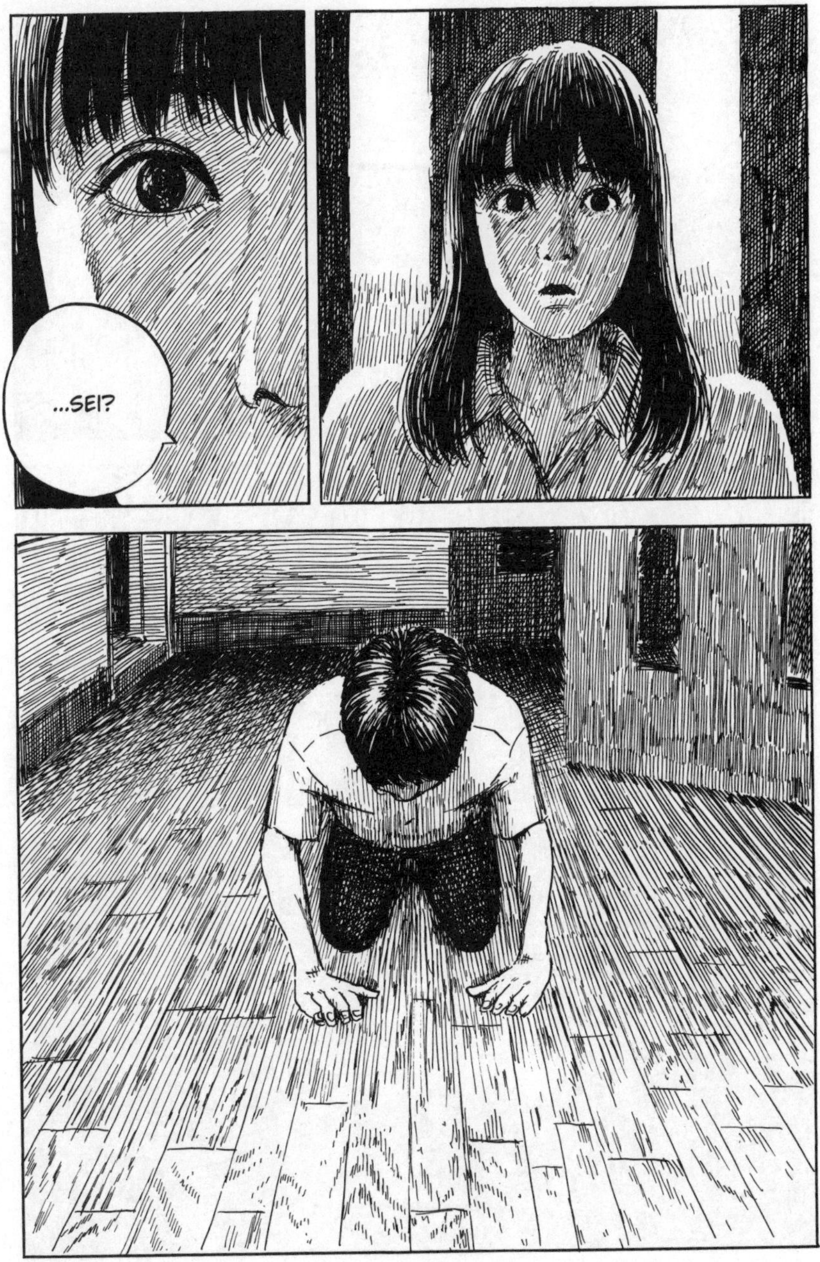
...SEI?

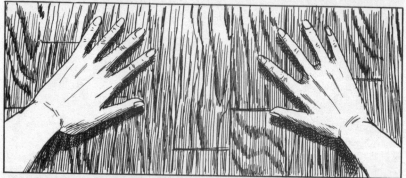

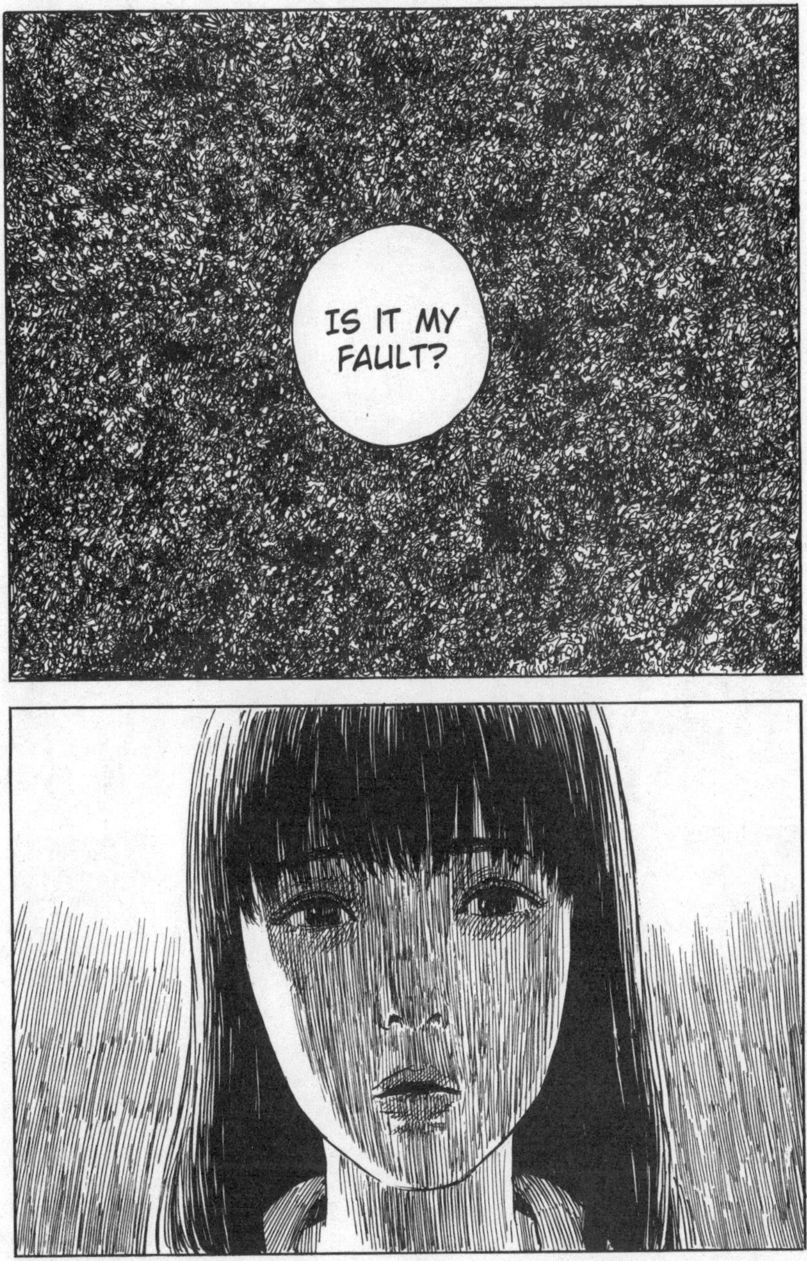
IS IT MY FAULT?

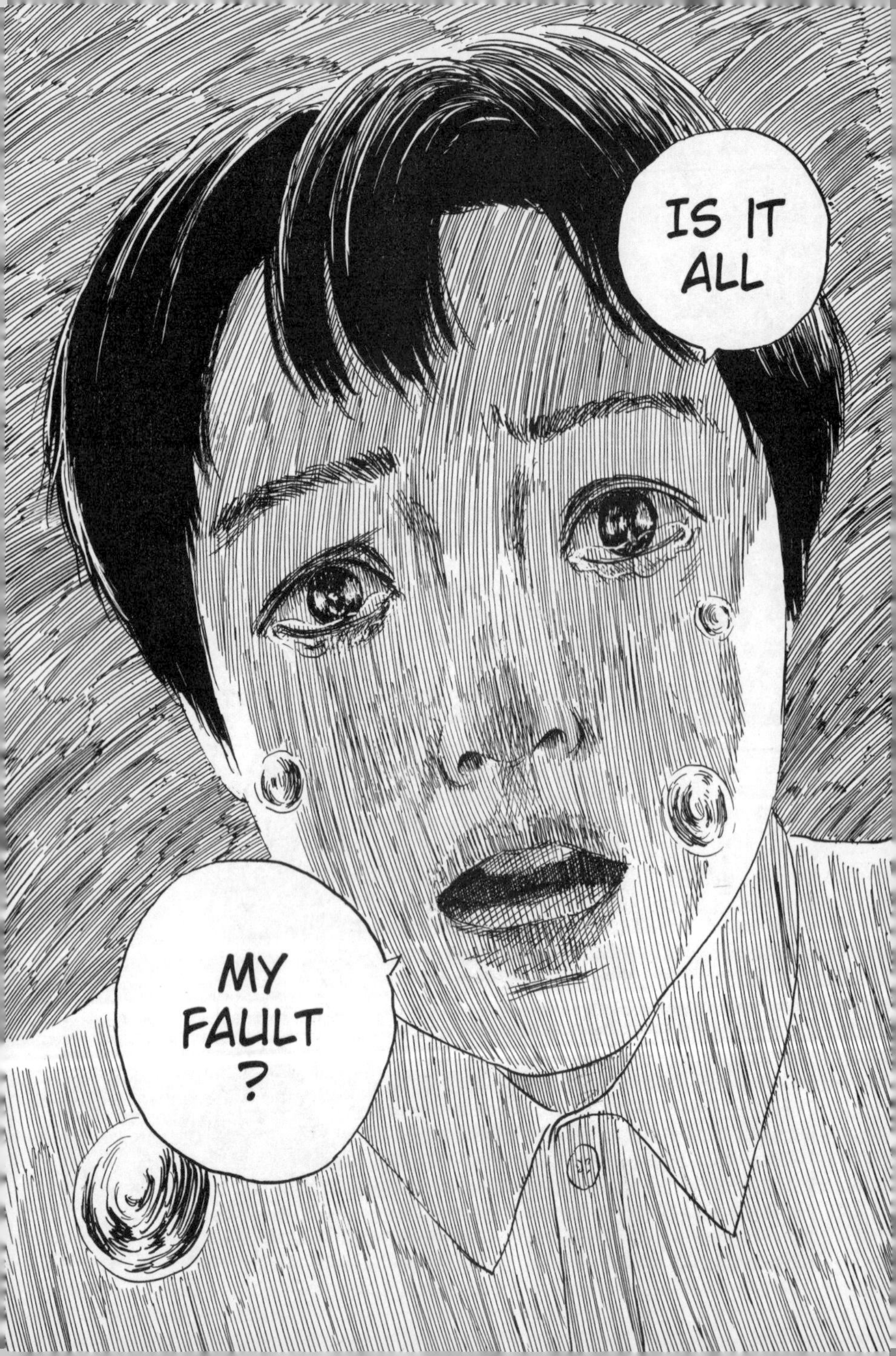
IS IT ALL
MY FAULT ?

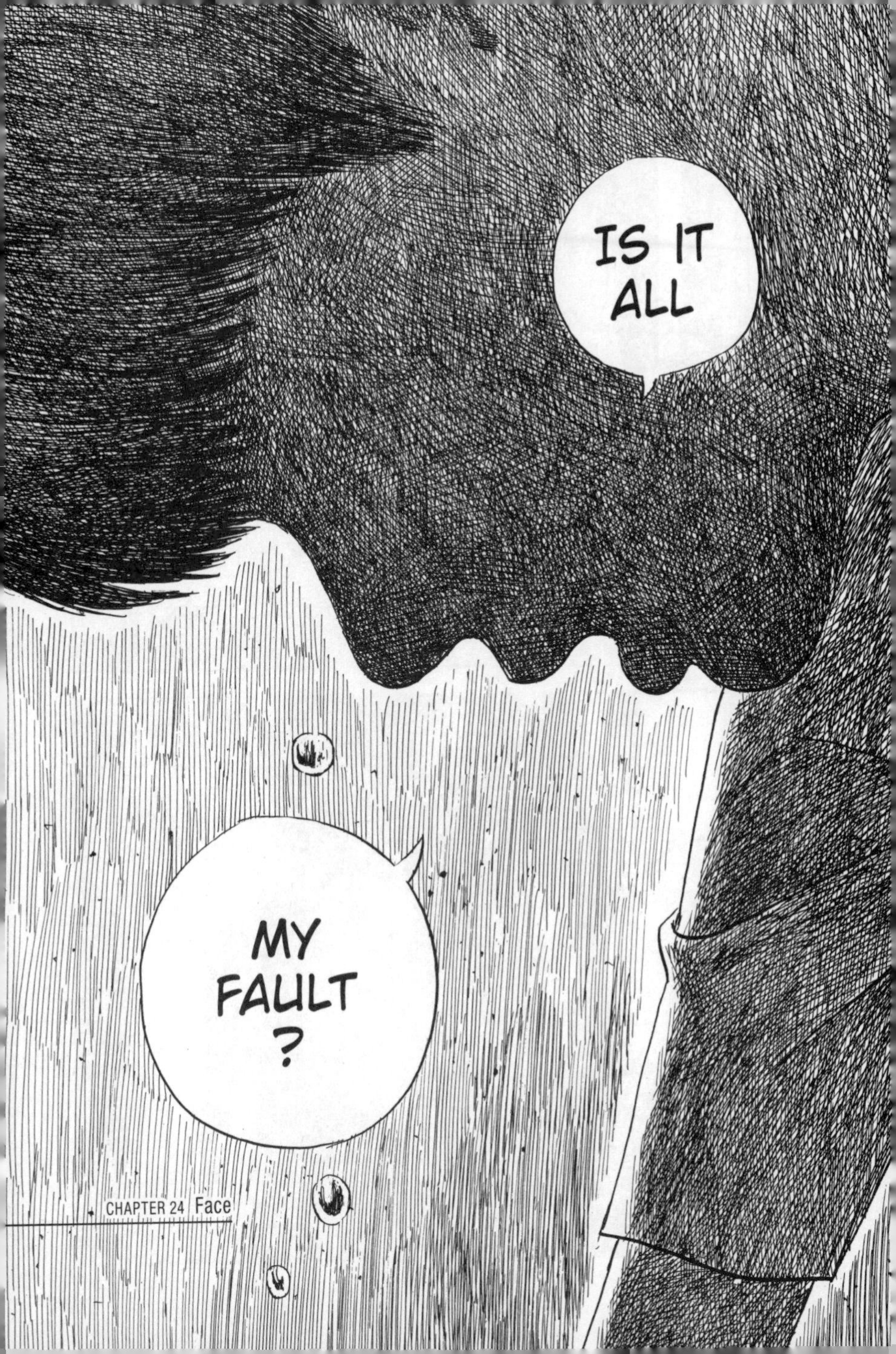
IS IT ALL
MY FAULT ?
CHAPTER 24 Face

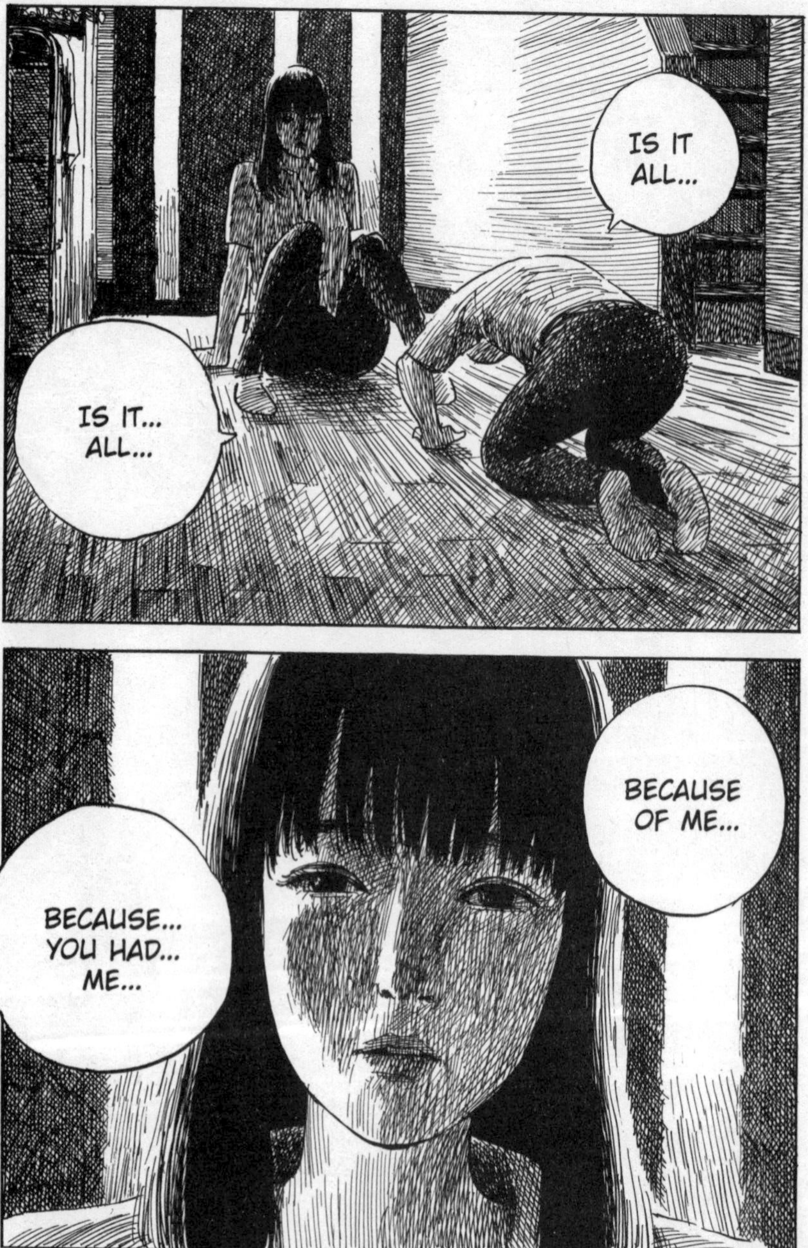
IS IT ALL...
IS IT... ALL...
BECAUSE OF ME...
BECAUSE... YOU HAD... ME...

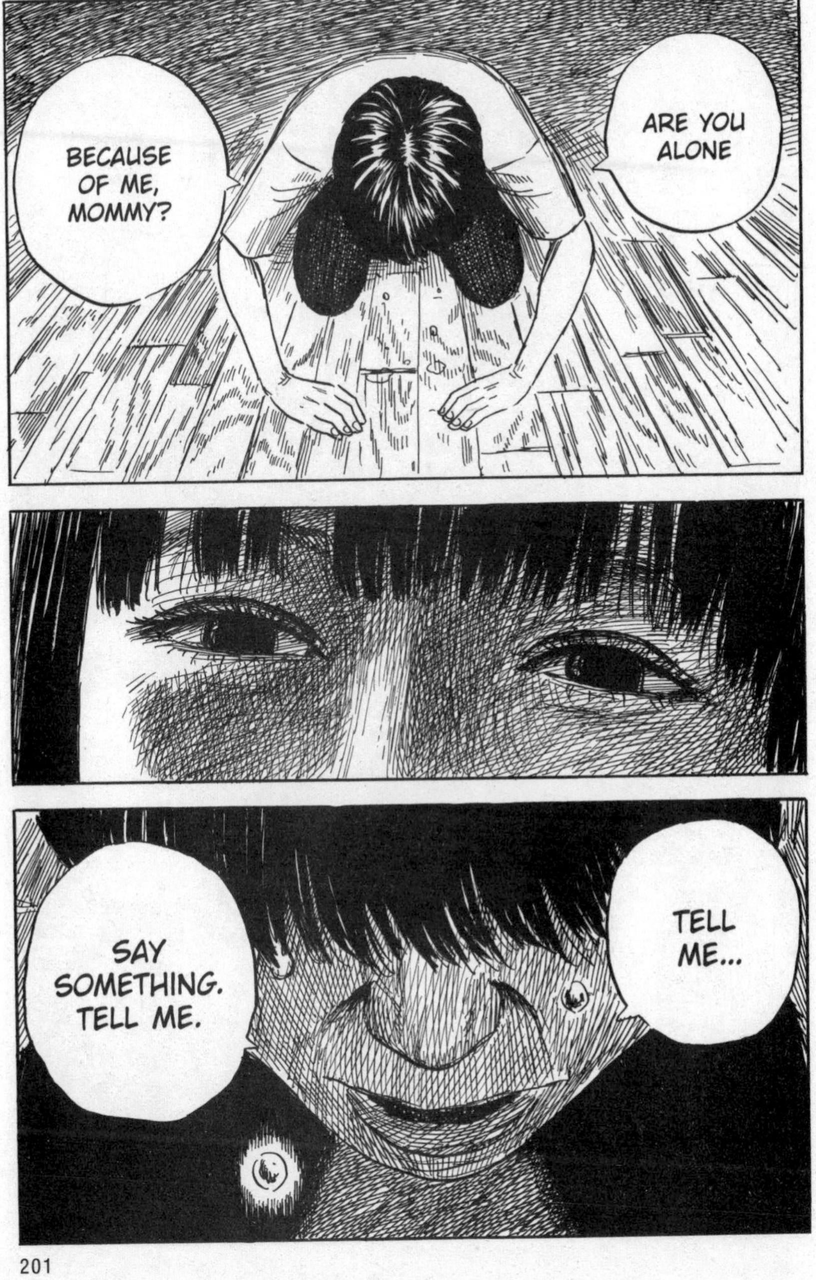
ARE YOU ALONE
BECAUSE OF ME, MOMMY?
TELL ME...
SAY SOMETHING. TELL ME.

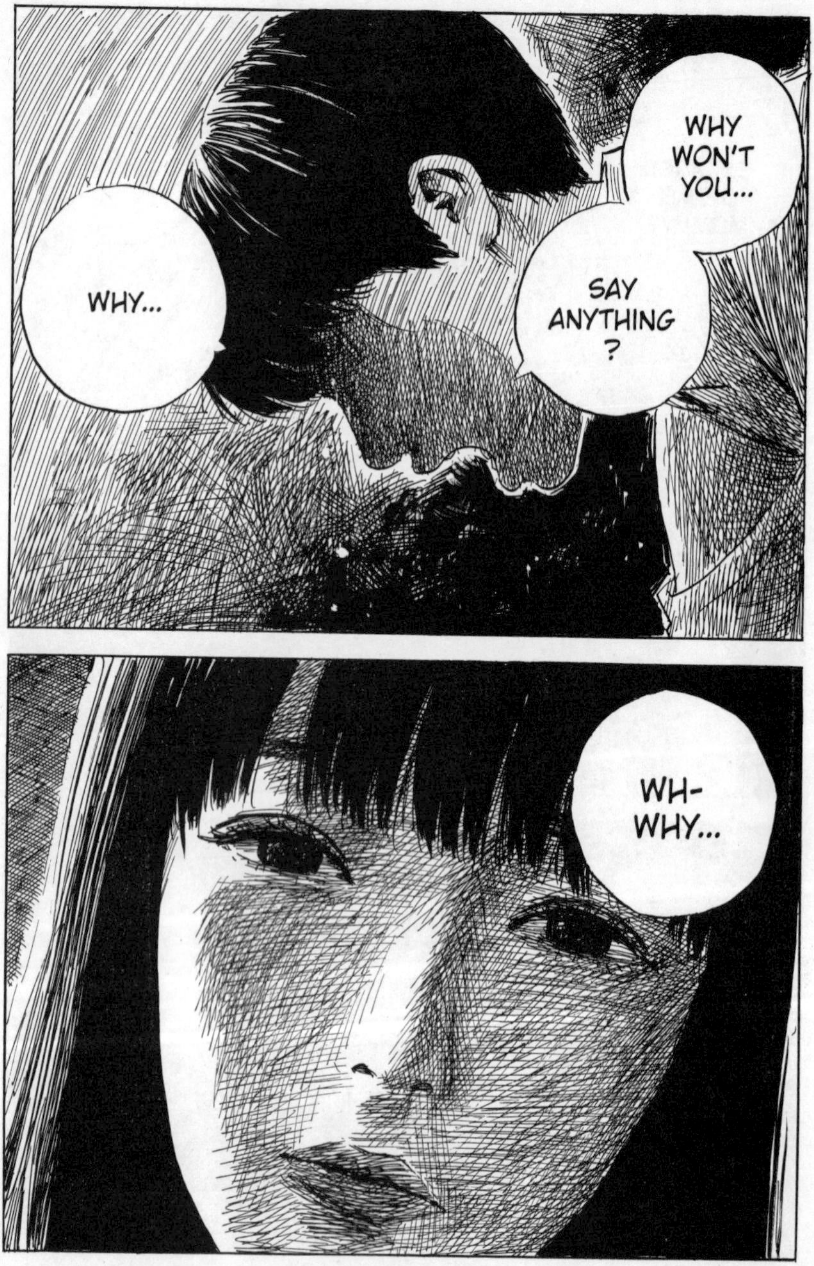
WHY WON'T YOU...
SAY ANYTHING ?
WHY...
WH- WHY...

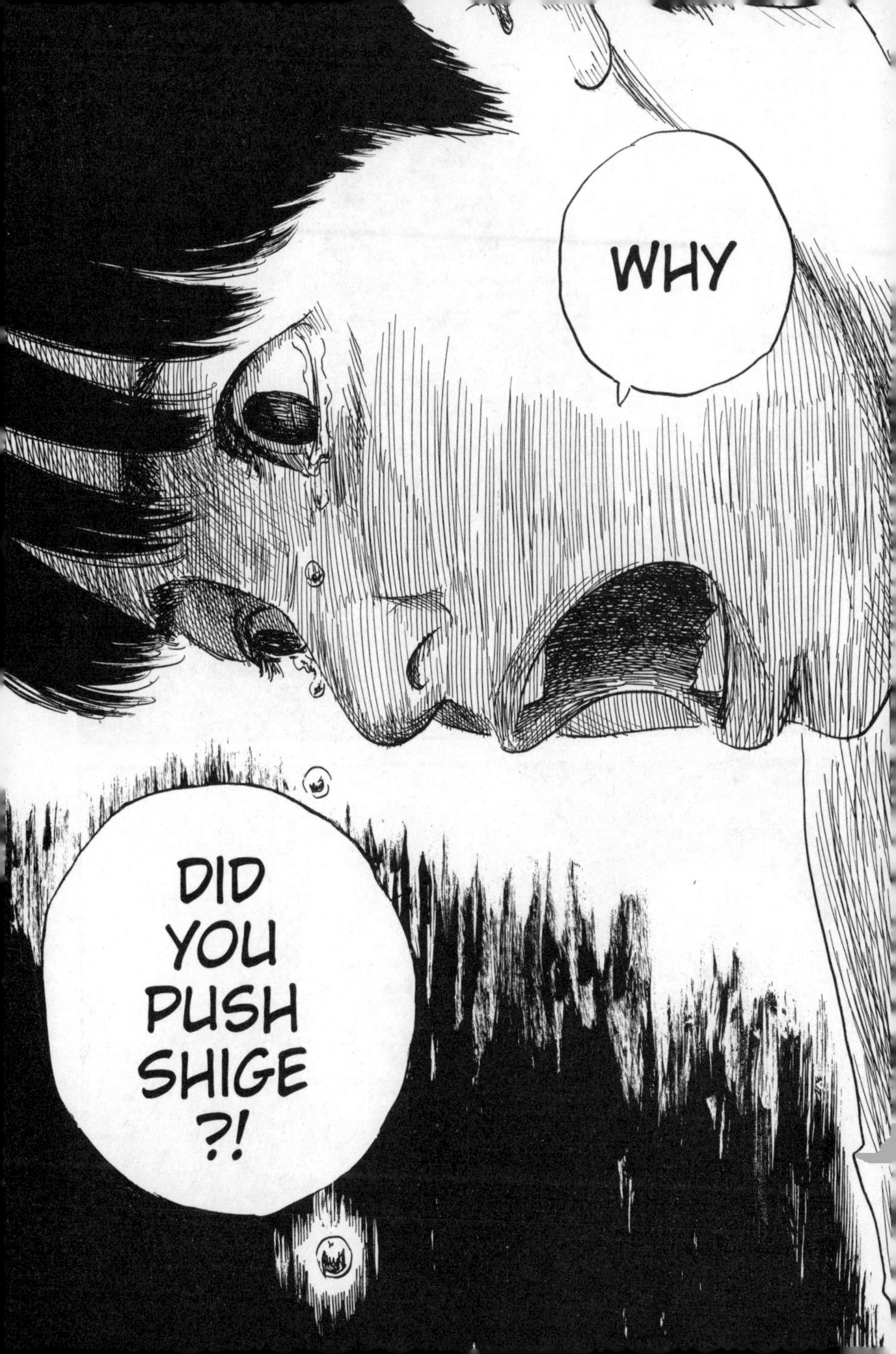
WHY
DID YOU PUSH SHIGE ?!

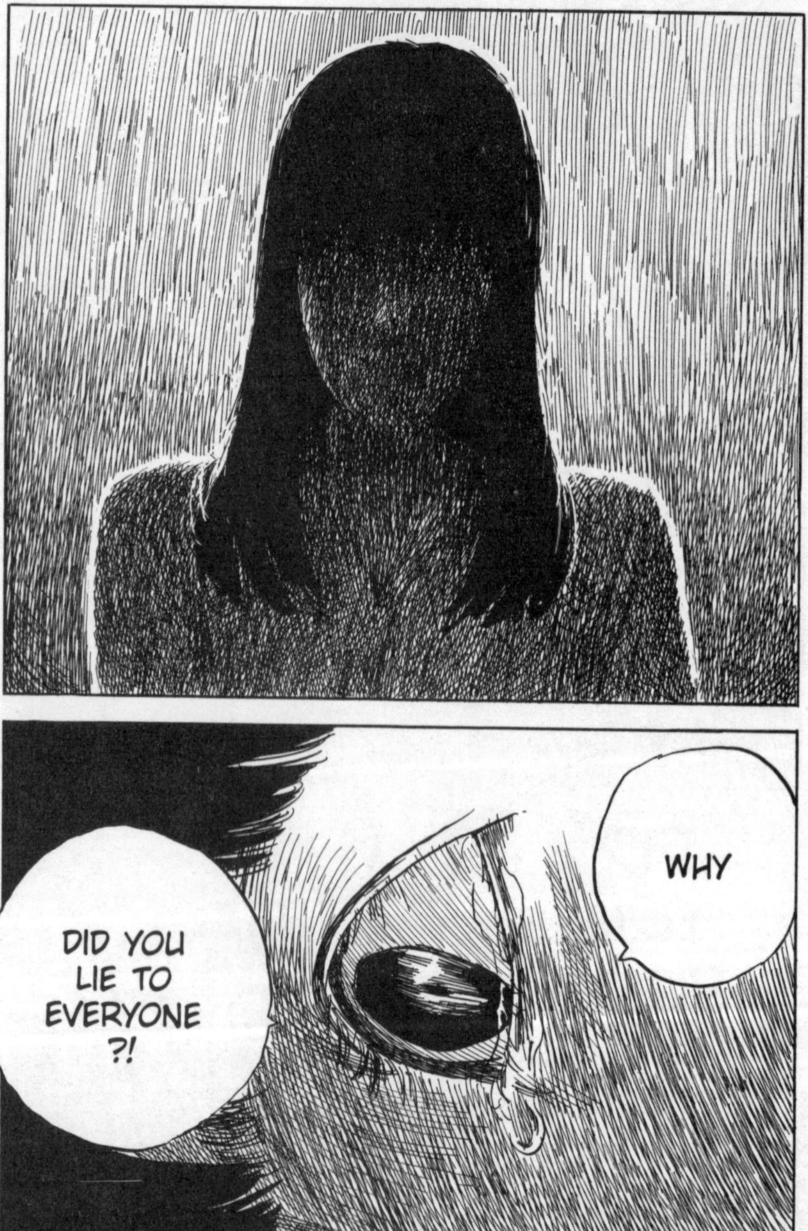
WHY
DID YOU LIE TO EVERYONE ?!

I...
I...
I...!
MOMMY !!

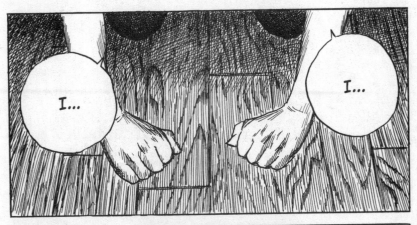

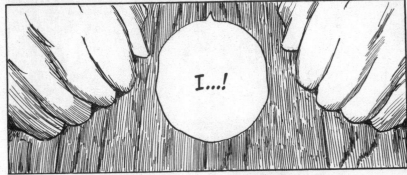

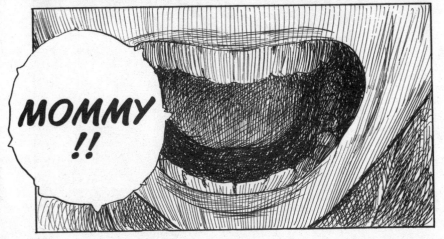

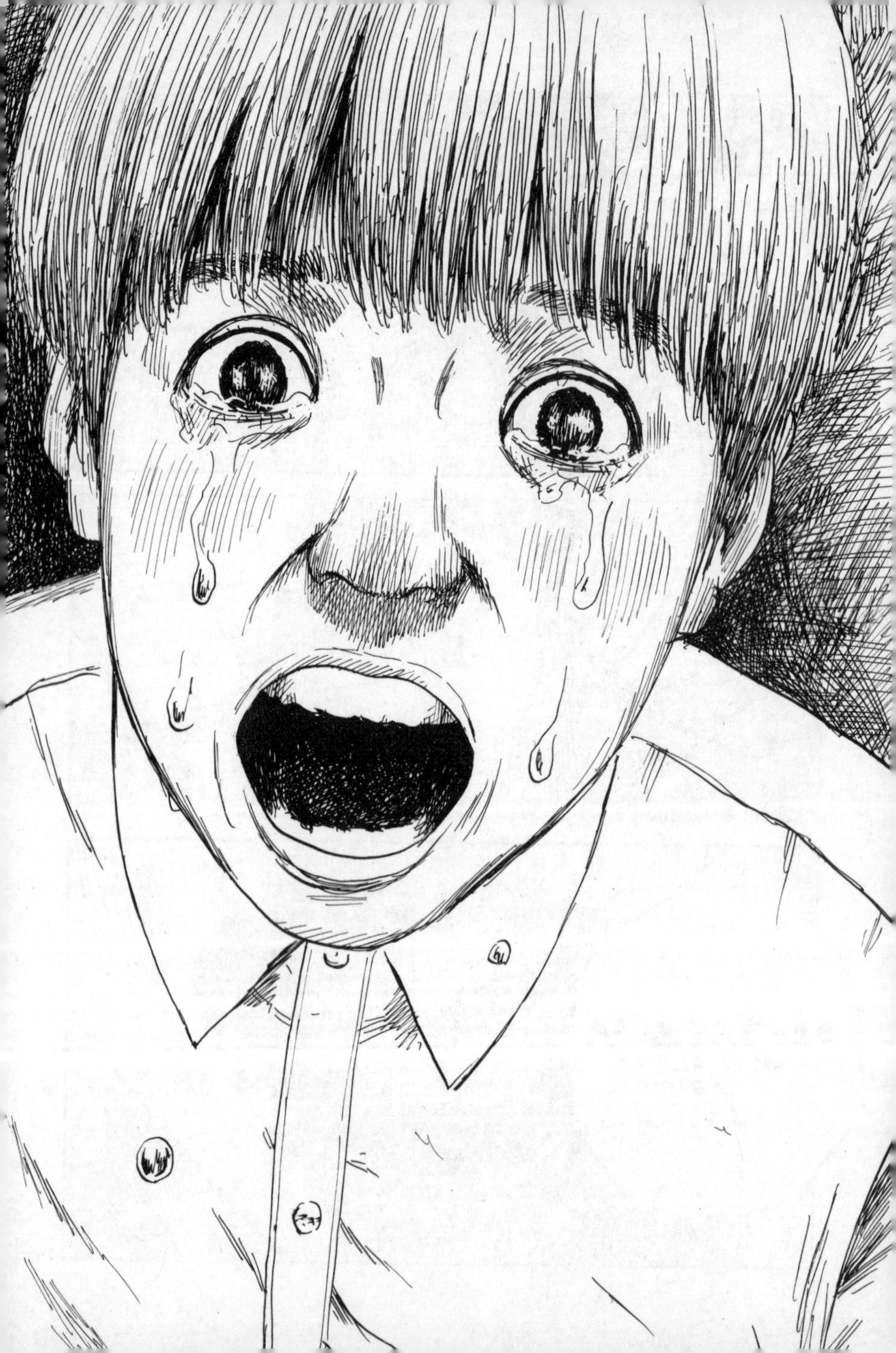

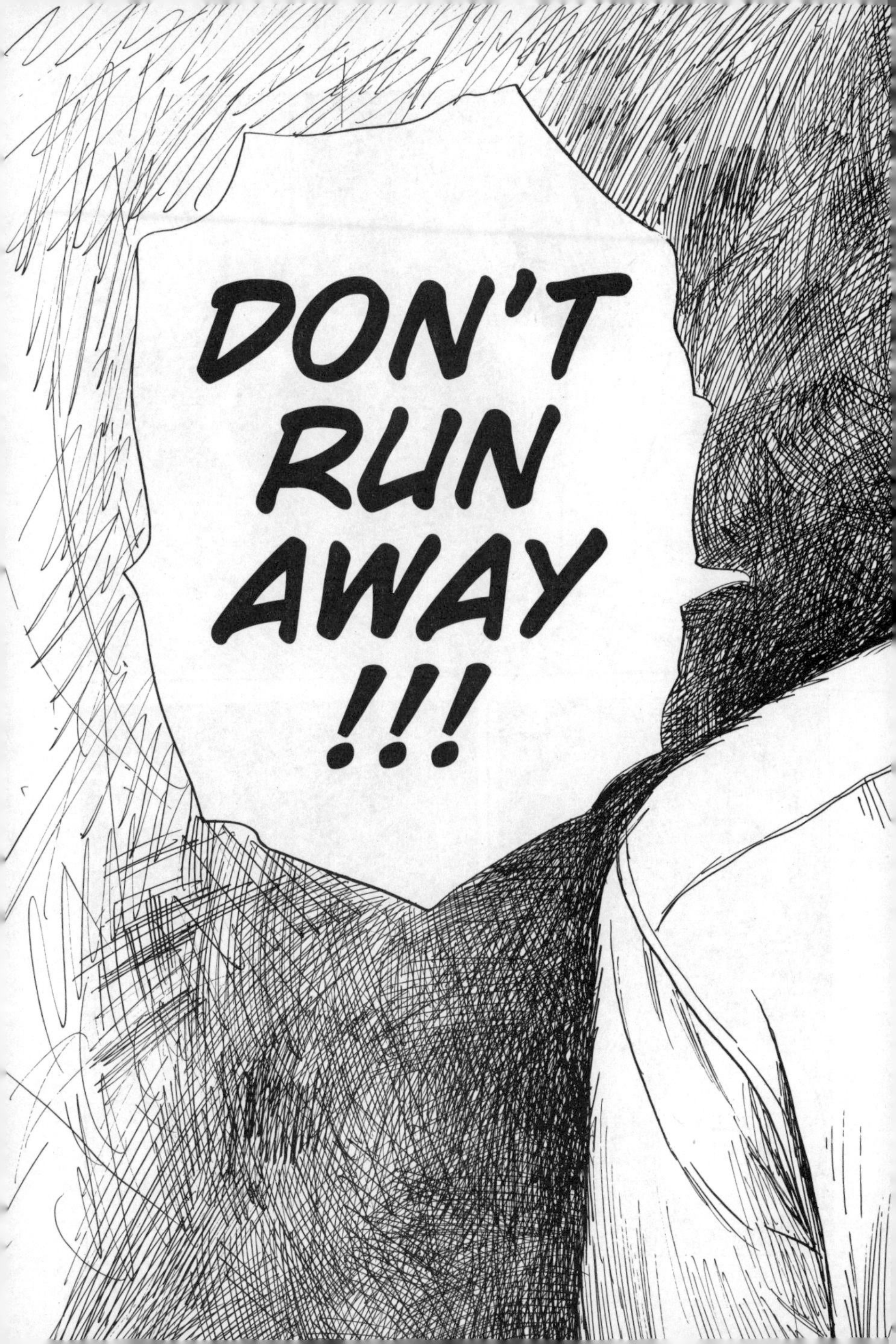
DON'T RUN AWAY!!!

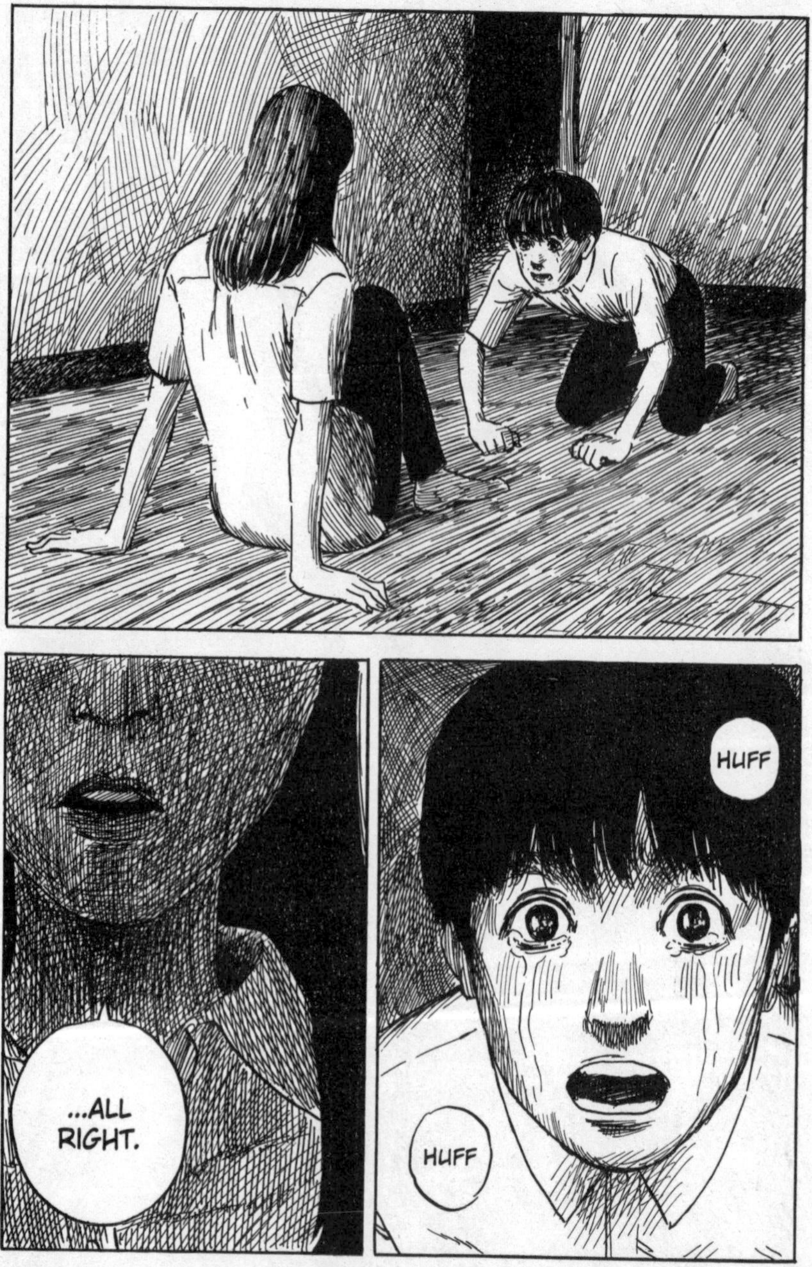
HUFF
HUFF
...ALL RIGHT.

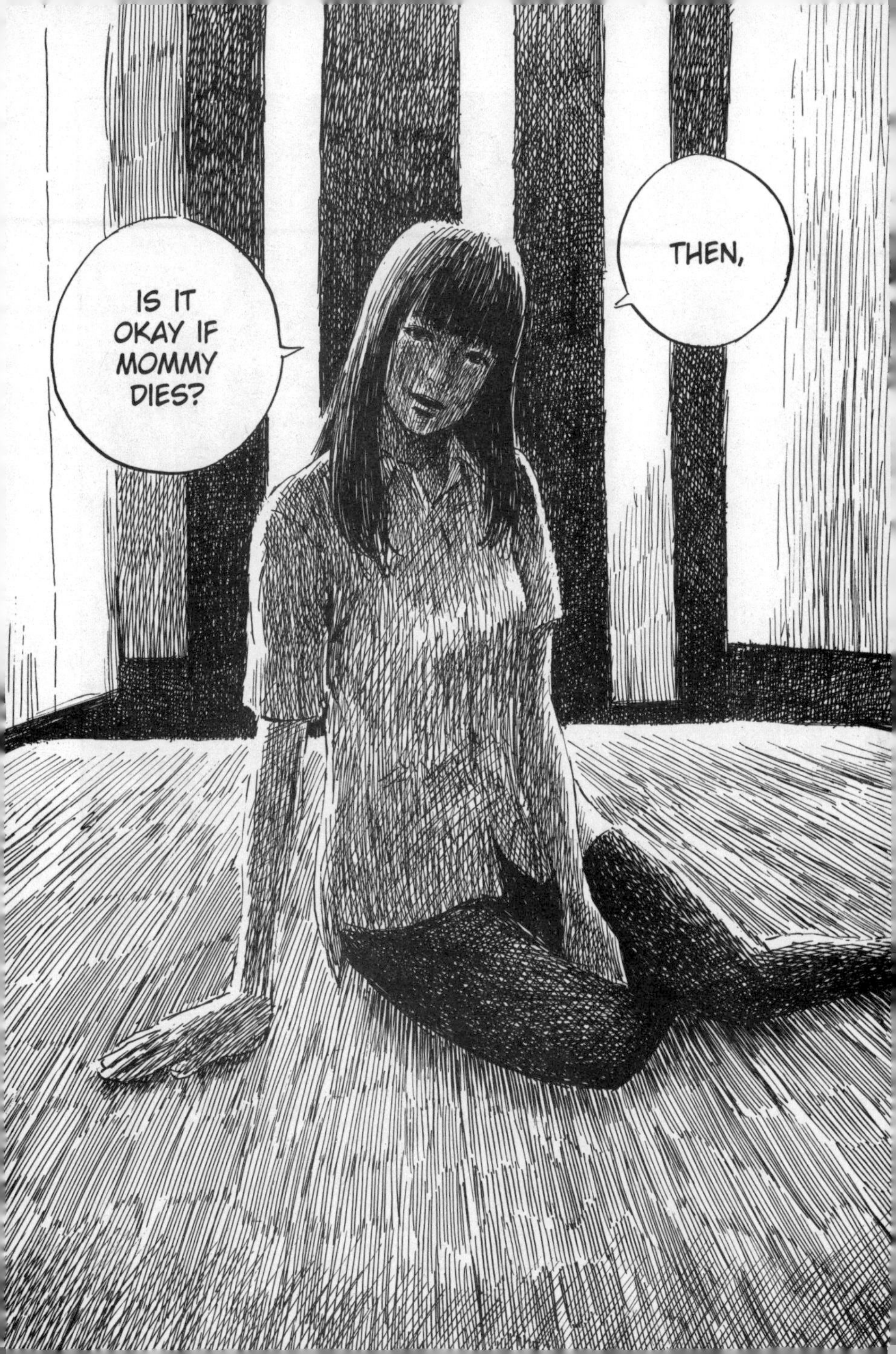
THEN,
IS IT OKAY IF MOMMY DIES?

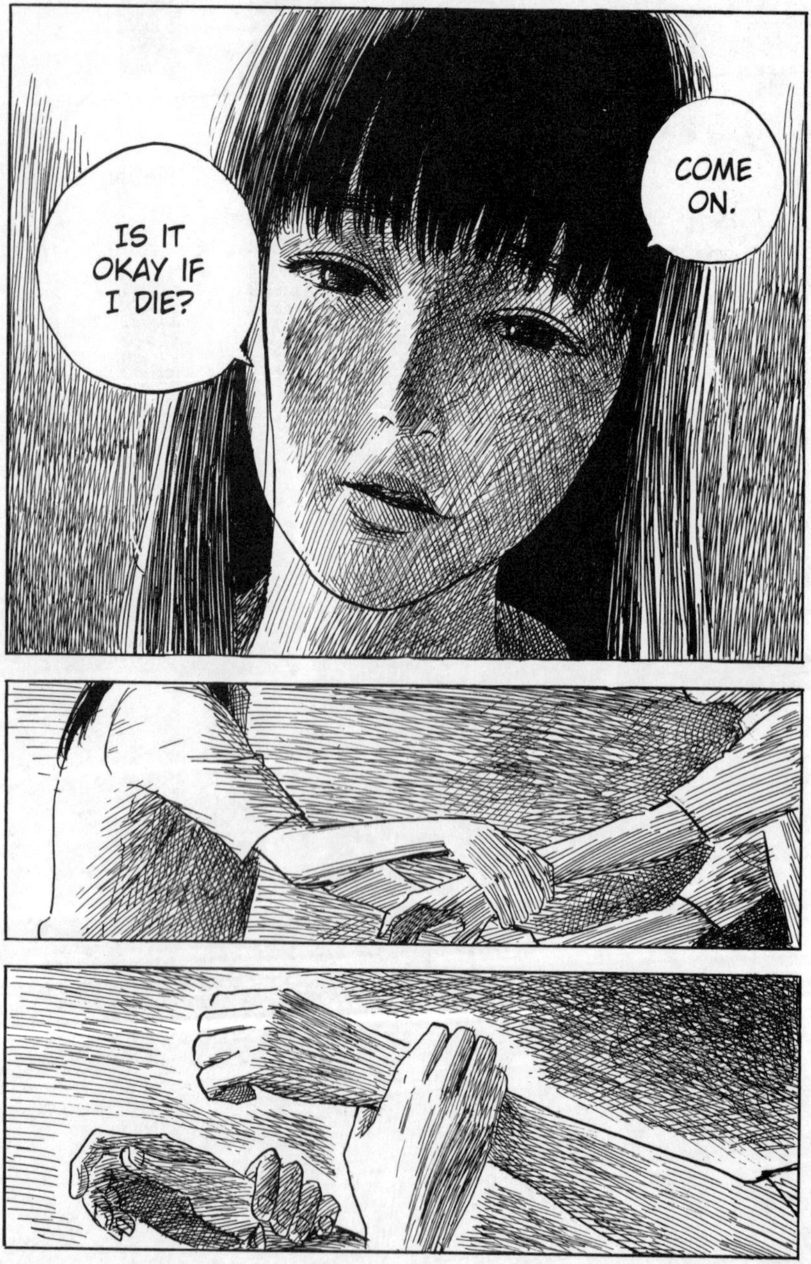
COME ON.
IS IT OKAY IF I DIE?

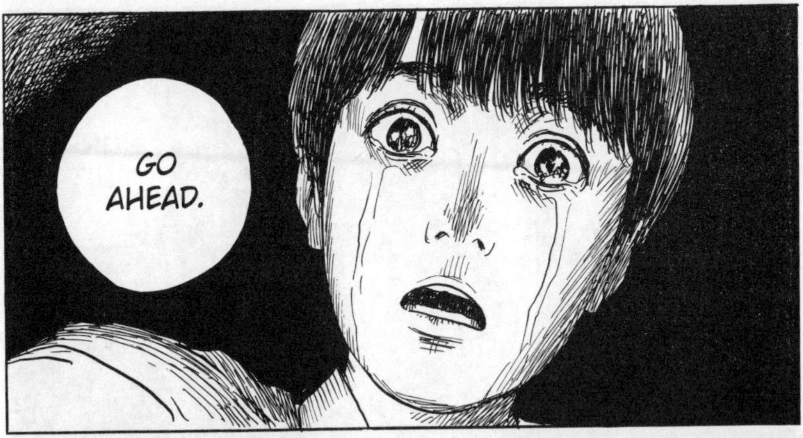
GO AHEAD.

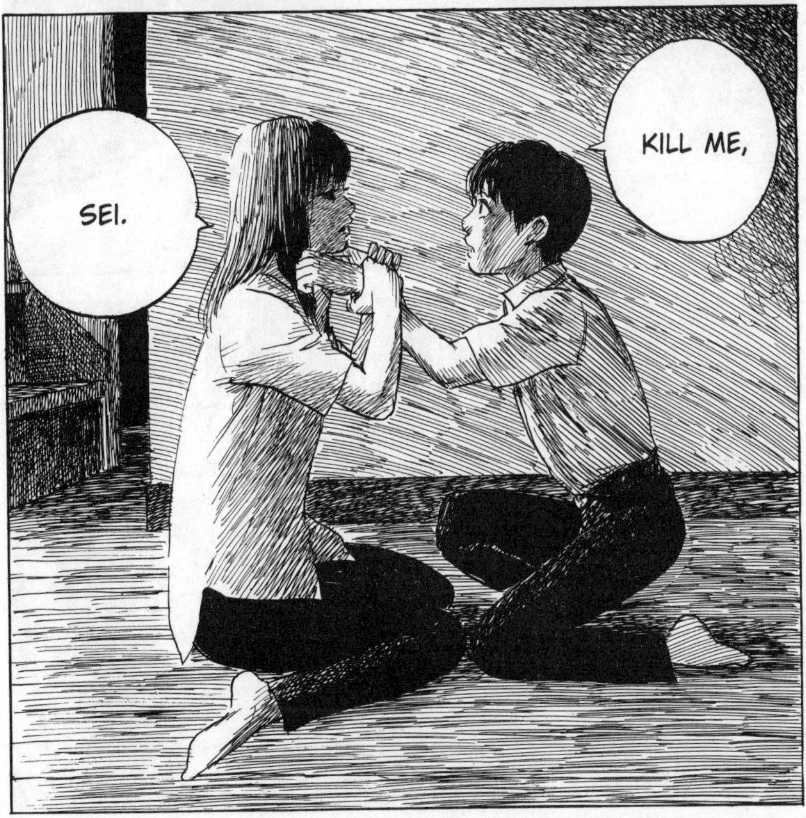
KILL ME,
SEI.

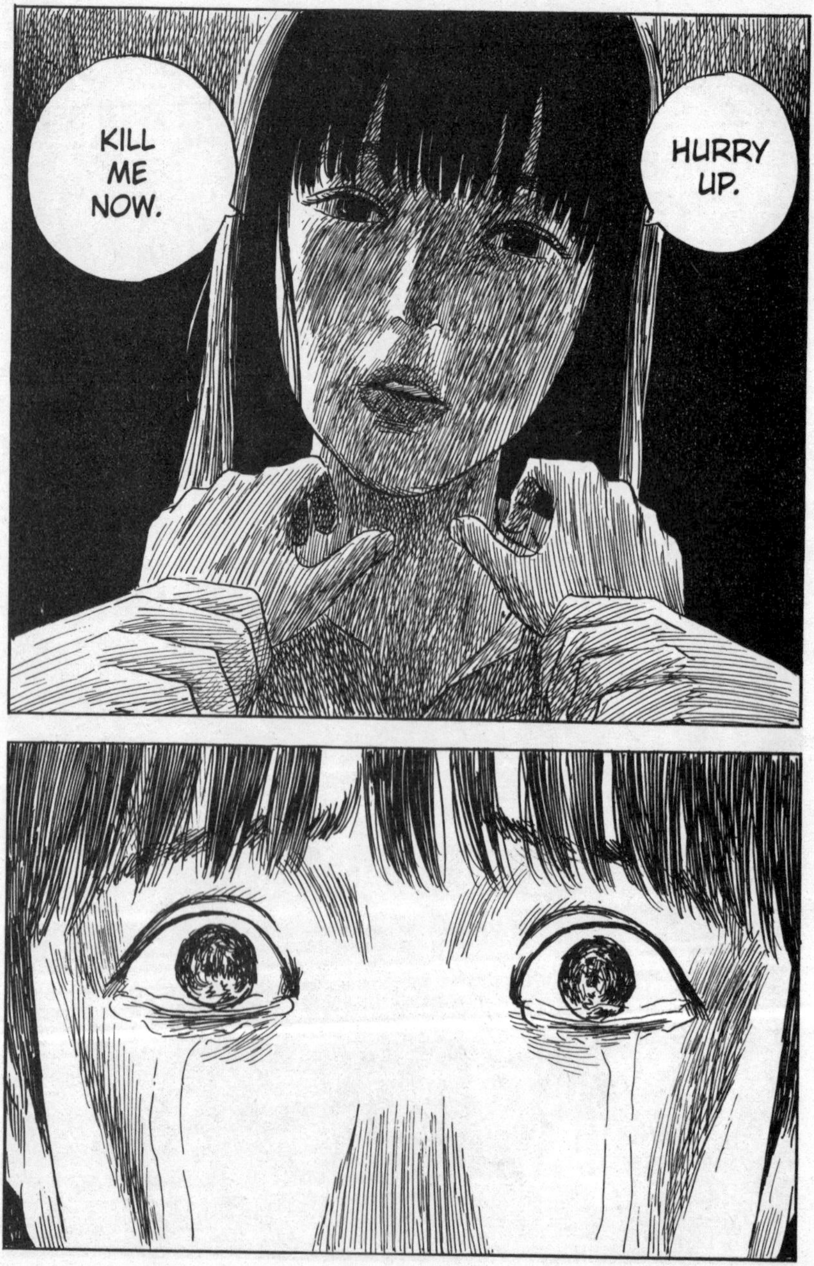
HURRY UP.
KILL ME NOW.

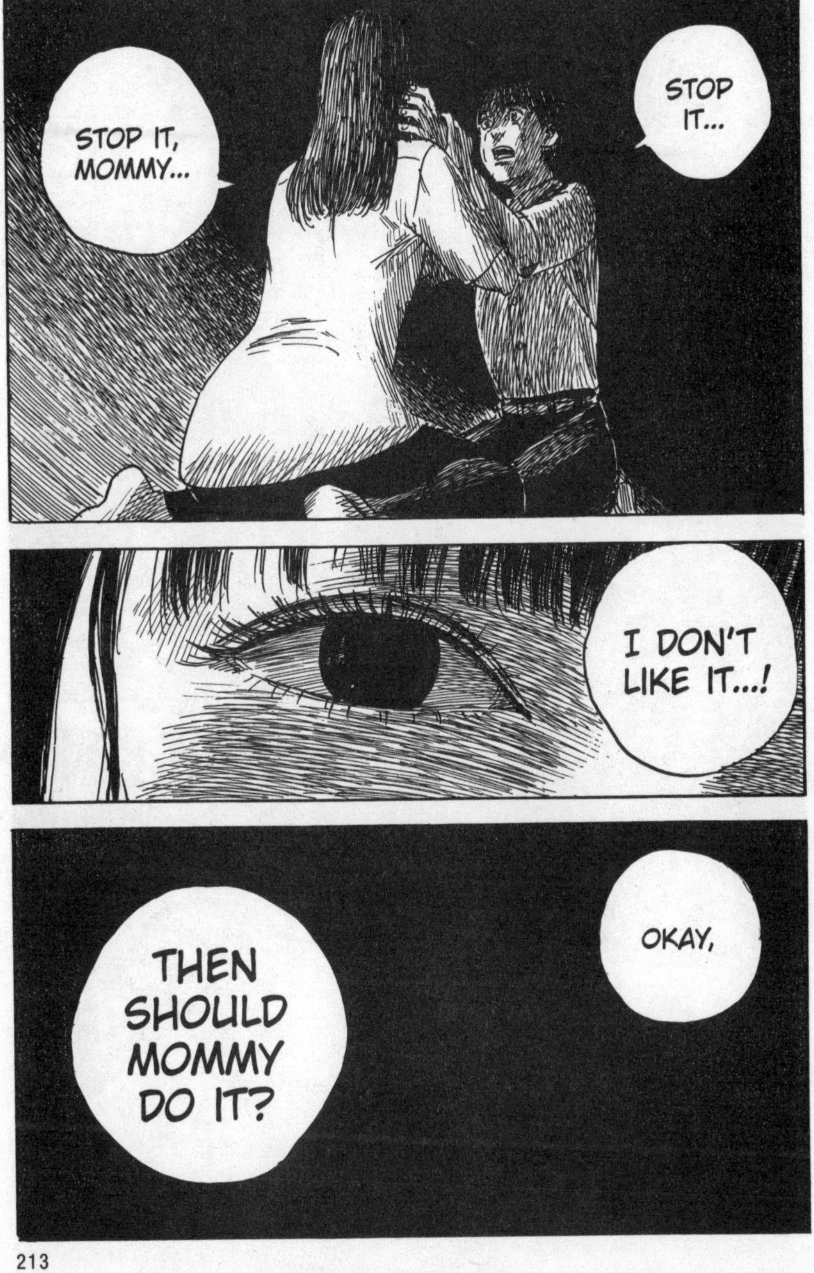
STOP IT...
STOP IT, MOMMY...
I DON'T LIKE IT...!
OKAY,
THEN SHOULD MOMMY DO IT?

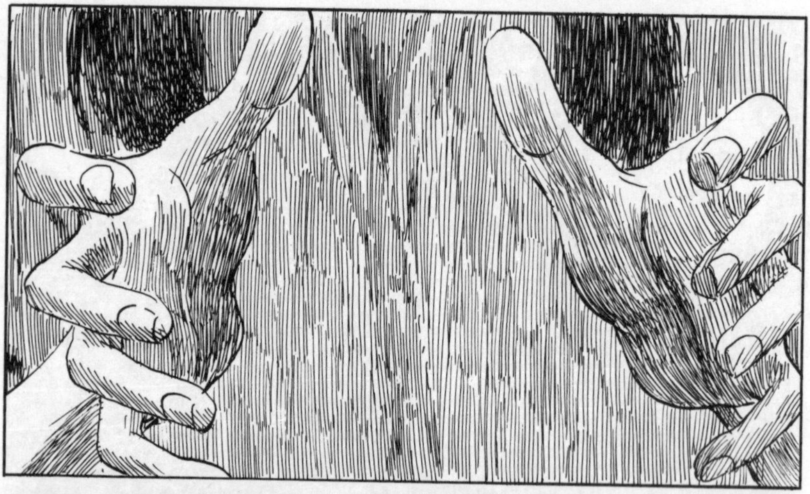
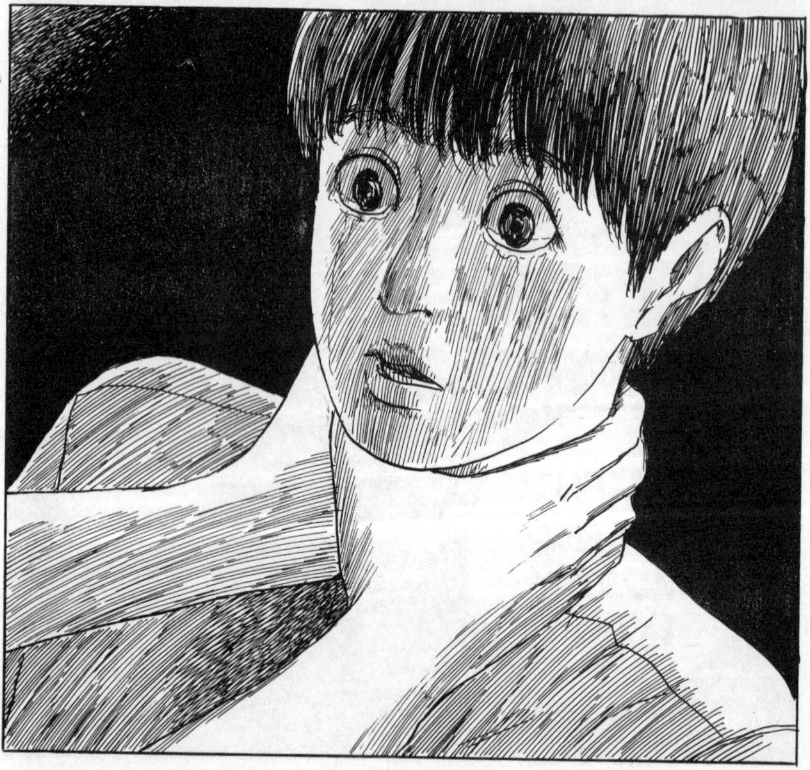

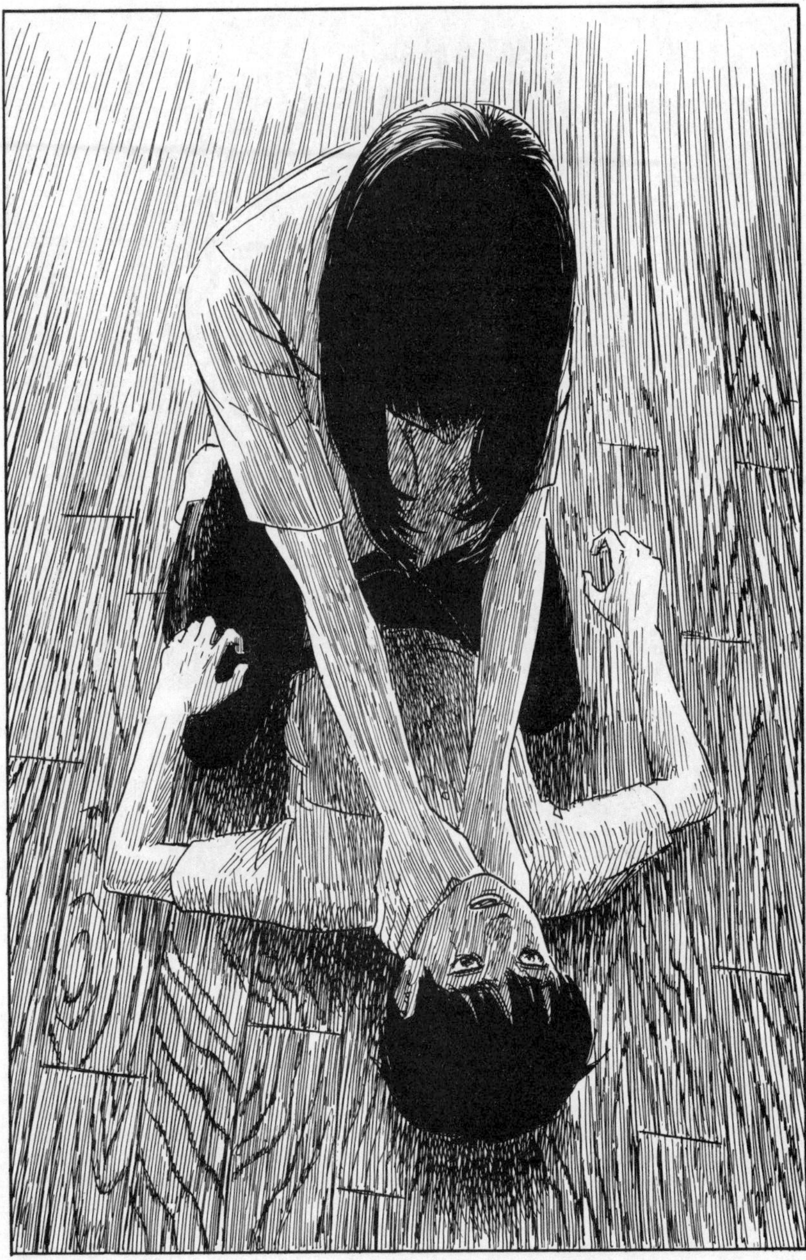

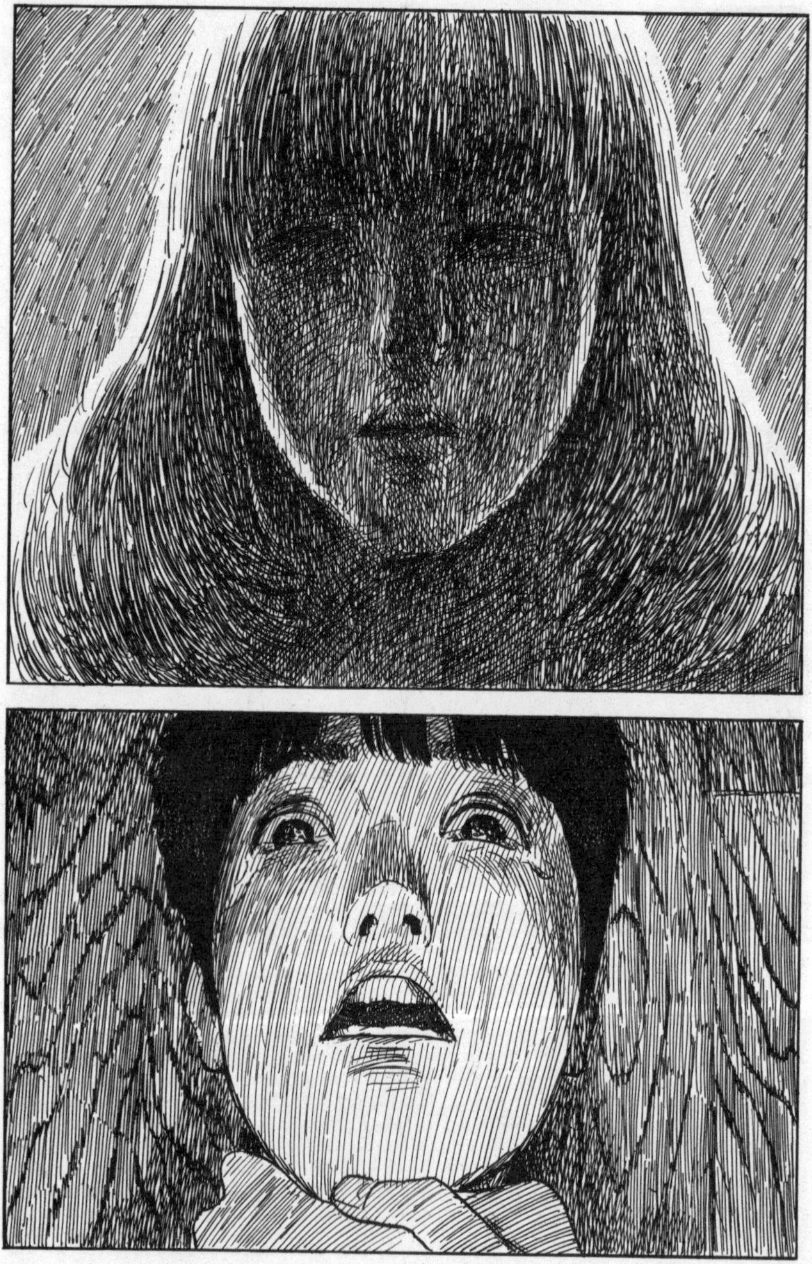

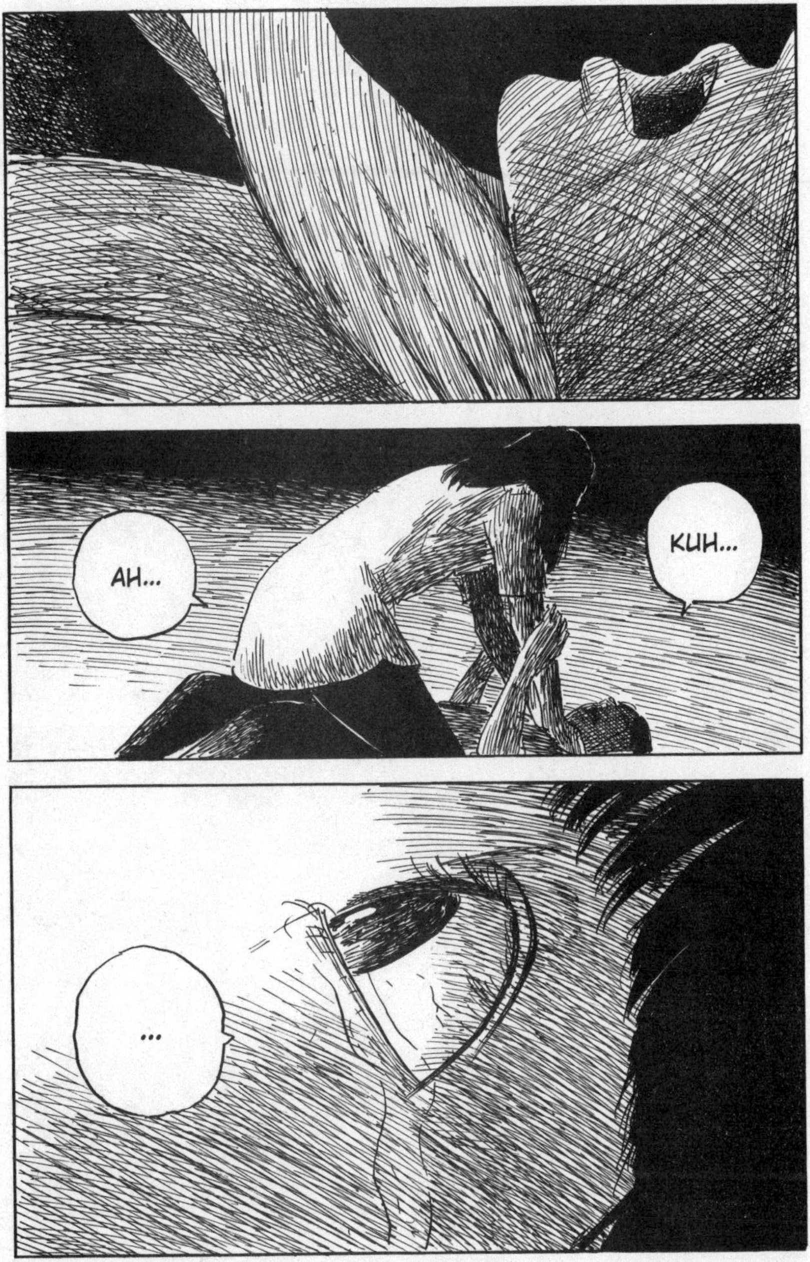
KUH...
AH...
...

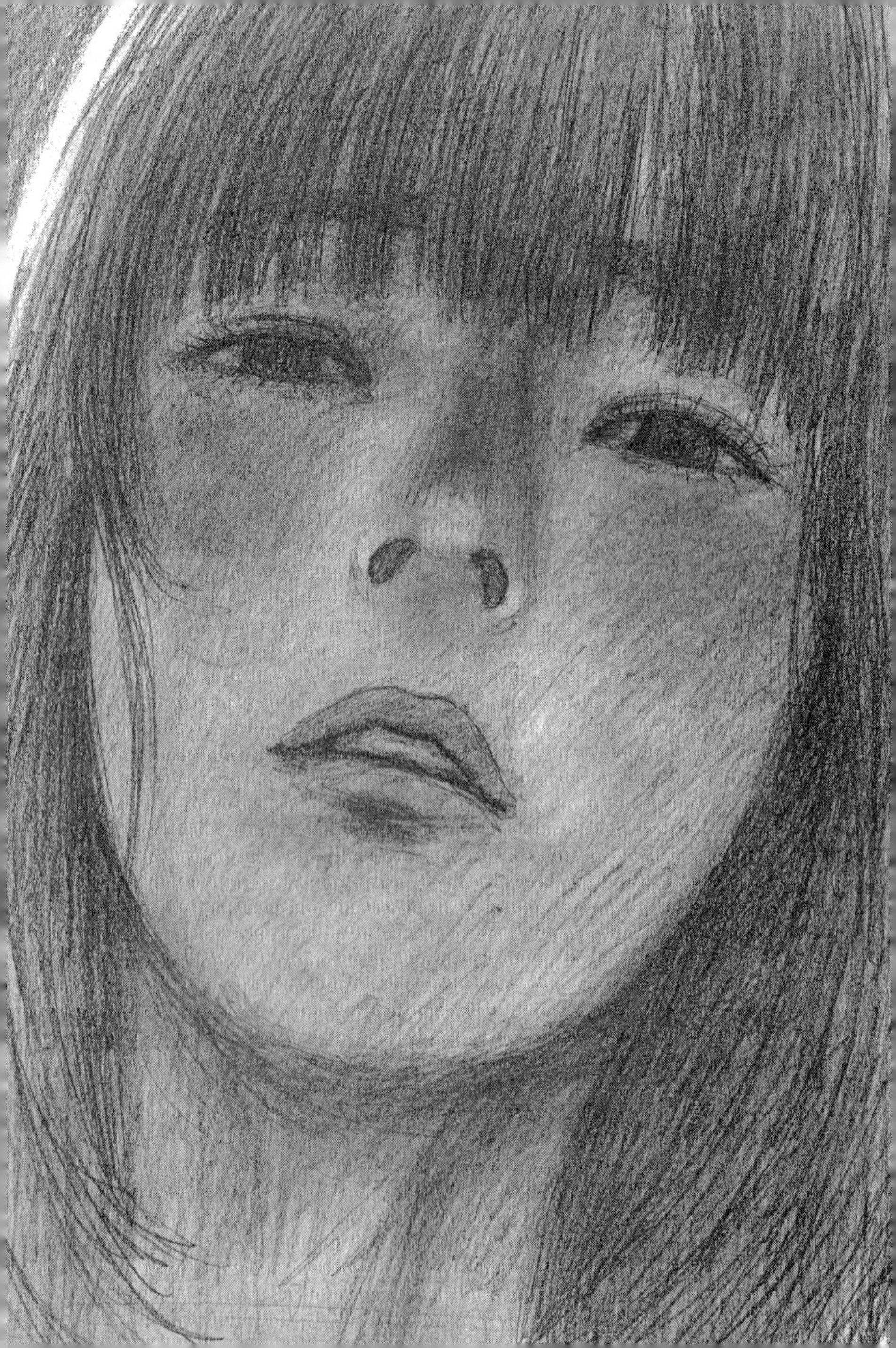

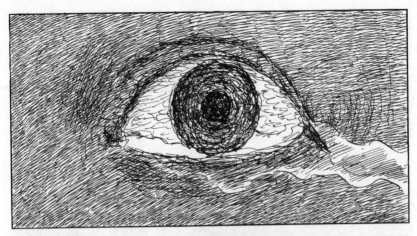

HA

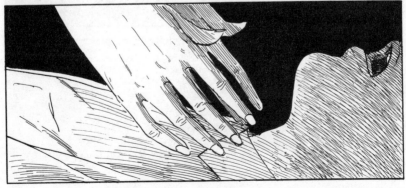

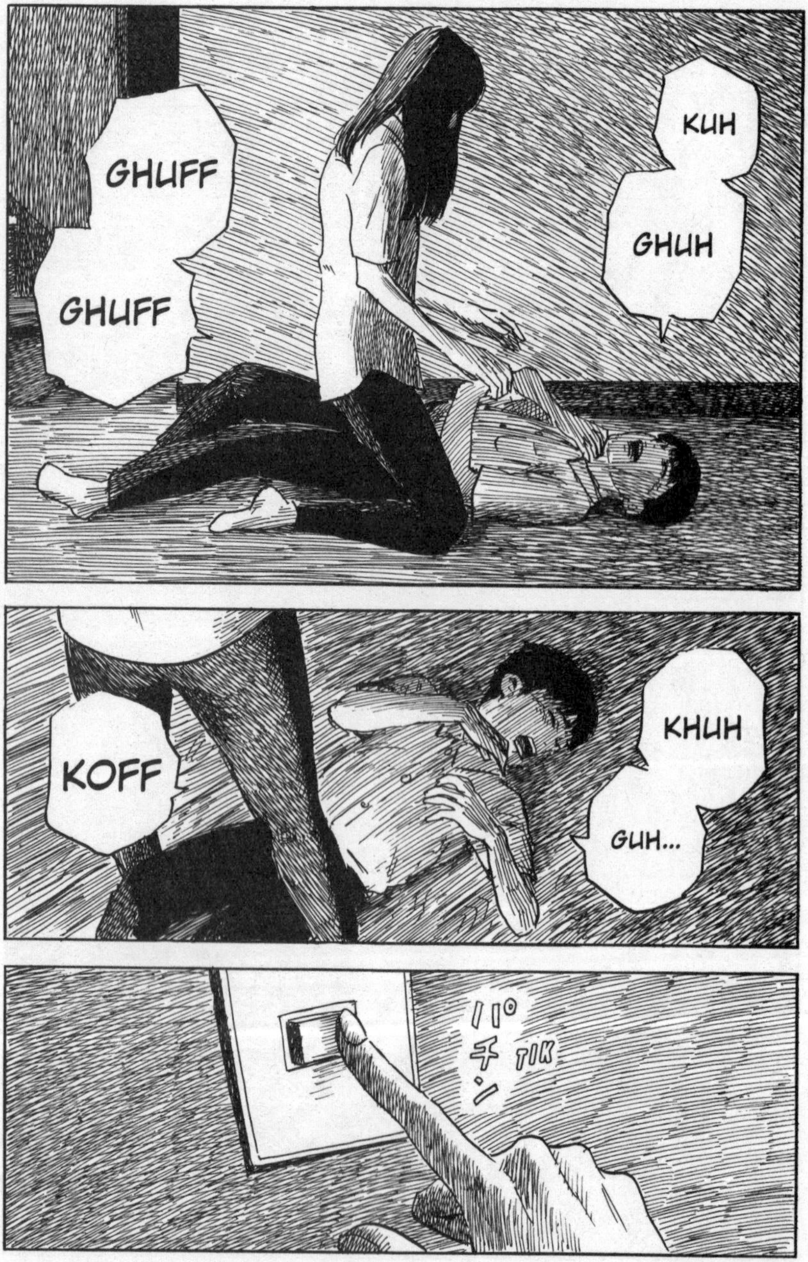
KUH
GHUH
GHUFF
GHUFF
KHUH
GUH...
KOFF
パチン
TIK

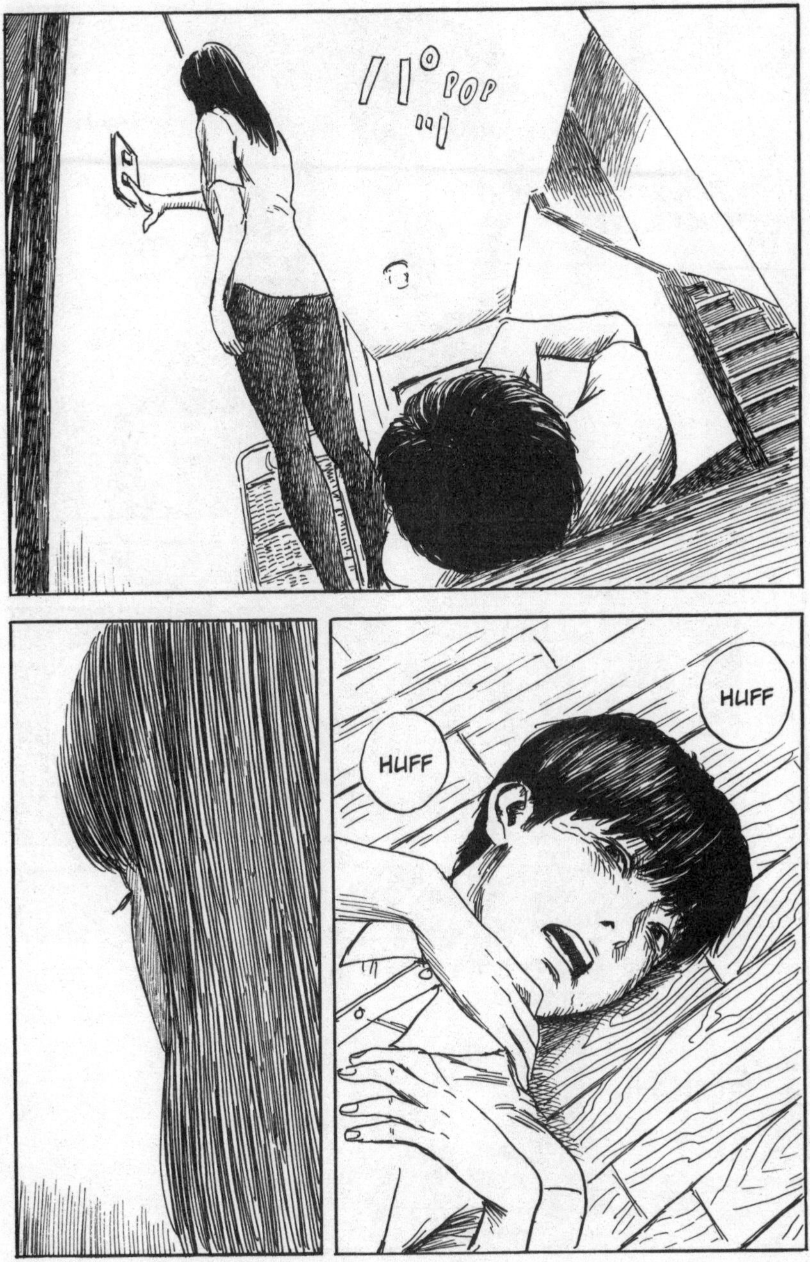
POP
HUFF
HUFF

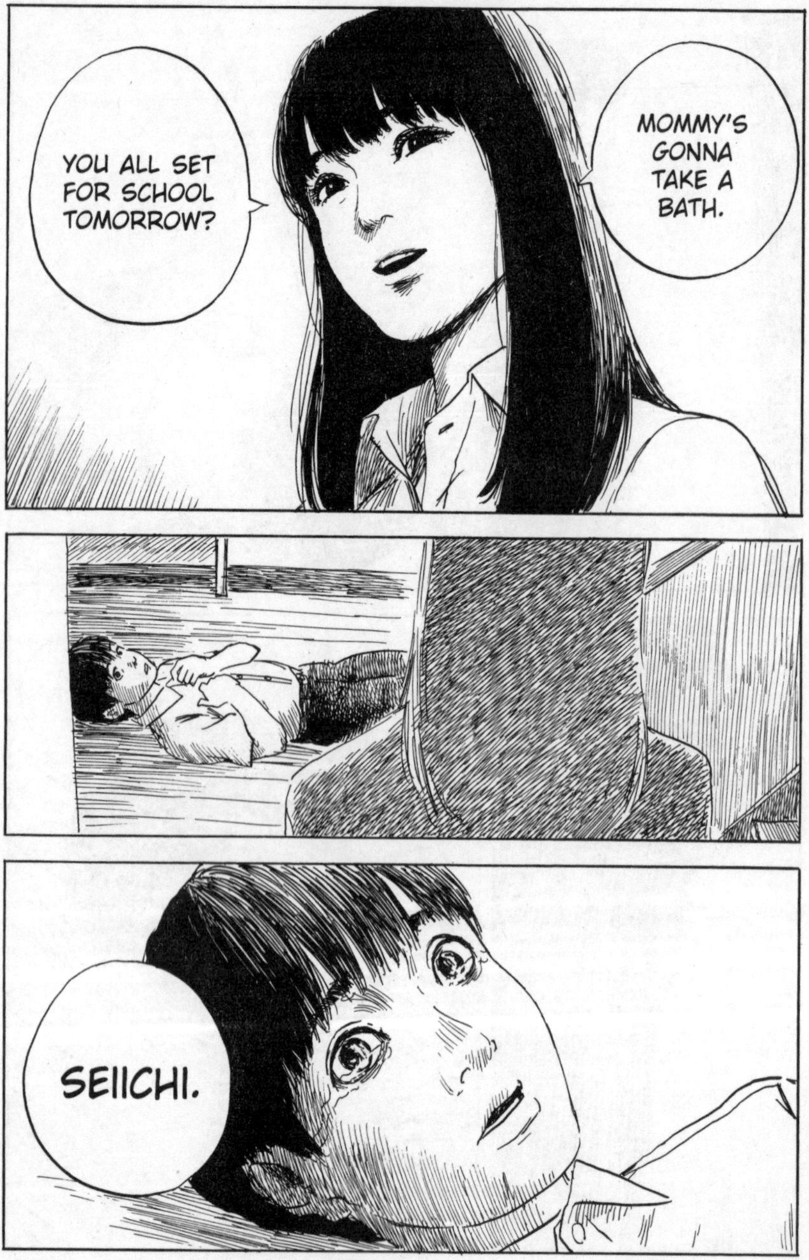
MOMMY'S GONNA TAKE A BATH.
YOU ALL SET FOR SCHOOL TOMORROW?
SEIICHI.

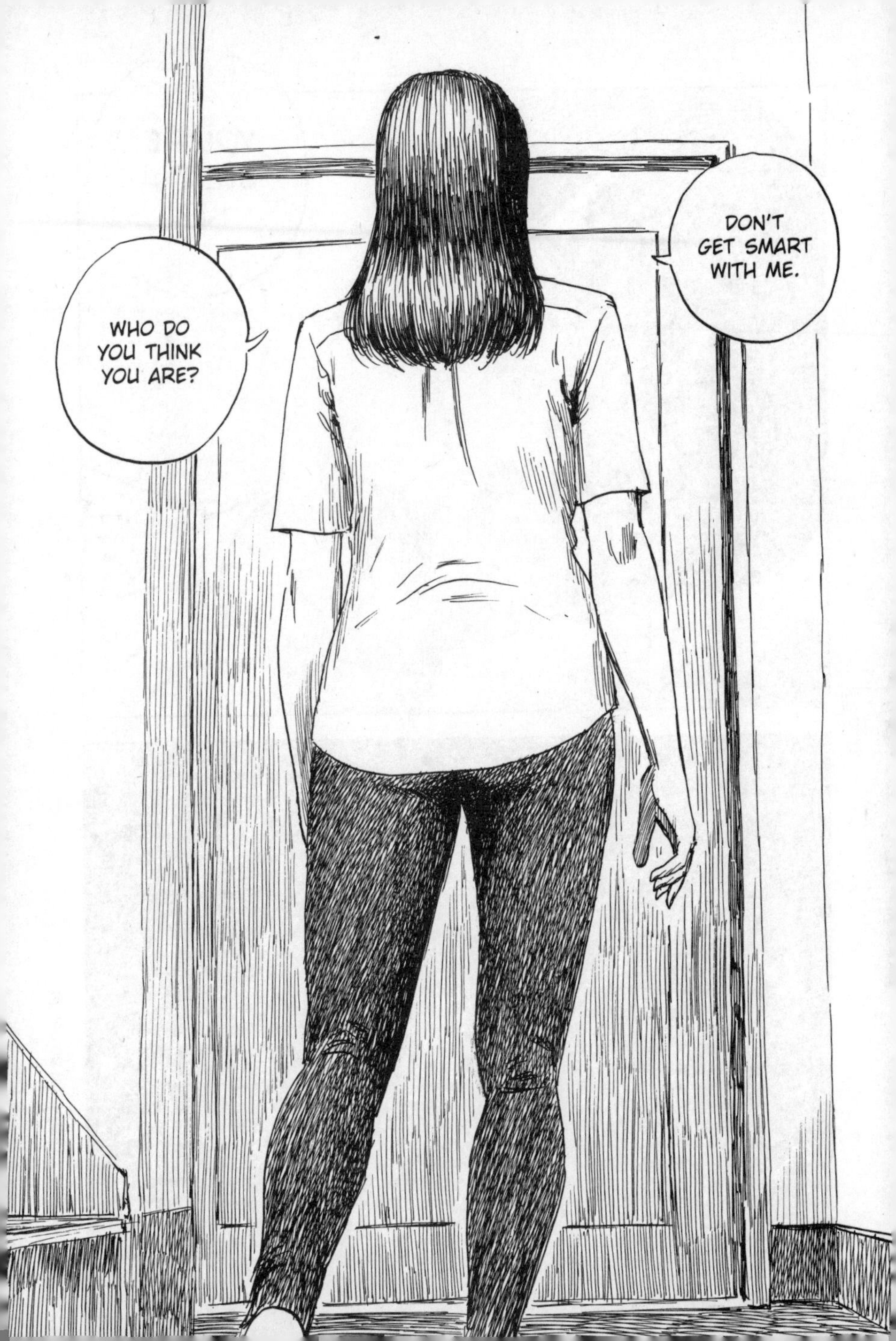
DON'T GET SMART WITH ME.
WHO DO YOU THINK YOU ARE?

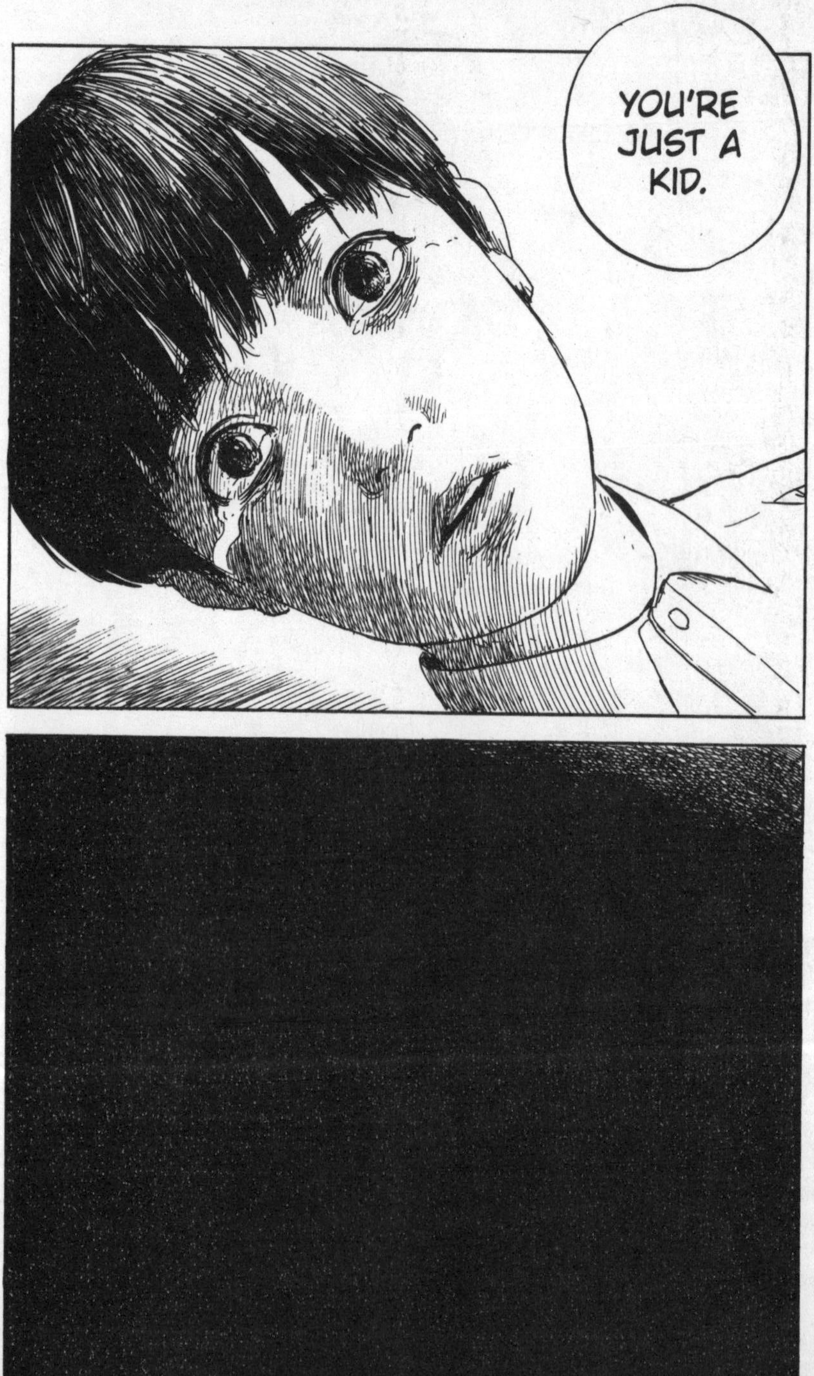
YOU'RE JUST A KID.

Blood on the Tracks VOLUME 3 • END

Photo
ALBUM

First
field day
1984
10
10

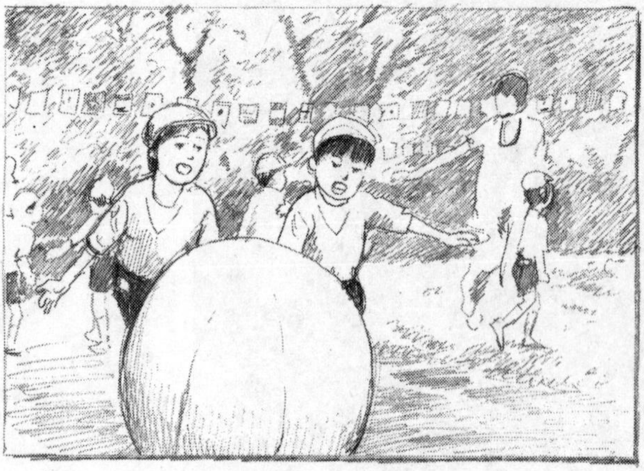

Go, Sei!

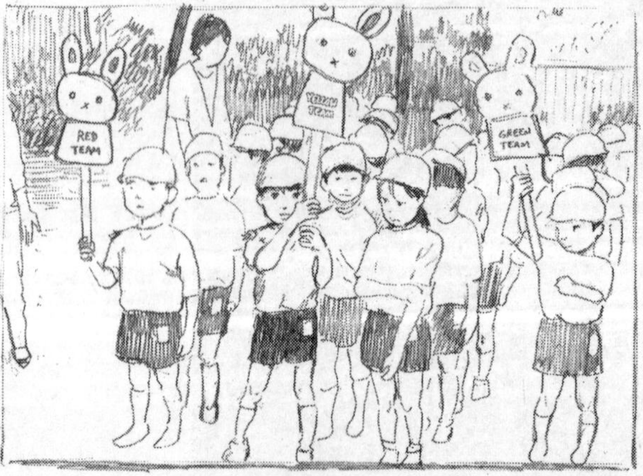
GREEN TEAM
YELLOW TEAM
RED TEAM

Kiryu City South   Kindergarten '84-85 School Performance 1985/2/28

Sei as
a goat!

At
Kiryu Hills
amusement
park

On a ferris wheel for the first time!

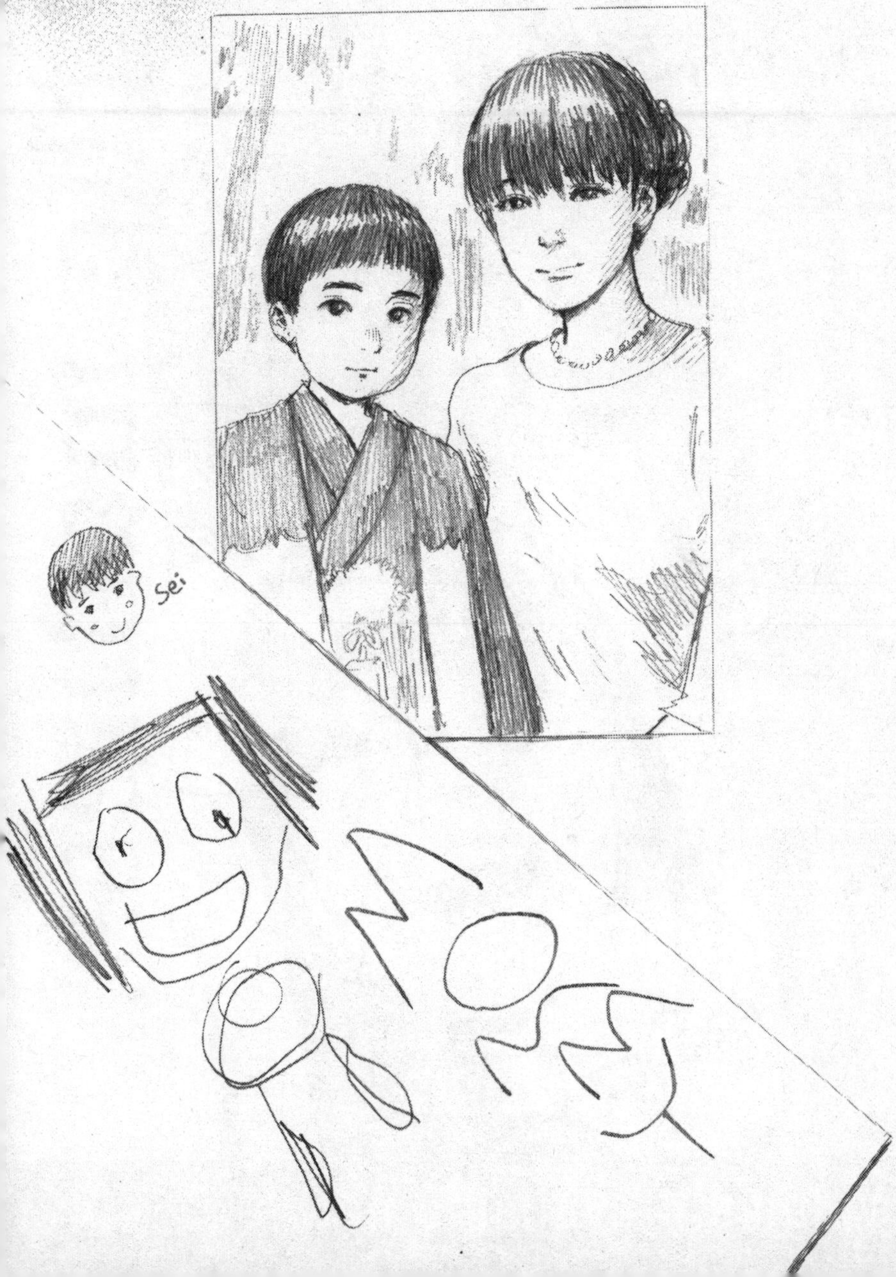
Sei

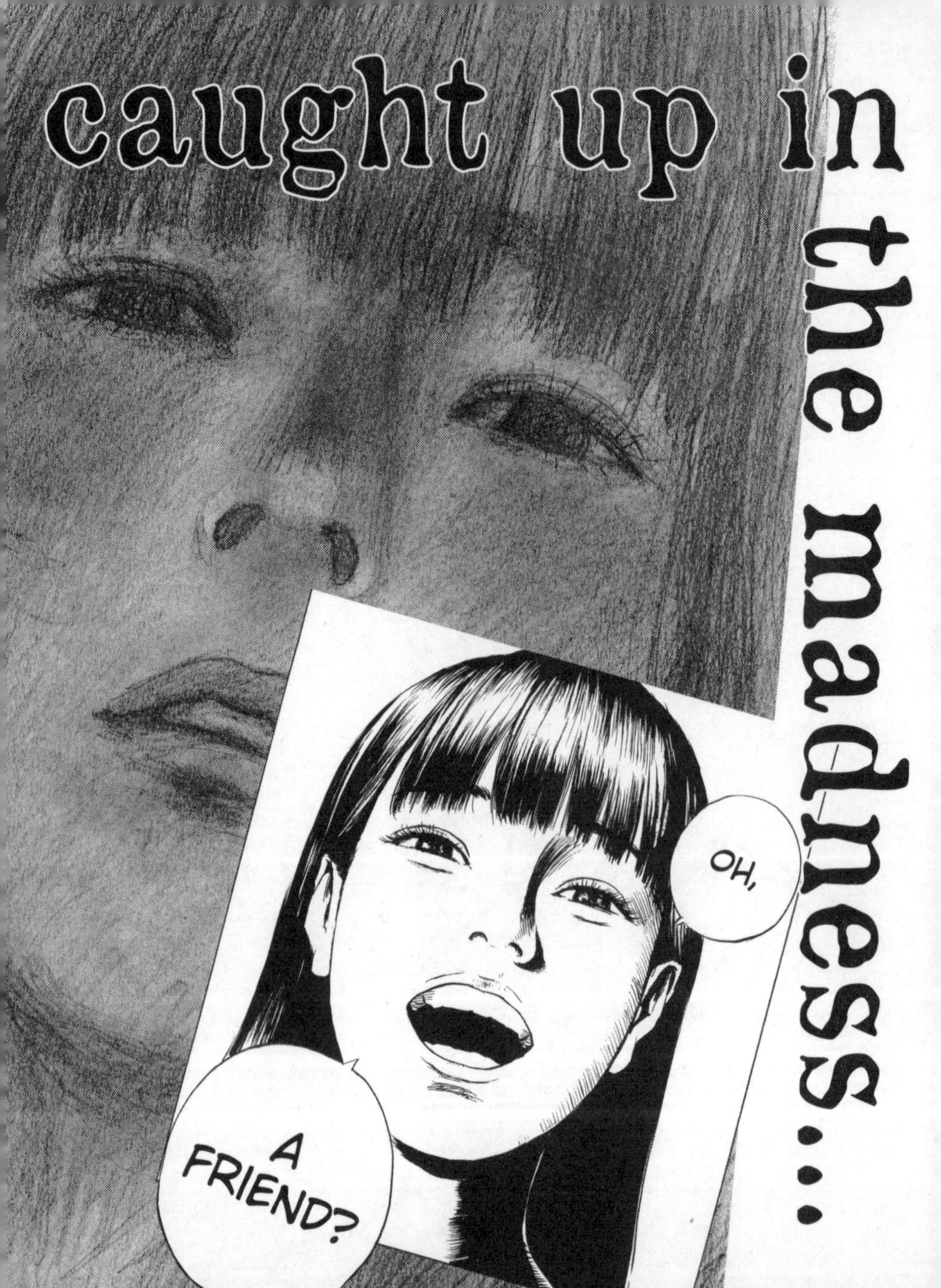
caught up in the madness...
OH,
A FRIEND?

Fukiishi gets

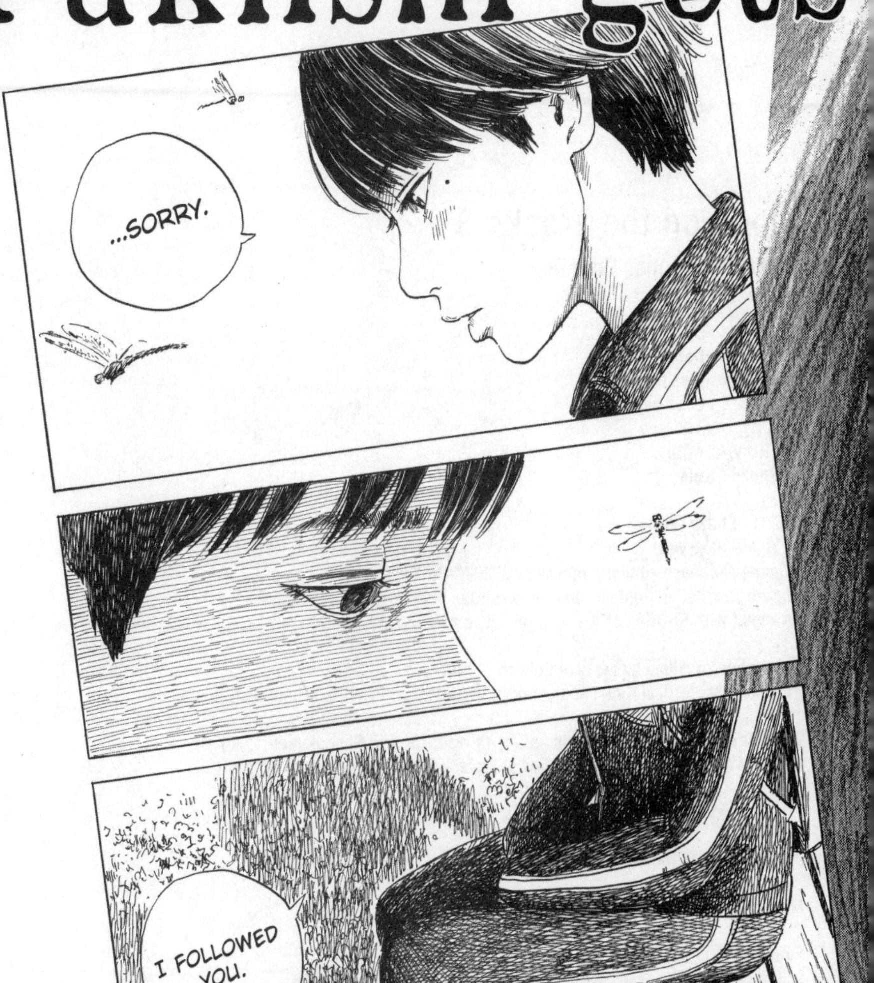
...SORRY.
I FOLLOWED YOU.

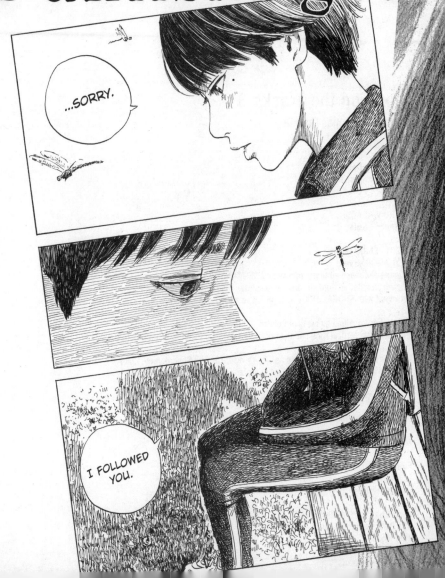

Blood on the Tracks 3
A Vertical Comics Edition

Editor: Daniel Joseph
Translation: Daniel Komen
Production: Risa Cho
             Evan Hayden

CHI NO WADACHI 3
by Shuzo OSHIMI

© 2017 Shuzo OSHIMI
All rights reserved.

Original Japanese edition published by SHOGAKUKAN.
English translation rights in the United States of America and Canada
arranged with SHOGAKUKAN through Tuttle-Mori Agency, Inc.

Translation provided by Vertical Comics, 2020.
Published by Vertical Comics, an imprint of Kodansha USA Publishing, LLC, New York

Originally published in Japanese as *Chi no Wadachi 3* by Shogakukan, 2018
Chi no Wadachi serialized in *Big Comic Superior*, Shogakukan, 2017-

This is a work of fiction.

ISBN: 978-1-949980-78-3

Manufactured in the United States of America

First Edition

Fourth Printing

Kodansha USA Publishing, LLC
451 Park Avenue South
7th Floor
New York, NY 10016
www.kodansha.us

Vertical books are distributed through Penguin-Random House Publisher Services.